Studies in Anglesey Hist◌

# MEDIEVAL ANGLESEY

## A D CARR

CYMDEITHAS HYNAFIAETHWYR A NATURIAETHWYR MÔN
THE ANGLESEY ANTIQUARIAN SOCIETY & FIELD CLUB

LLANGEFNI 2011

Published by
**Anglesey Antiquarian Society**
Llangefni, Ynys Môn
www.hanesmon.org.uk



**Designed & typeset by** Robert Williams
**Produced by** Llyfrau Magma, Llansadwrn
www.llyfrau–magma.co.uk


**Cover illustration**: Eglwys Llanrhwydrys
— a sketch by Kyffin Williams from the
collection of Oriel Ynys Môn, Rhosmeirch.
© Oriel Ynys Môn, 2011



First published in 1982
Second edition, 2011

ISBN 978-0-9568769-0-4

*— for Glenda : Semper eadem*

# Contents

*Page*

Foreword . . . . . . . . . . . . . . . . . . . . . . . . . . . . . . . . . ix
Preface . . . . . . . . . . . . . . . . . . . . . . . . . . . . . . . . . . xi
Abbreviations . . . . . . . . . . . . . . . . . . . . . . . . . . . . . . xiii
Glossary . . . . . . . . . . . . . . . . . . . . . . . . . . . . . . . . . xv

CHAPTERS

1   The Medieval Landscape . . . . . . . . . . . . . . . . . . . . . .   I
2   The Age of the Princes . . . . . . . . . . . . . . . . . . . . . .   21
3   The Government of the County . . . . . . . . . . . . . . . . . .   37
4   The Medieval Economy . . . . . . . . . . . . . . . . . . . . . .   63
5   The Social Order . . . . . . . . . . . . . . . . . . . . . . . . .   91
6   Rich Man, Poor Man . . . . . . . . . . . . . . . . . . . . . . .   119
7   The Making of the Gentry . . . . . . . . . . . . . . . . . . . .   159
8   The Towns . . . . . . . . . . . . . . . . . . . . . . . . . . . . .   185
9   The Church . . . . . . . . . . . . . . . . . . . . . . . . . . . .   211
10  Plague, Slump & Revolt . . . . . . . . . . . . . . . . . . . . . .   237

ILLUSTRATIONS

1   The coffin of Joan, wife of Llywelyn ab Iorwerth (the Great),
    now in Beaumaris church. (©*Mick Sharp*) . . . . . . . . . . . . . . . . .   143
2   Aerial view of Tal-y-llyn church; today it stands in isolation
    but archive evidence suggests the existence of a community
    of 22 households holding about 150 acres between them in 1306.
    (©*David Longley*) . . . . . . . . . . . . . . . . . . . . . . . . . . . . . . . . .   144
3   The site of the court complex at Rhosyr.
    (©*Gwynedd Archaeological Trust*) . . . . . . . . . . . . . . . . . . . . . . .   145
4   Aerial view of Penmon Priory. (©*Gwynedd Archaeological Trust*) . . . . .   146
5   The Romanesque arch in Aberffraw church. (©*Llyfrau Magma*) . .   147
6   Aerial view of Aberffraw; the court buildings lie beneath the
    present village. (©*Gwynedd Archaeological Trust*) . . . . . . . . . . . . . . .   148
7   Aerial view of Newborough: the street plan of the medieval
    town is clearly visible. (©*Gwynedd Archaeological Trust*) . . . . . . . . . .   148

8 The site of the town of Llan-faes in relation to Beaumaris;     *Page*
the nucleus of the town was probably around the church.
(©*Gwynedd Archaeological Trust*) . . . . . . . . . . . . . . . . . . . . . . . . . . . 149

9 Beaumaris castle from the north. (©*Gwynedd Archaeological Trust*) . . . 149

10 Possibly the earliest surviving Anglesey deed, recording the
conveyance in *tir prid* of land in Llangefni to Sir Gruffudd ap
Rhys (Sir Gruffudd Llwyd), 1313. (©*BUASC Mostyn 731*) . . . . . . . . 150

11 A page from the 1352 extent of Anglesey showing the entries for
the townships of Dinsylwy Rys, Penhwnllys, Trecastell and Twrgarw
in the commote of Dindaethwy. (©*BUASC Baron Hill 6714*) . . . . . . . 151

12-13 The birth of the Penrhyn estate: the will of Gwilym ap
Gruffudd ap Tudur, proved in 1376, and the fine relief of St Iestyn
in Llaniestyn church given by his widow and his nephew and heir.
(will ©*BUASC Penrhyn 5*; relief of St Iestyn ©*Mick Sharp*) . . . . . . . . 152–153

14-15 Tudor prehistory: the tomb of Goronwy ap Tudur (*d*.1382)
and his wife Myfanwy ferch Iorwerth Ddu, now in Penmynydd
church and a deed recording the conveyance in *tir prid* of lands
in Anglesey to Goronwy's brother Maredudd, the great-grandfather of Henry VII, 1389.
(tomb ©*RCAHMW*; deed ©*BUASC Mostyn 774*) . . . . . . . . . . . . . . . . 154

16 Part of a roll recording debts due to Gwilym ap Gruffudd of
Penmynydd and later of Penrhyn, 1406. This document sheds
light on the origins of the wealth of one of the greatest families
in north Wales in the fifteenth century.
(©*BUASC Penrhyn Further Additional, 1406*) . . . . . . . . . . . . . . . . . . . . 155

17 A house for Mr Bulkeley: the conveyance to William Bulkeley
the elder of the burgage in Beaumaris where he built his new
house, Henblas, 1474, and a plan of the house.
(conveyance ©*BUASC Baron Hill 510*; plan ©*RCAHMW*) . . . . . . . . . . . . 156

18 Henblas, Beaumaris, prior to its demolition in 1869.
(drawing ©*RCAHMW*; watercolour ©*Beaumaris Town Council*) . . . . . . . . 157

19 Hafoty, Llansadwrn, begun in the fifteenth century and probably
the best surviving example of a medieval house in Anglesey.
(©*Mick Sharp*) . . . . . . . . . . . . . . . . . . . . . . . . . . . . . . . . . . . . 158

20 The late fifteenth-century east window of Llangadwaladr church,
the gift of Meurig ap Llywelyn of Bodeon and his son Owain ap
Meurig and their wives. (©*Mick Sharp*) . . . . . . . . . . . . . . . . . . . 158

*RCAHMW* : Royal Commission on Ancient and Historical Monuments for Wales
*BUASC* : Bangor University Archives and Special Collections

APPENDICES                                                      *Page*

  **A**  Genealogical tables

     1  Wyrion Eden lineage ........................... 262

     2  Lineage of Llywarch ap Bran ..................... 264

     3  Lineage of Hwfa ap Cynddelw ................... 266

     4  Lineage of Iarddur ............................ 268

     5  Lineage of Carwed ............................ 269

  **B**  Maps

     1  Anglesey: cantrefs and commotes .................. 272

     2  Dindaethwy .................................. 273

     3  Menai ...................................... 274

     4  Malltraeth ................................... 275

     5  Llifon ...................................... 276

     6  Talybolion ................................... 277

     7  Twrcelyn ................................... 278

     8  Ecclesiastical lands ........................... 279

     9  Townships affected by the Black Death ............. 280

BIBLIOGRAPHY ....................................... 281

INDEX ............................................. 295

# Foreword

WHEN MEDIEVAL ANGLESEY was first published in 1982 it quickly became the definitive work and an indispensable guide to the development of the island during the Middle Ages. But no period of history can ever be known in its entirety, no historical work can even be judged to be complete; new facts emerge, either from the ground or from attics or from the less considered corners of estate offices, and the way we see ourselves now alters the way we see our past. All these processes have affected Anglesey in the twenty-nine years which have elapsed since the first edition was published, so this new version of the classic has many additions, modifications and adjustments: new material and new judgements on well-known material. An increase in quantity and quality of illustrations will be obvious at first opening and other aids, such as family trees of the princely lines, have been included. These will be welcomed by many readers who find Welsh patronymics difficult to hold in the mind.

The Society was delighted when Professor Carr agreed to write the original book since he was the recognised expert in the period and the area. He had full command of all the documentary sources and knew the terrain well; as Editor of the Society's *Transactions* for many years he had demonstrated his devotion to the study of the island's past. Everyone was equally delighted when he agreed to undertake the considerable work needed to fully revise his 1982 volume and distil into it all the insights gained in thirty additional years of studying the island and its context within the broader world of Britain and Europe. As Chairman of the Publication Committee I was especially pleased that his enthusiasm was undimmed and his professionalism was so strong that the task was completed to time without any exertion on my part. I must express my gratitude and that of the Committee to Professor Carr and to Robert Williams of Llyfrau Magma for the smooth and timely production of a book which I know will find a new and appreciative readership. The first edition sold out and we are sure this one will too, but now there are simpler ways of continuing to make this scholarship available electronically when that happens.

FRANCES LYNCH LLEWELLYN
Bangor   October 2011

# Preface

THE FIRST EDITION of this book appeared at the end of 1982 and the preface included various thanks and acknowledgements to friends and colleagues, some of whom are sadly no longer with us. Nearly three decades have now passed and after such a long interval there seems to be little point in repeating that preface, although my gratitude for and appreciation of so much help and advice has not diminished in any way. This second edition incorporates new material, both primary and secondary, including many documents, hitherto unknown and many of them dating from the middle ages and relating to Anglesey, which were discovered at Penrhyn Castle three months after the original publication; extensive use has been made of these. I have had second thoughts about some of the matters discussed in the original book and these, too, have been included. The original illustrations were less than satisfactory and they have been replaced; as a former archivist I make no apology for the inclusion of several significant documents. New maps have been prepared and I am particularly grateful to David Longley for drawing them.

It is always a pleasant task to acknowledge assistance and support. Once again I must thank the Anglesey Antiquarian Society and its officers for inviting me to prepare a second edition and especially the editor of Studies in Anglesey History, Frances Llewellyn, for her support and editorial guidance. My friends and former colleagues Tomos Roberts and Einion Thomas, successive University Archivists at Bangor, have been a tower of strength, in particular in making available the Penrhyn documents already mentioned. David Wilson of Stone Science scanned the first edition, thereby making the task of revision a great deal easier and Robert Williams of Llyfrau Magma has prepared the book for the press and lightened many burdens while doing so. I am particularly grateful to Mick Sharp and Jean Williamson, to David Longley and the Gwynedd Archaeological Trust, to the Royal Commission on Ancient and Historical Monuments for Wales, especially to Penny Icke, and to Einion Thomas for their help with the illustrations. As in 1982 my family has been unstinting in its interest and support and my wife Glenda's advice has changed the style substantially for the better. The first edition was dedicated to her; so is this. As I said then, there could be no other dedication.

A D CARR

# Abbreviations

**AHR**  *Agricultural History Review*

**Arch.Camb.**  *Archaeologia Cambrensis*

**BPR**  *Register of the Black Prince*

**BL**  British Library

**BBCS**  *Bulletin of the Board of Celtic Studies*

**BUASC**  Bangor University Archives and Special Collections

**CAC**  *Calendar of Ancient Correspondence concerning Wales*

**CAP**  *Calendar of Ancient Petitions relating to Wales*

**CChancRVar**  *Calendar of Chancery Rolls, Various*

**CCW**  *Calendar of Chancery Warrants*

**CChartR**  *Calendar of the Charter Rolls*

**CCR**  *Calendar of the Close Rolls*

**CFR**  *Calendar of the Fine Rolls*

**CIM**  *Calendar of Inquisitions Miscellaneous*

**CIPM**  *Calendar of Inquisitions Post Mortem*

**CPL**  *Calendar of Papal Letters*

**CPR**  *Calendar of the Patent Rolls*

**Camb. Econ. Hist.**  *The Cambridge Economic History of Europe I :*
  *the Agrarian Life of the Middle Ages*, ed. M. M. Postan (2nd edn., Cambridge, 1966)

**Econ. H.R.**  *Economic History Review*

**EHR**  *English Historical Review*

**Extent of Anglesey**  A. D. Carr: 'The Extent of Anglesey, 1352', *TAAS* 1971-2

**Fasti**  J. Le Neve: *Fasti Ecclesiae Anglicanae 1300-1541 : the Welsh Dioceses*

**JFHS** *Journal of the Flintshire Historical Society*

**JMHRS** *Journal of the Merioneth Historical and Record Society*

**NLW** National Library of Wales

**NLW Journal** *Journal of the National Library of Wales*

**Rec. Caern.** *Registrum vulgariter nuncupatum The Record of Caernarvon*

**RBH** *Red Book of Hergest*

**Reg. Chichele** *The Register of Henry Chichele, Archbishop of Canterbury, 1414-1443*

**Reg. Bothe** *Registrum Caroli Bothe, episcopi Herefordensis, A.D. MDXVI–MDXXXV*

**Reg. Mayew** *Registrum Richard Mayew, episcopi Herefordensis, A.D. MDIV–MDXVI*

**Reg. Millyng** *Registrum Thome Millyng, episcopi Herefordensis, A.D. MCCCCLXXIV – MCCCCXCII*

**Reg. Spofford** *Registrum Thome Spofford, episcopi Herefordensis, A.D. MCCCCXXII – MCCCCXLVIII*

**Reg. Winchelsey** *Registrum Roberti Winchelsey Cantuarensis Archiespiscopi*

**Rot. Parl.** *Rotuli Parliamentorum*

**RCAHM** Royal Commission on Ancient and Historical Monuments

**Taxatio Nich. IV** *Taxatio Ecciesiastica Angliae et Walliae, auctoritate Papae Nicholai IV circa 1291*

**TAAS** *Transactions of the Anglesey Antiquarian Society & Field Club*

**TCHS** *Transactions of the Caernarvonshire Historical Society*

**THSC** *Transactions of the Honourable Society of Cymmrodorion*

**TDHS** *Transactions of the Denbighshire Historical Society*

**TNA** The National Archives

**TRHS** *Transactions of the Royal Historical Society*

**Valor Ecclesiasticus** *Valor Ecciesiasticus temp. Henrici VIII auctoritate regia institutus*

**WHR** *Welsh History Review*

# Glossary

**Abjure** When a fugitive felon sought sanctuary in a church, the coroner offered him the choice of surrendering to justice or abjuring the realm. If he chose the latter, the coroner named a port; he then made his way there by the shortest possible route, carrying a cross. When he reached his destination he had to leave on the first available ship, never to return.

**Amercement** A monetary penalty imposed by a court, corresponding to the modern fine. If guilty a defendant placed himself on the mercy of the court and obtained it by this payment.

*Amobr* A fine for the loss of a woman's virginity, corresponding to the English *leyrwite* and paid to the lord when she married or on other relevant occasions. It was usually ten shillings for a free tenant and 6s 8d for an unfree one.

**Bailiff** In the principality of north Wales one of the two executive officials of a borough, elected at the court leet to hold office for one year.

**Bondman, villein** (W. *taeog*) An unfree member of the community, owing various rents, renders and services to his lord and subject to a number of restrictions. The status and the obligations and restrictions are discussed in detail on pp.91-107 below.

**Burgess** A resident of a chartered borough who was a full member of the civic community with all the rights that such membership conveyed.

**Cantref** The basic Welsh territorial administrative unit.

**Carucate** Originally the amount of land which could be worked by one plough team. It came to mean an area of land ranging from 60 to 120 acres; in Anglesey it was probably the lower figure.

*Clas* The name given to a pre-Norman monastic community in Wales, which consisted of an abbot and a body of canons attached to a mother church.

**Commote** A subdivision of the cantref, corresponding approximately to the English hundred.

**Commutation** The process whereby services in kind were replaced by cash payments called quit-rents or rents of assise.

**Court leet** A court similar to the sheriff's tourn (*qv*) held in boroughs (and in England on manors) at Easter and Michaelmas.

*Cylch* (pl. *cylchoedd*) The circuits or billeting rights of the king's stallion or warhorse, the rhaglaw, the falconers and the king's otter-hounds, all of which had been replaced by cash payments by the time of the Edwardian conquest.

**Demesne** The demesne was the land in the medieval manor set aside for the use and maintenance of the lord and his household and worked by his bondmen.

**Deodand** A payment corresponding to the value of the object by which a person met a violent or accidental death (i.e. the knife with which he was stabbed or the horse from which he fell), which was supposed to be devoted to pious uses.

**Escheat** The procedure whereby the tenement of a tenant who died without heirs, or in rebellion, or who was convicted of felony reverted to the lord.

**Estreat** An extract from the roll or record of a court, usually made to facilitate the collection of the profits of justice or as evidence of title to land.

**Farm** Farming was a practice used extensively by medieval rulers; a lump sum was paid for the lease of an office or some other piece of royal property and the income was then retained by the lessee. The ruler thus had an assured income without the trouble of collection.

**Fealty** An oath or declaration of fidelity taken by a tenant to the lord.

**Fine** A payment made, usually in court, for licence to do something not otherwise allowed, e.g. by a bondman for permission to take holy orders or to make a will or, in Wales, for a tenant to acquire land in fee. Also a collusive legal action whereby land could be conveyed.

**Gafael** (pl. **gafaelion**) Like the *gwely* a holding of land held by a kindred group. In some parts of north Wales it was the predominant unit of tenure but in Anglesey it was mainly the unit of tenure in the commotal centres of Cemais, Penrhosllugwy and Rhosyr and therefore unfree.

**Gobrestyn** An investiture fee paid in addition to relief to take up an inheritance when the heir was not a direct descendant of the deceased.

**Gwely** (pl. **gwelyau**) A kindred group descended from a common ancestor and sharing proprietary rights in its land; the term came to apply to the land as well.

**Heriot** A payment due to the lord on the death of a tenant, usually his best beast or the value thereof.

**Maerdref** The unfree township in each commote attached to the royal court there for its maintenance which corresponded, more or less, to the demesne.

**Mark** 13*s* 4*d* or two-thirds of one pound; the mark was a unit of account rather than of currency.

**Mease** A measure consisting of five long hundreds (i.e. 600) of herrings.

**Messuage** A building, usually a dwelling-house and its appurtenant lands.

**Moveables** Personal property on the value of which subsidies were assessed, usually crops and livestock as opposed to land (real property).

**Multure** The prince's or the lord's share of all the corn ground at his mill.

**Prise** The right of the crown to take a certain amount of wine from each incoming cargo for its own use.

**Quillet** A strip of land, often in an open field.

**Quit-rent** See 'commutation'.

**Raglotry** The office of *rhaglaw*.

**Relief** The fine paid to the lord by an heir to enable him to take up his inheritance; the term in Welsh law was *ebediw*. The sum of ten shillings was usually due from a free tenant and 6*s* 8*d* from an unfree one.

**Rent of assise** See 'commutation'.

*Rhaglaw* Before the Edwardian conquest the *rhaglaw* was the prince's representative in the cantref. In the principality of north Wales after 1284 there was one in each commote but he does not seem to have performed any official duties by the middle of the fourteenth century and the office was therefore a profitable sinecure.

**Ringildry** The office of *rhingyll*.

*Rhingyll* Formerly subordinate to the *rhaglaw*, by the middle of the fourteenth century the rhingyll had become the prince's executive representative in the commote, collecting and accounting for the royal revenue.

**Shrievalty** The office of sheriff.

**Suit of court** The obligation of tenants to attend the lord's court.

**Suit of mill** The obligation of tenants to have their corn ground at the lord's mill.

**Testator** The maker of a will.

**Tourn** A court established in 1284 which exercised the criminal jurisdiction of the sheriff. It was held twice a year in each commote of the county at Easter and Michaelmas and its principal function was the detection of crime through the interrogation on oath of representatives of each township.

**Township** The basic territorial unit of settlement and assessment. Each commote was made up of a number of free and bond townships of varying size.

**Trental** A sequence of thirty masses said for a special intention, usually the repose of the soul of the testator if provided for in a will.

**Tun** A cask for wine, usually containing 252 gallons.

**Turbary** A tract of land used for digging peat or turf, also the right to dig peat.

*Uchelwr, uchelwyr* The term generally used for the landowning class (later the gentry). It originally meant any free-born Welshman but it later came to apply to those families of good descent who were the social leaders of their communities and the patrons of the poets.

# I  *The Medieval Landscape*

WHOEVER ATTEMPTS to depict a community at any stage of its history should begin with a description. The famous third chapter of Macaulay's *History* has had many imitators and may be said to have started a fashion; such a description is a salutary exercise for the historian but it is not always easy. Vital documentary evidence may often have been lost, but, on the other hand, the land remains and Professor Hoskins reminded us many years ago that the English landscape '...to those who know how to read it aright, is the richest historical record we possess'.[1] This is as true of Wales as of England; the Welsh landscape cannot be dismissed out of hand as a world of mountains, sheepwalks and upland pastures. Nor can we delude ourselves that landscape is a mere natural phenomenon, untouched by human hand; since Neolithic times that hand has shaped its environment and it does so still. Even if the term 'man-made' as applied to landscape brings to mind the part played by such designers as Capability Brown in the eighteenth century, we cannot ignore the fact that most landscape is, to a greater or lesser degree, man-made. It has been said of a later period that 'the ravaging of Parys Mountain financed the landscape gardening of Llysdulas' and this sentence encapsulates the process of change.[2] The devastation wrought by copper mining on Mynydd Parys is there for all to see and if the glory of Llysdulas has long departed, the grounds at Plas Newydd were probably paid for from the same source. But neither mines nor grounds were to be seen in the middle ages and that sums up the argument. Landscape is dynamic; it has changed, is changing and will continue to change.

The basis of the landscape is land. Anglesey is an island. It covers an area of 290 square miles or 71,204 hectares and is approximately square in shape, measuring 23 miles from south-east to north-west and 21 miles from north-east to south-west.[3] It is separated from the mainland of Britain by the Menai Straits, which are some fifteen miles long and a smaller island, Holy Island or Ynys Cybi, lies to the west of it. Off the coast are various small islands and

---

1  W.G. Hoskins, *The Making of the English Landscape* (1970), p.14.

2  G.R.J. Jones, 'Anglesey portrayed', *TAAS* 1974, p.114. In this review Professor Jones made a number of salutary points which merit the attention of all who are interested in conservation.

3  The geographical background is discussed by Sir Cyril Fox in the Royal Commission on Ancient and Historical Monuments *Anglesey Inventory* (1937), pp.xxxi–xxxiv.

reefs. It is undulating and low; the grandeur and drama of Snowdonia will be sought in vain, although some of the finest views of the mountains are to be had from across the Menai Straits. In fact, the contrast with mainland Gwynedd is extreme; there is more low lying land in Anglesey than in any of the other historic counties of Wales and the highest point is only 219 metres above sea level. In geological terms the island is very old and it includes some of the oldest rock formations in Britain.[4] There are no large rivers but there are many small ones along with a number of lakes and marshy tracts. Drainage is mainly from north-east to south-west and this alignment is also to be seen in the Menai Straits and in the geological fault which runs from Red Wharf Bay to Malltraeth Marsh and which forms a natural division between the region known as Sir Fôn Fach to the south and that known as Sir Fôn Fawr to the north.

Much of the present-day landscape is the result of nineteenth-century changes. The island is linked to the mainland by two bridges, one built by Thomas Telford and completed in 1826 and the other built by Robert Stephenson in 1850 to carry the Chester and Holyhead Railway. Telford also built a new road linking his bridge with Holyhead, while the railway takes a more southerly route. The largest town by far is the port of Holyhead; next to it comes the county town, Llangefni, followed by Amlwch, Menai Bridge and Beaumaris. Other semi-urban settlements have developed, often as a result of the holiday industry and there has been a great deal of residential development along the Menai Straits. Nucleated villages do exist but these are far fewer than one would expect to find in an English county. The outstanding example of the impact of industry on the landscape is Mynydd Parys which has still not recovered from the pollution caused by copper mining at the end of the eighteenth century, but there is no shortage of other industrial remains. The twentieth century brought more industry, particularly a large aluminium smelter, now closed, near Holyhead and a nuclear power station at Wylfa and the presence of the latter, along with the universal availability of electric power, brought high-voltage power lines and the pylons which carry them; these, too, are part of an evolving landscape.

The rural landscape has also changed. One feature of Anglesey was its windmills, the bases of many of which are still to be seen. Although a few existed in the middle ages, these really spread in the eighteenth and nineteenth centuries, partly because of the problem of water supply in a dry summer; most medieval

---

4 The classic account of the geology of Anglesey is E. Greenly, *The Geology of Anglesey* (2 vols., 1919); see also A.E. Trueman, *Geology and Scenery in England and Wales* (1949), pp.196-8; E.G. Bowen, 'Anglesey and the North Wales coast', in E.G. Bowen, ed., *Wales, a Physical, Historical and Regional Geography* (1957), pp.306-12, and Melville Richards, ed., *An Atlas of Anglesey* (1972), pp. 9, 7, 17.

mills had depended on water power.[5] But the landscape is above all one of enclosed fields and consolidated farms and this is what can be seen today from
the top of any hill; fields are divided from each other by hedges and the depth
of the hedge-banks along many rural roads bears witness to their antiquity.
There are a few small tracts of woodland as well as some more recent afforesta-
tion, particularly by the Forestry Commission at Newborough and on Mynydd
Llwydiarth; another recent feature of the man-made landscape is the presence
of two large reservoirs at Llyn Cefni and Llyn Alaw, the latter now occupying
Cors y Bol.[6] There is not much common land; the main tracts are Penrhyn
Mawr on Holy Island, Tywyn Trewan between Valley and Rhosneigr, Tywyn
Aberffraw and Mynydd Bodafon.[7] Although there were no parliamentary en-
closures of open fields, a good deal of common land was enclosed by private
Act; Malltraeth Marsh, for example, was reclaimed and enclosed by a series of
Acts between 1788 and 1859. Some commons were voluntarily enclosed, as at
Llanfair Mathafarn Eithaf in 1815, and some were enclosed by illegal encroach-
ment, as on Mynydd Mechell.[8]

This, then, is the Anglesey landscape as it appears in the first quarter of the
twenty-first century. Its medieval counterpart would not be entirely unfamiliar
to the modern observer but it would be different. Unfortunately, there are few
contemporary descriptions; the earliest mention of it is by Bede who tells us
that in the seventh century the island supported a population of 960 families
and was more fertile than the Isle of Man which supported over 300.[9] The next
author to comment was Gerald of Wales. In his account of his journey through
Wales with Archbishop Baldwin of Canterbury in 1188 he said that Anglesey
contained 363 townships, by which he probably meant settlements.[10] He added
that it was 'an arid stony land, rough and unattractive in appearance'. To him
it was not unlike the area round St David's in his native Dyfed. He went on to
discuss its fertility, stating that it produced more grain than any other part of
Wales and providing us with the first recorded use of the phrase 'Môn Mam
Cymru' which stemmed from this.[11] Later descriptions are scarce. The first

---

5  *An Atlas of Anglesey*, p.97; see also R.O. Roberts, 'The mills of Anglesey', *TAAS* 1958, pp.1-15.
   In 1352 the heirs of Gwely Hywel ap Tudur in Trefdraeth Wastrodion in Malltraeth owed suit to
   the prince's mill at Dindryfwl but when it was not working they were free to mill where they wished
   (*Extent of Anglesey*, p.163); this suggests that there might sometimes have been a shortage of water.

6  For a brief summary of modern land use see *An Atlas of Anglesey*, p.139.

7  All common land registered in accordance with the Commons Registration Act, 1965, is shown
   in *An Atlas of Anglesey*, p.142; see also W.G. Hoskins and L. Dudley Stamp, *The Common Lands
   of England and Wales* (1963), p.228.

8  *An Atlas of Anglesey*, p.143. The standard account of enclosures in Anglesey is Evan J. Jones, 'The
   enclosure movement in Anglesey 1788-1866' reprinted in *TAAS* 2002, pp.23-61 and 2003, pp.48-69.

9  L. Sherley-Price, ed. and trans., Bede, *A History of the English Church and People* (1955), pp.112-3.

10  Gerald of Wales, *The Journey through Wales*, trans. Lewis Thorpe (1978), pp.186-7.

11  ibid. (*The Description of Wales*), p.230.

English topographical writer, William Worcester, did mention Anglesey in his *Itineraries*, written in 1478, but his description is rather garbled and much is lifted from Gerald. Of Llanddwyn he said that Dwynwen was buried in her chapel two miles from Newborough and that there were only two cottages in the township.[12] We are told elsewhere that Anglesey was well-populated with one thousand souls, that there was a monastery of white monks on the east side and another monastery on the west, and that the Skerries, one mile long and two bowshots wide, were not inhabited.[13] John Leland, writing at the end of the medieval period, is not much more informative since he does not seem to have visited Anglesey and what he has to say is not, therefore, the fruit of his own observation. He mentions that the roots of trees were often found in bogs when peat was being dug to be used as fuel and he also refers to the large numbers of rabbits around Llanddwyn.[14] One of his informants was Rowland Griffith of Plas Newydd who told him that within living memory men had not enclosed their land but that now they cleared the stones and separated their holdings in the Devonshire fashion; this probably means the construction of hedge banks with bushes growing on them.[15] In digging for the stones they often dug up 'yerthen pottes with the mouthis turnid douneward, conteyning (*cineres et ossa mortuorum*)'; in other words, Bronze Age burials were often disturbed. There also survives a list of churches and natural features in Anglesey, furnished by Mr Griffith and annotated by Leland himself.[16]

Contemporary descriptions are not, therefore, of much help. Gerald's description of Anglesey suggests that there was little woodland by the twelfth century and this is borne out by other evidence. The island was once heavily wooded, as was most of Britain, and Tacitus's description of the destruction of the sacred oak-groves of the druids by Suetonius Paulinus is well-known. Pollen analysis also reveals that there was once extensive woodland. Clearance began with the beginnings of agriculture in Neolithic times; there can be little doubt that the process has been essentially the work of man since the climate is favourable to forest growth.[17] It was certainly complete by the later middle

12  William Worcester, *Itineraries* (ed. J.H. Harvey, 1969), p.67.

13  ibid., pp. 135, 137.

14  L. Toulmin Smith, ed., *Leland's Itinerary in Wales* (1906), pp.52-3.

15  ibid., p.90. I am grateful to Professor G.R.J. Jones for this point.

16  ibid., pp.128-34.

17  Cyril Fox in *Anglesey Inventory*, pp.xxxii-xxxiii; for an analysis of plant remains from the excavations at Bryn yr Hen Bobl between 1929 and 1936 see ibid., p.xxxv, where it is suggested that oak and hazel predominated. Pollen analysis from the Bronze Age site at Bedd Branwen indicates the presence of oak, hazel and alder in the vicinity (Frances Lynch, 'Report on the re-excavation of two Bronze Age cairns in Anglesey: Bedd Branwen and Treiorwerth', *Arch Camb.* 120 (1971), 16). See also G.R.J. Jones and S.J. Eyre, eds., *Geography as Human Ecology* (1966), pp.199-203.

ages; no surviving deeds mention woodland and there seems to have been an acute shortage of building timber. When this was required it had to be imported; in 1305 the men of the county of Anglesey and the cantref of Llŷn sought leave to get 'commodities and things necessary for their buildings and ploughs' from the woods of Caernarfonshire and Merioneth as they had in the past and their request was granted.[18] The men of the commote of Menai asked for timber to rebuild the hall of the manor of Rhosyr and the burgesses of Newborough and Beaumaris sought wood from across the Menai Straits.[19] In 1336-7 timber for the repair of Melin y Bont and Melin Dindryfwl in the commote of Malltraeth was bought at Llanrwst and carried to Southcrook or Abermenai by sea.[20] It was also sought further afield; in 1395-6 payments were made to carpenters and sawyers in the king's forests in Cheshire for felling and lopping oaks for mills in Anglesey and Caernarfonshire, which may also indicate some degree of deforestation in Snowdonia by that time.[21] Another possible sign of the lack of woodland is that in the 1352 extent pigs are mentioned in only two townships, Tre Feibion Meurig and Bodynolwyn in Llifon; the presence of pigs was usually an indication of pannage in the lord's woods.[22] It is also significant that, while the commotal officials in Caernarfonshire and Merioneth included the forester or woodward, no such office existed in Anglesey after 1284.

Place-name evidence likewise tells us little about trees or woodland, although the names of two adjacent parishes in Dindaethwy, Llan-faes and Llan-goed, which described a church in the open fields and another in the woods, may have some significance.[23] The name Llannerch-y-medd also suggests the presence of forest at some time, since *llannerch* means a glade or a clearing. The only wood of any size in the late medieval period was that of Coedcadw near Beaumaris; this was also known as the wood of Llan-faes where in 1305 twenty shillings rent of assise was due from eighteen acres of underwood.[24] The accounts of Anglesey officials for 1353-4 include a transcript of an agreement between the Prince of Wales and a number of local men, most of them burgesses of Beaumaris, under which the prince had granted and sold the es-

---

18  *Rec.Caern.*, p.214.

19  ibid., pp. 214, 218, 223.

20  TNA SC6/1229/3; timber was also imported in 1339 for work on Melin Adda near Amlwch (TNA SC6/1229/6) and in 1344-5 it was obtained from the wood at Dolbadarn and carried by sea from Caernarfon to Beaumaris (TNA SC6/1229/7).

21  TNA SC6/1215/7.

22  *Extent of Anglesey*, pp. 189, 191. Pannage was the right to pasture pigs in the lord's woods and its payment was a sign of unfree status.

23  F.V. Emery, *Wales* (1969), p.59. The clearing of the woodlands in general is discussed here, pp.58-82.

24  Extent of the borough of Beaumaris (TNA SC11/767) printed in *Arch.Camb. Original Documents* (1877), p.xviii.

tovers of his wood of Llan-faes to them.[25] They were to enjoy this right in all
the wood, with the exception of eight acres granted to John de St Peter, the
constable of the castle; the bounds were from the road running across the
marsh of the wood to the hedge between the marsh and the rest of the wood
which it enclosed. They could lop branches off oak, maple and other trees and
sell them and they undertook to keep the wood in good condition. The main
reason for the clearance of woods from Neolithic times onwards was the need
of an expanding population for more cultivable land and the rapid rise in the
population of Europe in the twelfth century led to large-scale deforestation.
This is probably as true of Wales in general and Anglesey in particular as it is of
other countries and regions.[26] In the reign of Edward VI Dr Thomas Phaer said
of Anglesey that it was 'well inhabited, aboundant of corne, cattell and all good
provision except wood, good trade of merchandise and many gentlemen'.[27]

Obviously hills, lakes and rock-strewn pastures do not change very much,
but the outstanding example of man-made change in Anglesey is probably
Malltraeth Marsh or Cors Ddyga, through which the river Cefni flows to the
sea. This was drained and embanked between 1788 and 1859 and some three
thousand acres of land reclaimed, with the result that it looks very different
today; the original meander of the river is still to be seen to the west of the new
cut. Before the works were carried out, the marsh would have been an extensive
area of shallow water and mud flats through which the Cefni traced its course.
It would probably have been a major obstacle to travellers and it is not surprising that a wildfowler was among those from the commote of Malltraeth
who made their peace with the king in 1406.[28] The lack of any embankment
probably meant that the marshes could not be used for pasturing sheep as
could those in Essex and Kent. There were several lakes, along with considerable tracts of marsh, elsewhere and little was probably done to them. The
largest marshes were Cors y Bol and several in the commote of Dindaethwy,

25  TNA SC6/1149/4, m.8b. Estover was the right to collect dead wood or to cut a certain amount
    of standing wood. In 1355 the lessees of the mills of Llan-faes and Cefn-coch were allowed to
    have timber from the wood of Llan-faes when necessary for repairs (TNA SC6/1149/3, m.4b).
26  F.V. Emery, op.cit., pp.67-9.
27  W.R.B. Robinson, 'Dr. Thomas Phaer's report on the harbours and customs administration of
    Wales under Edward VI', BBCS 24 (1972), 502.
28  Guto'r Glyn composed a cywydd to Huw Lewis of Prysaeddfed giving thanks for his deliverance
    from drowning at Malltraeth and in his ymryson or battle of wits with Llywelyn ap Gutun the
    latter alleged that Guto had been drowned there when drunk. (Dafydd Wyn Wiliam, 'Y
    traddodiad barddol ym mhlwyf Bodedern, Môn', TAAS 1969-70, pp.75-7; Ifor Williams and J.
    Llywelyn Williams, eds. Gwaith Guto'r Glyn (2nd edn., 1961), pp.98-100). These references
    suggest that the perils of Malltraeth Marsh were well-known. Gruffudd Adarwr paid a fine of 5s
    in 1406 (Glyn Roberts, 'The Anglesey submissions of 1406', BBCS 15 (1952), 56). For a list of
    fords before the building of the embankment see BUASC Bangor 1790; I am grateful to my wife
    for drawing my attention to this reference.

especially Cors Erddreiniog and Cors Llanddyfnan. There are no surviving references to lakes but there are some to peat and to turbaries; peat or turf was valuable as a roofing material and as a fuel and its ash was an excellent fertiliser. Deeds mention turbaries in several townships; in 1472, for example, Hywel ap Dafydd ap Tudur of Llanddyfnan conveyed to Elen Bulkeley the turbary known as Mawnog Madog ap Gruffudd ab Einion along with another called Mawnog Ieuan Goch ap Madog ap Cynwrig and two un-named ones, all in that township. When Dafydd ap Gruffudd ap Dafydd ap Hywel conveyed Y Penrhyn Isaf in Dindryfwl to Gruffudd Gethin in 1459 he reserved the right to cut 'pyles or mawn' out of the moor called Y Gors.[29] In the few fourteenth-century court rolls which remain there are several references to stealing turves; at the sheriff's tourn held for the commote of Malltraeth on 23 March 1322 three from Dindryfwl and two from Rhosmor were amerced for this offence.[30] Rushes, useful as roofing material and floor covering, as well as for lighting, also grew on marshy land and at the Dindaethwy tourn on 20 September 1321 there were several cases of taking rushes in the townships of Carwad and Ucheldref.[31]

Marshes and turbaries had always been there but the landscape could be changed by natural disasters. In low-lying coastal areas this could often be the result of inundation following storms. In Anglesey the enemy was not the sea but sand and this happened particularly on the south coast. The classic case is that of Newborough; here a great storm on 6 December 1330 brought disaster.[32] According to the inquisition taken at Beaumaris on 26 August 1332 there had been about 600 acres of land in the manor of Newborough when it was first surveyed, each being worth sixpence a year. On 6 December 1330 183 acres were completely covered and destroyed by the sand and the tide and were now uncultivable and worthless.[33] Another inquisition a few days later found that the king's tenants at Rhosyr had held eleven cottages and 28 acres of land in villeinage; these, too, had been covered by the sand and the tide and there was no longer any profit to be had from them.[34] In 1359-60 a reduction of the rent from the manor of Rhosyr was still being allowed for the lands submerged by sea and sand and in his account for 1396-7 Hwlcyn ap Dafydd ab Ieuan, the farmer of the manor of Rhosyr, stated that during the year some 90 acres

29 BUASC Baron Hill 1111; NLW Sotheby 49.
30 TNA SC2/215/7, m.1a; similar offences had been committed in Llifon and Talybolion (mm.1b, 2a.)
31 TNA SC2/215/5, m.3b
32 The date is usually given as 1331 but the inquisition states that the disasters occurred on the feast of St Nicholas in the fourth year of Edward III which was 6 December 1330.
33 CIM ii, no.1275. For a detailed discussion of the coast see A.H.W. Robinson, 'The sandy coast of south-west Anglesey', TAAS 1980, pp.37-66.
34 CIM ii, no.1328; see also A.H.W. Robinson, op.cit., pp.55-56, where other fourteenth-century examples are cited.

of land in the townships of Tregarwed and Tre Feibion Pyll had been destroyed 'by the water and the sand of the sea'.[35] Thus the storm of 1330 was not an isolated event and this is borne out by the extent of the bishop of Bangor's lands made in 1306; in the township of Llanddwyn seven tenants held eight messuages without land.[36] Even then the dunes had begun their inexorable advance and something similar was probably happening on the other side of Malltraeth Marsh at Aberffraw.

The sandy beaches and rocky coves of the Anglesey coast are today attractions for the holiday visitor; the only real port is Holyhead. Beaumaris was the principal medieval port but many of the bays which indent the coast were ports as well. Abermenai or Southcrook at the southern end of the Menai Straits had a long history; Gruffudd ap Cynan had landed there in his first attempt to recover his inheritance and he had left it to his widow.[37] Other ports mentioned from time to time in medieval sources included Traeth Coch, Mathafarn, Dulas and Holyhead and there must have been many more in an age when the sea was the easiest means of communication. There survives among the records of the Exchequer a list of the harbours of Wales compiled by Dr Thomas Phaer during the reign of Edward VI and although it is from a slightly later period it does probably indicate the places which were regarded as ports in the middle ages.[38] The first Anglesey harbour in the list is Llanddwyn, described as 'a barred haven for litle boates'. Next comes Aberffraw, followed by St Bride's or Trearddur Bay and Holyhead, 'a roade and a good haven for all shippes at all wyndes to lie drie'; Holy Island is described as 'plenteous of corn', an interesting point since the landscape there is very similar to that of Llŷn which Phaer describes as 'verie bare of corn'. Beyond Holyhead were the ports of Trefednyfed, Cemlyn, St Patrick's, Dulas and Traeth Coch.[39] Ynys Seiriol was 'a meane rode for all shippes at sowthe wynde' and much the same was said of Round Table, presumably that part of Traeth Coch below Bwrdd Arthur. Beaumaris, the chief port of Anglesey, was 'a goodly haven and a rode for all shipps' serving 'a proper towne and a stronge castell'.

The effect of communications on the medieval landscape is hard to gauge. Many modern roads follow medieval routes and such features as hedge-banks can often be a guide to antiquity, especially along country lanes where there has been little or no realignment over the centuries; roads, too, are made to serve the needs of particular communities and when these needs no longer

35  TNA SC6/1149/10, m.6a; 1152/3, m.7a.

36  *Rec.Caern.* p.104

37  D. Simon Evans, ed., *Historia Gruffud vab Kenan* (1977), pp. 6, 32.

38  W.R.B. Robinson, op.cit., 485-503; the details of Anglesey harbours are on 501-2.

39  Trefednyfed must be Porth Trefadog although Porth Swtan or Church Bay to the north would seem to be a better anchorage; St Patrick's is Porth Wygyr, the present Cemais Bay.

exist they may be abandoned.[40] The question of the presence of Roman roads in Anglesey is still an open one.

There are a few references to roads in medieval deeds; in 1483, for example, lands are mentioned in Mathafarn Eithaf extending from the road near Ffynnon y Badell and a deed of 1339 refers to the highway in Newborough leading from the cross at the centre of the town to Abermenai, the present Chapel Street and originally the road to the ferry and hence one of the main arteries of southern Anglesey.[41] A 1325 conveyance of a holding in the common fields of Beaumaris refers to an abuttal on the way from the town to the friary.[42] One example of what is almost certainly a medieval road is that from the shore to Llan-faes church, which was probably the road from the port to the town of Llan-faes; the same might be said of the other roads which meet by the church. One would expect to find roads from each of the ferries; the old post road from Beaumaris to Holyhead, as mapped by John Ogilby in 1675, may, for example, have been the medieval one and the road from Moel-y-don ferry through to Llanddaniel may have a similar claim to antiquity. The best-documented medieval communications are the six ferries across the Menai Straits which before Thomas Telford came were Anglesey's only link with the mainland; these were at Abermenai, Caernarfon, Moel-y-don, Porthaethwy, Porthesgob (the bishop of Bangor's ferry between Bangor and Cadnant) and Beaumaris (originally Llan-faes).[43]

Roads had to cross rivers but medieval bridges are particularly difficult to trace. Fords were probably far more common, especially since Anglesey rivers are usually so small and it is possible that the element 'rhyd' in a place-name often indicates a medieval ford and consequently a medieval road or right-of-way. One example from the commote of Malltraeth is Rhyd-y-fotyn on a road, now a farm track, which runs from the Cefn Cwmwd-Aberffraw road in the direction of Dindryfwl. This is shown on the first edition of the Ordnance Survey one-inch map as a road running through to join the present one from Soar to Dothan and Llanbeulan and it may well have been a medieval road which was later abandoned. Another example from the same commote is Pont Rhyd-y-sbardun on the present B5109 from Llangefni to Bodedern between Llangefni and Bodffordd, which again may point to the antiquity of what was, in pre-Telford days, the post road to Holyhead. The Welsh name for Four Mile Bridge, Pont Rhyd-bont, suggests that this was the main crossing to Holy Is-

---

40  For general discussion of roads see W.G. Hoskins, *Fieldwork In Local History* (1967), pp.136-49 and Paul Hindle, *Medieval Roads and Tracks* (2002).
41  BUASC Baron Hill 1010; Mostyn 751.
42  NLW Pitchford Hall 1365.
43  The standard work on the ferries is H.R. Davies, *The Conway and the Menai Ferries* (1942).

land before the building of the Stanley Embankment. Rhyd-yr-arian in Llanfihangel Ysgeifiog could also testify to the age of an existing road, while Pont Rhyd-y-defaid today crosses Afon Caradog where it forms the boundary between Llandrygarn and Llechylched parishes and carries the B5112 between Treban and Llannerch-y-medd. Rhyd-y-clafdy in Llanbadrig is another which is now on a farm track which may once have been a road, and Rhyd-y-groes in the same parish is not on any existing route but may have had some connection with Afon Wygyr nearby. There is also a combined footpath and farm track which crosses a tributary of the Wygyr and which is shown as a road on the first edition of the Ordnance Survey map; this again may be a medieval road which has fallen into disuse. The same may be true of Rhyd-y-delyn Fawr and Rhyd-y-delyn Fach near Penmynydd church which are not connected with any existing road. These are only a few examples but a detailed study might prove rewarding.[44]

But it is the hand of man that has contributed most to the historical landscape. Forest clearance was, of course, a once-and-for-all activity but the basic feature of human settlement, which is the primary factor in shaping the landscape, is continuity.[45] The development of the landscape is a continuous process; in other words, landscape is dynamic and it cannot be described as a kind of fly in amber, caught at a particular moment in time. All one can hope to do is to try and give a general picture. When considering human settlement it is necessary to seek to understand its location and why men chose to settle where they did. One of the best examples of this continuity is to be found at Aberffraw, the traditional royal seat of Gwynedd, where the royal court, the ancient church of Llangadwaladr or Eglwys Ail associated with it and the Iron Age fort of Twyn-y-Parc are all in the same neighbourhood.[46] It obviously stands to reason that men will settle on the best soils and settlement and soil can be correlated.[47] The *maerdrefi* or royal demesne townships were all situated near the coast on good quality well-drained soils; Llifon, the only commote without a *maerdref* settlement, had no such soil near the coast although it did

44  Anglesey fords are discussed by Gwilym T. Jones, *The Fords of Anglesey / Rhydau Môn* (1992).

45  The best general discussion of the development of the Anglesey landscape is in Roy Millward and Adrian Robinson, *Landscapes of North Wales* (1978), pp.20-38; much of this is based on the work of Professor Glanville Jones.

46  G.R.J. Jones, 'Post-Roman Wales', in H.P.R. Finberg, ed., *The Agrarian History of England and Wales* 1 (ii), *A.D. 43-1042* (1972), p.376; idem., 'Anglesey portrayed', *TAAS* 1974, pp.114-6; idem., 'Multiple estates and early settlement', in P.H. Sawyer, ed., *English Medieval Settlement* (1979), pp.17-18.

47  Settlement in terms of soil quality was discussed by G.R.J. Jones, 'The distribution of medieval settlement in Anglesey', *TAAS* 1955, pp.35-45, and idem., 'Rural settlement in Anglesey', in Jones and Eyre, op.cit., pp.21-5; the standard work on Anglesey soils is E. Roberts, *The County of Anglesey* (Memoirs of the Soil Survey of Great Britain, 1958), which includes a valuable map.

contain one carucate of demesne land at Cleiflog near the Alaw estuary.[48] About three-quarters of the townships and hamlets of Anglesey were situated on well-drained soils and it has been suggested that primary settlement was where such soils were within easy reach of the coast, the interior of the island being used for summer grazing.[49] With the rapid rise in population that occurred all over Europe in the twelfth and thirteenth centuries, permanent settlement may have spread inland although some of this new settlement may have been the result of deliberate colonisation by the princes. It is possible that even in the *maerdrefi* there was expansion into less fertile land because of the pressure of a growing population.[50] In these circumstances it may not be without significance that a number of parishes had detached portions, some of which are shown on the first edition of the Ordnance Survey map; these may have been a consequence of the expansion of existing kindreds into new territory, thus creating hamlets some distance from the primary settlement.[51]

Thus the great expansion of settlement in Anglesey came in the twelfth and thirteenth centuries and it was probably, after the early clearance of the forests, the most important contributory factor to the shape of the medieval landscape.[52] The basic unit of settlement was the township. Anglesey, like every other part of Wales, was divided into a number of these, each eventually with fixed boundaries; a township might include a number of dependent hamlets which reflected later expansion. Townships could be free or bond; the free ones were those where the land was hereditary land, held by one or more kindred groups or *gwelyau,* often (but not necessarily) descended from a common ancestor.[53] The eponyms of these kindred groups seem generally to have lived in the late twelfth or early thirteenth centuries and their ancestors were probably settled in these places for generations previously.[54] For example, in the large township of Conysiog Lys and its dependent hamlets, which made up a large

---

48  G.R.J. Jones, *TAAS* 1955, p.46; for the development of the landscape in Cleifiog and Llanllibio see F.A. Barnes, 'Land tenure and landscape in Llanynghenedl, Anglesey', *TAAS* 1988, especially pp.35-45.

49  ibid., p.36.

50  Roy Millward and Adrian Robinson, op.cit., pp.32-3; G.R.J. Jones, *TAAS* 1955, pp.41-8.

51  G.R.J. Jones, op.cit., pp.41-2 and Fig.1. Examples which appear on the first edition of the one-inch Ordnance Survey map include Llwydiarth, a detached portion of Llangoed, both townships having formerly been among the lands of the bishop of Bangor, Bod-Ddeiniol which was a detached hamlet of Llanfechell township in 1352 and which was later a detached portion of that parish and Mynydd-mwyn, a detached portion of Gwredog, both townships having been episcopal ones in 1306.

52  For a recent overview of the medieval landscape and of settlement in Anglesey see David Longley, *Medieval Settlement on Anglesey: an assessment of the potential for fieldwork* (GAT, n.d.); see also idem, 'Medieval settlement and landscape change on Anglesey', *Landscape History* 23 (2001), 39-59.

53  For a detailed discussion of the *gwely* see G.R.J. Jones, 'Post-Roman Wales', pp.320-4. The term originally meant the kindred group but came to apply to its holding as well.

54  Dafydd Jenkins, 'A lawyer looks at Welsh land law', *THSC* 1967, pp.246-7, reminds us that these eponyms had ancestors as well as descendants.

part of the commote of Llifon and which may reflect an earlier pattern of social organisation, the land was held in 1352 by five free *gwelyau*, the eponyms of which were all sons of Hwfa ap Cynddelw.[55] The free township is generally regarded as having begun with the dwelling of the original proprietor but the rise in population, along with the operation of partible succession or *cyfran* led to the establishment of new homesteads away from the original settlement or *hendref*. These would be situated on the edges of the arable land and the result has been described as a 'girdle pattern' of settlement.[56] One of the best-documented free townships of Anglesey, thanks to the survival of a crown rental of 1549, is that of Llysdulas in Twrcelyn, held in 1352 by seven *gwelyau* descended from one Carwed.[57] Here there was a dispersed pattern of settlement and by 1549 the lands of these kindreds included holdings a long way from Llysdulas itself, a township the nucleus of which was the later parish of Llanwenllwyfo.[58] In fact, in 1549 there were Llysdulas lands at Llwydiarth Esgob in Llandyfrydog parish, at Madyn Dysw and several other places in Amlwch, at Trysglwyn and at Penbol; its hamlets in 1352 included Garddwr in Talybolion. Both Conysiog Lys and Llysdulas were large townships and free townships did tend, on the whole, to be larger than unfree ones.

The classic pattern of bond tenure was the *tir cyfrif* township. The settlement pattern here was similar to that in the royal demesne townships and it is important to remember that many bond townships had been granted to freemen by the princes and that their nature was therefore concealed in the 1352 extent. In *tir cyfrif* townships the bondmen lived in small nucleated hamlets and in return for labour services and renders 'heavy as compared with those of the freemen but light by English manorial standards' they enjoyed the use of small arable holdings along with grazing rights on the lord's waste.[59] Rights and obligations were shared equally among all the adult males, the total burden being a fixed one, and the arable land was reallocated from time to time according to the adult male population. In other bond settlements the tenants held by *tir gwelyog* tenure; here the *gwelyau* had less liberty than their free counterparts and the settlement pattern could be either one of dispersed homesteads or of nucleated communities.[60] In these cases the bond tenants may have been

55  *Extent of Anglesey*, p.179.

56  G.R.J. Jones, *TAAS* 1955, p.33.

57  *Extent of Anglesey*, p.217.

58  For Llysdulas see T. Jones Pierce, 'Medieval settlement in Anglesey', in *Medieval Welsh Society* (1972), pp.253-6, and 'An Anglesey crown rental of the sixteenth century', in ibid., pp.87-101; G.R.J. Jones, *TAAS* 1955, pp.68-73, and in Jones and Eyre, op.cit., pp.203-7.

59  G.R.J. Jones, 'The tribal system in Wales: a re-assessment in the light of settlement studies', *WHR* 1 (1961), 119; T. Jones Pierce, 'Medieval settlement in Anglesey', pp.276-7.

60  Some of these were examined by Professor Jones *TAAS* 1955, pp.75-81 where he discussed Twrllachied, Dwyran and Clorach, and in Jones and Eyre, op.cit., pp.207-11, he again examined Twrllachied and Dwyran.

granted the superior status to encourage settlement and cultivation in the interior of the island.[61] But the important point to remember about these bond townships is that they were generally nucleated communities or, in other words, hamlets. It was once customary to deny the existence of many such communities in Wales because of the lack of them today but this was the result of assumptions made on the basis of modern evidence. In fact, communities are born and communities die and the English and Welsh landscapes are scattered with deserted and abandoned villages.[62] In medieval Anglesey there would have been a number of nucleated communities which have now disappeared; all that often remains today is a single consolidated farm bearing the same name. The 1306 extent of the bishop of Bangor's lands is one source which may be used to illustrate this; all the episcopal bond townships were held by *tir gwelyog* tenure but the same argument may be valid. Llanfair-yn-y-cwmwd in the commote of Menai is the smallest parish in Anglesey and it is probably coterminous with the medieval episcopal township of Llanfair. In 1306 it was held by two bond *gwelyau* which consisted of ten named tenants along with an avowry tenant or incomer.[63] If this meant that there were eleven homesteads there, there must have been some nucleated settlement; there is none today. Another episcopal bond township was Conysiog Lan in Llifon, which must have formed an enclave in the large free township of Conysiog Lys. Here there were 49 tenants who held four carucates or 240 acres in common and this again suggests a considerable density of settlement.[64] The nucleus was presumably near Llanfaelog church; there are a few houses there today but nothing resembling a village. At Llanfflewin in Talybolion thirteen tenants held half a carucate, which again suggests some nucleation; today the parish church stands in a farmyard.[65] And at Tal-y-llyn, between Aberffraw and Gwalchmai, a medieval chapel stands alone at the side of the road near Llyn Badrig. Its present isolation must be misleading; such a chapel would not have been built had there not been a community for it to serve and in 1306 the episcopal township of Tal-y-llyn had three free tenants who held one carucate between them and nineteen unfree ones who held a carucate and a half in common.[66] This must have made for a not insubstantial population and would explain the chapel's existence; it may also indicate the site of a deserted medieval village.

61  G.R.J. Jones, *TAAS* 1955, pp.56-7.
62  The standard work on English deserted villages is M.W. Beresford, *The Lost Villages of England* (1954); there is a useful general discussion of the subject in W. G.Hoskins, *The Making of the English Landscape*, pp.117-23. See also G.R.J. Jones, op.cit., pp.32-3; investigation in north Wales is bedevilled by the lack of excavation.
63  *Rec.Caern.*, p.104.
64  ibid., p.105.
65  ibid., p.107.
66  ibid., p.105.

But it was the *tir cyfrif* communities which were particularly associated with nucleated settlements. One such community was Deri in Twrcelyn where there are now two farms which bear the name but no sign of any village.[67] Llanol, in the parish of Llanbabo in Talybolion, was another *tir cyfrif* township where no sign of a nucleated settlement has survived, while at Llanllibio in Llifon even the church has disappeared.[68] These are only three examples; Porthaethwy was another township, part of which was held by the same tenure, but here the settlement really dates from the nineteenth century.[69] Some, if not all, of the townships alienated to freemen were probably *tir cyfrif*, like Nantbychan in Twrcelyn, but again no nucleated settlement has survived.[70] The village at Bodffordd may owe its origin to the old post road and the same may be true of Bodedern, a free hamlet in 1352. Some such settlement may have been connected with another form of tenure, *tir corddlan* or nucleal land. This seems to have been particularly associated with those old-established churches which were the seats of religious communities or *clasau* around which hamlets grew up. Some traces persisted at Llangadwaladr in the eighteenth century and vestiges at Llanynys in the Vale of Clwyd survived well into the twentieth.[71] A similar pattern may well have existed at such religious centres as Caergybi and Llaneilian and the presence of a village at Llanfechell may also stem from this. The lack of medieval evidence for Llangefni is tantalising.

There is more evidence of nucleated settlement in the *maerdrefi*. Llan-faes, of course, was more than a village community; by the late thirteenth century it was probably the most important town in pre-conquest Gwynedd and although there is little above ground today its disappearance was the result of an act of state, not of natural decay. Llan-faes really died that Beaumaris might live; it was transferred to Rhosyr, the *maerdref* of the commote of Menai, and became the New Borough, a name which it used from the start. Anything that might have existed at Penrhosllugwy has disappeared completely. Cemais presents more of a problem because of the growth of the present village but there may be some continuity. Aberffraw is in many ways the most interesting of these sites because here the medieval village has survived, probably because of the rivalries of local landowners and because there were some other sources of income for the inhabitants.[72] The Anglesey landscape today is essentially one

67  *Extent of Anglesey*, pp.226-7.
68  ibid., pp. 209-10, 191
69  ibid., p.245.
70  ibid., p.226.
71  For *tir corddlan* see G.R.J. Jones, 'Post-Roman Wales', pp.340-9, where Amlwch is also mentioned, and 'Early customary tenures in Wales and open-field agriculture', in Trevor Rowley, ed., *The Origin of Open Field Agriculture* (1980), pp.206-15.
72  For discussion of Aberffraw see G.R.J. Jones, *TAAS* 1955, pp.81-4, Jones and Eyre, op.cit., pp.211-4, and P.H. Sawyer, op.cit., pp.15-18.

of scattered farms and dispersed settlement, as modern maps show, but although such settlement did exist in the middle ages, particularly in the free townships, the nucleated hamlet was also common. Nor should the two boroughs of Beaumaris and Newborough be forgotten and there were other small urban settlements like Llannerch-y-medd which is unfortunately undocumented but which lay where the boundaries of the commotes of Twrcelyn, Talybolion, Llifon and Menai met and which owed any development to its convenience as a trading centre.

But why did these settlements disappear and why does one consolidated farm so often stand today where there was once a community? Why do villages die? In fact, most bond communities which existed in medieval Wales have vanished; they only survived where there were conditions conducive to their survival.[73] The reasons for their decay often lie in the middle ages and they derive, at least in part, from the general crisis of the fourteenth century. The burdens of *tir cyfrif* tenure themselves contributed; the community was responsible for a fixed burden of rents and services so that if only one tenant remained he was responsible for everything. At Llanllibio, for example, the tenants owed a total of £7 10s as well as labour and carrying services.[74] If twenty adult males lived there, each would therefore have owed 7s 6d, but if only one survived he was liable for the whole sum. Similarly, at Llanol the total rent was £4 17s 8d with labour services at the mill of Aberalaw and at the manor of Cemais, both of which were some distance away and carrying services within Anglesey; the same rule applied.[75] Any substantial fall in the bond population therefore meant hardship for the survivors; the mortality caused by the Black Death started the rot if, indeed, it had not started already. Matters were made worse by the Glyn Dŵr revolt, which made it easy for many bondmen to move; fifteenth-century accounts tell a story of depopulation and decay in many bond townships. The ultimate result was the acquisition of bond lands by free landed proprietors and the beginning of a process of estate-building and consolidation which led eventually to the emergence of single farms.[76] It was not only plague that was responsible for depopulation; the demographic crisis of the fourteenth century, caused, to some extent, by overpopulation and climatic change had also played its part.[77] In many places, too, landowners abandoned arable farm-

---

73  G.R.J. Jones, *WHR* 1, 121.

74  *Extent of Anglesey*, p.191.

75  ibid., pp.207-8.

76  G.R.J. Jones, *WHR* 1, 121; Jones and Eyre, op.cit., p.223, *TAAS* 1955, p.75. The depopulation of bond townships is also briefly discussed in J. Beverley Smith, 'Crown and community in the principality of north Wales in the reign of Henry Tudor', *WHR* 3 (1966), 152, 154-7.

77  Trevor Rowley, *Villages in the Landscape* (1978), pp.120-1.

ing and went over to grass; there was no need for a pool of labour and 'without villagers there was no village'.[78] In Wales the process worked in the same way, helped by the demand for Welsh cattle in England, especially for the London market.[79] Even the *maerdrefi* were not exempt and this may perhaps explain the disappearance of Penrhosllugwy.

Thus the picture of human settlement has changed over the centuries. Viewed from any vantage point today, the Anglesey landscape or, indeed, any British agrarian landscape, is a patchwork of enclosed fields. Often this is a landscape which has only emerged in the past two hundred years and in many parts of England it is the result of parliamentary enclosure. But before this the pattern of agrarian organisation all over Europe was the open field. Every set- tlement had its common fields in which each occupant's holding was made up of a number of scattered strips. This was as true of Wales as of anywhere else and there is no lack of evidence, particularly in legal texts.[80] Medieval deeds bear this out although they do reveal some closes like the great close called Y Cae Glas in Llanbedr-goch in 1516 and the close in Penhwnllys called Cae Maes Yrron in 1520.[81] Some of this early enclosure had a particular purpose; in 1492 in Llanfechell there was an orchard called Cae Mawr.[82] Many deeds relate to the conveyance of small parcels and many of these parcels were obvi- ously one or more holdings in open fields. In Mathafarn Eithaf in 1498 Dafydd ap Hywel ap Gruffudd, otherwise known as Dafydd ab Angharad ferch Iolyn, conveyed to Gruffudd ap Hywel ap Tudur ap Dafydd of Llanddyfnan his ten- ement near Y Borth Wen which contained Yr Erw Fawr, Dryll y Ddôl, Y Fron Serth, Pen Coed Cadfor and Dryll y Garnedd.[83] These names do suggest a tenement made up of scattered holdings in open fields. The names of many parcels in these deeds are enough to indicate their nature and in the great sur- vey of escheat lands in Anglesey made in 1608 there are many more references to scattered parcels in fields, many of them amounting to only an acre or so.[84] Many of the names of these parcels are clear evidence of their having been strips or sharelands in open fields and there can be no doubt that in Anglesey, as elsewhere, the open field was the basis of arable farming.[85]

78  ibid., p.121.
79  G.R.J. Jones in Jones and Eyre, op.cit. p.223.
80  G.R.J. Jones, *TAAS* 1955, p.30.
81  BUASC Baron Hill 765, 766
82  BUASC Baron Hill 1462.
83  BUASC Baron Hill 1016.
84  TNA LR 2/205. This survey is an immensely valuable source and could serve as the basis for a considerable amount of topographical reconstruction.
85  In the manor of Rhosyr, for example, there was a parcel of land lying in an open field (the Latin word *campus* is used) (TNA LR 2/205, f.11) and in the same manor there were parcels called Llain yr Orsedd and Dryll ar yr Orsedd (ibid.). In Rhoscolyn there was a parcel called Y Llain dan y Sinach Fawr and in Aberffraw the survey included eight acres in Maes y Maerdref (ibid., ff. 37, 51).

The enclosure of these open fields was a gradual process, generally brought about by consolidation, by the patient accumulation of adjacent strips by the more enterprising proprietors and sometimes by exchange. It had already begun in the middle ages and it went on, probably into the nineteenth century. In Llandyfrydog township in 1524 the lands conveyed by Dafydd ap Rhys ap Llywelyn ap Gruffudd included a house by the churchyard, a close or enclosed field and various parcels in other, presumably open, fields.[86] In 1499 Llywelyn ap Rhys ap Gruffudd ab Einion of Berw Isaf conveyed three closes there with a house standing on them and half a meadow belonging to these closes between them and Cors Ddyga.[87] Anglesey in the middle ages was a region where men lived in both scattered homesteads and nucleated settlements, where arable farming was carried on in open fields and where livestock was pastured on waste or common. Unenclosed quillets survived at Aberffraw until well into the nineteenth century and the overall pattern there has been shown to have corresponded to that which prevailed on the medieval English manor.[88] Something similar must have existed in many medieval townships in Anglesey, especially since some, like Penmynydd and Trecastell, resembled the English manor in other ways. The absence of evidence is often frustrating.

One feature of the Anglesey landscape and, indeed, of the Welsh landscape in general, is the large number of isolated churches, remote from any centres of population and often only accompanied by a single farm, usually bearing the name Ty'n llan. This has in the past led to speculation about the siting of churches, speculation which generally ignores the fact that settlement patterns have changed a great deal since the middle ages. The fact that a church is isolated today, even if it is as isolated as, for example, Bodwrog, or Llanrhwydrys, or Gwredog, does not mean that it was isolated seven centuries ago. The combined effects of the consolidation of bond land and of depopulation have already been mentioned and dispersal of settlement could lead to the collapse of communities which had already diminished in size as the population fell.[89] Recent investigation suggests that most churches were, in fact, established near existing bond communities and it is interesting that the Norwich Taxation of 1254 associates many churches with townships. Churches were usually founded for public worship and although some may well bear the names of landowners rather than of saintly founders, the fact remains that even then they would have been founded for the use of those landowners, their bondmen and their de-

---

86  NLW Sotheby 108.
87  NLW Carreglwyd i, 2100.
88  G.R.J. Jones in Jones and Eyre, op.cit., pp.210-2, where he also describes the remains of an open-field pattern which survived in Dwyran Esgob in the nineteenth century.
89  The point was made by G.R.J. Jones in *WHR* 1, 127-8.

pendents who must have lived in some kind of settled community. In other words, churches were not built in a topographical vacuum and the sight of one standing on its own in a field should not inspire romantic visions of Celtic hermits fleeing a sinful world. They were not originally isolated but were within easy reach of the inhabitants of the local community. But, although churches were near bond communities, few of the latter had their own. The platonic bond settlement of the Laws had nine houses, a plough, a kiln, a churn, a cat, a cock, a bull and a herdsman. It was surrounded by one or more open fields and beyond them lay the common pasture.[90] It therefore had all that was necessary to make it a self-sufficient agricultural community but it had no church; indeed, the Laws state that the consecration of a church in a bond township made it free.[91] Churches tended, therefore, to be in free townships but bond settlements might nevertheless grow up around them and this was even more likely to be the case in mixed communities where one might suggest that the bondmen often lived in the vicinity of the church.

Not all these churches became parish churches in their own right. Many were originally chapels-of-ease, but as territorial parishes developed they became parish churches although many medieval livings included several. These were the chapels which have survived, but there were many which have not. Like churches, chapels-of-ease existed to serve communities, particularly those which were some distance from an existing place of worship. They were more common in the highland zone, not only in Wales but also in the immense upland parishes of northern England like Halifax in Yorkshire and Whalley in Lancashire.[92] Many seem to have been established in the twelfth century, presumably in response to the needs of a growing population, and as the pattern of settlement changed they ceased to serve any useful purpose. But their existence meant that the medieval landscape included rather more churches than are to be found today.[93] The *clas* church at Caergybi had three chapels or daughter churches at Bodedern, Bodwrog and Llandrygarn and the fact that

---

90  ibid., 121.

91  Dafydd Jenkins, ed., *Llyfr Colan* (1963), p.34, 1.573. In fact, of the *tir cyfrif* townships in Anglesey only Llanllibio had a church and all the lay bond *tir gwelyog* townships, with the exception of Rhosmor (Llangwyfan), were also without churches. The picture in the episcopal bond *tir gwelyog* townships was very different; many had churches, among them Y Dafarn (Llanallgo), Crafgoed (Llanddona) and Llanfflewin. Some mixed townships had churches, examples being Hirdre-faig (Llanffinan) and Nantmawr (Llaneugrad). Few alienated townships, most, if not all of which had a servile basis, had churches; not all free townships had them but many did.

92  W.G. Hoskins, *The Making of the English Landscape*, p.132. For a brief discussion of chapels see Dorothy Owen, 'Chapelries and rural settlement: an examination of some of the Kesteven evidence', in P.H. Sawyer, op.cit., pp.35-40.

93  For lists of Anglesey chapels see A.W. Wade-Evans, ed., 'Parochiale Wallicanum', *Y Cymmrodor* 22 (1910), 87-95, and E. Neil Baynes, 'The old monasteries, abbeys and chapels of Anglesey', *TAAS* 1920, pp.33-43.

these churches were dependent on Caergybi suggests that there were very early settlements nearby. The discovery some years ago of an early Christian cemetery near Bodedern may be significant in this respect.[94] The chapel at Tal-y-llyn has already been discussed. The ruined Hen Gapel Llugwy may indicate settlement near the fourth-century village site at Din Llugwy and Capel Halen at Penrhosllugwy was probably the chapel of the court complex there. The chapel at Dindryfwl near Aberffraw may have served the large mixed township of that name where there must certainly have been a fairly large nucleated settlement; the existence of a hill-fort there may suggest continuity.[95]

Many chapels have disappeared completely but the important point about them is that they reflected settlement and an increase in population in the twelfth and thirteenth centuries. Ecclesiastical topography can shed some light on landscape change but the medieval Anglesey landscape calls for more investigation and many questions have still to be asked as well as answered. But, above all, it must be stressed that the medieval landscape cannot be judged in today's terms.

94 Richard B. White, 'Excavations at Arfryn, Bodedern: long-cist cemeteries and the origins of Christianity in Britain', *TAAS* 1971-2, pp.19-45.
95 Tomos Roberts, 'Safle Capel Mair o Ddindryfwl', *TAAS* 1976-7, pp.51-2; *Extent of Anglesey*, pp.168-72.

# 2 *The Age of the Princes*

THE FACT that Anglesey is an island may have helped to give it its distinct character, but it also made it more exposed to attack from the sea. Indeed, many of the references to it before the thirteenth century have to do with such attacks; at least eleven Norse raids were recorded between 855 and 993. The foundation of the kingdom of Dublin in the ninth century made the island particularly vulnerable and recent investigation, especially the excavation of a Scandinavian settlement at Llanbedr-goch, bears this out. It is even possible that Dublin exercised a measure of political control in Gwynedd.[1] When Gruffudd ap Llywelyn seized the kingship of Gwynedd in 1039 it was to Dublin that Cynan ab Iago, possibly a member of the Gwynedd dynasty, fled. There he married the king's daughter and there his son Gruffudd was born and brought up. Gruffudd ap Cynan came to Gwynedd after the death of Bleddyn ap Cynfyn in 1075 to make his first bid for power; he is said to have landed at Abermenai and in Anglesey and Arfon he found his strongest support. Anglesey seems to have played an important part in his early career. When the behaviour of his Norse retinue proved too much for the men of Llŷn, those of Anglesey remained loyal and 75 of them fell in battle when he was defeated at Bron-yr-Erw. He escaped to Abermenai and went from there to the Skerries on his way back to Ireland. The following year he landed at Abermenai once again but had to leave when his Norse mercenaries plundered the island.[2] An Anglesey man, Cynddelw ap Conws, is said to have led the men of Gwynedd when Gruffudd and Rhys ap Tewdwr of Deuheubarth won their victory at Mynydd Carn in 1081.[3] The victory may have been followed by Gruffudd's capture and imprisonment by Earl Hugh of Chester and Gwynedd now lay at the mercy of Hugh's cousin Robert of Rhuddlan, Gruffudd's one-time ally. Domesday Book

1 Mark Redknap, 'Llanbedrgoch: an early medieval settlement and its significance', *TAAS* 2007, pp.53-73. Relations with Ireland are discussed by David Moore, 'Gruffudd ap Cynan and the medieval Welsh polity' in K.L. Maund, ed., *Gruffudd ap Cynan: a collaborative biography* (1996), pp.24-7; see also Wendy Davies, *Patterns of Power in Early Wales* (1990), pp.56-60.
2 *Historia Gruffud vab Kenan*, pp. 6-8, 10-11, 12; according to this source two brothers from Anglesey turned traitor (p.10).
3 According to the pedigrees he was the father of Hwfa ap Cynddelw, ancestor of so many Anglesey families (ibid., p.75); Bartrum, *WG*, p.44.

describes Robert as holding north Wales of the king, which suggests that he was recognised by William the Conqueror as ruler of Gwynedd in 1086. Nothing is known of events in Anglesey, or whether or not Robert of Rhuddlan ever succeeded in crossing the Menai Straits, but to have held Aberffraw might somehow have made legitimate his hold on Gwynedd.

The chronology of the period is obscure, to say the least, and it is important to remember that the twelfth-century biography of Gruffudd is the only source for most of the information about his career.[4] According to his biographer he escaped, or was released, from his captivity. The story of how Robert of Rhuddlan met his end is open to dispute; his place in Gwynedd was taken by Earl Hugh who, we are told by the same biographer, built castles at Bangor and Caernarfon, in Meirionnydd and in Anglesey.[5] In 1093 the earl refounded the Benedictine abbey of St Werburgh in Chester and among his grants to the monks were two manors in Anglesey, the tithe of the fisheries there and the right to operate a ship of ten nets in those same fisheries.[6] The *History* describes Gruffudd's clandestine activities in pursuit of his inheritance and he spent some time in hiding on the island.[7] But the tide was about to turn, and on the departure of William II for Normandy in 1094 a major revolt broke out in Gwynedd. Gruffudd seems to have sought the aid of the Manx king Godred Crovan, whom the *History* describes as his friend, a clear indication that Gruffudd ap Cynan, half Welsh and half Norseman, had a foot in both camps.[8] With the fleet lent to him by Godred he attacked Anglesey but a day-long battle was inconclusive and the Manxmen withdrew. With one ship Gruffudd remained on the Skerries and then sailed to Nefyn where he assembled an army, invaded Anglesey and besieged and took the Norman castle at Aber Lleiniog.[9]

It was not long before the Normans had been ejected from Gwynedd west of the Conwy and the revolt had spread to south Wales. An expedition led by William on his return from Normandy was defeated by the weather and it was not until the summer of 1098 that any further moves were made against Gruffudd. This campaign was led by the two marcher earls, Hugh of Chester and Hugh of Shrewsbury, with some Welsh assistance. Gruffudd and Cadwgan ap Bleddyn of Powys fell back on Anglesey and hired a Norse fleet from Dublin

4  *Historia Gruffud vab Kenan*; its limitations are discussed by Moore, op.cit., pp.1-2. There are fewer references to Gruffudd in *Brut y Tywysogyon*.

5  *Hist. Wales*, p.391; *Historia Gruffud vab Kenan*, p.18.

6  J. Tait, ed., *Chartulary of Chester Abbey* (Chetham Soc., N.S. 79, 1920), 17, 30.

7  *Historia Gruffud vab Kenan*, pp.18-9.

8  ibid., pp.19-20; *Hist. Wales*, p.392.

9  *Historia Gruffud vab Kenan*, pp.20-1; *Florentii Wigorniensis Monachi Chronicon ex Chronicis* (ed. B. Thorpe, 1848-9), ii, p.35.

to defend them, but the invaders bribed the sailors to change sides and the two rulers had to flee to Ireland.[10] The island was ransacked and many were killed and mutilated. The earl of Shrewsbury was said to have kennelled his dogs in Llandyfrydog church but by morning they had gone mad and the earl was dead within a week.[11]

Deliverance came from what was, to all appearances, an unexpected direction. Magnus Bareleg, king of Norway, appeared on the scene with his fleet and attacked the invaders. Hugh of Shrewsbury was killed, shot in the eye, according to the saga, by the king himself. The Normans withdrew and Gerald of Wales tells us that their power ceased in Anglesey from that time.[12] The withdrawal is understandable; the appearance of the Norwegian fleet made it clear that neither Anglesey nor Gwynedd could be subjugated permanently without sea power and at this time the Norsemen still controlled the Irish Sea.[13] Magnus's sudden and providential appearance was hardly likely to have been a coincidence. He had come from the Isle of Man, being engaged in an expedition against the king of Munster and, bearing in mind Gruffudd's previous alliance with the Manx and his Irish and Scandinavian connections, there must be a strong suspicion of collusion.[14]

Gruffudd and Cadwgan soon returned and Gruffudd spent the rest of his life securing his position in Gwynedd. His possession of Anglesey may have been recognised in 1099 and his biographer saw these years as a new age of peace and plenty.[15] He died in 1137, full of years and honour. Two Anglesey churches, Penmon and Caergybi, were among those which he remembered at the end, and to his wife Angharad he left that port of Abermenai which had played such a part in his early life.[16] Progress continued under his son and successor, Owain Gwynedd, and it cannot be without significance that the priory church at Penmon, the tower at Llaneilian and part of the parish church of Aberffraw all date from this period. It was a time of change in Gwynedd in general and Anglesey in particular; the twelfth century saw a rise in population all over Europe and a consequent increase in migration and colonisation and

10 *Hist. Wales*, pp.408-9; *Historia Gruffud vab Kenan*, pp.23-5; Thomas Jones, ed. *Brut y Tywysogyon* (RBH) (1955), pp.37-9.

11 Gerald of Wales, *The Journey through Wales*, p.188.

12 *Historia Gruffud vab Kenan.*, pp.25-7; *Hist. Wales*, pp.409-10; Snorri Sturluson, *Heimskringla: The Norse King Sagas* (trans. S. Laing, ed. P. Foote, 1961), p.263; Gerald of Wales, *Journey*, p.188.

13 The point about the events of 1098 showing that Anglesey could not he held without sea-power was made by J.E. Lloyd in RCAHM *Anglesey Inventory*, p.xxxvii.

14 For a discussion of the relevant sources, see *Historia Gruffud vab Kenan*, pp.94-5nn. and p.xcvii, and Arthur Jones, ed., *The History of Gruffudd ap Cynan* (1910), pp.178-9. Magnus visited Anglesey again in 1102 (*Brut y Tywysogyon*, (RBH), pp.45-7).

15 *Brut y Tywysogyon* (RBH), p.39; *Historia Gruffud vab Kenan*, p.30.

16 ibid., p.31.

lands in the interior of Anglesey may have been colonised at this time.[17] What was happening in the borderlands of eastern Europe and the Iberian peninsula was also happening in Wales.

Anglesey consisted of three cantrefs, Aberffraw, Cemais and Rhosyr, each of which was divided into two commotes; these were Malltraeth and Llifon, Talybolion and Twrcelyn and Dindaethwy and Menai. In many parts of Wales the origin of cantrefs seems to have lain in lesser political units which were later absorbed by larger neighbours but those in Anglesey would appear to be artificial creations, as J.E. Lloyd suggested a century ago.[18] By the thirteenth century each of the six commotes, apart from Llifon, had its own court centre and excavation of the court complex at Rhosyr, the commotal centre of Menai, where a charter of Llywelyn ab Iorwerth was dated in 1237, has revealed the layout of such a site for the first time.[19] It was to these centres that the prince and his court came as he travelled around his dominions and it was here, too, that the food renders due from his subjects were consumed and their services performed.

Although we know little of the general history of the island at this time, it appears to have been among the lands held by Owain Gwynedd's troublesome younger brother Cadwaladr, since he was expelled from it in 1152.[20] In 1157 a major campaign was mounted against Gwynedd by Henry II, probably because Owain's eastern border was too near Chester, strategically one of the most sensitive cities in England, for comfort. The royal army was to advance from Chester along the coast and at the same time a fleet sailed north from Pembroke to make a rendezvous with the king. On the way it raided Anglesey and the result was the battle of Tal Moelfre in which the men of the island were victorious. There is some uncertainty about the site of the battle; it was generally assumed to have been at the present Moelfre in Twrcelyn, but both Gwalchmai and Hywel ab Owain Gwynedd in their poems celebrating the

---

17 J. Beverley Smith, 'Owain Gwynedd', *TCHS* 32 (1971), 11; T. Jones Pierce, 'Medieval settlement in Anglesey', pp.267-9; G.R.J. Jones, *TAAS* 1955, pp.56-7. Contemporary colonisation in eastern Europe is discussed by R.Koebner, 'The settlement and colonisation of Europe', in M.M. Postan, ed., *The Cambridge Economic History of Europe*, i (2nd edn., 1966), pp.82-90 and more recently, by Robert Bartlett, *The Making of Europe: conquest, colonization and cultural change 950-1350* (1993), especially pp.106-66.

18 *Hist. Wales*, pp.229-32; see also D. Longley, 'The royal courts of the Welsh princes in Gwynedd' in Nancy Edwards, ed., *Landscape and Settlement in Medieval Wales* (Oxford, 1997), pp.41-54 and Rhys Jones, 'The formation of the *cantref* and the commote in medieval Gwynedd', *Studia Celtica* 32 (1998), 169-77.

19 Neil Johnstone, 'Cae Llys, Rhosyr: a court of the princes of Gwynedd', *Studia Celtica* 33 (1999), 251-95; idem, '*Llys* and *maerdref*: the royal courts of the princes of Gwynedd', *Studia Celtica* 34 (2000), especially 172-4, 176-7, 179-80, 180, 184.

20 *Brut y Tywysogyon* (RBH), p.131. Cadwaladr had landed at Abermenai in 1144 when he brought a fleet and mercenaries from Ireland after being expelled from Gwynedd by Owain for the murder of Anarawd ap Gruffudd of Deheubarth (ibid., p.119).

Welsh victory referred to the Menai Straits and there is a Tal-y-foel on the Straits in the parish of Llangeinwen.[21] The victims included Henry Fitz Henry, one of the illegitimate sons of Henry I. The advance from Chester under the king's personal command was rather more successful (although the army came very near to disaster in a battle near Hawarden) and Owain was obliged to relinquish the territory between the Clwyd and the Dee.

The death of Owain Gwynedd in 1170 led to a disputed succession in which the competitors were his son Hywel, probably his chosen successor and Dafydd and Rhodri, his sons by his second wife Cristin: Hywel was defeated and killed in a battle fought at Pentraeth.[22] The kingship seems to have gone to Dafydd; each of his brothers received a share of the lands and Anglesey fell to Maelgwn. But he was not to hold it for long; as so often happened when the inheritance was partitioned one brother, in this case Dafydd, sought to dominate the others and in 1173 Maelgwn was forced to flee to Ireland. He returned the following year and was promptly imprisoned.[23] This added Anglesey to Dafydd's territory and he soon overcame Rhodri; the poem in which Gwilym Rhyfel hailed him as 'king of Cemais' must date from this period.[24] Rhodri escaped from captivity in 1175 and drove Dafydd out of Gwynedd west of the Conwy. This resolved the rivalry between the two brothers and produced a balance of power which was to persist for nearly twenty years.

In 1188 Archbishop Baldwin of Canterbury made his famous tour of Wales to preach the crusade and display his metropolitical authority, a tour immortalised by the pen of Gerald of Wales. From Bangor the party crossed to Anglesey where the archbishop preached.[25] Rhodri himself was in the congregation but none of the young men in his retinue would take the cross. Within three days, however, divine retribution came upon them for their lack of enthusiasm, while Rhodri, who had ignored the admonitions of the archbishop on the subject of his marriage within the prohibited degrees, was eventually to pay for his obduracy by losing all his lands.[26] Gerald also described various wonders to be seen in Anglesey and commented on its fertility.[27]

At the time of Gerald's visit Dafydd and Rhodri were already being challenged by their young nephew Llywelyn ab Iorwerth. A contest between Rhodri

---

21  The topographical arguments are put forward in *Hist. Wales.*, p.499, n.54. The attack is described in *Brut y Tywysogyon* (RBH), pp.135-7, and Gerald of Wales, *Journey*, pp.188-9.

22  *Hist. Wales*, p.549.

23  *Brut y Tywysogyon* (RBH), p.163.

24  J. Morris-Jones and T.H. Parry-Williams, eds., *Llawysgrif Hendregadredd* (1933), p.184.

25  Gerald of Wales, *Journey*, pp.185-6; see also the earlier translation by W. Llywelyn Williams (1908), pp.118-9, where the possible location is discussed in n.2 where the views of the antiquaries Henry Rowlands and Richard Llwyd are cited.

26  ibid., p.186.

27  ibid., 186-91.

and the sons of his brother Cynan had ended about 1190 with him being driven out of Anglesey. Rhodri then sought the aid of the Manx king Rognvaldr I and appears to have married his daughter. But there was later some doubt about the consummation of this marriage and it is possible that it never went beyond the stage of an agreement between the two rulers.[28] In 1193 Manx aid was forthcoming and Rhodri regained Anglesey. This episode was long remembered as 'Haf y Gwyddyl', but within a few months he had again been expelled by the sons of Cynan.[29] The stage was now set for the emergence of Llywelyn ab Iorwerth; the following year he and the sons of Cynan turned on Dafydd and defeated him near Aberconwy and this was followed by his two victories at Porthaethwy and 'Coedaneu'.[30] These may have been won over Rhodri but, whatever his fate, death removed him from the contest in 1195; he was buried at Caergybi.[31] For the next five years Gwynedd west of the Conwy was ruled by Gruffudd ap Cynan ab Owain Gwynedd and Gwynedd east of the Conwy by Llywelyn ab Iorwerth.[32]

In 1200 Gruffudd ap Cynan ab Owain Gwynedd died after taking the Cistercian habit at Aberconwy. It was not long before Llywelyn brought Gwynedd west of the Conwy under his rule; he was eventually to associate his power with the traditional seat of kingship. About 1230 he assumed the title of Prince of Aberffraw and Lord of Snowdon in place of that of Prince of North Wales.[33] The strength of Llywelyn's position after 1215 meant that there was no external threat to Gwynedd for the rest of his reign. But Henry III, for all the adverse criticism that has been heaped on him, was to come to understand Wales and Welsh politics better than most English kings. The capture of Dublin by the Normans in 1170 meant the end of the main Scandinavian base on the Irish Sea and the presence of the power of the English crown opposite Gwynedd. The former ally was now as much the seat of a potential enemy as was Chester or Shrewsbury. Scandinavian power had helped to save Gwynedd in 1098 but English rulers had often realised that a maritime attack on Anglesey could be the key to success; this strategy had, after all, been used by Harold Godwinson

28  *Hist. Wales*, p.588 and nn. 69, 70, where the evidence is reviewed; 617 and n.29 where the Manx marriage is discussed in connection with Llywelyn ab Iorwerth's bid to marry the same princess.

29  ibid., p.588; *Brut y Tywysogyon* (RBH), p.173.

30  *Hist. Wales*, p.589. As Lloyd says, there is nothing to indicate whom Llywelyn defeated in these two battles. The Porthaethwy victory is mentioned by Prydydd y Moch in an *awdl* to Llywelyn and the same poem suggests that it was won over Rhodri (*Gwaith Llywarch ap Llywelyn 'Prydydd y Moch'*, ed. Elin M. Jones (Cardiff, 1991)), pp.214, 217.

31  Sir John Wynn, *History of the Gwydir Family and Memoirs* (ed. J. Gwynfor Jones, 1990), p.7.

32  Gruffudd's tenure of Anglesey is confirmed by his grant of Gelliniog, Rhuddgaer and the mill of Tal-y-bont in Menai to Aberconwy Abbey; for the text of the charter and discussion of its date see Huw Pryce, ed., *The Acts of Welsh Rulers 1120-1283* (2005), no.206.

33  *Hist. Wales*, p.669. The earliest surviving use of the title in a document is in about May 1230 (*CAC* (1935), p.51).

in 1063 and by Henry II in 1157. Now Dublin was available as an offensive base and in the 1231 campaign against Llywelyn Henry III saw the possibility of an attack on Anglesey from the sea while he and Hubert de Burgh were occupied in central Wales. In September he wrote to the justiciar of Ireland with a plan for an army from Ireland to cross to Wales the following summer and land on the island. The project came to nothing since a truce was concluded two months later, but it shows the direction of Henry's strategic thinking.[34]

After Llywelyn's death in 1240 came the long-drawn-out crisis in Anglo-Welsh relations over the succession to Gwynedd and the dismembering of his principality. Dafydd ap Llywelyn renewed hostilities after the death of his elder brother Gruffudd in 1244 and again Henry was faced with the need for a major campaign in Wales. He advanced as far as Degannwy, where he stayed for two months, unable to advance into Snowdonia and suffering much discomfort at the hands of the Welsh. But once again he was able to take advantage of his hold on Dublin. A force was brought over from Ireland and although it arrived too late to be of any use at Degannwy, Anglesey was ravaged and the harvest destroyed in an operation which foreshadowed the tactics used with such success by Edward I in 1276.[35] Dafydd ap Llywelyn died in 1246 and was succeeded by two of his nephews, Owain and Llywelyn ap Gruffudd. There was a real danger of civil war in Gwynedd but the brothers were persuaded to divide the principality between them. In Anglesey Owain seems to have had Malltraeth and Menai and possibly Llifon, while Llywelyn had Twrcelyn and Dindaethwy. This would indicate a north-south division and one would expect Aberffraw to have been part of Owain's share as the older of the two.[36] Owain and Llywelyn were soon forced to come to terms with the king and the Treaty of Woodstock was the nadir of Gwynedd's fortunes before 1282. However, Llywelyn ap Gruffudd was able to remove his brother and he gradually built up his position, taking advantage of Henry's troubles in England, until he was recognised by the crown as prince of Wales in the Treaty of Montgomery of 1267. In 1257 the king had once again planned to land a force from Ireland in Anglesey but Llywelyn appears to have used his fleet to prevent this.[37] Not until

34  *Close Rolls, 1227-1231*, 600; *Hist. Wales*, p.676.

35  *Hist. Wales*, pp.703-5; M. Dolley, *Anglo-Norman Ireland* (Dublin, 1972), p.139. Some Irishmen had been killed in Anglesey and in 1248 it was ordered that their deaths be investigated (*Close Rolls 1247-1251*, 118).

36  David Stephenson, *The Governance of Gwynedd* (1984), pp.155-7 and the evidence there cited. See also *CIPM* ii, no.538, which states that Gruffudd ap Maredudd had held a fourth part of Clegyrog which he had from Dafydd ap Llywelyn and the townships of Bodwrdin in Malltraeth and Llyslew in Menai which he had 'of the gift of Owain, sometime prince'. See also J. Beverley Smith, *Llywelyn ap Gruffudd, Prince of Wales* (1998), pp.66-7.

37  *Close Rolls, 1256-1259*, 91; T.F. Tout, 'Wales and the march in the Barons' Wars', in T.F. Tout, *Collected Papers*, ii (1934), p.61.

1276 was a royal army to appear again on the island.

Post-conquest evidence does shed some light on Anglesey before 1282. One of the most important sources for the economic and social history of medieval Gwynedd is the great survey or extent of Anglesey and Caernarfonshire made by the deputy-justice of north Wales, John de Delves, in 1352; the social structure reflected in it is, to a very considerable degree, that which existed before the Edwardian conquest.[38] There can be no doubt that the twelfth and thirteenth centuries were a period of great change.[39] The growth of trade and the development of a cash economy led to the emergence of urban commercial centres; Llan-faes was the main commercial centre in Gwynedd by 1282 and there was also trade at Llannerch-y-medd and Rhosyr.[40] Although the thirteenth century saw the reorganisation of Gwynedd's defences there is nothing to be found in Anglesey comparable with the careful arrangements which existed in Arfon and Llŷn for the removal of stock and provisions to the mountains in time of danger. This may possibly be explained by the potential threat from the sea and the consequent need to keep the island victualled and defended.[41]

Grants of land in Anglesey were made by successive princes to kinsmen and servants. Many of these grants were of bond townships and they included the delegation of royal rights and of jurisdiction over the unfree inhabitants.[42] Lands held by royal kindred included those in the possession of descendants of Rhodri ab Owain Gwynedd at Cleifiog in Llifon and those at Lledwigan Llan in Malltraeth and Llanllibio in Llifon which had been granted by Llywelyn ap Gruffudd to the sons of Llywelyn ap Maredudd, a descendant of Cynan ab Owain Gwynedd and the last lord of Meirionnydd, after his expulsion in 1256.[43] Other lands were held on privileged terms by descendants of the poet

38  The original extent is BUASC Baron Hill 6714; the text printed in *Rec.Caern.* pp.1-89, was taken by the editor from BLHarl. 696 and 4776. A.D. Carr, 'The extent of Anglesey, 1352', *TAAS* 1971-2, pp.150-272, is an English translation of the Anglesey section.

39  These changes are discussed by T. Jones Pierce, 'Medieval settlement in Anglesey', pp.251-84; G.R.J. Jones, 'The distribution of medieval settlement in Anglesey', *TAAS* 1955, pp.27-95; 'The tribal system in Wales: a re-assessment in the light of settlement studies', *WHR* 1 (1961), 111-32, and 'The distribution of bond settlements in north-west Wales', ibid., 2 (1964), 19-36. See also Dafydd Jenkins, 'A lawyer looks at Welsh land law', *THSC* 1967, pp.241-7.

40  T. Jones Pierce, 'The growth of commutation in Gwynedd in the thirteenth century', in *Medieval Welsh Society*, pp.120-3.

41  G.R.J. Jones, 'The defences of Gwynedd in the thirteenth century', *TCHS* 30 (1969), 38.

42  For these townships see *An Atlas of Anglesey*, p.40. A clear example was the grant made by Llywelyn ab Iorwerth to Maredudd ab Iorwerth of lands at Ysgeifiog in Menai (*Extent of Anglesey*, p.248). T. Jones Pierce in *Medieval Welsh Society*, pp.269-71, and G.R.J. Jones in *TAAS* 1955, pp.56-7.

43  *Extent of Anglesey* pp. 182 (Cleifiog), 162 (Lledwigan Llan); *CPR 1307-1313*, 461-2 (Llanllibio). The position of royal cadets and kinsmen in Gwynedd is discussed by David Stephenson, op.cit, pp.138-52.

Gwalchmai ap Meilir.[44] But the outstanding examples of grants of this kind were those made to the descendants of Llywelyn ab Iorwerth's great seneschal, Ednyfed Fychan. These grants seem to have had a twofold significance, being at once rewards for services rendered and yet to come. The townships were held by a particularly free tenure which generally involved nothing more than the obligation to attend the prince's court. The heirs had jurisdiction over their bondmen and in 1348 some descendants of Ednyfed Fychan claimed the right to hold a court which resembled the English manorial court in their lands.[45] More significant than this, perhaps, was the obligation of military service; in most cases the proprietors followed the prince to war at their own expense within Wales and at the prince's expense outside. Grants on these terms were a new departure in thirteenth-century Gwynedd and were part and parcel of the military policy of the princes, the object being to keep an army in being for more than the forty days customary service which every free man owed his lord. It may be seen as a form of tenure by knight service and as yet another example of the way in which feudal influences were coming into Gwynedd and being encouraged by the house of Aberffraw.[46]

Since Anglesey formed part of the nucleus of Gwynedd, it is not surprising that it is not as well documented during this period as are many parts of the march or the more peripheral areas of Llywelyn ap Gruffudd's principality. Llywelyn's very success brought serious problems in its wake. The heavy annual tribute which he agreed to pay in the Treaty of Montgomery was to prove more than the fragile economy of his principality could bear and the last decade of Welsh independence was a period during which the shoe had begun to pinch.[47] Many examples of this came to light after 1282, especially when Edward I's tax-collectors assumed that the heavy payments exacted in Llewelyn's last years were the rule rather than the exception and some of these examples are from Anglesey. The best-known case is probably that of the bondmen of the *maer-*

---

44 The descendants of Gwalchmai held lands in Lledwigan Llys, Trefdraeth Wastrodion, Trefdraeth Ddisteiniaid and Trewalchmai in Malltraeth and Castellior in Dindaethwy (*Extent of Anglesey*, pp. 161, 163. 171, 243).

45 These townships are shown in the commote maps, Appendix B. The tenure, described in the fourteenth century as that of 'Wyrion Eden', also existed in a number of townships in the Abergele area in the lordship of Denbigh (Glyn Roberts, 'Wyrion Eden', in Glyn Roberts, *Aspects of Welsh History* (1969), pp.182-3); *Rec.Caern.*, pp.150 (Penmynydd, Trecastell and Erddrein-iog), 167 (Tregarnedd), 168 (Trecastell and Gwredog), *Extent of Anglesey*, pp. 223, 227, 235, 245. The Wyrion Eden lands are also discussed in Smith, *Llywelyn ap Gruffudd*, pp.217-9.

46 Military service was also due from the tenants of Bodffordd and of Gafael Gwenllian in Grugor in Malltraeth (*Extent of Anglesey*, pp. 158, 170), and from Nantmawr in Twrcelyn (*CIM* ii, no. 1030). Glyn Roberts, op.cit., pp. 181-4 and 184, n.1; G.R.J. Jones, *TCHS* 30, 40-1; Ceri W. Lewis, 'The Treaty of Woodstock, 1247, its background and significance', *WHR* 2 (1964), 63-4; David Stephenson, op.cit., pp.89-91.

47 W.H. Waters, *The Edwardian Settlement of North Wales in its Administrative and Legal Aspects, 1284-1343* (1935), pp.27-8; Keith Williams-Jones, *The Merioneth Lay Subsidy Roll, 1292-3* (1976), pp.xix-xxi.

*dref* of Penrhosllugwy who were still fighting the excessive burden of rents and services imposed on them in the extent of 1284 well into the reign of Edward II.[48] Another case was that of the inheritance of Iorwerth ap Philip Goch, a free tenant of Llechog in Twrcelyn. In 1322 he petitioned the king, stating that his father had died during the reign of Llywelyn ap Gruffudd and that he was then in wardship; the prince had taken the inheritance into his hands until a relief of seven pounds was paid.[49] Here again we see Llywelyn pressing on his subjects and demanding an arbitrary fine from an heir.

The steady deterioration in Anglo-Welsh relations after the accession of Edward I in 1272 came to a head in 1276 when the king assembled an army and planned a major campaign to teach Llywelyn ap Gruffudd a lesson.[50] Anglesey played a key part in Edward's strategy and he had one great advantage which none of his predecessors had enjoyed. It was now possible for an English fleet to operate in the Irish Sea without any risk of a Scandinavian challenge, thanks to the Scottish victory at Largs in 1263 and the cession of Man and the Hebrides to the Scots by Magnus Haakonson of Norway three years later.[51]

According to *Brut y Tywysogyon* Edward 'sent a large section of his host to Anglesey to burn much of the land and to carry off much of its corn'.[52] Most of the fleet came from the Cinque Ports and its purpose was to seize Anglesey, to cut it off from the rest of Gwynedd and then to carry troops across the Menai Straits. A force of some 2,000 men seems to have been sent to secure the island once the king reached Degannwy. They do not appear to have destroyed the crops but to have harvested them for the use of the royal forces; 120 mowers and 240 reapers were sent across in four ships.[53] But the blow to Llywelyn's morale was every bit as great as it would have been had the harvest been destroyed; not only had he been deprived of the harvest but it was being used by Edward. The occupation of Anglesey and the loss of the harvest was one of the factors which persuaded the prince to seek terms; the result was the Treaty of Aberconwy of November 1277.[54]

---

48  For the extent of Penrhosllugwy see G.Rex Smith, 'The extent of Anglesey, 1284', *TAAS* 2009, pp.93-116; *CAP*, pp.261-2; *CIM* ii, no.563; *Rec.Caern.*, p.217; *CCR 1323-1327*, 304. The episode is discussed by A.D. Carr, 'The bondmen of Penrhosllugwy: a community's complaint', *TAAS* 1988, pp.15-29.

49  *CAP*, pp. 335-6, 478; *CIM* ii, no.2102. Iorwerth and Dafydd Chwith complained in 1297 that the extent of their lands in Glasgrug and Llechog was unjust (*CIM* i, no.1744). See also David Stephenson, op.cit., pp.75-7.

50  The succession of crises in Anglo-Welsh relations is discussed by F.M. Powicke, *The Thirteenth Century* (1953), pp.406-12, *Hist. Wales*, pp.704-9 and Smith, *Llywelyn ap Gruffudd*, pp.338-89.

51  F.M. Powicke, op.cit., p.596 & n.1. It may also be borne in mind that the ability of any English king to maintain a fleet in the Irish Sea depended to a considerable degree on the state of Anglo-Scottish relations.

52  *Brut y Tywysogyon* (RBH), p.267.

53  J.E. Morris, *The Welsh Wars of King Edward the First* (1901), pp.134-5.

54  J.G. Edwards, ed., *Littere Wallie* (1940), pp.118-22.

Under the treaty Llywelyn's principality was reduced to the territory to the west of the Conwy. All the lands conquered by Edward during the war were to be ceded to him with the exception of Anglesey. This was granted to Llywelyn and his lawful heirs to be held as he had held it previously at an annual rent of 1000 marks. The day after the treaty the king announced that he had made this grant to Llywelyn with the exception of the portion in Anglesey of his brother Dafydd after his death, for which he had compensated Dafydd; the island would revert to the king if Llywelyn died without heirs.[55] At one stage during the campaign Edward had made other arrangements, presumably on the assumption that Llywelyn would have fought to the end. On 23 August 1277 he had promised Dafydd that, in the event of Llywelyn being defeated, he would restore half Snowdon, Llŷn, half Anglesey and Penllyn to him and his imprisoned brother Owain, or, if he kept all of Anglesey in his own hand, the whole of Snowdon and Penllyn.[56] But, since Llywelyn submitted, this grant did not take effect.

The final crisis came in 1282. This is not the place to discuss its causes nor the way in which Llywelyn was drawn into the war and then to his destruction, but it was preceded by a number of local disputes, some of which were in Anglesey.[57] In January 1278 a commission was appointed; among its duties was that of receiving amends for the injuries done to the king's men in Anglesey after the conclusion of the peace treaty.[58] One who had suffered in this way was Iorwerth Foel, who was a man of some standing in Anglesey. In 1278 he complained that, when he had made his peace with the king and had then served in his army, Llywelyn had seized his horses and corn and the plunder taken by his men and had later burned all his houses; as a result he dared not cultivate or inhabit his hereditary lands or enter the principality.[59] This case was just one of many which showed that Llywelyn could no longer rely on the support of his own subjects, let alone on that of leading Welshmen outside Gwynedd; it also shows that he had a short way with dissenters. The record of a meeting of representatives of the community of Gwynedd in August 1283 lists a number of complaints about the late prince's heavy hand, including one that the free men of Dindaethwy had been forced to provide *porthiant* or billeting dues for the prince's men.[60] There were other issues too; Llywelyn's

55  *CChancRVar*, 158.
56  *Littere Wallie*, pp.103-4; *CPR 1272-1281*, 225.
57  The crisis is discussed by F.M. Powicke, op.cit., pp.412-9, and Smith, *Llywelyn ap Gruffudd*, pp.451-509.
58  *CChancRVar*, 162, 170, 177; *CAC*, p.111.
59  J. Conway Davies, ed., *The Welsh Assize Roll, 1277-1284* (1940), p.158.
60  Llinos Beverley Smith, 'The *gravamina* of the community of Gwynedd against Llywelyn ap Gruffudd', *BBCS* 31 (1984), 175. Dr Smith suggests that these demands might be connected with the maintenance of a substantial garrison in eastern Anglesey (ibid., 168).

brother Rhodri, who had sold his interests to him some years previously, now put forward a claim for his share of the inheritance, while the proceedings of the king's justices in Anglesey were among the grievances which the prince brought to the attention of the archbishop of Canterbury during the latter's well-intentioned but maladroit attempt to mediate.[61]

After the revolt of the Welsh lords in 1282 it was only a matter of time before Llywelyn was forced to join in. Edward again used the tactics which had proved so successful five years earlier. A fleet was summoned from the Cinque Ports and an army under the personal command of the king advanced from Chester. The fleet began with 28 ships and another 12, with two great galleys, followed later.[62] The forward base for both fleet and army was at Rhuddlan and a force was detached from the main body and put under the command of Luke de Tany to cross to Anglesey. His orders were to occupy the island and then to build a bridge of boats across the Menai Straits. The plan was to attack Snowdonia from east and west and de Tany had strict instructions not to cross his bridge until Edward gave the word. Anglesey was occupied in August 1282; de Tany's first task was to secure his hold on the southern coast, especially the commote of Menai, and to seize the harvest.[63] Work on the bridge began at the end of August and by November a concerted attack was possible, but then came the archbishop's peace mission. Why Luke de Tany crossed the Straits on 6 November 1282 will probably never be known. One English chronicler suggested that it was an act of treachery during the archbishop's negotiations and it certainly seems to have been in defiance of the king's orders. But cross he did and as the force was on the bridge at high tide it was ambushed by the Welsh.[64] Many jumped off and were drowned; the victims included de Tany himself, Hywel ap Gruffudd ab Ednyfed Fychan and two sons of Robert Burnell, Edward's chancellor.[65] This was a crushing defeat for Edward and it was only the unexpected death of Llywelyn in a skirmish near Builth a month later that helped to bring the war to an end. The disaster did not mean the end of the bridge; it was still in use early in 1283, but by the summer it was dismantled to enable the ships carrying building materials to Caernarfon to pass through the Straits.[66]

61  *Welsh Assize Roll.*, pp. 238-9, 228.

62  J.E. Morris, op.cit., p.173.

63  ibid., pp.176-7; for the building of the bridge see A.J.Taylor, *The King's Works in Wales, 1277-1330* (1974), pp.354-6. During construction a base was established at Llan-faes and 14 ships were involved in the work along with 200 carpenters from the Cinque Ports (ibid., p.356).

64  The episode and the possible location of the bridge are discussed by Smith, *Llywelyn ap Gruffudd*, pp.536-42.

65  J.E. Morris, op.cit., pp.179-80; A.J.Taylor, op.cit., pp.356-7; Thomas Jones, ed., *Brut y Tywysogyon* (Peniarth 20 version) (1952), p.120.

66  A.J.Taylor, op.cit., p.357.

The time Edward spent in Wales after the fall of Llywelyn included a visit to Anglesey. In July and August 1283 he was successively at Rhosyr, Aberffraw, Holyhead, Penrhosllugwy and Llan-faes.[67] It was not until March 1284 that arrangements were made for the government of his new lands in the shape of the Statute of Wales, issued at Rhuddlan. Under the Statute Anglesey became one of three new counties in north Wales with its own sheriff and county court and all the other attributes of its new status.[68] Those who had supported the king received their due reward; Iorwerth Foel was granted lands in Aberffraw along with the farm of the ringildry of the cantref at a reduced rate and he was the richest taxpayer there in 1292-3.[69] His son Gruffudd was one of the most prosperous burgesses of Newborough in 1352.[70] Another grant for good service was that of Nantmawr in Twrcelyn made by Edward I to Tudur Fychan for life in 1284; he was followed there by his son and his grandson.[71] Others must have been rewarded but there were also losers. In 1307-8 the sheriff accounted for the issues of 60 acres in Gwydryn in Menai which were in the king's hand because Cynwrig Teg had died against the peace in the war of Llywelyn.[72] In 1350-1 account was rendered for one carucate in Trewalchmai, formerly of Hywel Ddu ap Goronwy, who also died in the war of Llywelyn and for lands in Cefn-coch in Dindaethwy once held by Rhirid ab Iorwerth who had been killed in the war of Dafydd ap Gruffudd, Llywelyn's brother.[73] Some, at least, had made the ultimate sacrifice for their prince.

Edward was to visit Anglesey again in 1295 after an episode which can be seen, at least in part, as a consequence of the abnormal conditions of the last years of Llywelyn's reign. This was the revolt of Madog ap Llywelyn.[74] Madog was a descendant of Cynan ab Owain Gwynedd and one of the four sons of

67  *CPR 1281-1292*, 71-2 (Aberffraw, 2-3 Aug.);  72 (Holyhead, 4 Aug.; Llan-faes, 8-11 Aug.); *CCW*, 10 (Rhosyr, 29 July); *CCR 1279-1288*, 214 (Penrhosllugwy, 6 Aug.).

68  The text of the Statute is in Ivor Bowen, *The Statutes of Wales* (1908), pp.2-27.

69  Iorwerth was granted a carucate and a half in Aberffraw free of rent in 1314 (*CPR 1313-1317*, 78); in 1320 he petitioned parliament, seeking to hold the land for himself and his heirs but the request was refused (*CAP*, pp.113-4). He also held land of the bishop of Bangor in the nearby township of Llanfeirian (*Record of Caernarvon*, p.105); for the ringildry see ibid., p.225. TNA E179/242/49.

70  *Extent of Anglesey*, p.262; he also held lands in Trefdraeth Ddisteiniaid and Rhosyr (ibid., pp. 166, 259-60).

71  *CChancRVar*, 288; in 1290 he was paid £20 for his good and faithful service to the king (ibid., 326).

72  TNA SC6/1227/7.

73  TNA SC6/1149/1, m.3a. In 1320 Gruffudd ap Hywel of Anglesey petitioned the king for the lands of his kinsman Hywel ap Goronwy 'who died in the king's prison in the war with Llywelyn' (*CAP*, p.27).

74  The revolt is described by John Griffiths, 'The revolt of Madog ap Llywelyn', in *TCHS* 16 (1955), 12-34, and by R.F. Walker in E.B. Fryde, ed., *A Book of Prests of the King's Wardrobe. 1294-5* (1962), pp.xxvi-liii. For the military details see J.E. Morris, op.cit., pp.240-70.

the last ruler of Meirionnydd, who had been driven out by Llywelyn in 1256 and had sought refuge in England. In 1278 Madog had appeared before the royal justices to claim his inheritance but in 1284 it became part of the new county of Merioneth.[75] An inquisition taken in 1308 revealed that Madog and his brother Dafydd had been granted certain lands in Anglesey for their maintenance.[76] Anglesey was one of the centres of the revolt; the church and probably much of the town of Llan-faes were burned and the island devastated.[77]

This was followed by an attack on Caernarfon in which the borough records, the unfinished town walls and part of the castle were destroyed and Roger de Pulesdon, the unpopular and extortionate sheriff of Anglesey, was hanged. The hanging was the work of two Anglesey men, Goronwy, the rhingyll of Twrcelyn and Trahaearn ap Bleddyn of the commote of Talybolion. Both Goronwy and Trahaearn were later executed and their lands in Bodewryd and Dronwy escheated to the crown; they were not the only Anglesey men to die in rebellion.[78] As the revolt began in Anglesey, so, in a way, did it end there. On 11 April 1295 Edward crossed from Bangor to Llan-faes, which he made his headquarters.[79] He remained there for some three weeks and it was during his stay that he gave instructions for the establishment of the castle and town of Beaumaris; in fact, the decision had been taken the previous November.[80] As order was gradually restored a number of hostages were taken. On 23 April 1295 nine from Anglesey were taken to Shrewsbury and kept there until 20 August 1296. Another five were taken to Hereford and released on 27 August 1296 and six were moved from Shrewsbury to St Briavels and freed on 25 August 1296.[81]

Madog himself was captured, probably in Meirionnydd, at the end of July 1295.[82] His life was spared but he spent the rest of his days as a prisoner in the Tower of London and he was still there in 1312.[83] But, although his revolt had disrupted Edward's planned campaign in France and although the unforeseen expenditure its suppression had entailed was to be one of the causes of a major financial and constitutional crisis in England, the king was not vindictive and he seems to have realised that something was radically wrong with the royal

75  *Welsh Assize Roll*, pp. 237-8, 251.
76  *CIM* ii, no.49; see also *Governance of Gwynedd*, pp.144-6. The brothers Dafydd and Madog had no connection with Edeirnion (ibid., p.145).
77  *CCR 1318-1323*, 70-1; *CIM* ii, no.327; *CAP*, p.82.
78  TNA SC6/1149/1, m.5a, 6a. E.A. Lewis, 'The decay of tribalism in north Wales', *THSC* 1902-3, p.36; TNA SC6/1227/7 (Llanidan, Llywarch ap Maredudd); 1149/1, m.3a (Einion ap Gruffudd).
79  J.E. Morris, op.cit., p.263.
80  A.J.Taylor, op.cit., pp.395-6.
81  Natalie Fryde, *List of Welsh Entries in the Memoranda Rolls, 1282-1343* (1974), p.xvi.
82  John Griffiths, op.cit., 22
83  *CPR 1307-1313*, 461-2.

administration in Wales. There was no corruption of the blood; Madog had held the township of Lledwigan Llan and his brother Dafydd had held Llanllibio but there were no forfeitures. In 1305 Gwenllian, Dafydd's widow, petitioned the prince of Wales for dower in her late husband's land and Llanllibio was granted in 1312 to Madog's son Maredudd, who was in the king's service despite his father's imprisonment.[84] A further grant of the adjacent township of Cleifiog was made to Maredudd for life in 1327 on account of his services to Edward II and Queen Isabella; it was worth ten pounds a year and one cannot but wonder what lay behind such a grant for services to Edward II so soon after that king's fall.[85] Maredudd was dead by 1334 when Llanllibio and Cleifiog were granted to William Trussell. His brother Hywel still held Lledwigan Llan in 1352, but he, too, was dead by 1363-4 when the escheator accounted for the issues of the lands there once held by Madog ap Llywelyn.[86] And with that reference the line of Gruffudd ap Cynan and Owain Gwynedd disappears from view.

84 *Rec.Caern.*, p.216; TNA SC6/1227/8; *CPR 1307-1313*, 461-2; *CFR 1307-1319*, 135.

85 *CPR 1327-1330*, 101. Maredudd produced this charter at the sessions held on 16 May 1328 (NLW Peniarth 405, pp.424-5).

86 *CCR 1333-1337*, 267; *Extent of Anglesey*, p.162; TNA SC6/1150/2, m.7a. At Lledwigan Llan Hywel owed suit to the county court at Michaelmas and to the sheriff's tourn but nothing else.

# 3 The Government of the County

WHEN DISCUSSING local government in the middle ages it is important to remember that the concept of a local authority as we understand the term is totally irrelevant. Medieval local government was concerned with two things, the maintenance of order and the collection of revenue. There was no question of the provision of services, nor were there any elected bodies and the only supervision from above was by means of the audit. Most of the legal and administrative changes made by Edward I in the lands which came into his possession in 1282 were contained in the document issued by the king at Rhuddlan on 19 March 1284 which is usually known as the Statute of Wales.[1] They involved the introduction of superior administrative units and courts and for the purposes of local government Gwynedd was divided into three counties, one of which was Anglesey.[2] The commote was retained as the basic unit of local administration, being similar in so many respects to the English hundred, and the English county and sheriff were grafted on to it.

The chief royal official in the county was the sheriff. In north Wales he was both a judicial and a financial officer, as his English counterpart had been in his prime.[3] In his judicial capacity he presided over the county court and the tourn and possibly over the commote court as well.[4] His administrative duties were included in his financial responsibilities which had mainly to do with the collection of the royal revenue and the enforcement of services. Any necessary expenditure was met out of revenue and he rendered account at the Caernarfon

---

1  Ivor Bowen, *The Statutes of Wales*, pp.2-27.

2  The standard account of the working of the legal and administrative settlement during its first fifty years is W.H. Waters, *The Edwardian Settlement of North Wales in its Administrative and Legal Aspects 1284-1343* (1935).

3  Local government in the southern counties of the principality is examined by Ralph A. Griffiths, *The Principality of Wales in the Later Middle Ages: the structure and personnel of government*, i (*South Wales, 1277-1536*) (1972); the sheriff is discussed on p.47. See also W.H. Waters, *The Edwardian Settlement of West Wales 1277-1343* (Abergele, 2000). The county and the hundred in thirteenth-century England are discussed.by Helen M. Cam, *The Hundred and the Hundred Rolls* (1930), pp.59-194.

4  The point about the commote court is made by W.H. Waters, op.cit., p.109.

Exchequer. The chamberlain of north Wales then accounted for the whole principality at the main Exchequer at Westminster.[5] The revenue for which the sheriff accounted consisted, first of all, of the rents of assise from the various commotes. These were fixed sums, based after 1284 on the extent of the county made in that year. He also answered for the profits of justice, which were mainly the fines and amercements levied in the different courts, and for the sums paid for the farms of offices. Some income came from escheat lands, that is, from hereditary lands which had come into the crown's possession through lack of heirs or through forfeiture and which were then rented out and there was usually a certain amount of casual revenue like wrecks and the goods and chattels of fugitive felons and of those who had died intestate. The account also included arrears from previous years. Disbursements included such things as the repair of ferry-boats and of royal mills and allowance was made for decay or items which no longer contributed to the royal income although they were still regarded as part of the formal revenue. The sheriff was personally responsible for all arrears and might be liable to meet them out of his own resources. This could cause him considerable embarrassment, as in 1302 when Walter de Winchester left office in arrears and his land and property in Beaumaris were seized by the chamberlain.[6]

A new system of accounting was introduced in 1350. Under this the commote officials and some others accounted directly to the auditors and this meant a change in the form of the sheriff's account. In 1350-1 William de Ellerton answered first of all for the sum of seventy pounds paid by him for the farm of the shrievalty.[7] This covered the income from the hundred courts and the tourns but not rents. He then accounted for the county's share of the fixed sums which replaced the community's traditional obligation to maintain the prince's stallions and otter-hounds and for the income from the highest court, the justice's sessions, during the year. Fines and amercements collected from the tenants of the king's mother, Queen Isabella, and the bishop of Bangor were handed over to their representatives. Finally, there came instalments of arrears from their terms of office paid by former officials. In later accounts the sheriff accounted for the issues of the different courts, for reliefs and *gobrestyn* due from heirs on taking up their inheritances and for respites. These were usually the unpaid portions of fines and other payments which were due in instalments as well as fines which, for some reason or other, could not be collected. He would also account for necessary expenditure. By the end of the fourteenth century his English counterpart was in decline and fifteenth-century accounts

5  ibid., pp.26, 21.
6  ibid., p.40.
7  TNA SC6/1149/1, m.8a.

suggest that in north Wales, too, his main concern was with the collection and transmission of the profits of justice. His other responsibilities, which are not reflected in the surviving records, included the custody of the county gaol and its inmates and the execution and return of writs emanating from the central administration at Caernarfon.[8]

The second official mentioned in the Statute of Wales was the coroner. This office had existed in England since the end of the twelfth century but little is known of its working in north Wales.[9] According to the Statute one was to be elected in the county court for each commote but in practice there were two for each county; in Anglesey one was responsible for Talybolion, Twrcelyn and Dindaethwy and the other for Llifon, Malltraeth and Menai. The coroner had to view the bodies of all who had died by misadventure and also of those who were so badly injured that their lives were despaired of; afterwards he held an inquest with a jury drawn from the township where the death had occurred and the four adjacent townships. He was also responsible for the supervision of the process when any felon chose to abjure the realm.[10] A few Anglesey coroners' accounts have survived; in 1328-9 Madog ab Einion, the coroner of Talybolion, Twrcelyn and Dindaethwy, held inquests at Cornwy Lys and Llaneilian.[11] In 1303 the township of Trewalchmai was amerced two pounds for burying a body before the coroner had seen it.[12] There is a reference to the election of one coroner at the county court; Hywel Lipa was chosen for Talybolion, Twrcelyn and Dindaethwy in 1346 by the prince's writ and the assent of the suitors.[13] Later accounts suggest that it was the escheator rather than the coroner who came to answer for the goods and chattels of the victims of misadventure, but the coroner was still holding inquests in the early sixteenth century and he continues to do so.[14] The decline of the office may be explained by the fact that it was unpaid and conferred no advantages or perquisites.

---

8  In fact in Gwynedd, where the county gaol was in the castle of the county town, the constable of the castle seems to have been responsible for the custody of prisoners and answerable for their escape. In 1318-9 John de Sapy, the constable of Beaumaris, made fine before the justice for the escape of Ieuan Cwta and his companions from his custody (TNA SC6/1170/1). In 1320 he was pardoned for their escape (*CPR 1317-1321*, 446).

9  For a general discussion of the work of the coroner in north Wales based on transcripts by Robert Vaughan of inquest records from Merioneth, 1336-1347, see A.D. Carr, 'The coroner in fourteenth-century Merioneth', *JMHRS* 11 (1992), 247-54.

10  This is discussed in detail in W.H. Waters, op.cit., pp.140-2.

11  TNA SC6/1170/19.

12  TNA E101/119/33, m.5.

13  G.P. Jones, 'Anglesey court rolls 1346', in *TAAS* 1933, p.48.

14  This point is also made by Ralph A. Griffiths, op.cit., pp.56-7; he points out that in England, too, the escheator was encroaching on the coroner's province (R.F. Hunnisett, *The Medieval Coroner* (1961), p.198). There are some references to the coroner and to inquests held by him in BUASC Porth-yr-Aur Add. 178, an Anglesey indictment roll from the early sixteenth century; see mm.5b, 9, 13-4, 34, 35-6.

The escheator was originally responsible for lands and property which had escheated or passed to the crown through lack of heirs or through forfeiture. The office first appeared in north Wales in 1306; from 1323 it was held by the chamberlain and the first surviving reference to an escheator of Anglesey is in 1347 when Gwilym ap Gruffudd ap Hywel was appointed escheator, controller of the sheriff and coroner and keeper of the prince's millstone quarries.[15] It was almost certainly the Black Death and its catastrophic effects that changed the nature of the escheator's duties and laid far heavier burdens on his shoulders; surviving accounts suggest that before this the sheriff, rather than the coroner, answered for many of the issues which later fell within his province.[16] In 1350-1 the office was farmed by the sheriff for £13 6s 8d; by 1363-4 it had been separated from the shrievalty and was held jointly by two leading local figures, Dafydd Fychan ap Dafydd Llwyd and Ieuan ap Tudur Llwyd.[17] Lands could be in the escheator's hands for a number of reasons as can be seen in the account of William de Huntingdon for 1377-8.[18] Tenements were in his custody because of outlawry, because a free tenant had married a bondwoman, because of conviction for treason, because the proprietor had been hanged, because the heir was illegitimate and because the proprietor had abjured the realm. He also accounted for the goods and chattels of several who had died intestate, for the value of livestock bought outside the market and for a fine from two brothers for the redemption of their possessions which had been seized because they had knowingly received an outlaw. From time to time he disposed of stray animals and stolen goods. In the fifteenth century the accounts rendered for goods and chattels become much more detailed although they are never as informative as, for example, a seventeenth-century probate inventory. But all this shows that in many ways the escheator had superseded the coroner and had become one of the principal accounting officers of the county.[19]

The commote was not one of the innovations of 1284; it had been the unit of local administration under the princes and as it remained, so did its two officials, the *rhaglaw* or bailiff and the *rhingyll* or beadle.[20] The former had been the chief official under the princes; in the march he exercised the right of purveyance or the compulsory collection of supplies on behalf of the lord and he

15  W.H. Waters, op.cit., pp.43-4;  the early history of the office in north Wales is further discussed
    in ibid., pp.59-61. *BPR* i, 155.
16  Ralph A. Griffiths, op.cit., p.56.
17  TNA SC6/1149/1, m.8a; 1150/2, m.7a.
18  TNA SC6/1150/4, m.6a.
19  Although the coroner had been responsible for wrecks and treasure trove in England in the early
    13th century, the sheriff also retained responsibility and during the 14th century it passed to the
    escheator (R.F. Hunnisett, op.cit., pp.6-7).
20  For the commote see Smith, *Llywelyn ap Gruffudd*, pp.193-6.

also supervised the collection of rents, issued summonses and arrested suspected felons and other offenders. But by the middle of the fourteenth century he seems to have ceased to perform any administrative duties.[21] After 1350, when commotal officials accounted directly to the prince's auditors, it was the *rhingyll* who did so. The office of *rhaglaw* remained, but only as a profitable sinecure. In 1348 the *rhaglaw* of Twrcelyn stated that he was entitled to a graduated levy on fines from the hundred court, the tourn and the Penrhosllugwy manorial court, to twenty shillings from every township that presented at the tourn, to a penny from every suitor at the hundred court and to two shillings from every relief. From every brewing of ale for sale he had sixpence and from every execution for debt two shillings and every unfree tenant in the commote owed him provender for his horse and food for one servant for a day and a night.[22]

The *rhingyll*, therefore, became the more responsible of the two commote officials.[23] In the commote of Malltraeth in 1350-1 he accounted for the rent of assise and other renders from each township and the income from escheat lands, for goods of intestates and shipwrecks, for the farms of the commote offices, for the *staurum* or render of supplies for Beaumaris castle, for the income from land which was untenanted because of the Black Death and for land which did not yield any revenue because no tenants could be found for it.[24] In 1348 the perquisites of the office in Twrcelyn included a fee of fourpence for each amercement, twenty shillings from each community presenting at the tourn, two shillings for each relief and a penny from each suitor at the hundred court.[25] His responsibilities had changed not at all by the fifteenth century. In some parts of Wales the *rhaglaw* seems after the conquest to have dealt with the free population and the *rhingyll* with the unfree, but in Gwynedd the *rhingyll* was, for most people, the executive arm of royal government.

A change in the system of accounting in the 1340s meant that the accounts became much more detailed. Two things were responsible for this change; one was the general overhaul of the administration of the principality and the earldom of Chester which followed the grant of both to the Black Prince in 1343 and the other was the Black Death.[26] The disruption caused by the plague ne-

---

21 See particularly William Rees, *South Wales and the March, 1284-1415* (1924), pp.95-8; for the office in Flintshire see Arthur Jones, ed., *Flintshire Ministers' Accounts, 1301-1328* (1913), pp. xxxiii-xxxv, and for Cardiganshire and Carmarthenshire Ralph A. Griffiths, op.cit., pp.59-62.

22 *Rec.Caern.* p.170.

23 William Rees, op.cit., pp.99-103.

24 TNA SC6/1149/1, mm.3a-b.

25 *Rec.Caern*, p.170

26 In future individual accounts were written out in full for the convenience of the auditors. In Flintshire the new pattern began in 1349 (D.L. Evans, ed., *Flintshire Ministers' Accounts, 1328-1353* (1929), pp.xiii-xvi).

cessitated a more rigorous supervision of the principality's resources and with this was associated the need of the prince for as much revenue as possible. The first Anglesey account was that for 1350-1, rendered at Beaumaris before the auditors; there was a further change in the commotal accounts from Anglesey and Caernarfonshire in 1353-4, following the new extent of the two counties drawn up by the deputy-justice, John de Delves, in 1352.[27] Expenditure by the authorities at Caernarfon continued to be entered on the chamberlain's account.

The only formal bodies which were concerned with the administration of the county and the commotes were the courts. Like all courts of law, these dealt with the punishment of crime, the maintenance of order, the collection of the profits of justice and the hearing of civil actions between individuals. At the head of the hierarchy of courts stood the sessions, held several times a year in each county by the justice of north Wales.[28] Only one pre-1500 plea roll, for Caernarfonshire from the reign of Richard II, has survived, but two rolls of estreats from the early years of the fourteenth century shed some light on the kind of business that came before the sessions.[29] Other actions were mentioned from time to time by the sheriff in his accounts and in notes made by the seventeenth-century antiquary Robert Vaughan of Hengwrt from plea rolls that have since been lost.[30] The sheriff also accounted for the fines and amercements imposed at the court and later accounts state the number of sessions held. Trial of pleas of the crown was reserved to the justice, but when those subject to some of the private jurisdictions which existed in Anglesey were tried at the sessions the ensuing amercements were handed over to their lords.[31] The total amercements levied at the sessions held by the deputy-justice, John de Delves, at Beaumaris in December 1355, for example, came to £7 17s 8d, and of this sum sixpence was paid to the representatives of the king's mother, Queen Isabella, who held the commote of Menai, 13s 4d to the bishop of Bangor and ten shillings to the abbot of Aberconwy.[32] Other sheriffs' accounts include similar payments.

Fifteenth-century accounts are more informative than those of the fourteenth since by then the sheriff answered for respites of fines; respites were the unpaid balances of fines which were paid in instalments. These do reflect certain aspects of the business that came before the justice; in 1437-8 they included

27  TNA SC6/1149/1, 1149/4.
28  For a discussion of the sessions in north Wales between 1284 and 1343 see W.H. Waters, op.cit., pp.123-33.
29  TNA E101/119/33, 120/1; they are discussed by W.H. Waters, op.cit.
30  For Vaughan's notes see NLW Peniarth 405, pp.417-55.
31  Pleas of the crown were homicide, wounding, rape and arson
32  TNA SC6/1149/6, m.5a.

ten fines for licence to acquire land, one paid by a free tenant to purge his trespass in marrying an unfree woman and another from a free woman for licence to marry her daughter, who was unfree on her father's side, to any free man she wished.[33] Later accounts included fines to purge outlawry, one from a bondman to dwell wherever he liked in England or Wales to follow his trade as a mason and others from bondmen for licence to make wills. The fines varied from case to case, but what they do show is the importance of the sessions as a means of raising revenue. Conveyances of land by the collusive actions of fine and common recovery also took place there. As far as can be seen from surviving accounts, no attempt was ever made in Anglesey to redeem the sessions. When this was done the authorities accepted a lump sum from the community equivalent to the expected profits instead of holding the court; it was a common practice in the march and in the southern counties of the principality in the fifteenth century.[34]

Next in importance to the justice's sessions was the county court.[35] Its real importance was administrative rather than judicial. As a legal tribunal there was nothing the county court could do that the hundred court could not and the latter body had the added advantages of being familiar and near at hand. But the county court was the place where the county community, which meant the leading free tenants, was assembled. Here royal proclamations were read and explained, here coroners were elected and here the community probably gave voice to its grievances. It was a new institution in Gwynedd but it had existed in England since Anglo-Saxon times and there, too, its importance was as 'the public expression of the county community'.[36] The court met once a month; in Anglesey it met at Beaumaris on a Thursday according to the surviving rolls. Suit to the county was an obligation attached to the free tenure of land as the 1352 extent shows; few, if any, were excused attendance. Its jurisdiction was limited to trespass, detention of chattels and other minor civil actions involving less than forty shillings.[37] Most of the surviving Anglesey rolls are lists of estreats containing details of amercements, largely for non-prosecution of pleas and non-appearance of defendants.[38] Only one true court

33 TNA SC6/1153/6, mm.16b-17a.
34 Ralph A. Griffiths, op.cit. pp.27-30; T.B. Pugh, *The Marcher Lordships of South Wales, 1415-1536* (1963), pp.39-40. The office of justice and the working of the sessions in south Wales are discussed by Professor Griffiths, pp.19-33.
35 The working of the county court in north Wales is discussed in detail by W.H. Waters, op.cit., pp.99-105.
36 Alan Harding, *The Law Courts of Medieval England* (1973), p.116.
37 W.H. Waters, op.cit., p.102.
38 In 1325-6 there are estreats of three actions of trespass, five of unjust detention, one of unjust caption, one of non-prosecution, one of false plaint and two defaulting defendants (TNA SC2/215/11).

roll exists, for six courts held between April and September 1346 and here again there was little business of importance; most of the actions were of debt and wrongful detention.[39] But the bare record of the court roll says nothing of the county court's significance as the monthly gathering of the community where views were exchanged, grievances expressed and the royal will made known.

Under the Welsh princes the only local court had been that of the commote. It remained because there was no reason to abolish it. It was the most familiar and convenient of all the courts, and since the commote had become the hundred it was natural for the commote court to become the hundred court.[40] Like the county court, it was attended by the freeholders, most of whom owed suit to the hundred. This was the court which was closest to the life of the community. It met every three weeks with the sheriff presiding, and in Anglesey the meeting-place varied from court to court. The hundred court dealt with all manner of breaches of law and custom, with minor civil actions and with the grant of licences. In 1325-6, for example, the matters dealt with by the court included failure to repair court buildings and mills, neglect of coastguard duty, false claims, unjust detention, trespass, buying and selling outside the market and unlicensed brewing.[41] Bond tenants were granted licence to marry and heirs took up their inheritance on payment of relief and, where applicable, *gobrestyn*. At the Llifon court held at Bodedern on 19 September 1346 the servants of the *rhaglaw* and the *rhingyll* were amerced because they neither kept order in the court nor revealed the names of those who were making a noise.[42] It is not possible to say much about the court's frequency because the rolls of only eighteen survive, six each from Dindaethwy, Llifon and Twrcelyn in 1346 and there is no regular pattern. The intervals between these courts varied a great deal; in Dindaethwy they were 24 days, 27 days, 14 days, 43 days and 32 days and the pattern was much the same in the other commotes.

The fourth court was the sheriff's tourn. This had existed in England at least since the twelfth century but it was entirely new to Gwynedd.[43] Here was exercised the sheriff's criminal jurisdiction and the court was attended by all freeholders and others who held land in the commote. It was held twice yearly, at Easter and Michaelmas. In Anglesey each township seems to have been represented by five members of the community.[44] A jury was empanelled by the sheriff and the articles of the tourn, a series of questions, were laid before it.[45]

39  G.P.Jones, 'Anglesey court rolls, 1346', in *TAAS* 1933, pp.44-9.
40  The court is discussed by W.H.Waters, op.cit., pp.105-13; see also Alan Harding, op.cit., pp.72-3.
41  TNA SC2/215/11, mm.7-10
42  G.P. Jones, op.cit., p.47.
43  W.H.Waters, op.cit., pp.113-23.
44  ibid., pp.116-17.
45  The articles are set out in Ivor Bowen, op.cit., pp.5-7.

The representatives of the townships were then questioned on oath and thus all the offences and breaches of law which had been committed during the past six months were brought to light. The surviving tourn rolls reveal the kind of offences with which the court dealt; at the Malltraeth tourn held on 12 March 1321 the townships of Heneglwys and Bodffordd presented one case of unlicensed brewing and one of begging.[46] Other offences presented by other townships included the drawing of blood and similar injuries, trading outside the market and looting wrecks; other rolls record neglect of coastguard duty, harbouring lepers, usury, suspicious wandering and all kinds of stealing. Thus the tourn was concerned with minor breaches of public order. It also uncovered offences which had not come to light elsewhere. This was made possible by its inquisitorial procedure since concealment was not easy in the face of direct questioning under oath. The jurors decided if there was a case to answer; some were amerced on the spot but serious offenders were reported secretly to the sheriff so that they would not escape and they would eventually stand trial before the justice In some rolls reference is made to the common fine paid by each community; this was paid by the unfree to 'avoid being troubled at the tourn with the small articles which did not touch the crown'.[47] The rolls indicate that courts were held on successive days and two might be held on the same day. Attendance was compulsory; according to the Statute only 'Men of Religion, Clerks and Women' were excused. Many fines were paid for non-suit to the county and hundred courts, but these were probably for licence to be absent rather than amercements.[48]

No court rolls from the commote of Menai have survived. This was because that commote was set apart from the rest of the county at those periods for which records are available, having been granted to Queen Isabella, first the wife and then the widow of Edward II, in 1309.[49] It had previously been granted by Edward I to his wife, Eleanor of Castile.[50] Even after it came back into the possession of the principality after Isabella's death in 1358 it was still to some degree separate from the rest of the county. The first account rendered for it was that for 1359-60. The profits of the courts were farmed by the *rhingyll* and

46 TNA SC2/215/5, m.1.
47 W.H.Waters, op.cit., p.119. This is how it was explained in the roll for the commote of Talybont in Merioneth in 1325-6.
48 ibid., pp. 100 (county), 106 (hundred).
49 *CPR 1307-1313*, 101. Menai and Rhosyr formed part of her dower and were later surrendered by her in exchange for Cornwall (*CPR 1317-1321*, 116, 202, 223, 268). They were subsequently earmarked for the maintenance of the king's son John and his daughter Eleanor (ibid., 453). After the fall of Roger Mortimer in 1330 they were again granted to Isabella in 1331 (*CPR 1330-1334*, 225, 271, 529-30).
50 *CChancRVar*, 291-2.

during the fourteenth century it had its own escheator.[51] When the sheriff accounted for the profits of justice he did so for the tourns and hundred courts in the other five commotes. Menai also had its own steward, who was presumably responsible for holding the tourn and the hundred courts.

The two boroughs of Beaumaris and Newborough had their own hierarchy of court leet, borough court and market and fair courts; the court leet was the equivalent of the tourn. But these were not the only courts in Anglesey; there were several private jurisdictions, the most important being that of the greatest landowner after the prince, the bishop of Bangor, who held lands in each of the six commotes. In 1348 he claimed a number of privileges, including the right to exclude the sheriff from his lands, the right to hold his own tourn, the authority to try all pleas except those of the crown in his court before his steward and the fines and amercements of those of his tenants who were convicted in the prince's courts.[52] He also claimed the right to hang felons from his lands after their conviction before the justice. In 1306 the profits of the bishop's courts in Anglesey were valued at £3 2s 8d and all his tenants owed suit.[53] The earliest surviving Anglesey plea roll includes a case committed to the sessions in 1515 from the bishop's court held at Llandyfrydog by his steward.[54] Similar privileges were enjoyed by the abbot of Aberconwy in his Anglesey lands and in 1348 he cited a charter of Llywelyn ab Iorwerth, confirmed by Edward III, in support of his claim.[55] He, too, claimed jurisdiction over his tenants and the exercise of that jurisdiction in a court held by his steward as well as his own gallows. Like that of the bishop, his jurisdiction was that of the hundred and the tourn; neither lord's townships were represented at the latter court. In 1535 the profits of the abbot's court at Gelliniog in Menai were valued at one pound.[56] The prior of Penmon also had his own court for the regulation of his tenants, but he did not enjoy the jurisdiction of the tourn, nor did he appear before the prince's justices in 1348 since he did not claim any delegated royal authority. In 1374 it was recorded that the prior's tenants owed suit to his court, held every three weeks, and in 1535 its profits were valued at ten shillings.[57] Those tenants in the commote of Menai who held of Clynnog Fawr do not appear to have owed any suit of court at all; in 1412 the commote officials were

---

51  TNA SC6/1149/9, m.6a.

52  *Rec.Caern.*, pp.133-8; the significance of these proceedings is discussed by Gwilym Usher, 'The Black Prince's Quo Warranto', in *WHR* 7 (1974), 1-12.

53  *Rec.Caern.* pp. 100, 104, 106.

54  Hugh Owen, ed., *Plea Rolls of Anglesey, 1509-1516* (1927), p.48

55  *Rec.Caern.*, pp.144-50; Gwilym Usher, op.cit., 9-10. *Valor Ecclesiasticus*, iv, 441-2. For the text and a critical examination of this charter see Huw Pryce, ed., *The Acts of Welsh Rulers 1120-1283* (Cardiff, 2005), no.218.

56  *Valor Ecclesiasticus* iv, 441-2.

57  A.D. Carr, 'The Penmon Valor 1374', *TAAS* 2005, p.18; *Valor Ecclesiasticus* iv, 430.

told by the sheriff that they should not annoy or distrain the tenants of Beuno at Tre'r-dryw who did not owe suit.[58]

Not only churchmen had their own courts. Several laymen who claimed them appeared before the justices in 1348 and three of these, all descended from Ednyfed Fychan, were from Anglesey. Hywel ap Goronwy claimed his own court held by his steward in his manors of Penmynydd and Trecastell, and the township of Erddreiniog and similar claims were made by Ieuan ap Gruffudd, the son of Sir Gruffudd Llwyd, in Tregarnedd and by Llywelyn ap Goronwy Fychan in Trecastell and Gwredog.[59] Ieuan claimed that his court had cognisance of pleas of trespass, debt and contract, while Llywelyn claimed all pleas except those of the crown and of the shedding of blood. They all claimed their privileges by prescription, which meant that their ancestors had enjoyed them before 1282; the original grants were probably made by Llywelyn ab Iorwerth to his seneschal, Ednyfed Fychan.[60] No records of any of these courts have survived, nor have any records of any other private jurisdictions. Each commotal centre seems to have had its own court, a body which must have resembled the manorial court so common in England, and there were at least two examples of grants of a similar jurisdiction after 1282.[61] In 1284 Edward I granted the township of Nantmawr in Twrcelyn to Tudur Fychan for his good service. He was followed there by his son and his grandson and an inquisition taken there on 12 March 1328 found that the tenants there owed suit of court every three weeks and valued the annual profits of the court at ten shillings. In 1320-1 the profits of justice had been leased to Madog Llwyd, a former sheriff, at an annual rent of fifteen shillings.[62] The other example was Gafrogwy in Menai, where the profits of the courts were valued at £1 10s in 1359-60 and which had its own court leet.[63] The manor of Gafrogwy comprised the townships of Gafrogwy, Bodwrog, Cerrigdewi, Ynys-gnud, Bryncir and Lledwigan Llan, the last of which was held in 1352 by a very free tenure by one of the sons of Madog ap Llywelyn, the leader of the rebellion of 1294-5.[64] These scattered townships may originally have been brought together to provide an

---

58 Henry Rowlands, 'Antiquitates parochiales', in *Arch.Camb.* 1848, p.58.

59 *Rec.Caern.*, pp. 150, 167-9; this Gwredog is the one in Twrcelyn near Rhosgoch, not the one in Llifon which belonged to the bishop of Bangor.

60 Glyn Roberts, 'Wyrion Eden', in *Aspects of Welsh History*, pp.181-3.

61 In 1348 the holder of the offices of *rhaglaw* and *rhingyll* of Twrcelyn claimed fees on every amercement in the manor court of Penrhosllugwy (*Rec.Caern.*, p.170). For a fragment of an Aberffraw court roll 1529-31 see W. Ogwen Williams, ed., *Calendar of Caernarvonshire Quarter Sessions Records, 1541-1558* (1956), pp.241-2

62 *CIM* ii, no 1030; TNA SC6/1228/7.

63 TNA SC6/1149/9, m.6a; 1150 m.4b. It was described as a manor in 1356 when Robert de Hambury was pardoned for acquiring it without licence (*BPR* iii, 495).

64 TNA SC6/1153/4, m 2b; *Extent of Anglesey*, p.162.

endowment for Madog after he had failed to recover Meirionnydd; in 1357 the manor was granted to the Caernarfon burgess Robert de Parys.[65]

Not one of the various Anglesey courts in private hands exercised a jurisdiction the derivation of which was independent of the crown; they had no more than delegated royal authority.[66] But all courts were concerned with the maintenance of order and although the evidence of courts of law is not the only guide to standards of civic morality and social behaviour in any community, it does shed some light on the question.[67] One petition from the middle of the fourteenth century shows that even the most eminent families were not above the law.[68] The king was asked by the kinsmen of Tudur ap Goronwy Fychan, who was accused of having killed Tudur ap Madog and, fearing vengeance, had fled the country, to receive him to his grace so that he could answer in court, but the petition was endorsed that the king was not advised to pardon him and the sequel bears this out. In 1377-8 the escheator accounted for the issues of a quarter of the township of Gwredog, once held by Tudur ap Goronwy Fychan who had been hanged.[69] The Gwredog connection is enough to identify Tudur as the grandson of Goronwy ab Ednyfed Fychan, the seneschal of Gwynedd, who died in 1268.[70] The fact that a descendant of Ednyfed Fychan could pay the ultimate penalty may say something about the efficiency of the administration at that time.

The accounts rendered for escheat lands refer from time to time to those who paid for their crimes with their lives. In March 1320 the constable of Beaumaris castle was pardoned for the escape of three prisoners from his custody. One of them, Ieuan Cwta, was run to earth and killed in Llanallgo church, and in 1350-1 the *rhingyll* of Twrcelyn was still accounting for the issues of his lands in Bodafon.[71] In 1311-2 the escheats included four acres in Trefadog in Talybolion, once held by Iorwerth ap Dafydd who killed his father, while in 1317-8 the sheriff accounted for lands in Pentraeth formerly held by Coluddyn Ci, hanged in the lordship of Denbigh the previous year.[72] There are many similar escheats and they indicate that felony, when detected, did not go unpunished.

65  Ralph A. Griffiths, 'An immigrant elite in the later middle ages: locating the de Parys family in north Wales and Chester', *WHR* 25 (2010), 177-9.
66  Gwilym Usher, op.cit., 1-4.
67  Criminal procedure in the courts between 1284 and 1343 is discussed by W.H. Waters, op.cit., pp.134-48; see also J. Conway Davies, 'Felony in Edwardian Wales', *THSC* 1916-7, pp.145-96.
68  *CAP*, p.395.
69  TNA SC6/1150/4, m.6a.
70  There is no mention of Tudur in any pedigree; this may be explained by the circumstances of his death.
71  *CPR 1317-1321*, 446; TNA SC6/1149/1, m.6a.
72  TNA SC6/1227/8, SC6/1227/14; Coluddyn Ci means 'Dog's Guts', which suggests that there was a story behind the nickname.

On the other hand, they also indicate that some did manage to escape the consequences of their actions, as did Philip Ffwlbart of Trefdraeth Wastrodion who fled after killing Ieuan ap Dafydd.[73] Another who ended on the gallows was Adda Goch of Bodednyfed in Twrcelyn, who was hanged in Caernarfon castle for killing Dafydd ab Elis, while Ieuan ap Dafydd ab Ieuan of Eglwys Ail or Llangadwaladr abjured the realm after killing Tegwared ap Dafydd Gest.[74] Thus felons were identified and, if caught, tried, sentenced and executed; what cannot be known is the rate of detection and the effectiveness of the law as a deterrent.

Lesser crimes were dealt with at the tourn and these proceedings must often have reflected local tensions and jealousies. At the Malltraeth tourn held on 12 March 1321 a man from Lledwigan Llys was amerced sixpence for drawing blood, while Iocyn Fach of Trefdraeth Wastrodion paid threepence for drawing a knife on Ieuan Ddu.[75] There were several cases of looting; the townships of Trefdraeth Ddisteiniaid and Trefdraeth Wastrodion were amerced 13s 4d for taking wine from a ship wrecked at Abermalltraeth and several men from Aberffraw were punished for stealing wood and ropes from a wreck. Other crimes included housebreaking, stealing turves and stealing livestock. Violence was not restricted to the male sex; at the Twrcelyn tourn on 5 September 1346 Efa *Tope* of Bodafon was amerced for shedding the blood of Gwerfyl Goch and this was not the only such case.[76] Men might also assault women, as did Madog ab Ieuan of Llaneilian; it cost him one shilling.[77] As in English manorial courts, those who wandered abroad without good reason were suspect; Tudur ap Gruffudd ap Meurig was amerced two shillings at the Talybolion tourn on 4 September 1346 for it.[78] At the Malltraeth tourn three days earlier Rhys ap Madyn Espyn was presented; he had been arrested after a breach of the peace in the market at Aberffraw and had then escaped from custody.[79] The *rhaglaw* and the porter were amerced for their negligence. These crimes were the small change of everyday life; petty theft must have been commonplace and in a society where every man carried a knife and where tempers could run high, bloodshed must have been frequent. It is worth remembering that the order and public peace we take for granted today are comparatively new and did not exist before the nineteenth century.

Among the King's Bench indictments are some which arose from proceed-

73  TNA SC6/1149/1, m.3a; *ffwlbart* means polecat.
74  TNA SC6/1149/1, mm.6a, 3a.
75  TNA SC2/215/5, m.1.
76  G.P. Jones, 'Anglesey court rolls, 1346', *TAAS* 1930, p.34.
77  ibid., p.35.
78  ibid., p.36.
79  G.P. Jones, 'Anglesey court rolls, 1346', *TAAS* 1932, p.48.

ings in Anglesey at the beginning of the reign of Henry V. Most of these are connected with the Glyn Dŵr revolt but a few deal with the activities of some Anglesey men who were pursuing a career of crime at the time. Such cases would normally have come before the justice, but it might have been more convenient for the royal commissioners to hear them. On 7 February 1414 Hywel ap Dafydd *Llorpe* and Dafydd ab Ithel ap Gwyddel, a tinker, broke into the house of Mato ap Tudur Hen in Dwygyfylchi in Caernarfonshire and stole a mare and other things.[80] In the same month they carried out robberies at Amlwch and at Boduan in Llŷn and they had also stolen cloth, a doublet and shoes from Ieuan Llwyd Crydd at Newborough.[81] These offences were not the small thefts from neighbours which one finds in court rolls; they were planned and premeditated robberies over a wide area and as such they reflect another aspect of the problem of law and order. Then, as now, men might be tempted to live by taking what did not belong to them. Had the plea rolls of the justice's sessions survived we would know a great deal more about serious crime; as it is we have to be content with the occasional reference in the accounts as in 1420-1 when Mato ab Ieuan Llwyd of Newborough, a former bailiff of the town, was killed there by Edward, son of Thomas Haryot.[82] Mato had survived an earlier attempt on his life by Nicholas Feddyg in 1414.[83]

Breaches of order might come before the courts but one might reasonably ask how order was maintained and some measure of public peace secured. The answer is that the burden was laid on the community. Like the English hundred, the commote was responsible for crimes committed within its boundaries and it was liable to pay compensation if they were not detected.[84] The hue and cry, well-established in England, is not mentioned in the Statute but it was introduced in 1284. If a crime was committed the four adjacent townships were obliged to pursue the culprit until he was caught; after 1305 the obligation only applied as far as the next township which then took up the chase. At the Malltraeth tourn held on 12 March 1321 the communities of Trefdraeth Wastrodion and Trefdraeth Ddisteiniaid were each amerced ten shillings for not joining the hue and cry, and at the Dindaethwy tourn four days later the township of Penmon was amerced one shilling for not joining it at Bodfa and that of Mathafarn Eithaf for not joining it at Erddreiniog.[85] The effectiveness of local government obviously depended on the efficiency of those who held office. The sheriff was the key man in the county and he was generally an Englishman although nine

---

80  TNA KB9/204/3/K18.
81  TNA KB9/204/3KC20, 21, 19.
82  TNA SC6/1152/9, m.8b.
83  TNA KB9/204/3/K19.
84  Communal responsibility is discussed by W.H. Waters, op.cit., pp.136-9.
85  TNA SC2/215/5, mm.1, 3a; the hue and cry is discussed by W.H. Waters, op.cit., pp.136-7.

Welshmen held the office during the fourteenth century. The first of these was Sir Gruffudd ap Rhys, better known as Sir Gruffudd Llwyd, in 1305-6.[86] He was followed by Gruffudd ab Owain (1306-8), Madog Llwyd (1308-12), Einion ab Ieuan (1316-27), Cynwrig ap Gruffudd (1334), Gruffudd ap Madog Gloddaith (1355-9), Ieuan Chwerw (1372-3), Rhys ap Tudur ap Goronwy (1374-5) and Gwilym ap Gruffudd ap Gwilym (1395-7).[87] These men belonged to leading local families; the last two were descendants of Ednyfed Fychan while Ieuan Chwerw of Bodafon in Twrcelyn was *rhingyll* of that commote in 1352-3 and *rhaglaw* in 1386-7.[88] Einion ab Ieuan was a prominent burgess of Beaumaris and Gruffudd ap Madog Gloddaith belonged to a family which held lands in Anglesey and Caernarfonshire and his father had also played some part in the administration of the principality.[89] Such men were more than fit to be sheriffs. They were the natural leaders of the community and the authorities depended on them for efficient administration. As long ago as 1244 the officers of the earl of Pembroke had told the royal justice in south Wales that it was not easy to control the Welsh except through one of their own race and the point was usually well taken.[90] But they were not always regarded as reliable, especially in the climate of the fourteenth century and as early as the 1330s an attempt was made to restrict the office to Englishmen.[91] The Glyn Dŵr revolt marks a watershed; no Welshman was appointed to the office again until after the coming of the Tudors.

The earliest sheriffs were royal servants Some might be clerics; the Thomas Harborough who held the office from 1352 to 1355 might be the man of that name who was archdeacon of Anglesey from 1368 to 1395.[92] Many were burgesses, like Richard de Pykemere, a burgess of Caernarfon who was sheriff of Anglesey from 1376 to 1385 and again from 1387 to 1390 and sheriff of Caernarfonshire in 1395; Richard Golding (1385-1387) and Adam Clerk (1390-1395) were burgesses of Beaumaris.[93] This suggests that there were two classes of social leaders, the Welsh landed proprietors and the leading families in Conwy, Caernarfon and Beaumaris whose interests now extended beyond the towns. Three early fifteenth-century sheriffs, Ralph de Barton, John del Wode

86  W.H.Waters, op.cit., p.72; for his career see J.G. Edwards, 'Sir Gruffudd Llwyd', *EHR* 30 (1915), 589-601, and *Y Bywgraffiadur Cymreig*, p.299.

87  *TNA List of Sheriffs*, 236. For Ieuan Chwerw and Rhys ap Tudur ap Goronwy see TNA E163/24/1, mm.1a, 1b.

88  TNA SC6/1149, m.6a; 1151/3, m.4a.

89  For the Gloddaith family see A.D. Carr, 'Medieval Gloddaith', *TCHS* 38 (1977), 7-32.

90  *CAC*, p.48.

91  W.H.Waters, op.cit., p.73.

92  Le Neve, *Fasti* 11, p.9; *TNA List of Sheriffs*, 236.

93  Glyn Roberts, 'Wyrion Eden', p.202; *TNA List of Sheriffs*. 236.

and John Walsh, were Cheshire men.[94] There was nothing unusual in this; many former servants of the prince in north Wales had come from Cheshire and one has only to think of John de Delves, the man responsible for the 1352 extent. Another sheriff, Roger Strangeways (1418-1424), was from Lancashire. None of these had any local connections; they had all been in the service of Henry V and it was on men like them that he depended to staff the higher levels of his administration and to bring about a return to normality. In 1425 John Stanley, yet another Cheshire esquire of Henry V, was appointed. In 1437 he was granted the office for life and he was also sheriff of Merioneth in 1433 as well as being constable of Caernarfon and serjeant of the armoury with a house in the Tower of London.[95] A man who had so much could hardly have been expected to give Anglesey his undivided attention; he needed a deputy and it was as deputies to English officials that members of so many Welsh families rose to prominence in the fifteenth-century.[96] As the century progressed, the shrievalty came to have less and less connection with the world of day-to-day administration and eventually passed permanently into the hands of the leading local families.

The office of escheator was entrusted to Welshmen rather more often than was the shrievalty in the fourteenth century. Between 1350 and 1360 the office was held by the sheriff, but between the latter date and the end of the century seven of the ten whose names are known were Welsh. They included Maredudd ap Tudur (1388-1390), the great-grandfather of Henry VII, and the last Welsh-man to hold the office before the revolt was Maredudd ap Cynwrig of Porthaml, perhaps the greatest accumulator of farms and offices in medieval Anglesey.[97] English escheators were drawn from the ranks of the burgesses; Richard de Pykemere (1383-4 and 1394-5) also served as sheriff, while William de Huntingdon (1377-8) was a burgess of Caernarfon and Henry Clerk (1391-2) was a burgess of Beaumaris and bailiff there on four occasions between 1378 and 1396. After the revolt the office was sometimes held by royal officials and sometimes by burgesses; no Welshman served again as escheator.

At commote level the officials were generally Welsh, although there were oc-casional exceptions. If it was the leading local families which provided sheriffs and escheators, the same was equally true of offices lower down the scale. As one would expect, the commote of Menai was dominated by the descendants of Llywarch ap Bran. Maredudd Ddu ap Goronwy was *rhaglaw* from 1306 to

94  Ralph A. Griffiths, 'Patronage, politics and the Principality of Wales, 1413-1461', in H. Hearder and H.R. Loyn, eds., *British Government and Administration: studies presented to S.B. Chrimes* (1974), p.77.
95  ibid., p.81; *CPR 1436-1441*, 153; *CPR 1441-1446*, 272.
96  The point is made by W. Ogwen Williams, *Tudor Gwynedd* (1958), p.19.
97  For the career of Maredudd ap Cynwrig see A.D. Carr, 'Maredudd ap Cynwrig: a medieval public person', *TAAS* 1998, pp.13-21.

1308 and his grandson, Dafydd ab Ieuan Wyddel, in 1359-60. Dafydd's son Llywelyn was *rhaglaw* from 1388 to 1393 and *rhingyll* in 1377-80, 1381-3 and from 1384 to 1388.[98] Llywelyn's son Hywel was *rhingyll* in 1418-9 and 1421-2, and another son, Rhys, held the same office in 1441-2, while Llywelyn ap Hwlcyn ap Dafydd ab Ieuan was *rhingyll* in 1414-5.[99] This Llywelyn's brother Madog was *rhingyll* in 1437-8 and an approver of the commote in 1449-50.[100] Ithel ap Hywel ap Llywelyn was joint *rhingyll* in 1437-8 and an approver in 1449-50 and 1456-7 while his cousin, Hywel ap Rhys ap Llywelyn, was steward of the commote between 1465 and 1468 and *rhingyll* in 1471-2; Ithel's son Owain was an approver in 1480-1.[101] These were not the only descendants of Maredudd Ddu to hold office. The great Maredudd ap Cynwrig, for example, was his grandson and his tally of offices included the ringildry of the commote, the farms of the tolls of Llannerch-y-medd fair and the *maerdrefi* of Rhosyr, Cemais and Penrhosllugwy, the farms of ferries, royal mills and escheats in Menai and of the borough of Newborough and the offices of under-sheriff of Anglesey and serjeant-at-arms in the county at various times.[102] This record shows how a single lineage could dominate a commote. A similar dominance was exercised by the descendants of Carwed in Twrcelyn and by those of Hwfa ap Cynddelw in Llifon. Some holders of these offices, like the poets Gruffudd Gryg and Gruffudd ap Maredudd ap Dafydd, attained distinction in other fields. The greatest official family of them all was, of course, that of the descendants of Ednyfed Fychan.[103]

Most of these men held their offices at farm; in other words, they leased them. The farmer paid a lump sum for the right to collect the perquisites of the office. The advantage for the crown was the lump sum; the advantage for the farmer was that he could make a profit. The *rhingyll* accounted for the royal revenue and paid it over and there were many opportunities for him to make more personal profit by way of additional fees to oil the wheels of administration and justice.[104] The farm of the commote was really a contract; like the hundred bailiff in England the *rhingyll* agreed to pay the farm and was then

---

98 TNA SC6/1170/5; 1227/7; 1149/9, m.6a; 1151/5, m.4b; 1151/8, m.4b; 1150/4, m.3b; 1150/6, m.4a; 1150/8, m.4a; 1150/9, m.4b; 1151/1, m.6a; 1151/4, m.4b.

99 TNA SC6/1152/7, m.4a; 1153/1, m.6a; 1153/5, m.6a; 1152/6, m.7a.

100 TNA SC6/1153/4, m.7a; 1153/6, m.7a.

101 TNA SC6/1153/4, m.7a; 1153/6, m.7a; 1154/2, m.8a; 1154/6, m.8a; 1217/6; 1155/2, m.5a; 1155/5, m.5a.

102 Carr, 'Maredudd ap Cynwrig', pp. 14, 18-19; for a genealogical table of the leading members of the lineage see Appendix A, Table 2.

103 Gruffudd *Grek*, *rhingyll* of Malltraeth in 1357-8, may be the poet and Gruffudd ap Maredudd ap Dafydd was *rhaglaw* of Talybolion in 1372-3 and 1374-5 (TNA SC6/1149/8, m.1a; E163/24/1, mm.1a-b).

104 Helen M. Cam, *The Hundred and the Hundred Rolls*, pp.150-2.

given the office.[105] But the mid-fourteenth century appointments appear to have been the result of a kind of auction; candidates came to the Exchequer at Caernarfon and made proffers or bids.[106] The farms varied a great deal but on the whole the sums paid for commotal offices showed a gradual decline over the years. In Dindaethwy, for example, the farm of the raglotry ranged from £5 10s between 1351 and 1379 to 13s 4d in 1424-5, while the upper and lower limits for the ringildry were £8 16s 8d in 1356-7 and two shillings in the second hall of the fifteenth century. The general pattern in the other commotes was much the same; farms were sometimes higher than in Dindaethwy but it is hard to tell to what extent higher farms reflected higher profitability or more competition for office. What we cannot know is just how much competition there was and who the unsuccessful bidders were.

The shrievalty and escheatorship were also farmed for a time in the four-teenth century as was the stewardship of Menai; the last-named office included all the profits of justice from the commote. Some farms of commotal offices in the 1370s were very low indeed and this, combined with the figures for the 1380s, suggests that this may have been a difficult time, But farmers were not always to be found; in the fifteenth century there seems often to have been no demand for the ringildry and the authorities were obliged to appoint approvers in each commote who collected as much of the royal revenue as they could. It had ceased to be an office which brought much profit by the late fifteenth cen-tury. The farm, when paid, had become a derisory sum; in 1472-3 Dindaethwy, Malltraeth and Llifon were each worth 3s 4d, Talybolion and Menai two shillings and Twrcelyn 6s 8d.[107]

There was another way in which appointments might be made; since all these offices were in the prince's gift they might from time to time be used to meet the demands made on his patronage. The pattern of patronage varied considerably over the years. Grants were made by Edward I as rewards for good service and many who held raglotries and ringildries before 1284 re-mained in office. In 1305 Goronwy Crach, the *rhingyll* of Menai, complained to Edward of Caernarfon that he and his ancestors had held the office without paying any rent until the keeper of the queen's lands imposed an annual farm of three pounds.[108] An inquisition had found that he should pay nothing, but the justice had then raised the farm to five pounds and had demanded arrears. The prince ruled that Goronwy should hold the office for life at an annual farm

105  ibid., p.146.
106  For examples see TNA SC6/1305/16, m.1a (1352-3) and E163/24/1, mm.1a-b (1372, 1374), where the successful candidates and the sums they offered are listed. For 1373 see ibid., m.2b, where the pledges are also named. Bids were also made for escheat lands.
107  TNA SC6/1155/3; the raglotry of Menai was worth 6s 8d, but no other raglotry is mentioned.
108  *Rec.Caern.* p.219.

of three pounds; he was pardoned the arrears but in return he had to relinquish all the rights which he and his heirs had in the office. This is an interesting decision which may reflect a compromise. Although Edward I was prepared to respect the rights of those who had held office under Llywelyn ap Gruffudd and had made their peace in 1282, he might not have been willing to allow continued hereditary tenure which would deprive him and his successors of patronage. The fact that many offices appeared to have been held by particular lineages might have given them a lien on them which had to be broken in the interests of effective government. There were several other petitions in and around 1305, some seeking grants of office and some complaining that they had been deprived of offices or forced to pay farms for those which they had been granted free of any rent.[109]

Although commotal offices were largely a Welsh preserve, they were not a monopoly; there were sometimes English appointments. Since the king or the prince was the fount of patronage and had clerks and servants to reward, it was inevitable that the principality of Wales should sometimes be a source of royal bounty. It is unlikely that some of these grantees ever actually performed the duties of those offices, the profits of which they enjoyed. Not every Englishman was a royal clerk. Thomas de Chebsay, the former *rhingyll* of Aberffraw and Talybolion, who still owed £33 0s 1d arrears in 1347, was probably a member of the Beaumaris family of that name, and William de Hampton, *rhaglaw* of Menai in 1381-2, belonged to a Caernarfon family and was himself a burgess of Beaumaris and one of the bailiffs of the town in 1388.[110] Both Edward III and the Black Prince granted many offices to absentees. Many were granted for life, as rewards for service or in settlement of debts, and several might be granted to a single individual. Such grants were made in each county but there was nothing in Anglesey to compare with the grant of all the king's rights in Merioneth to Walter de Mauny in 1341.[111] In 1339 a royal yeoman, Thomas de Colle, was granted the raglotry and ringildry of Twrcelyn for life, while Roger de Heyton, the king's surgeon, was *rhingyll* of the cantref of Aberffraw in 1337-8 and was later granted the manor of Aberffraw for life.[112]

There was some repetition of the practice in the reign of Richard II, the most blatant example being the life grant of the whole county to Sir William le Scrope in consideration of his service at home and abroad in 1397.[113] A similar

109 *CAP*, p.395; *Rec.Caern.* p.215.
110 *BPR* i, 133; Keith Williams-Jones, 'Caernarvon', in Ralph A. Griffiths, ed., *Boroughs of Medieval Wales* (1978), pp. 83, 90; TNA SC6/1151/5, m.5a.
111 W.H. Waters, op.cit., p.76; D.L. Evans, 'Walter de Mauny, sheriff of Merioneth, 1332-72', *JMHRS.*, 4 (1963), 197-8.
112 *CFR 1337-1347.* 152; TNA SC6/1229/4; *CPR 1340-1343*, 295.
113 *CPR 1396-1399*, 82. The commotal officials and others seem to have retained their offices under Scrope (TNA SC6/1152/3; NLW Llanfair and Brynodol M2).

grant was made in 1399 to Henry Percy, better known as Hotspur.[114] Again, Welshmen were being excluded from office in both principality and march although grants were now made to royal servants rather than to royal creditors.[115] But it was in the fifteenth century that the use of patronage reached its peak. In theory it should have been used to ensure the efficient working of the royal administration but in practice it was used to reward good service and secure loyalty. In the early years of the century practically every office in Anglesey was held by a Welshman despite the Glyn Dŵr revolt, but as soon as Henry VI came of age in 1437 the floodgates were opened and within the next few months more than half the offices in north Wales had been granted out, mainly to members of the king's household.[116] The practice was as common in Anglesey as anywhere else and most grants were for life. In 1437 there were seven grants of offices and farms in the county, all to members of the household, and they were followed in the next few years by further ones, some of which were in survivorship. Such grants were not uncommon and they inhibited royal control of patronage even more.[117] When Thomas Babham, groom of the chamber, was granted the raglotry of Twrcelyn in 1442 every commotal office in Anglesey except the ringildry of Twrcelyn had come into the hands of an absentee member of the royal household.[118] And the death of a grantee did not mean any change; there must always have been a queue of hungry household officers awaiting vacancies. When Nicholas Middlemore, a yeoman of the crown who had obtained the raglotries of Menai, Llifon, Malltraeth and Dindaethwy in 1437, died in 1442 all four offices were granted to the king's serjeant Robert Cookes, yeoman of the chamber.[119]

This practice did nothing for efficient administration or for the morale of the leaders of the local community, although some might serve as deputies to absent *rhingylliaid*. An Act of Resumption could cancel all existing grants and restore the king's patronage to him, but between 1449 and 1451 most officeholders in Wales obtained exemption.[120] After the fall of the duke of Suffolk in 1455 offices again went largely to local men, although ringildries were no longer

114  *CPR. 1399-1401*, 155.
115  Glanmor Williams, *Owen Glendower* (1966), p.15.
116  Ralph A. Griffiths, 'Patronage, politics and the Principality of Wales, 1413-1461', in H. Hearder and H.R. Loyn, op.cit., pp.69-86.
117  *CPR 1436-1441*, 45, 64, 69, 94, 100, 118, 155, 177, 196, 280; *CPR 1441-1446*, 63, 143. Grants in survivorship are discussed by Ralph A. Griffiths, op.cit., p.75.
118  *CPR 1441-1446*, 96. The *rhingyll* of Twrcelyn was Dafydd ab Ieuan ap Hywel of Llwydiarth Esgob (TNA SC6/1153/5, m.7a). He was a man of some standing in the commote, with a long record of service and this might have protected him.
119  *CPR 1441-1446*, 98. In 1446-7 these offices went to yet another royal servant, Henry Rossington, a yeoman of the crown (TNA SC6/1154/2, m.2a.)
120  Ralph A. Griffiths, op.cit., pp.84-5.

so attractive and commotes were frequently in the hands of approvers. In 1472-3 no farmer could be found for the raglotry of Malltraeth, which indicates that these offices, which were a survival from the pre-1282 world, no longer counted for much. But, however many offices might be conferred on outsiders and however anachronistic the traditional commote offices might have become, real power and influence remained in the hands of those local families whose dominance of their communities was to be consecrated in the next century by their inclusion in the Commission of the Peace.

The exercise of patronage was not restricted to commotal offices; there were also several townships which were held separately. These consisted of four *maerdrefi* or commotal centres, Aberffraw, Cemais, Penrhosllugwy and Rhosyr and three other townships, Nantmawr, Gafrogwy and Cleifiog and Llanllibio. The farm of each *maerdref* stemmed originally from the office of porter there; the porter was, in effect, the *rhingyll* of the *maerdref*. The perquisites which made the office worth-while were fees from each prisoner and from certain fines as well as the profits of justice.[121] In the early years of the fourteenth century the office was often held jointly with that of *rhingyll* of the commote and it was usually held by a Welshman. Under the Black Prince, however, many grants were made to members of his household. Penrhosllugwy was granted in 1347 to Sir John de Ravensholme and Cemais to Thomas de Missenden, while Aberffraw was sometimes farmed by local Welshmen and sometimes by Englishmen.[122] Some of the English farmers were burgesses and some outsiders and in 1473-4 the farm was taken up by the younger William Bulkeley of Beaumaris.[123] Penrhosllugwy and Cemais followed much the same pattern although in each case there were rather more Welsh farmers, usually members of leading local families. From time to time they were farmed by the local community as at Aberffraw and Penrhosllugwy in 1376-7 and Cemais in 1424-5; Penrhosllugwy was farmed by its bond tenants in 1480-1.[124] Rhosyr was usually farmed by members of the leading families in Menai; like everything else in that commote it was very much the preserve of the descendants of Llywarch ap Bran. The other three townships were usually farmed in the same way. One interesting grant was that of Nantmawr in 1347 to Sir Edmund de Wauncey, later steward of the Black Prince's household and captor of the king of France's son at the battle of Poitiers.[125]

---

121 *Governance of Gwynedd*, p.51.

122 *BPR* i, 112.

123 TNA SC6/1155/4, m.8a; he also farmed Penrhosllugwy and Nantmawr.

124 TNA SC6/1150/3, mm.1a, 3b; 1153/2, m.6a; 1155/5, m.7a.

125 *BPR* i, 101; T.F. Tout, *Chapters in the Administrative History of Medieval England* v (1930), p.432; *BPR* iii, 452.

In addition to grants of offices, annuities might be charged on particular sources of revenue. In 1418 an annuity of one hundred pounds was granted to Sir William Harrington, the king's standard-bearer, out of the issues of Twrcelyn; he was dead by 1439 when both office and annuity were granted to Sir Ralph Boteler, later Lord Sudeley, a prominent royal servant whose other offices included that of constable of Conwy castle.[126] The grant made to Henry V's widow, Katherine de Valois, in 1422 included most of the issues of Anglesey, an inclusion which turned out to be particularly appropriate in the light of her second marriage.[127]

Of the conduct of officials there is less evidence. One would not expect to find much mention of good and conscientious service; only the oppressive and the extortionate would call forth protests and petitions. In 1298 the tenants of Menai complained that Hugh de Leominster, the keeper of the commote, was claiming an annual rent of £22 from certain tenants; because of their poverty their rent had been reduced to ten pounds but he had taken no notice.[128] The community of the same commote complained in 1330-1 that William de Shalford, when farmer of Menai, had done so much damage that the tenants could no longer pay their rents nor render their services.[129] Such petitions, along with those of individuals, show the kind of complaints that did arise, but nothing has survived to compare with the evidence of official extortion and corruption in Flintshire in the forties and fifties of the fourteenth-century.[130]

The fact that most of the surviving records are financial ones may distort the picture to some extent, but finance has always played a vital part in local government; the Welsh proverb 'Diwedd y gân yw'r geiniog' expresses a universally accepted truth. Medieval local government was not concerned with services; it was concerned with revenue. Nor was the revenue likely to be applied to the well-being of the local community; it was part of the profits of kingship. It came from a number of sources, the principal ones being the fixed revenue from each commote, which consisted mainly of the quit-rents due from each township, the variable revenue from royal mills and the profits of justice, casual income and farms of offices. All these were the issues of the county.[131] They formed the accounting officer's charge, for which he had to answer. What was actually collected and paid over was his discharge. This com-

126 *CPR 1413-1416*, 143; *CPR 1436-1441*, 252. Annuities are discussed by Ralph A. Griffiths, op.cit., pp.78-9.
127 *Rot. Parl.*, iv, 184.
128 Natalie Fryde, *List of Welsh Entries in the Memoranda Rolls. 1284-1343*, no.144.
129 *CAP*, p.284.
130 D.L. Evans, ed., *Flintshire Ministers' Accounts, 1328-1353*, pp. xxi-xxviii, xxxiv-xxxix; A.D. Carr, 'Rhys ap Roppert', *TDHS*, 25 (1976), 157-62.
131 For a discussion of the form of accounting see R. Ian Jack, *Medieval Wales* (1972), pp.116-8.

prised money received, expenditure met from income, respites and decayed
rents which still formed part of the charge but which had ceased to exist or
had not been paid. In a perfect world, charge and discharge would balance,
but this rarely happened. If the charge exceeded the discharge the accounting
officer was in arrear, and if it were the other way round he was in surplus and
out of pocket. Arrears or surplus would be carried forward to the following
year's account.

The quit-rents from the townships were based on the 1284 extent of Anglesey after that year and on the new extent of 1352 from 1353-4 onwards. The
total value of the county in 1284 was £483 10s 11d. From this total was sub-
tracted the value of certain lands granted by Edward I to the bishop of Bangor
and the abbot of Aberconwy and some other small sums and after these de-
ductions the annual income came to £430 2s 6½d. Everything over and above
this sum was increment. In the account which he rendered for 1305-6 the
chamberlain of north Wales accounted for a total revenue of £821 3s 7d.[132] The
fixed income based on the extent amounted to £435 2s 6¼d; the rest was made
up of farms of lands, mills, ferries and offices, profits of justice and various
fines made before the justice of north Wales. The boroughs of Beaumaris and
Newborough accounted separately. Against the total charge for Anglesey were
offset decayed rents, among them the income entered in the extent for the borough of Llan-faes which by now had ceased to exist.

This was the kind of income which the king or prince might expect to receive
from Anglesey. The perquisites of the courts or profits of justice varied from
year to year, as did casual revenue. This could come from many sources; in
1311-2 the sheriff accounted for the value of a small porpoise that had been
washed ashore and in 1315-6 for a stray horse.[133] Much of this income came
from wrecks, as in 1339 when the account included 6s 8d, the value of a boat
wrecked in a storm.[134]

Out of his revenue the sheriff had to meet the cost of repairs to royal property, such as mills and ferry boats; many accounts from the first half of the
fourteenth century contained detailed accounts of this expenditure. He ceased
to account for all the issues after the change in the system of accounting in
1350; in subsequent accounts the *rhingyll* answered for the fixed income from
the commote and the farms of the raglotry and ringildry. Goods of intestates
and shipwrecks were the responsibility of the escheator, while the profits of the
tourns and the hundred courts were accounted for by the sheriff. The total

---

132  John Griffiths. 'Early accounts relating to north Wales, temp., Edward I', *BBCS*, 16 (1954-6),
      112-6.
133  TNA SC6/1227/8, m.2a; 1227/11.
134  TNA SC6/1229/3.

sum due from the *rhingyll* of Dindaethwy in 1350-1 was £46 15s 7¾d; at the end of the year he still owed 18s 4¼d.[135]

The other commote accounts followed a similar pattern; the *rhingyll* of Malltraeth managed to make his account balance while his colleague in Llifon ended the year in surplus because of a respite. In this they were more fortunate than Peter de Overton in Talybolion; even with respites he still owed £19 18s 10½d and because of this he was arrested and imprisoned in Beaumaris castle.[136] The bailiffs of Beaumaris and the sheriff were also in arrear, owing £29 15s 3½d and £22 14s 8¾d respectively. Arrears were entered on the rolls of debts and were usually paid off over the next few years. They were often higher in the fifteenth century. In 1441-2 the total brought forward from the previous year was £245 11s 11½d; the arrears carried forward to the following year were £118 3s 11½d.[137] As these figures suggest, some officials were more successful than others in clearing them. The total issues of Anglesey for each financial year, which began at Michaelmas, were contained in the chamberlains' accounts. The following figures show how they could fluctuate:

| | | |
|---|---|---|
| 1321-2 | : | £ 675 18s 17¾d |
| 1343-4 | : | £ 734 12s 15½d |
| 1394-5 | : | £ 651 17s 12½d |
| 1448-9 | : | £ 348 17s 16½d |
| 1459-60 | : | £ 321 12s 11¾d |
| 1467-8 | : | £ 498 19s 11½d |
| 1483-4 | : | £ 307 18s 15d½   [138] |

This suggests that the fifteenth century showed a substantial decrease in revenue although there was considerable variation, depending on the level of arrears; the profits of justice certainly showed a diminishing return.

Anglesey produced less revenue than Caernarfonshire but more than Merioneth. In 1328-9 it yielded £641 7s 10d; the other two counties produced £820 15s 11½d and £480 5s 11d.[139] In the 1370s Caernarfonshire brought in about £1,100 annually, Merioneth about £750 and Anglesey about £800.[140] By 1453-4 the yield from Anglesey was £439 15s 2½d and that from Caernarfonshire £578 12s 4d; Merioneth only produced £28 4s 5½d but by this time it had be-

135  TNA SC6/1149/1, mm.1a-b.
136  TNA SC6/1149/1, m.5b.
137  TNA SC6/1153/5, m.1a.
138  TNA SC6/1212/7; 1214/2; 1215/6; 1216/7; 1217/3; 1217/6; 1217/7.
139  TNA SC6/1213/6.
140  D.L. Evans, 'Walter de Mauny, sheriff of Merioneth, 1332-1372', 203.

come 'ungoverned and ungovernable'.[141] The totals in the chamberlains' accounts were, of course, the actual sums collected rather than the sums with which the counties were charged and respites and decayed rents had taken their toll. Under Edward I and during the principate of Edward of Caernarfon the government of north Wales had been subject to close and vigorous supervision from the centre. Attempts to revive this supervision under Edward III had been less than successful and by the middle of the fifteenth century the central government was no longer in a position to supervise. There was certainly a gradual deterioration in administrative standards and this deterioration was reflected in the financial management of the principality. In 1466 a commission was issued to the justice and some of the leading men of north Wales to investigate a report that many of the rents and revenues of Caernarfonshire and common fines in that county and Anglesey had not been paid since Edward IV had become king in 1461 and to make arrangements for the payment of the arrears.[142]

There were other occasional demands in the form of subsidies. The first of these was the fifteenth on moveables levied by Edward I in 1290, which was extended to Wales at the beginning of 1291.[143] For north Wales only the subsidy rolls for Flintshire and Merioneth have survived; all that remains from Anglesey is the detailed assessment for the manor of Aberffraw, and the commote of Malltraeth.[144] Keith Williams-Jones, however, suggested a figure of £812 for the county, basing it on the usual proportion of Merioneth contributions to those from Anglesey.[145] The significance of this subsidy as a contributory factor to the revolt of Madog ap Llywelyn is well-known; it certainly seems to have been one of the heaviest imposed on the royal lands in Wales. Despite Edward's promise that it would not be regarded as a precedent, there was no lack of subsequent demands on the taxpayers of north Wales, but later subsidies were not parliamentary ones; they were probably based on the taxes levied from time to time by marcher lords.[146]

Another subsidy from the royal lands in Wales was levied in 1300. North Wales yielded the sum of two thousand marks (£1,333 6s 8d), but no breakdown for individual counties has survived. If the formula suggested by Mr Williams-Jones (3 : 4.3 : 5 for Merioneth : Anglesey : Caernarfonshire) is applied,

141 TNA SC6/1217/2; Ralph A. Griffiths, 'Wales and the marches' in S.B. Chrimes, C.D. Ross and Ralph A. Griffiths, eds., *Fifteenth Century England, 1399-1509* (1972), p.155.

142 *CPR1461-1467*, 529.

143 Keith Williams-Jones, *The Merioneth Lay Subsidy Roll, 1292-3*, *p.*viii; the object of the subsidy was to pay off the debts incurred by the king in paying the ransom of Charles of Salerno, the king of Sicily.

144 TNA E179/242/49.

145 Keith Williams-Jones, op.cit., p.xxv.

146 ibid., p.ix.

the Anglesey contribution would be about £466.[147] Anglesey contributed £325 5s 2d to the fifteenth granted to Edward II in 1318 and a payment called mise, hornyeld or *cymorth*, traditionally levied on the accession of a new prince or lord, raised 500 marks from the three counties of north Wales in 1344.[148] Further subsidies were granted in 1353-4, 1381-2 and 1395, each payable in instalments and even after the outbreak of the Glyn Dŵr revolt the crown demanded one.[149] During the years after the revolt a good deal of extra income came from the fines paid to purge rebellion in 1406 and subsequent fines for a charter of pardon and for the restitution of rights and liberties. There was certainly an increase in the incidence of extraordinary taxation in the fifteenth century, so much so, in fact, as to make that adjective seem inappropriate. In 1437, for example, a commission was issued to induce the communities of Anglesey, Flintshire, Chirkland, Hawarden and Moldsdale, the lands formerly held by Queen Katherine, to 'grant to the king in his difficult circumstances certain gifts, aids or subsidies as the custom has been hitherto'.[150] One reason for these subsidies may have been the need to make up the deficiency caused by the decrease in the regular income from the county; they were also intended as a substitute for the common fine of the sheriff's tourn.[151] But these sums, although raised locally, were not for local use, although necessary military expenditure was met out of income. It was not until the sixteenth century that rates were raised in the county or the parish to pay for such things as highways and poor relief.

---

147  ibid., p.xxv.
148  Natalie Fryde, op.cit., p.xix; TNA SC6/1214/3
149  TNA SC6/1305/16, mm.3a-b; 1214/9; 1215/8.
150  *CPR 1436-1441*, 148; for other subsidies see TNA SC6/1216/3 (1417-8); 1216/6 (1446); *CPR 1452-1461*, 124 (1453); TNA SC6/1217/3, m.2 (1457); 1217/5 (1466); 1217/7, m.2 (1483).
151  J. Beverley Smith, 'Crown and community in the principality of north Wales in the reign of Henry Tudor', 154; the financial problems of the fifteenth century are discussed in this article.

# 4 *The Medieval Economy*

DURING THE WAR OF 1276-7 an English force landed in Anglesey and seized the harvest. The fact that this was one of the blows which forced Llywelyn ap Gruffudd to seek terms reflects the importance of the island's contribution to the economy of Gwynedd. As early as the seventh century Bede had commented on its fertility while at the end of the twelfth Gerald wrote that Anglesey was 'so productive that it could supply the whole of Wales with corn over a long period'.[1] In addition to the political consequences of the seizure, Edward I seems to have been able to make a useful profit. In 1278 Dafydd ab Einion, possibly that burgess of Llan-faes who was later to be one of the richest men in Beaumaris, complained that certain men had claimed that corn bought by him from William Burnell and his men in Anglesey belonged to them and had, in accordance with local custom, caused a cross to be placed on the corn, which meant that he could not touch it.[2] Dafydd was a merchant and a man of considerable enterprise and the timing of the episode suggests that he had bought up part of the 1277 harvest and that its original owners had proceeded against him.

The most fertile land in Anglesey was that occupied by the *maerdref* of Llanfaes which contained 13 carucates or about 780 acres. In 1291-2 far more oats were grown there than any other crop. The total yield for that year, according to the chamberlain's account, was 250 bushels of wheat, 186 bushels of maslin (a mixture of grains) and 1,630 bushels of oats.[3] This came from that part of the demesne which was farmed directly; the king's share of the corn ground in his mills for the tenants came to 44 bushels of maslin, 32 bushels of wheat malt, 228 bushels of oats for malting, eight bushels of oatmeal and sixteen bushels of barley. A total of £17 9s 7d was spent on iron and steel for carts and ploughs, on the smith's wages and on wages for the various activities involved in the growing of corn, namely sowing, harrowing, weeding, reaping, carrying, threshing and winnowing, as well as for mowing and haymaking. The presence in the

---

1 L. Sherley Price, trans., Bede, *A History of the English Church and People*, pp.112-3; Gerald of Wales, *The Description of Wales* (trans. and ed., Lewis Thorpe), p.230.

2 *CChancRVar*,170. The erection of a cross on land was a way of claiming it or, presumably, its fruits (A.R. Wiliam, ed., *Llyfr Iorwerth* (1960), pp. 102, 134).

3 John Griffiths, 'Two early ministers' accounts for north Wales, in *BBCS* 9 (1937), 63-70.

account of malt and of oats for malting is a clear indication of brewing on a substantial scale, as one might expect in a town; this is confirmed by the 1284 extent.[4] Arable farming seems to have predominated at Llan-faes. The only livestock mentioned in the account were 33 oxen and three affers or draught beasts which were presumably working stock, although the borough account included receipts of 13s 7d from herbage or grazing.[5] The number of oxen suggests that the ox-drawn plough was still the rule; there were enough to make up four plough-teams. The other *maerdrefi* were leased out, so no figures are available from them. But the Llan-faes figures do suggest that Anglesey produced a marketable surplus of corn and in 1298 66 bushels of wheat and 168 bushels of oats were received from various Welshmen of the commote of Menai for the king's use.[6]

Only four detailed assessments for the lay subsidy of 1292-3 have survived from Wales and these are all from Gwynedd, from the commote of Malltraeth in Anglesey and the town of Nefyn and the commotes of Cafflogion and Creuddyn in Caernarfonshire.[7] That for Malltraeth was long thought to relate only to the *maerdref* of Aberffraw since this was the section of it published by Frederic Seebohm in 1895, but Professor Glanville Jones found that the original assessment in the then Public Record Office included several other townships in the commote.[8] These assessments were the original documents on which the subsidy was based and they list all the taxable property of the taxpayers; they were assessed on horses, cattle, oxen and sheep and on crops.

In the commote of Malltraeth there were 548 oxen, 388 horses, 164 mares and 565 affers or draught beasts. Of the 313 taxpaying households in the commote 198 had at least one ox but only eleven had the eight necessary to make up a plough-team. At Aberffraw Iorwerth Foel had twenty and Einion ab Iocyn sixteen; no other taxpayer had more than nine, which suggests a considerable degree of co-operation. 275 households owned at least one horse or one mare although not one of them owned both; the highest number owned by any individual was seven, in Trefdraeth Ddisteiniaid. The horse was increasingly used

4  Ale was brewed from oats as well as from barley (C. Parain, 'The evolution of agricultural technique', in *Camb.Econ.Hist.*i, p.162), where the use of various cereals in the middle ages is discussed.
5  An affer is usually taken to have been a small horse, particularly one used for ploughing.
6  J. Griffiths, 'Early accounts relating to north Wales *temp.* Edward I', in *BBCS*, 15 (1953), 148.
7  Keith Williams-Jones, *The Merioneth Lay Subsidy Roll, 1292-3*, pp.ix-xi.
8  F. Seebohm, *The Tribal System in Wales* (1895), App., pp.37-46; the original commotal assessment is TNA E179/242/49. This assessment is discussed and analysed as a whole by G.R.J. Jones, 'The multiple estate: a model for tracing the inter-relationships of society, economy, and habitat' in Kathleen Biddick, ed., *Archaeological Approaches to Medieval Europe* (Kalamazoo, 1984), pp.9-41. The Aberffraw section is discussed by Colin Thomas, 'Thirteenth-century farm economies in north Wales', *AHR* 16 (1968), 1-14, and 'Peasant agriculture in medieval Gwynedd: an interpretation of the documentary evidence', *Folk Life*, 1975, 24-37.

for ploughing in the thirteenth century. The ox, which thrived on grass and which, when too old to work, could be turned into meat or leather, was more economical, whereas the horse, although it needed oats, was far more efficient.[9] As a rule the ox seems to have been used for ploughing and horses and affers for carting and harrowing, although oxen and horses could also be used together in the plough-team.[10] At Aberffraw and Penrhosllugwy in 1284 horses had been provided by the tenants to harrow the prince's land in the winter and the spring.[11]

Malltraeth contained 1306 head of cattle; 306 of the taxpaying households had at least one cow and fourteen had ten or more. The largest herds were again those of Iorwerth Foel who had sixteen and Einion ab Iocyn, Llywelyn ab Owain of Lledwigan Llan and Gwrgeneu ap Tegwared of Trefdraeth Wastrodion who each had fifteen. Sheep amounted to 1816 of which 747 were at Aberffraw; 161 households had them and 72 had flocks of ten or more, 27 of these being at Aberffraw. The largest of these flocks was the 50 of Adda ab Einion of Aberffraw followed by the 46 of Einion ap Deicws. Altogether there were eight flocks of more than 40, six of them being at Aberffraw. Such flocks were substantially larger than any which were to be found in the other areas for which assessments have survived; there were, for example, 710 sheep in the commote of Cafflogion in Llŷn where the largest flock contained no more than 20.[12] The large number of sheep at Aberffraw may possibly be explained by the grazing available on the sand-dunes and the fact that only just over half the households in the commote had them may suggest that sheep-farming, in which 46 taxpayers were involved, was a rather more specialised activity than the usual pattern of mixed farming.[13] Sheep were kept for their wool and their meat and for their milk, which was often made into cheese. The cow furnished dairy products when alive and meat and leather when dead. There is no mention in Malltraeth or Llŷn of that most economical of all animals, the pig, or of the goat; it is possible that in Wales they were not taxed.[14]

The presence of large numbers of oxen, as in Malltraeth, may be an indication of extensive crop husbandry.[15] Wheat, barley, oats and peas were grown,

---

9  The use of horses in medieval agriculture is discussed by C. Parain, op.cit., pp.142-4, and Georges Duby, *Rural Economy and Country Life in the Medieval West* (trans. Cynthia Postan, 1968), pp.110-11.

10  Keith Williams-Jones, op.cit, p.cxvii; K.C. Newton, *The Manor of Writtle* (1970), p.62.

11  Smith, 'Extent of Anglesey, 1284', pp. 99, 105.

12  Keith Williams-Jones, op.cit., p.cxv, where sheep-farming in north Wales at that time is discussed.

13  The point about the preponderance of sheep at Aberffraw is made by Dr Thomas in *AHR* 16, 3-4 although he does not suggest an explanation.

14  Keith Williams-Jones, op.cit., p.xiv.

15  Colin Thomas, 'Livestock numbers in medieval Gwynedd: some additional evidence', in *JMHRS* 7 (1974), 116.

but oats were by far the dominant crop. The 313 taxpayers owned a total of 4,708 bushels of oats, 1,644 of wheat and 758 of barley, with another 751 of mixed barley and peas. 237 taxpayers had wheat, 283 oatmeal and 132 barley; the largest quantity of wheat owned by a single individual was the 80 bushels owned by Iorwerth Foel at Aberffraw, while Iorwerth and Einion ab Iocyn each had 160 bushels of oatmeal. Einion ab Iocyn also had 48 bushels of wheat. Only one other taxpayer in the commote, in the township of Trefdraeth Ddisteiniaid, had as many as 40. Nineteen other taxpayers had 40 or more bushels of oatmeal and one, in Trefdraeth Wastrodion, had 80 bushels of unthreshed oats. If the amount of wheat as a percentage of the total crops in each township can be taken as an indicator of fertility, the best land in the commote was in Lledwigan Llan where wheat comprised 27.64 per cent of the crops. At Trefdraeth Ddisteiniaid wheat made up 27 per cent of the total and at Aberffraw 23.57 per cent. By the same standard the least fertile township was Lledwigan Llys where wheat only amounted to 11.3 per cent, followed by Trefdraeth Wastrodion (16.76 per cent). Comparisons with other north Wales commotes in 1292-3 are not really helpful since the only complete surviving assessment is that for Cafflogion where wheat made up 14.63 per cent of the total as compared with 22.24 per cent in Malltraeth.[16] It has been suggested that the figures for Aberffraw may indicate that the township was more like southern England than Llŷn and that the taxpayers there were well-off by comparison with the inhabitants of some parts of England. It is important however to remember that Aberffraw, being a *maerdref* settlement, occupied some of the best land in Anglesey and may therefore be untypical of much of the island.[17]

More information about contemporary agriculture may be found in the extent of Anglesey made in 1284.[18] At Llan-faes reaping, carrying and harrowing works were valued at £1 6s 8d. while the extent assumed that nearly 3,000 gallons of ale were brewed there each year. At Aberffraw the prince's share of the corn ground at his three mills came to 240 bushels annually and the bond tenants of the hamlet of Treberfedd owed sixteen bushels of barley meal, nine sheep, nine lambs, nine hens, 180 eggs and butter. Similar renders were due from the other bond tenants of Aberffraw. The works owed by the tenants illustrate the importance of arable farming. Three day-works were due from each of nine bondmen in Aberffraw itself at the hoeing of the corn and 300 were due from fifteen bondmen at harvest-time, along with 80 from the other bondmen of the cantref. There were also 550 day-works from men and horses for

---

16  These figures and their significance are discussed by Jones, 'The multiple estate', pp.21-33.

17  H.E. Hallam, *Rural England* (1981), pp. 223, 238. The complete commotal assessment had not been identified at the time of this publication, which explains why only Aberffraw is discussed.

18  Smith, 'Extent of Anglesey, 1284', pp.93-116.

harrowing, and the bondmen of Aberffraw owed an annual render of 40 bushels of oats as fodder for the prince's horses. In the cantref of Aberffraw the township of Conysiog and its subsidiary hamlets, the territory of the lineage of Hwfa ap Cynddelw, owed 160 bushels of oatmeal and 40 of wheat, and a number of unfree townships owed renders in kind and works. At Tre Feibion Meurig and Bodynolwyn each bondman who kept pigs owed a render of one; by 1352 this had been replaced by the payment of pannage of twopence for each pig.[19] Most of the other renders were of wheat or oatmeal, and in addition to those from individual townships the whole bond community of the cantref owed wheat, oatmeal, oats for fodder, 27 hens and one annual ploughing-work. The total corn render from the cantref of Aberffraw came to 32 bushels of barley, 157 of wheat and 468 of oats, both unthreshed and ground, which confirms that here again oats were the predominant crop.

The same was true of Talybolion. Although all renders and works there seem to have been commuted by 1284, the prince's share of the produce of the three royal mills in the commote was estimated at 320 bushels of oatmeal. At Penrhosllugwy in Twrcelyn some bond tenants owed renders of milk as *maeronaeth* and butter; they also owed fodder, lambs, hens, eggs and straw and they had to carry turf and peat.[20] The second part of the Penrhosllugwy extent mentions reaping works and carrying services and the harrowing of wheat, barley, beans, peas and rye. Three times a year 100 stacks of peat had to be provided for the prince from his turbary; at other times the tenants had the use of it. The whole community owed 40 bushels each of wheat, oatmeal and barley meal each year and renders of milk were due in summer and autumn. In the rest of the commote the tenants owed almost 180 bushels of oats and oatmeal and 54 of wheat with reaping and carrying works. In Menai the three royal mills yielded 320 bushels of ground corn; since each bushel was valued at fourpence it must have been barley.[21] The bond tenants of the *maerdref* of Rhosyr owed 24 bushels of wheat, 62 of oats and oatmeal and 119 of barley meal; this preponderance of barley, both in the issues of the mills and in the renders, is interesting. They also owed hens, eggs and lambs and harrowing, reaping, carrying and manuring works and they had to find fuel and straw for the prince when the need arose. The corn renders due from the rest of the commote came to 64 bushels of wheat, 39 of barley and 36 of oats and oatmeal. The two townships of Tre Feibion Pyll and Tregarwed between them owed 86 bushels of oat malt. This was a heavy burden and they owed a great deal less in rent in 1352, possibly

---

19 *Extent of Anglesey*, p.189.

20 *Maeronaeth* was a rent in kind of milk and corn for the use of the lord's pastures and vaccaries in the summer. (Stephenson, *Governance of Gwynedd*, pp.61-2.)

21 In the extent of Menai wheat was valued at 7½d the bushel, oatmeal at 6d, barley at 4d, oat malt at 3d and whole or unthreshed oats at 2d.

because of the loss of some land there by the action of the sea.[22]

Although the most detailed information in the extent comes from the *maer-drefi*, which were situated on the best soil, it does offer a general view of the nature of agricultural activity at the end of the thirteenth century. Like any similar region elsewhere in Europe, Anglesey was an area of mixed farming and this is confirmed by the extent made of the lands of the bishop of Bangor in 1306.[23] The bond tenants of the townships nearest to the bishop's manor of Treffos owed renders of barley and bread on 1 May, presumably for the epis-copal household. At Llangoed in Dindaethwy the bond tenants owed wheat at Christmas and oats during Lent and each individual tenant owed reaping works in the autumn and a hen at Christmas. Renders from other townships consisted of varying quantities of wheat and oats, both in the form of grain and of malt. Many had been commuted, especially in Menai and in those parts of Talybolion and Twrcelyn which were furthest from Treffos. The heaviest render from an individual township was from Gwredog in Llifon and its hamlet of Mynydd-mwyn; this included four times as many oats as wheat.[24] Anglesey was the only part of Gwynedd where the bishop's bond tenants owed substan-tial renders of cereals; those in Llŷn and on the manor of Gogarth in Creuddyn only owed cash rents and reaping works and the latter was the only labour serv-ice due in Anglesey. The tenants of Talybolion, Twrcelyn and the cantref of Aberffraw owed far more oats than anything else, but in Dindaethwy the prin-cipal cereal was wheat and this is also suggested by the valuation of the tem-poralities of the priory of Penmon made in 1374.[25] Here the bond tenants owed 54 bushels of wheat and no oats. By 1352 all renders in kind had been com-muted but carrying works and labour services survived in many townships. At Tre Feibion Meurig in Llifon the tenants carried the lord's victuals and fuel from his own township and at Aberalaw in Talybolion they had to carry hay, oats, straw and turf, for which they received reasonable payment; this suggests that it was no longer a service in the original sense of the term.[26]

The few surviving judicial records reflect the local economy to some extent. In September 1321 Dafydd Fychan of Eiriannell in Llifon was amerced fifteen

22  *Extent of Anglesey*, pp.256-7; TNA SC6/1152/3, m.7a.
23  For examples of rents and services elsewhere by way of comparison see K.C. Newton, *Thaxted in the Fourteenth Century* (1960), pp.48-58 (1393); Georges Duby, op.cit., pp.479-82 (Boughton, Hunts., 1252), 487-9 (Mons and Roosbeck, 1280-1308). The most recent discussions of thirteenth-century farming in England are E. Miller and J. Hatcher, *Medieval England: Rural Society and Economic Change, 1086-1348* (1978), pp.213-24, and H.E. Hallam, ed., *The Agrarian History of England and Wales*.ii: *1042-1350* (1988); *Rec.Caern.*, pp.100-9.
24  *Rec.Caern.* p.105.
25  ibid., pp.249-51; for a translation and brief discussion see A.D. Carr, 'The Penmon Valor 1374', *TAAS* 2005, pp.13-19. In 1291 the priory had 53 cows and 44 sheep (*Taxatio Nich.IV*, p.293); there was also some income from rabbit skins.
26  *Extent of Anglesey*, pp. 188, 202.

pence for ploughing the land of Dafydd Ddu and the amercement of two tenants at the Malltraeth tourn in March 1323 may be connected with the joint
ploughing of open fields.[27] At one of the Twrcelyn hundred courts in 1324
Ieuan ap Philip was amerced for not ploughing with his neighbours, which may
have been the result of a failure to perform a joint-ploughing contract.[28] In
September 1346 a Trefednyfed tenant was amerced at the Talybolion tourn for
wrongfully impounding another person's animals, which suggests that they had
strayed among his crops. At the Malltraeth tourn in March 1322 Cynwrig ap
Meurig had paid a heavy amercement of two shillings for sending his pigs outside his house.[29] Pigs were scavengers and Cynwrig's pigs may have been scav-
enging on his neighbour's land. If the surviving court rolls are typical, there
must have been a great deal of petty theft of stock and produce; at the Llifon
tourn in March 1322 a man from Eiriannell was amerced two shillings for stealing cheese, and in the 1346 rolls there are references to the theft of peas, corn,
flour, horses, sheep, lambs and wool.[30] The references to the theft of peas are
a reminder of the importance of leguminous crops which played an important
part in the medieval diet as well as being good for the soil.

After about 1550 wills and probate inventories are among the most important sources for the study of agriculture. Few medieval Anglesey wills survive,
but those which are available include references to both stock and crops. The
earliest is that of Gwilym ap Gruffudd ap Tudur of Llaniestyn, who died in
1376; this includes an inventory which reveals that Gwilym had two horses and
22 beasts, presumably cattle.[31] Bequests included three cows and a calf. Cynwrig ab Ieuan ap Llywelyn of Rhosyr, who died in 1430, mentioned a number
of debts due to him which included corn and the milk from particular cows.[32]
This may suggest that the testator had lent cows to some of his neighbours in
return for a share of their milk. Elen, the daughter of Gruffudd ap Hywel Escut
of Llechgynfarwy, who died in 1433, left eight sheep, a calf and an affer in her
will, while the unbequeathed property of Madog ab Ieuan ap Hywel of Llanedwen amounted to two oxen, five cows, four affers, six sheep, one mare and one
piglet when he died in 1447.[33] Some debts of unthreshed oats and of oatmeal
and flour were due to him at his death. His son Ieuan died in 1483 and he left
all his sheep to his wife, some corn to the Dominican friars of Bangor and one

27  TNA SC2/215/5, m.5b; 215/8, m.2a.
28  TNA SC2/215/11, m.9.
29  G.P. Jones, 'Anglesey court rolls, 1346', *TAAS* 1930, p.37; TNA SC6/215/7, m.1a.
30  TNA SC6/215/7, m.1b; G.P.Jones, op.cit., *TAAS* 1930, pp.34-48; 1932, pp.42-9.
31  BUASC Penrhyn 5.
32  NLW Sotheby 26.
33  NLW Sotheby 32; BUASC Plas Coch 3.

affer each to two clerics.[34]

More interesting and more informative are the accounts of coroners and escheators. The former, of course, dealt only with the property of those who died
by misadventure or who fled to escape the consequences of their actions, but
they can give a rough idea of the kind of property a tenant might have. Iorwerth
Gam of Tre Feibion Meurig, who fatally wounded Iorwerth ap Dafydd in 1312-
3, had rye flour and oats worth twelve pence and standing corn worth five
pence. Einion Grach of Lledwigan Llys, who killed Dafydd ap Cynwrig in the
same year, had one cow, three sheep, three lambs and standing corn valued at
twelve pence.[35] These figures may be typical of the goods of smallholders. In
late fourteenth-century accounts the escheator often accounted for sheep, as
in 1378-9 when he answered for six which Angharad ferch Madog *Talior* had
stolen from Tegwared ap Rhys ap Hwfa.[36] In the 1392-3 account a stolen hive
of bees was valued at 1s 4d.[37] Bees, of course, provided honey, the only sweet-
ening agent generally available and the basic ingredient of mead; they also produced wax, the raw material for candles. Wax candles were probably beyond
the means of most people but they were in constant demand by the church for
its liturgical needs.

Fifteenth-century accounts contain much useful detail. Nest ferch Ieuan
Ddu of the commote of Malltraeth, who died in 1413-4, owned one cow and
ten sheep, and in 1420-1 Efa ferch Madog ap Wyn had nine affers and a flock
of 51 sheep.[38] In the latter year Dafydd Hir ap Madog ab Ieuan ab Einion had
three cows, one calf, 24 sheep and lambs, four piglets and wheat and oats, and
Dafydd ab Iocyn had five affers, 13 sheep, one horse and one mare. Two fugitive
felons for whose goods the escheator answered in 1441-2 seem to have been
moderately prosperous farmers; Hywel ap Dafydd ab Ednyfed had two cows
with calves, 14 sheep and six lambs, three hives and three swarms of bees and
a quantity of wheat, barley and oats, while Hywel ap Dafydd Hir, a bond tenant
of Penrhosllugwy, had four piglets, three hives and a swarm of bees and wheat,
barley, oats and peas, as well as five ells of Welsh linen cloth.[39] He also owned
no fewer than 21 affers. A number of others had a few animals and a small
quantity of corn, but it is, of course, the better-off who are the most interesting.
Hywel ab Ieuan ap Gruffudd Ddu of Clorach in Twrcelyn, a fugitive felon for
whose goods the escheator answered in 1471-2, had twelve oxen, 25 cows and

34  BUASC Plas Coch 17.
35  TNA SC6/1170/8.
36  TNA SC6/1150/4, m.6b.
37  TNA SC6/1151/8, m.8b. A swarm of bees was valued at the same sum in the Welsh laws (*Llyfr
    Iorwerth*, p.89); I am grateful to Mr Tomos Roberts for drawing my attention to this reference.
38  TNA SC6/1152/5, m.7b; 1152/9, m.8b. TNA SC6/1153/5, m.11b.
39  TNA SC6/1153/5, m.11b.

bullocks, bees, oats, eight geese, six hens and a cock, and in 1481-2 Ieuan ab Iorwerth ap Heilin of Tre Feibion Meurig had two horses, two mares, two cows, a bullock and a calf, 61 sheep and a stack of corn.[40] But all these were over-shadowed by the wealth of a bond tenant of the commote of Menai, Dafydd ab Ieuan Moel. He owned thirteen mares and foals, a total which may suggest an interest in breeding, eleven oxen, 23 cows, fourteen bullocks, 176 sheep, a stack of corn, two pigs and three hives of bees.[41] This was, by any standards, a substantial estate.

The escheators' accounts are too few in number to provide a meaningful sample, but they do suggest the emergence of a class of substantial farmers. Some details of tithes are given in the *Valor Ecclesiasticus* of 1535.[42] The canons of Penmon had tithes of wheat, hemp, flax and barley from Penmon itself; wool and lamb tithes there were valued at 6s 8d and lactuals (milk, butter and cheese) at two shillings. For the other churches held by the priory corn tithes amounted to by far the largest part of the total, but at Llanddona and Pen-rhosllugwy the tithes on lambs, wool and lactuals were higher than elsewhere At Amlwch, one of the churches attached to the archdeaconry of Anglesey, the corn tithes were £20 6s 8d and at Llangristiolus and Cerrigceinwen eleven pounds; lactuals were five pounds and £1 6s 8d. At Llanddwyn the corn tithes were fivepence, which was hardly surprising since most of the parish was sand by then. Lactuals were eightpence and wool and lamb tithes ten shillings, which shows that the sand-dunes did offer some grazing.[43] Thus the available infor-mation about Anglesey agriculture in the later middle ages suggests a pattern of mixed farming with oats the predominant crop. The size of some flocks of sheep recorded in escheators' accounts during the fifteenth century hints at an increase in sheep-farming and this may possibly be confirmed by the steady decline in the farms paid for royal mills from the late fifteenth century onwards. An inquisition taken in 1495 revealed that many of the royal and private mills listed in the 1352 extent were derelict or had ceased to exist altogether. Al-though milling was probably being concentrated in fewer and larger mills, it is possible that the fall in population after the Black Death and the consequent decay of so many bond townships led to a fall in the acreage under cultivation and the conversion of untenanted land to grazing; this was, after all, a common trend.[44]

---

40 TNA SC6/1155/2, m.10b; 1155/6, m.10a.
41 TNA SC6/1155/6, m.10a.
42 *Valor Ecclesiasticus*, iv, 430; vi, xix-xx.
43 ibid., xxiv.
44 TNA E315/166, ff. 11a-b; the point is made by Georges Duby, op.cit., pp.327-30, and by M.M. Postan in *Camb. Econ. Hist.*, i, pp.590-1.

The surviving documents tell us nothing about such things as rotation although this was provided for in the laws.[45] It is clear that most farming was carried out in open fields, but there are no references to assarts and very few to manuring. In 1284 the tenants of Penrhosllugwy owed twenty horses and men to spend a day drawing out manure and the second part of the extent of that township includes an obligation to supply ten horses to manure the prince's land around Easter, while at Rhosyr the tenants had to provide fourteen horses for one day to draw out manure.[46] Henry Rowlands, writing in 1704, claimed that shell-sand, marling and liming had not been used in Anglesey before the seventeenth century; before that the only techniques used to enrich the soil had been manuring, surface-burning, pinfolding and the application of seaweed.[47] The provision of ten horses at Penrhosllugwy may possibly be a reference to pinfolding.

In a society based on agriculture most economic activity must be derived from it. The most important medieval manufacturing industry met a need almost as fundamental as that for food, namely clothing. Sheep produced wool and the wool was woven into cloth; the cloth industry was the backbone of the medieval English economy and it must have played a similar part in Wales.[48] Examination of personal names and patronymics reveals a number of weavers in medieval Anglesey and four shearmen and a fuller were among those who made their peace with the crown in 1406. There was a fulling-mill at Caerdegog in Talybolion in 1430 and another at Tre'r-ddôl in Llifon in 1515, while a deed of 1520 mentions a parcel of land called Dryll y Pandy in Mathafarn Eithaf.[49] The existence of such mills indicates a degree of investment, although most weavers and fullers were probably also farmers, and spinning and weaving were essentially domestic crafts.[50] Much of the local cloth was probably sold at the fairs held at Beaumaris and Newborough and also at Llannerch-y-medd and Aberffraw; in 1350-1 the account of the *rhingyll* of Twrcelyn included a total of 10s 8d for tolls collected on Welsh cloths at the two Llannerch-y-medd fairs.[51] The tolls the following year came to 12s 8d and in 1352-3 to eleven shillings,

---

45  This is discussed by G.R.J. Jones, 'The distribution of medieval settlement in Anglesey', *TAAS* 1955, pp.48-9.

46  Smith, 'Extent of Anglesey, 1284', pp. 105, 115, 109.

47  Henry Rowlands, *Ideae Agriculturaee* (1934-6), i, pp. 91, 93-5; iii, pp.58-61. Pinfolding was the folding of a number of beasts on a particular tract of soil which would be enriched by their manure.

49  The most recent account of the industry is R. Ian Jack, 'The cloth industry in medieval Wales', in *WHR* 10 (1981), 443-60.

49  BUASC Penrhos vii 1;  NLW Sotheby 94;  BUASC Baron Hill 1027.

50  R. Ian Jack, op.cit., 455.

51  TNA SC6/1149/1, m.6b. The fairs were on 25 March and 15 August.

but subsequent accounts make no mention of cloth.[52] An Aberalaw tenant was amerced sixpence at the Talybolion tourn in March 1322 for selling wool outside the market, presumably to a weaver. At the Llifon tourn in September 1346 Tegwared ab Owain of Llechgynfarwy was amerced one shilling for selling cloth at Llannerch-y-medd on the queen's land, that is, in that part of the township which was in the commote of Menai and not in the market.[53] In the fifteenth century wool and cloth were among the principal exports of the port of Beaumaris, although these probably came from all over Gwynedd.[54]

At the Dindaethwy hundred court held on 6 May 1346 it was ordered that all weavers should attend the next court with their looms, and on 10 July five, three of whom were women, were amerced for failing to appear, while four, two of whom were women, were in mercy for producing additional looms.[55] The inspection of looms was probably a means of quality control to make sure that the finished product was of the right size, while the restriction on their number may have been intended to protect the interests of large-scale producers in the old-established urban centres of the industry in England. In 1414 two Anglesey men were accused of various crimes, among them the nocturnal theft at Newborough of goods which included four yards of red cloth; at Amlwch two days earlier they had stolen cloth, flax and wool.[56] Cloth also appears from time to time in escheators' accounts. Hywel ap Dafydd Hir, a bond tenant of Penrhosllugwy, had four ells of Welsh linen cloth in 1441-2, while Hywel ab Ieuan ap Gruffudd Ddu of Clorach had 54 yards of woollen cloth and thread in 1471-2, which suggests that he might have been a weaver as well as a substantial farmer.[57]

If sheep provided wool, cattle provided leather, an essential item for shoes and for harness; analysis of personal names reveals a number of cobblers. The cattle trade with England is particularly associated with medieval and early modern Wales but this is scarcely mentioned in surviving Anglesey documents although the account of the chamberlain of north Wales for 1407-10 included the receipt of £1 14s for the passage of beasts at Porthaethwy.[58] There is one reference to a drover, Tegwared Porthmon, who was a tenant of St Beuno in the commote of Menai in 1418-9.[59] Another occupation which was based on

52 TNA SC6/1149/2, m.5a: 1149/3, m.6b.
53 TNA SC2/215/7, m.2a; G.P. Jones, 'Anglesey court rolls, 1346', *TAAS* 1932, p.49.
54 E.A. Lewis, 'A contribution to the commercial history of medieval Wales', *Y Cymmrodor*, 24 (1913), 128-71.
55 G.P. Jones, 'Anglesey court rolls, 1346', *TAAS* 1930, pp.39-40.
56 TNA KB9/204/3/K18-21.
57 TNA SC6/1155/2, m.10b.
58 TNA SC6/1216/2.
59 TNA SC6/1152/7, m.10a.

agriculture was brewing, which was particularly important in an age when ale was the staple drink. Licences to brew for sale were granted at the hundred court. Brewing in the middle ages is generally regarded as having been a female activity but most licensed brewers in Anglesey whose names have survived were men. Of 77 named in the court rolls in 1322-3, 1324-5 and 1325-6, only nine were women.[60] The total annual yield from fines for licences to brew, where figures exist, ranged from one pound in 1337-8 to £2 11s in 1325-6.[61] The court rolls also record amercements for unlicensed brewing and for breaches of the assize of ale. At the Malltraeth tourn held on 12 March 1321 there were four convictions for unlicensed brewing, and at the Llifon hundred court on 17 August 1346 Dafydd Ddu ap Tegwared was convicted of brewing six times without licence.[62] Not only was ale the usual drink of most people but the alehouse was probably as much the social centre of the community in Wales as it was in England.

Next to the working of the land came the exploitation of the minerals which lay in it. The Romans had worked the copper deposits of Mynydd Trysglwyn but there is no mention of any medieval metal mining. In 1441-2, however, a new activity appeared in the records; the farm of the township of Ysgeifiog in the commote of Menai, let to John Pykemere and Hywel ap Llywelyn ap Dafydd ab Ieuan for £7 5s 8d, included coal mines.[63] This is the earliest reference to the working of coal in Ysgeifiog and around Cors Ddyga. But Anglesey's most important product was one which was absolutely essential in any agricultural community; Anglesey millstones were famous in the middle ages and for a long time afterwards.[64] The principal quarries were at Mathafarn Eithaf and Mathafarn Wion and at Penmon, the best stone being the carboniferous limestone found in that part of Anglesey.[65] The working of millstones was generally a royal monopoly, but the Penmon quarries belonged to the priory. Accounts for the repair of royal mills refer frequently to local stones. For the new windmill

60 TNA SC2/215/8, m.9; 215/10, m.1; 215/11, m.6; see also R.H. Hilton, *The English Peasantry in the Later Middle Ages* (1979), p.45.
61 TNA SC6/1229/4; 1228/9.
62 TNA SC2/215/5, m.1; G.P. Jones, 'Anglesey court rolls, 1346'. *TAAS* 1930, p.46.
63 TNA SC6/1153/5, m.6a; the most recent account of coal-mining in Anglesey is T.M. Bassett and Geraint James, 'Coalmining in Anglesey', *TAAS* 1969-70, pp.137-63.
64 For reference to the use of Anglesey millstones in the twentieth century see G.O. Heald, 'Pentrefoelas mill, 1900-49', *TDHS* 25 (1976), 212; this article also includes a most interesting account of the dressing of millstones and the working of a water mill.
65 There are various scattered references to Anglesey millstones, in particular Geraint Dyfnallt Owen, *Elizabethan Wales* (1964), p.158. Several quarries are mentioned in seventeenth-century Exchequer actions (T.I. Jeffreys-Jones, ed., *Exchequer proceedings concerning Wales* in tempore *James I* (1955), pp. 9, 22, 49). Leland commented on the quality of Anglesey stones (L. Toulmin Smith, ed., *Leland's Itinerary in Wales*, p.134).

built at Newborough in 1303 stones were brought from Mathafarn.[66] In 1325-6 stones for Melin y Bont at Aberffraw, Dindryfwl, Bryn Gwydded and Cemais were bought from Einion Felyn's quarry at Castell Bwlchgwyn, while Einion Goch furnished stones for Aberalaw and Llan-faes and Ieuan ap Dafydd for Bodronyn and Cefn-coch.[67] Nothing was paid for the carriage of the stones for Melin y Bont because the king's bondmen had always been obliged to carry them. Stones seem to have been replaced often; Bodronyn mill in Talybolion had a new pair in 1333-4 and it needed replacements three years later, and Dulas mill in Twrcelyn also needed new stones after a similar interval.[68]

Anglesey millstones were known far beyond the island. In 1314 stones worth £1 8s 9d were exported from Mathafarn for the royal mills in Dublin, and in 1338 a pair was taken by sea to Barmouth and from there by land to the mill of Llanegryn in Merioneth.[69] In 1350-1 three pairs of stones were bought in Anglesey for the Dee mills at Chester at a cost of £1 6s 9d. Their carriage to Chester by sea cost a further £1 2s, and in 1357-8 the manufacture of thirteen pairs in Anglesey for the Chester mills had cost £6 10s.[70] At £6 15s 8d their transport by sea to Burton in the Wirral cost more than the stones themselves and the cost of six pairs of stones from the quarry at Castell Bwlchgwyn and their conveyance to Chester in 1384-5 was more than ten pounds.[71] Attempts were made to enforce the royal monopoly from time to time. In 1347 William ap Gruffudd ap Hywel was appointed escheator of the county and keeper of the prince's millstone quarries and in the same year the sheriff was ordered to arrest and seize all millstones found in mines and quarries; they were not to be worked without the prince's special licence.[72] The lands granted in 1422 to Queen Katherine to support her in her widowhood included the millstone quarries in Twrcelyn (more probably in Dindaethwy) which were valued annually at seven pounds. After her death in 1437 the king's quarries in Anglesey were let at an annual farm of £3 6s 8d.[73] Nothing was rendered for them in 1441-2 and there is no mention of the farm in any subsequent accounts.[74] The decline may be connected with the decline in milling in the fifteenth century;

---

66  TNA SC6/1170/3, m.5.

67  TNA SC6/1228/9.

68  TNA SC6/1229/2, 3.

69  R.O. Roberts, 'The mills of Anglesey', *TAAS* 1958, p.5;  E.A. Lewis, 'The development of industry and commerce in Wales during the middle ages', *TRHS* (New Series), 17 (1903), 144, n.5, citing TNA SC6/1232/10.

70  R. Stewart-Brown, ed., *Chester Chamberlains' Accounts, 1301-1360* (1910), pp. 167, 241.

71  Jane Laughton, *Life in a Late Medieval City: Chester 1275-1520* (2008), pp.176-7.

72  *BPR*, i, 155; TNA E315/166, f13a. A similar order was issued to the sheriff of Caernarfonshire concerning slates.

73  *Rot Parl.* iv, 184; TNA SC6/1153/4, m.2a.

74  TNA SC6/1153/5, m.1b.

another factor may have been the existence of private quarries. In 1457 Ieuan ap Dafydd ab Einion of Mathafarn Eithaf conveyed all his lands and tenements in Dindaethwy and his share in a millstone quarry in the commote to William Griffith of Penrhyn.[75] An action was brought by the prior of Penmon in the Court of Requests in 1517 or 1518 over an attempt by the farmer of the royal quarries to seize millstones which had been dug on the priory's land.[76]

In any maritime community the sea contributed as much as the land to the economy.[77] Fish formed an important part of the medieval diet, and fisheries, particularly the Irish Sea herring fishery, played a significant part in the island's economic activity. A flourishing herring fishery was centred on Llan-faes at the end of the thirteenth century. A custom of a penny on every five mease of herrings landed brought in an annual total of ten shillings, and each herring-smack entering or leaving the port owed a mease, valued at two shillings.[78] The total custom of ten shillings meant 600 mease and this indicates that some £60 worth of fish was landed at Llan-faes each year. The custom, like the other commercial profits of Llan-faes, was taken over by the burgesses of Beaumaris, but by the middle of the fourteenth century there had been a substantial decline. In 1350-1 the custom on herrings brought in twopence since only ten mease had been landed during the year, a figure which may reflect the migration of that very temperamental fish.[79]

There are also references to fisheries at Beaumaris in the fifteenth century. Thomas Norreys was farming a fishery between the limekiln below the town and the ferry wharf in 1439 and nine years later another, lying between Norreys's weir and Llan-faes friary, was leased to Thomas Sherwin; both leases were for terms of 20 years at an annual rent of sixpence.[80] From about 1451 a weir near Gallows Point was leased for 40 years at an annual rent of fourpence.[81] The fishery of Ynys Gadarn or Ynys Dulas was farmed regularly during the fourteenth and fifteenth centuries, although the farm gradually went down from ten shillings in 1357-8 to two shillings in 1464-5. In 1377-8 the *rhingyll* of Talybolion answered for the farm of a new fishery or weir in the Alaw estuary.[82] Weirs also appear from time to time among the properties conveyed

75  BUASC Penrhyn 395.

76  TNA Req. 2/6/214.

77  For a brief account of medieval fisheries see A.D. Carr, 'Medieval fisheries in Anglesey', *Maritime Wales*, 3 (1978), 5-8.

78  Smith, 'Extent of Anglesey, 1284', pp.93-4. A mease was usually five long hundreds of herrings (i.e. 600).

79  TNA SC6/1149/1, m.7a.

80  TNA SC6/1153/5, m.10a; 1153/6, m.13a.

81  TNA SC6/1154/2, m.15a

82  TNA SC6/1149/8, m.5a; 1154/5, m.6b; 1150/4, m.6a.

in deeds.[83] At the Talybolion tourn on 15 March 1322 Dafydd Don was amerced for taking eels in the Alaw estuary, and at the same court two years later two men were amerced for fishing there without licence.[84] The goods of Hywel ap Tegwared of Twrcelyn, who died intestate in 1312-3, included a net and two mease of herrings as well as livestock, a reminder that fishing and farming often went together.[85]

The best-documented medieval fisheries are those which belonged to the bishop of Bangor. In the 1306 extent the bond tenants of Trefelias, Buarth-brych and Brynberfi in Dindaethwy each owed 1s 9½d on 1 May for the repair of a weir. However the most profitable of the bishop's fishing interests was that on the north-west coast of Anglesey around the Skerries, part of the episcopal township of Cornwy Lan.[86] Not only fish were caught there; the Welsh name for the group is Ynysoedd y Moelrhoniaid (the Seal Islands) and there are three references to the poaching of seals, in 1349, 1352 and 1466.[87] The nineteen seals taken in 1466 were described as the property of William Griffith and William Griffith I (Gwilym Fychan) of Penrhyn seems to have bought up the rights of the various heirs of local kindreds in the fishery, as the list of his shares in the Skerries printed in the *Record of Caernarvon* suggests.[88] This list and the list of deeds which follows it have generally been taken to refer to shares in land and have been used to argue for extreme population pressure on the main-land, since they concern the *gwelyau* which held land in Cornwy, Dronwy and Cnwchdyrnog.[89] But there could not possibly have been room for so many landed interests on the Skerries and it therefore seems more likely that these shares, many of which were acquired by Ieuan Chwerw of Bodafon in Twrce-lyn, a prominent local figure in the second half of the fourteenth century, were in an important and profitable fishery. The reference to William Griffith is also a reminder of a dispute with the bishop over fishing rights which was not re-solved until the end of the fifteenth century. In 1498 bishop Henry Dean drew up a statement of the position.[90] He stated that the fishing rights belonged to the bishop but that they had not been exercised for a long time because of the non-residence of his predecessors. In the absence of successive bishops, the

83 BUASC Mostyn 716, 717, 4084 (Porthaethwy 1316, 1378, 1394); NLW Carreglwyd i, 545, 535 (Alaw estuary, 1437, 1442).

84 TNA SC2/215/5, m.2a; 215/7, m.2b.

85 TNA SC6/1170/8.

86 *Rec.Caern.*, pp.102-3.

87 TNA E315/166, ff. 20b, 14b-15a; SC6/1155/1, m.10b. They are discussed in A.D. Carr, op.cit., 7.

88 *Rec.Caern.* p.253.

89 For the suggestion of settlement see G.R.J. Jones, 'The distribution of medieval settlement in Anglesey', pp.47-8.

90 NLW Church in Wales Records, B/MISC.VOLS./27, p.194, printed in Browne Willis, *A Survey of the Cathedral Church of Bangor* (1721), p.189.

Griffith family had moved in and when the bishop, with the agreement of his tenants, had gone to the islands to assert his rights there had been a clash. Law-suits were pending but all the other tenants acknowledged the bishop's rights and had released all their title in the fishery to him in order to keep Griffith out.[91]

The sea was more than a source of food. Before the coming of the railway it was the main means of transport and was thus one of the most important el-ements in the local economy. In 1291-2 the custom on ships and herrings at the port of Llan-faes came to £1 0s 2d and that on boats to sixteen shillings.[92] The port dues from ships calling there were estimated in 1284 at £1 6s 8d which, at fourpence a ship, suggests that no fewer than 80 cleared the port each year.[93] A duty of tenpence was levied on each tun of wine or ale imported there. Llan-faes had been the principal port, not only of Anglesey but also of Gwynedd, but after 1296 it was superseded by Beaumaris. In 1297 an ordi-nance provided that no messengers or merchants should come into Wales ex-cept through the ports of Chester, Beaumaris, Milford or Haverfordwest.[94] This was probably connected with the king's plans for his campaign in Flanders but it shows that Beaumaris was regarded as an important port only a year after its incorporation. About 1315 the burgesses asked the king for a quay to be built and a return of ships of over 40 tons burthen in west coast ports in 1325 showed that at Beaumaris Adam Sandbach had one of 60 tons.[95]

Few statistics for the port of Beaumaris have survived. In 1350-1 the total income was eightpence from two foreign ships, a consequence, perhaps, of the Black Death, but the following year saw an improvement with four foreign ships and four with their own boats which yielded a total of four shillings.[96] The bailiffs accounted for 1s 4d from four ships leaving the port and two shillings from three ships with boats that called in 1357-8, but there are no fur-ther figures since the burgesses farmed the customs, court perquisites and tolls in subsequent years.[97] Some chamberlains' accounts refer to the purchase of wine for the castle from ships calling at the port. Ships bringing it included the *Saint Mary* cog of Bristol in 1378-9, the *George* of Plymouth in 1388-9 and the *Mary* of St Ives in 1464-5 as well as un-named ships belonging to various mer-chants.[98] Wine was the main dutiable import; the first reference to the trade

91  Two of these releases are BUASC Baron Hill 1500-1.
92  John Griffiths, 'Two early ministers' accounts from north Wales', 64.
93  Smith, 'Extent of Anglesey, 1284', p.94.
94  *CCR 1296-1302*, 86-7.
95  *CAP*, p.117; *CAC*, p.219.
97  TNA SC6/1149/1, m.7a; 1149/2, m.6a.
97  E.A. Lewis, 'A contribution to the commercial history of medieval Wales', 108-20.
98  TNA SC6/1149/8, m.5a.

comes from 1304-5 when two tuns were taken as prise from a cargo of 40 which belonged to the Chester merchant William de Doncaster.[99] The principal exports were wool, cloth and hides.[100] Most of the foreign ships recorded in the fifteenth century came from Brittany. Their home ports included St Malo, St-Pol-de-Leon, Conquet, Penmarc, Paimpol and Le Croisic and there are also references to ships belonging to Lisbon and Honfleur. This suggests that most of Beaumaris's foreign trade was with Breton ports, but these statistics only relate to such trade; there is nothing to cast any light on domestic commerce.

Some coastal shipping activity is, however, reflected in the victualling accounts for the castles. Although Anglesey seems to have been able to produce enough of a surplus of corn at least to supply the needs of Beaumaris castle in the years immediately after the conquest, there are later references to imports. In 1324-5 224 bushels of wheat were bought from a Liverpool merchant and 128 bushels of beans from merchants of Drogheda, and 60 years later, in 1384-5, 60 bushels of wheat and 60 of beans were bought at Chester.[101] This seems strange, considering the well-known fertility of Anglesey, but in the absence of a series of victualling accounts it would be unsafe to try to draw any conclusions; these may, however, have been exceptional purchases following bad harvests. Honey was also imported; in 1324 a cask of Spanish honey was bought for the castle from a Beaumaris burgess, Edward Friend, and in 1384-5 two pipes were bought at Chester.[102] Some of this honey was taken on to Caernarfon by Cadwgan Boatman and his crew. Lead was bought at Chester in 1323 and Daykyn Kat was paid £1 15s for bringing it in his small boat. More lead was brought from Chester in 1324-5 and Thomas Maykyn received three shillings for carrying lead for the king's works in his boat from Liverpool to Beaumaris in 1448-9.[103] As the principal port of Gwynedd, Beaumaris was the centre for distribution. Wine for the castles was bought there in 1328-9; 12 casks and two pipes were taken to Caernarfon in the king's boat by Richard Shedle, while William Walker took four casks in his boat to Conwy and Adam Laurenz two casks in his to Cricieth.[104] More wine was bought in 1331-2 at Priestholm, presumably from a ship which had dropped anchor there, and some of this, too, was shipped to Caernarfon and Conwy.[105]

99 E.A. Lewis, 'The account roll of the chamberlain of the principality of north Wales from Michaelmas 1304 to Michaelmas 1305', in *BBCS*. i (1923), 265.

100 E.A. Lewis, 'A contribution to the commercial history of medieval Wales', 128-30, 170-l.

101 TNA SC6/1212/11; 1214/11.

102 TNA SC6/1212/10; 1214/11.

103 TNA SC6/1212/10; 1212/11; 1216/6.

104 TNA SC6/1213/6.

105 TNA SC6/1213/10.

Other ports do appear in the records from time to time. The burgesses of Beaumaris complained to the prince in 1305 that, although the king had ordered that all ships coming to Anglesey should call at Beaumaris and nowhere else to offer goods for sale, some were calling at other places.[106] This suggests that some of the other ports were more attractive or more convenient. In the 1291-2 account the issues of the port of Dulas in Twrcelyn were estimated at 1s 8d annually; it was the only port, other than Llan-faes, mentioned in the 1284 extent.[107] In 1351-2 and 1352-3 the *rhingyll* of Twrcelyn reported that no ships had called, but in 1379-80 he accounted for harbour dues from two vessels.[108] In 1502 the *Michael* of Dulas carried cargoes from Chester to Conwy and back and from Beaumaris to the Isle of Man.[109] The annual income from the port of Mathafarn in Dindaethwy was estimated at 4s 4d in 1302-3; dues from ships calling there in 1311-2 brought in 8s 10d, but in 1350-1 the *rhingyll* only answered for three ships.[110] An instruction in 1312 to the justice of north Wales to investigate the right of Dafydd Rwth ap Dafydd ap Goronwy to the Mathafarn port dues suggests that some ports may have been in private hands before 1282.[111] In his account for 1407-10 the chamberlain answered for port dues of 16s 8d from Traeth Coch (which may well be Mathafarn), which suggests some considerable activity there and there are references in Chester records to ships plying between the two ports.[112] After the Glyn Dŵr revolt all the Dindaethwy port dues seem to have been farmed. The farm fluctuated between £1 2s in 1418-9 and 6s 8d in 1437-8 and it stood at seven shillings when it came eventually to William Bulkeley the elder in 1464-5.[113]

Of the other Anglesey ports, Abermenai or Southcrook had a long history and played a significant part in the economy of south-east Anglesey and such harbours as Cemlyn, Cemais and Aberffraw must have been involved in the coastal trade. They do not appear in any surviving records but this may be because port dues were only collected from foreign or foreign-going vessels. Mathafarn had a flourishing export trade in millstones, while timber for royal mills was often imported through Abermenai.[114] There are few references to the port which was eventually to become the most important in Anglesey and these do not reflect any commercial activity. In September 1315 Thomas Dun,

---

106  *Rec.Caern.*, p.223.
107  Smith, 'Extent of Anglesey, 1284', p.107.
108  TNA SC6/1149/2, m.5a; 1149/3, m.6b; 1150/6, m.3a.
109  Laughton, *Life in a Late Medieval City*, p.177
110  TNA SC6/1227/4; 1227/8; 1149/1, m.1a; fourpence was collected from each ship.
111  *CCR 1307-1313*, 429.
112  TNA SC6/1216/2; Laughton, op.cit., p.177.
113  TNA SC6/1152/7, m.1b; 1153/4, m.2a; 1154/5, m.1b.
114  TNA SC6/1170/3 (1303); 1229/3 (1336-7); 1229/6 (1339).

with a 'great navy' of Scots, descended on Holyhead, seized a ship called the
*James* of Caernarfon and took it away to Scotland.[115] The subsequent investigation revealed a story of incompetence on the part of local officials. Holyhead's importance seems to have been as much military as commercial. In 1332
the justiciar of Ireland was ordered to arrest all suitable ships in Irish ports and
bring them to Holyhead in readiness for the king's forthcoming expedition to
Ireland, and in 1395 ships were to be brought from Chester and adjacent ports
for the passage of the archbishop of York and the bishop of London across the
Irish Sea.[116]

Such references only appear in the records when royal interests were involved but they are sufficient to show the importance of coastal shipping to
the local economy. It was far cheaper and far more convenient to move goods
by sea and the maritime tradition of Gwynedd is a long-standing one. But, just
as roads are often dangerous today, the sea had its casualties and the coast of
Anglesey was to claim many medieval victims, especially since the route up the
Irish Sea led to such busy ports as Chester, Liverpool, Dublin and Drogheda
as well as to Beaumaris. This was the main shipping lane to and from Ireland
and western Britain and it was no backwater. On 15 July 1297 the king in-
formed the keeper of north Wales that he had received a petition from Juliana,
widow of Simon de Faversham of Dublin.[117] A large part of the subsidy recently
collected in Ireland had been entrusted to a ship belonging to Simon, but on
1 November 1295 this ship was wrecked in Porth Eilian during a storm and
Simon and his three sons were drowned. The money, the ship's tackle and
Simon's own property, valued at 60 marks, came into the hands of various local
men and as the king naturally wanted to recover the money as well as help Juliana he called for an investigation. Occasionally the sheriff answered for the
value of wrecks and wreckage; a small ship wrecked at Cemlyn in 1302-3 was
worth one pound.[118] Looting could be a serious problem and in 1343-4 two
casks of wine 'which Welshmen took and consumed' were cast ashore but the
imbibers could not be traced.[119] Casks of wine thrown up on the beach would
have been too much of a temptation, as they were for the communities of Trefdraeth Wastrodion and Trefdraeth Ddisteiniaid who were presented at the
Malltraeth tourn on 12 March 1321 for helping themselves from a vessel
wrecked at Abermalltraeth.[120]

115  *CPR 1313-1317*, 421; *CIM* ii, no.248; *CCW* i, 426. The episode is discussed by Gwilym Usher,
     'Holyhead as a fourteenth century port' *BBCS* 15 (1954), 209-12.
116  *CCR 1330-1333*, 488; *CPR1391-1396*, 587.
117  *CCR 1296-1302*, 117.
118  TNA SC6/1227/4.
119  TNA SC6/1229/7.
120  TNA SC2/215/5, m.1.

Personal names can be a useful guide to medieval occupations. Those connected with the manufacture of cloth have already been mentioned. The finished cloth was made up into garments and there was a number of tailors, many of whom may have been itinerant craftsmen. Surprisingly the sea is hardly represented at all in medieval personal names in Anglesey; the only maritime names are of two boatmen. The single wildfowler was in the commote of Malltraeth in 1406 and one would expect to find him pursuing his occupation around Cors Ddyga. The needs of the community would account for the thatchers and for those men described as *eurych* a trade far more likely to be that of a general metal worker rather than a goldsmith. At Llandyfrydog in 1306 there was an innkeeper and other occupations included some sextons, a baker and a herdsman. The most common trade, on the evidence of personal names, was that of the carpenter. This was only to be expected; the trade had nothing to do with any specific industrial activity but a great deal to do with the fact that this was the basic craft in a society where most things were made of wood. The carpenter was builder, joiner and shipwright and his services must have been in constant demand.[121] Next in order of frequency came the smiths, again a vital part of the agricultural community; they were the makers and maintainers of tools and implements and in Welsh law they enjoyed a status which suggests that their craft once had supernatural overtones.[122] One thing must be remembered about all these craftsmen; there was probably no hard and fast division between agriculture and the pursuit of a trade. Many of these rural weavers, carpenters, cobblers and the rest were also smallholders or sharers in family landholdings and this would have been true of most of Europe.[123]

One craft illustrates the most complicated technological aspect of this kind of economy, that of the miller. Anglesey was always famous for its mills, although most medieval ones were powered by water rather than by wind.[124] The miller and his mill were an essential part of society; without them the corn was useless. In Anglesey, as elsewhere, some mills belonged to the prince and some to kindreds or private individuals and those who did not have their own for themselves and their bondmen owed suit to royal ones. Suit of mill was valuable

---

121 Keith Williams-Jones, *The Merioneth Lay Subsidy Roll, 1292-93.* p.ci; the point is made here that the personal name may have been the traditional occupation of the family without being that of the individual. Occupational names in Merioneth in 1292-3 are discussed in ibid., pp.ci-cxi.

122 A.R. Wiliam, ed., *Llyfr Iorwerth.* p.23; all the crafts named here conferred freedom. Priesthood and the craft of the poet had supernatural connotations; the idea that the smith had them must go back to the first appearance of an iron-using people.

123 For a brief discussion of crafts and craftsmen in medieval England and in medieval Europe generally see M.M. Postan, 'Medieval agrarian society in its prime: England', in *Camb. Econ. Hist.*, i, pp.622-4, and G. Duby, op.cit., pp.152-5.

124 R.O. Roberts, 'The mills of Anglesey', pp.1-15; see also G. Duby, op.cit., pp.106-7

because the prince was entitled to multure or a share of all the corn that was ground. There were altogether seventeen royal mills in the county in 1352, two in Dindaethwy and three in each of the other commotes. A good deal of attention was paid to their upkeep and repair and the sheriff's accounts from the first half of the fourteenth century do contain a good deal of information about the cost of labour and materials. These were the mills to which suit was owed but the prince was not directly interested in the corn that they yielded; they were almost invariably farmed or leased to private individuals or communities and it was the farmer who took the multure. Sometimes no farmers could he found. This happened at Llan-faes and Cefn-coch in Dindaethwy in 1350-1, perhaps as a result of the plague, and the *rhingyll* accounted for the issues.[125] At Llan-faes there were 24 bushels of wheat, 80 of oat malt and twelve of maslin (in this case a mixture of oat and barley meal). Cefn-coch yielded three bushels of wheat, four of oat malt, six of oats and nineteen of maslin. These figures confirm the preponderance of oats. The multure figures would be a great deal more informative if the account had stated what the prince's share was. At Aberffraw in 1352 the heirs of the free Gwely Porthorion who owed suit to the prince's mill had their wheat and malt milled free of toll, but for other corn the prince had each thirtieth measure and at Nantmawr in Twrcelyn the heirs of four and a half *tir gwelyog gwelyau* owed each twenty-ninth measure.[126] At Rhandirgadog in Menai the free tenants and their bondmen owed suit to the mill of Melin Newydd; the free tenants paid every thirtieth measure and the bond tenants every twenty-fifth.[127] These figures suggest that multure was not as great an exaction in Anglesey as it was in parts of England; at Hodsock in Nottinghamshire in 1324 the free tenants owed the twentieth measure and the bondmen the sixteenth.[128]

New royal mills were occasionally built. In 1297 three water-mills in the commote of Menai were farmed at ten pounds a year, but the foundation of the borough of Newborough must have meant a need for additional milling capacity.[129] The new mill was a windmill, the first of which there is any record in Anglesey. It was begun in 1303; it cost £18 3s ½d to build and it began to work on 28 June 1305.[130] The millers were called John, Henry and Philip; John was paid 1s 6d weekly before August and two shillings from 3 August to

125 TNA SC6/1149/1, m.1a.
126 *Extent of Anglesey.* pp. 172, 225;  the same applied at Trefdraeth Wastrodion (p.163) and Tregornor (p.167).
127 ibid., p.251.
128 J.Z. Titow, *English Rural Society, 1200-1350* (1969), p.152.
129 John Griffiths, 'Early accounts relating to north Wales, *temp.* Edward I', *BBCS* 15 (1953), 151.
130 TNA SC6/1170/3, m.5; E.A. Lewis, 'The account roll of the chamberlain of north Wales', 262, 269.

Michaelmas, presumably because the mill was then at its busiest. During that period the multure amounted to five bushels of barley, half a bushel of malt and six bushels of oat malt. There are a few other references to windmills; in 1327 Einion ab Ieuan of Beaumaris was permitted to build a windmill on the Mill Hill by the town and in 1495 an inquisition revealed that Rhys ap Llywelyn ap Hwlcyn, the sheriff of the county, had built a windmill with four sails, although it did not say where.[131] The property of the abbey of Aberconwy at its dissolution included a windmill at Rhuddgaer in Menai.[132] But most medieval mills were powered by water and, given the lack of large and fast-running rivers in Anglesey, most of them must have needed ponds and dams and sluices. Accounts for work done on royal mills include payments for cleaning mill-ponds, as at Aberffraw in 1333, for a new pond at Cemais in 1336-7, for repairs to the dam at Aberffraw in 1337-8 and for new sluices at Aberalaw and Bryn Gwydded in Twrcelyn in 1339.[133]

Although most of the surviving evidence relates to royal mills, there were far more private ones; the 1352 extent lists 45 and the list is certainly not a complete one. Sometimes the ramifications of kinship links and inheritance could lead to a kindred having an interest in a mill a long way from the township where their lands were situated. At Trefadog in Talybolion in 1352 the free *gwelyau* of Cuhelyn ap Cadrod and Gwythur ap Cadrod had shares in the mill of Llaneilian, while at Nantmawr the free *gwely* of Hywel ap Llywelyn had a share in Melin Braint in Dindaethwy.[134] In those townships where free kindreds had their own mills their bondmen owed suit to them. New mills were sometimes built; William de Cranwell was allowed to erect a mill on his land in Beaumaris and to divert water to make a watercourse for it in 1355 and in 1396-7 Ieuan ap Tegwared ap Dafydd was granted a licence to move his corn-mill called Melin Pwllfanog in Dindaethwy and to build a new one.[135] The 1495 inquisition also mentions a number of private mills built since 1352; three had been built in Talybolion since 1447-8.

Ecclesiastical landowners also had their own mills. According to the 1306 extent the bishop of Bangor had mills at Treffos and Moelfre. There is no mention there of his mill of Melin Esgob in Llandyfrydog but it is mentioned in the 1291 *Taxation* where its issues were valued at 15s 4d and it was still working in 1495.[136] There is no mention in the extent of any suit of mill but it must

---

131  *CPR 1327-1330*, 94; TNA E315/166, f.116. Rhys had also built a tide-mill at Holyhead.

132  R.W. Hays, *The History of the Abbey of Aberconway. 1184-1537* (1963), p.171.

133  TNA SC6/1229/2, m.1b; 1229/3; 1229/4; 1229/6.

134  *Extent of Anglesey*, pp. 195, 225.

135  TNA SC6/1149/5, m.4b; 1153/3, m.7a.

136  *Record of Caernarvon*, pp. 100, 109; *Taxatio Nich.IV*, p.292; TNA E315/166, f.11a.

have been due from the bond tenants. Penmon had mills at Bancenyn, mentioned in 1374 and 1535 and Bodiordderch and the monks of Aberconwy had them at Penmynydd and Cornwy as well as the windmill at Rhuddgaer.[137] Before the end of the twelfth century Gruffudd ap Cynan ab Owain Gwynedd had granted the monks the mill of Tal-y-bont in Menai and this is the earliest reference to a mill in Anglesey.[138]

According to the 1352 extent all the prince's bond tenants owed labour services on the royal mills as well as suit. The *tir gwelyog* tenants of Dindryfwl had to repair the ditch and maintain the roof and part of the wall of the mill there and carry timber and millstones within Anglesey and their fellows elsewhere owed the same services on their local mills.[139] In 1304-5 the *rhingyll* of Menai was amerced two shillings at the sessions for failing to summon the prince's bondmen of three townships in the commote to carry millstones for the new windmill at Newborough as he had been ordered to do; they had been brought from Mathafarn to Abermenai by sea.[140] And suit was certainly enforced; some cases of failure to perform it were presented at the Twrcelyn tourn in March 1321 and there were others.[141] Several cases were also heard at the sessions held at Caernarfon on 5 September 1327. These seem to have been brought by the farmer of royal mills in the cantref of Aberffraw and most of them involved free tenants who were able to prove that they had mills of their own and therefore owed nothing.[142] Royal officials could certainly be over-enthusiastic in their claims at times and at the beginning of the fourteenth century the 'commonalty of the free men of Anglesey' complained that they were being compelled to perform suit, which they had not been under the princes.[143] Since mills were a source of profit, hand-mills were regarded with particular disapproval and at the Twrcelyn tourn in September 1321 a Rhosmynach tenant was presented for having one. However, in 1352 the tenants of Eglwys Ail, who held of St Cadwaladr, were described as being free to mill in their own houses, which suggests that they enjoyed the privilege, probably long-established, of using hand-mills.[144]

137  *Record of Caernarvon*, p.251; *Valor Ecclesiasticus*, iv, 429; TNA SC6/Hen.VIII/4705; R.W. Hays, op.cit., pp.114-5.
138  R.W. Hays, op.cit., p.6; the charter is published and discussed in Huw Pryce, ed., *The Acts of Welsh Rulers 1120-1283* (2005), pp.338-9.
139  *Extent of Anglesey*, p.169.
140  TNA E101/120/1.
141  TNA SC2/215/5, m.2b; 215/11, m.1b (Dindaethwy, 1326); G.P. Jones, 'Anglesey court rolls, 1346', in *TAAS* 1930, p.35 (Twrcelyn).
142  NLW Peniarth 405, pp.418-9.
143  *CAP*, p.452.
144  TNA SC2/215/5, m.6b; *Extent of Anglesey*, p.166.

Any discussion of the medieval economy should include wages and prices. For these, too, the Anglesey evidence is sparse and what information there is comes once again from the accounts of royal officials which are mainly concerned with work on royal buildings and the repair of mills. The discussion of wages is also complicated by the fact that so much was done by piecework. In 1312-3 the chamberlain of north Wales rendered account for expenditure on the repair of a stone house in Beaumaris which had belonged to the former sheriff of Anglesey, Thomas Danvers.[145] One thousand slates for the roof cost 2s 6d and lime cost twelve pence; the slater's labour came to three shillings and a mason and a carpenter were paid twelve pence each for repairing the door of the cellar and the roof of the solar. The sheriff's account for 1337-8 includes expenditure on the court buildings at Cemais, Penrhosllugwy and Aberffraw.[146] The work at Aberffraw included a new tiled roof for the king's chamber, the materials and labour for which cost £1 5s 7d, which shows that part, at least, of the court complex there was still standing and in use at this time.[147]

Such detailed accounts are only available during the first half of the fourteenth century. Later chamberlains' accounts include the total annual expenditure on repairs to Beaumaris castle and later to the town walls but they do not mention labour or materials and after the middle of the century the farmers of individual mills were responsible for their maintenance. But before 1350 there is some information about wages. In 1300-1 Iorwerth the carpenter was paid fourpence a day for five days' work on the Llan-faes ferry-boat and his mate Madog was paid twopence.[148] Three carpenters were paid a total of 3s 5d for seven days' work on the Porthaethwy boat in 1318-9, which suggests that their daily rate was twopence.[149] A carpenter received three shillings for six days' work on the bridge and the granary at Beaumaris castle in 1339 and there are other references to carpenters' wages in the sheriffs' accounts for work on mills.[150] At Cemais in 1325-6 Cynwrig ap Madog was paid fourpence a day for six days' work making new wheels and Henry the carpenter was paid at the same rate at Llan-faes and Cefn-coch.[151] In Twrcelyn in 1339 a carpenter working on the mills of Bryn Gwydded and Melin Adda for a total of 23 days was paid twopence a day at the former and threepence at the latter, and in 1344-5 two carpenters at Dolbadarn making a shaft for the mill of Llan-faes were paid

145  TNA SC6/1211/6.
146  TNA SC6/1229/4.
147  198 pieces of timber from the court complex at Aberffraw were shipped to Caernarfon for the castle works in 1317 (A.J. Taylor, The King's Works in Wales, p.386, n.6).
148  TNA SC6/1227/3.
149  TNA SC6/1228/2.
150  TNA SC6/1229/6.
151  TNA SC6/1228/9.

at a daily rate of sixpence.[152] In the latter year two carpenters at Cefn-coch were being paid twopence-halfpenny a day, while another was paid fourpence; at Llan-faes two were paid twopence daily for twelve days' work.[153]

Thus carpenters' wages fluctuated; this may possibly be explained in part by the skill of the individual and in part by the amount of work available at any particular time. Often he was paid according to the job and not according to the time spent on it and the rate was probably agreed at the outset; the 'bargen' has a long history. The construction of the windmill at Newborough in 1303 was paid for in this way. The carpenter Matthew de Sylkeston was paid five pounds for work on the mill and £1 2s 8d for work on the town cross which was built at the same time, while David the ditcher received £2 4s for digging the mill's foundations.[154] Philip the carpenter was paid 11s 6d for shaping a large piece of timber at Aberffraw in 1326-7 and Ieuan the carpenter's payment for repairing the outside of the wheel at Aberalaw in 1328-9 was five shillings.[155]

One interesting feature revealed by these accounts is that for many mills there was some kind of maintenance contract with particular carpenters; in 1325-6 Madog Saer was responsible for the upkeep of Melin y Bont at Aberffraw and Dindryfwl while Cynwrig ap Madog looked after the mills in Talybolion and Twrcelyn.[156] These agreements included the responsibility for carrying new stones from the quarry to the mill, a task which was normally the duty of bond tenants; in 1328-9 Madog ab Ithel carried stones from Mathafarn to Cemais as part of the work of maintenance.[157]

There are a few references to other trades. At Aberalaw in 1339 one mason was paid threepence a day for four days' work and another twopence and at Beaumaris in 1347 John de Sardon the mason received 2s 6d for making a stone wall within the passage of the great wall of the castle; this suggests that one of the wall-passages was being adapted to make a prison or a dungeon, especially since fourpence was spent on a pound of candles as the mason could not work there without light.[158] Two boys were each paid three-halfpence a day for carrying stone and lime and generally helping the mason. Smiths seem usually to have been paid by the job, but in 1339 Stephen the smith was paid 2s 6d for seven days' work at Beaumaris castle and his boy was paid twopence a day.[159] In the week ending 17 June 1347 Einion Bach, the smith's mate at the castle,

152  TNA SC6/1229/6, 7.
153  TNA SC6/1229/7.
154  TNA SC6/1170/3.
155  TNA SC6/1228/10; 1229/1.
156  TNA SC6/1228/9.
157  TNA SC6/1229/1.
158  TNA SC6/1229/8.
159  TNA SC6/1229/6.

was paid sixpence-halfpenny for four and a half days; the smith's weekly wage here seems to have been 1s 2d and Einion the locksmith received eightpence for four days' work making locks and keys for the prison.[160] A thatcher at Aberalaw in 1339 was paid twopence-halfpenny a day and his boy two pence for five days' work and at Dindryfwl in the same year the thatcher's daily wage was twopence.[161] Four men received threepence a day each in 1344-5 for cutting down trees at Dolbadarn to provide timber for Cefn-coch and two men were paid three-halfpence a day each for general work there. In 1347 fourteen men had the same wage for cleaning the pond and the watercourse and eighteen women had a penny a day each for collecting stones for lime.[162]

These few figures may be compared with wages elsewhere. The standard series is that compiled by Lord Beveridge from the accounts of the bishop of Winchester's manors.[163] Here the average daily wage of a carpenter was 3.39d between 1320 and 1329, 3.18d between 1330 and 1339 and 2.96d between 1340 and 1349. For thatchers the rates were 2.08d, 2.09d and 2.21d. On the manor of Thaxted in Essex in 1377-8 a carpenter's daily wage was fourpence.[164] Professor William Rees put the daily wages of a carpenter in south Wales at three to four pence in the reign of Edward II and two to three pence between 1327 and 1349.[165] The rates for a thatcher were two pence and twopence-halfpenny and for a mason threepence and twopence-three farthings to fourpence; the rates for masons on the Winchester manor of Taunton were 3.27d, 3.1d and 2.89d. Thus the Anglesey figures, such as they are, suggest that wages were much the same as in the rest of England and Wales. By way of comparison, the three prisoners from the Isle of Man imprisoned at Beaumaris during the reign of Edward II were each allowed threepence a day for their upkeep. One man's day-work was valued at one penny on the lands of the bishop of Bangor in 1306; at Aberffraw in 1294 it was worth three-halfpence and at Penmon in 1374 twopence, but these figures were no more than a basis for commutation. There is certainly not enough evidence to venture any suggestions as to whether wages rose or fell during the whole period.

There is even less information about prices than there is about wages. The richest source of such information is in manorial accounts and there were none of these in Gwynedd. There are a few isolated figures; at Llan-faes in 1291-2

---

160  TNA SC6/1229/8.

161  TNA SC6/1229/6.

162  TNA SC6/1229/7, 8.

163  These are set out in M.M. Postan, 'Some agrarian evidence of declining population in the later middle ages', in idem., *Essays on Medieval Agriculture and General problems of the Medieval Economy* (1973), p.199.

164  K.C. Newton, *Thaxted in the Fourteenth Century*. p.83.

165  William Rees, *South Wales and the March. 1284-1415*, p.265.

wheat was 6s 8d a quarter (eight bushels), oats three shillings and maslin five shillings.[166] Barley, oatmeal and malt were each six shillings a quarter. These prices seem considerably higher than the ones prevailing in England at this time, which may reflect a bad harvest in Anglesey.[167] The subsidy of 1292-3 was based on fixed valuations, as was the 1284 extent in all probability.[168] A crannock or four bushels of wheat at Llan-faes in 1350-1 was worth four shillings, one of oat malt 2s 3d and one of maslin 2s 4d.[169] Escheators' accounts in the fifteenth century often include stocks of corn, but since the valuations do not differentiate between wheat, oats and barley they are of little help. The values of livestock are not much better; there are various isolated examples but not enough to draw any conclusions. All that can be said is that prices seem to have been increasing in the fifteenth century; the average value of a sheep, according to the escheator, was fourpence in 1449-50 and just over five pence in 1481-2, while a pig was worth eightpence in 1457-8 and tenpence in 1481-2.[170] In 1471-2 25 cows and bullocks and three calves were worth £6 10s.[171] How reliable these figures are as a guide to current prices is difficult to say; the sample is far too small to mean very much and the escheator's valuations may well have been based on a fixed scale. The prices of building materials included in accounts for work on royal buildings are more reliable but they relate mainly to the purchase of timber and iron. There is certainly not enough information about wages or prices to make any kind of statistical analysis possible. Few conclusions can therefore be drawn and even then they can only be tentative.

166 John Griffiths, 'Two early ministers' accounts for north Wales', 64.
167 For a series of prices see J.M. Stratton and J. Houghton Brown, *Agricultural Records A.D. 220-1977* (2nd. edn., 1978), p.240. The average price of wheat in England in 1291 was 5s 7½d a quarter and of oats 2s 2d. See also D.L. Farmer, 'Prices and wages' in *The Agrarian History of England and Wales*, ii, *1042-1350*, pp.716-817 and idem, 'Prices and wages' in E. Miller, ed., *The Agrarian History of England and Wales* iii: *1350-1500* (1991), pp.431-525.
168 The scales are set out in Keith Williams-Jones, op.cit., p.xiv.
169 TNA SC6/1149/1, m.1a.
170 TNA SC6/1153/6, m.15a; 1155/6, m.11b; 1154/3, m.16a.
171 TNA SC6/1155/2, m.10b.

# 5   *The Social Order*

MEDIEVAL MEN AND WOMEN often saw their society as one divided between those who fought, those who prayed and those who worked.[1] It was, according to its lights, a logical and functional division but alongside it there
existed that line of demarcation between the free and the unfree which was
common to all European societies. The villein, bondman, or *taeog* was a universal figure and the main features of his status were common knowledge. He
was bound to the soil and could not leave it without his lord's consent. It was
said of him that he did not know of an evening what he would be called upon
to do on the morrow. He and his offspring could be bought and sold. He owed
heavy labour services and food-renders to his lord and in return he had a plot
of land where he grew what crops were necessary to feed himself and his family
and perhaps kept a pig or two, a cow, or some hens. The basic fact about his
status was that he was born to it; it could not be achieved nor, unlike penal
slavery in an earlier age, could it be thrust upon him. At the same time he
could, under certain circumstances, become free. It has several times been suggested that the bond element in Welsh society was descended from the neolithic
inhabitants of Wales who were depressed in status as a result of successive
Celtic invasions and that until the twelfth century bondmen formed a majority
of the population.[2]

Another essential feature of servile status was what might be called the lack
of blood. For the free Welshman blood was of paramount importance; his position in society and his title to his land stemmed from his descent and his pedigree was as much an abstract of title as a statement of his ancestry. Both he
and his neighbours knew exactly who he was. But the bondman's status in society was completely different. He has been aptly described as 'a man without
ancestry', indicating that his position was expressed in terms of his dependence

---

1   E. Miller and J. Hatcher, *Medieval England: Rural Society and Economic Change, 1086-1348*, p.xiii;
W. Ogwen Williams, 'The social order in Tudor Wales', *THSC* 1967, pp.171-2. For a very clear
and comprehensive picture of society in the march of Wales which is in many ways applicable to
the principality see R.R. Davies, *Lordship and Society in the March of Wales, 1282-1400* (1978), pp
354-91.
2   W. Ogwen Williams, op.cit., p.172; G.R.J. Jones, 'The tribal system in Wales: a re-assessment in
the light of settlement studies', 125.

on his lord.[3] He was far from being a landless labourer; every bondman living in a bond community had his share of its land. But his interest in it did not flow from his membership of any kindred; the strips in the fields of the township where he lived were distributed at intervals by the reeve among the tenants. All this meant that he was regarded as the lord's personal possession and that he could consequently be bought and sold.[4] He could have one of several masters; he might be a royal bondman whose direct lord had been the prince before 1282 and the king or the prince of Wales after that year. He could in Anglesey be a bondman of the bishop of Bangor, the abbot of Aberconwy, or the prior of Penmon. Or he could be subject to a layman, perhaps as a result of the grant of the township where he lived to a lay magnate in the twelfth or thirteenth century. All these categories existed in Anglesey but it was only the last which bought and sold bondmen, generally along with the land where they lived.[5] In 1330 four of the sons of Bleddyn ap Llywelyn Croen of the commote of Dindaethwy and their cousin Gwenllian ferch Dafydd sold four bondmen and their issue to Gwilym ap Gruffudd ap Tudur of Llaniestyn for ten pounds and when Gwilym died in 1376 he left more than twenty bondmen, all named, in his will.[6]

There are several other examples of bondmen being conveyed, either with land or on their own.[7] General releases of land tended to include them as a matter of course, as in 1410 when John Woodhouse conveyed all his lands, tenements and bondmen, formerly the property of Gwilym ap Tudur ap Goronwy, to Gwilym ap Gruffudd ap Gwilym.[8] Such transactions were still taking place in the sixteenth century. In 1501 Nicholas ap Dafydd ap Gwilym of Amlwch conveyed his share of the lands of his father, along with twelve named bondmen, to Rowland Bulkeley and as late as 1509 a conveyance of the township of Dinsylwy Rys in Dindaethwy included bond tenants.[9] This buying and selling should not be seen as a cruel and heartless traffic in human flesh; indeed, to refer to bondmen being bought and sold may over-simplify the whole issue.[10]

---

3  R.R. Davies, op.cit., p.384.

4  Paul R. Hyams, *Kings, Lords and Peasants in Medieval England: the common law of villeinage in the twelfth and thirteenth centuries* (1980), pp.3-5, discusses the sale of bondmen in England.

5  R.R. Davies, op.cit., p.385 and n.104, which gives examples.

6  BUASC Penrhyn 407;  Penrhyn 5.

7  NLW Sotheby 5 (1378); 8 (1391); BUASC Penrhyn 10 (1410); 11 (1413); 23 (1443); 386 (1413); 392 (1446); 397 (1472); 394 (1456); BUASC Penrhyn Further Additional 4 July 1389; 24 January 1418; 24/5 January 1419; 23 August 1423; 27 July 1425; 22 July 1426; 20 June 1449; BUASC Baron Hill 1276 (1501); 1278 (1503); 959 (1509). For three deeds relating to the sale of bondmen in Dwyran in 1399, 1422 and 1449 see Henry Rowlands, 'Antiquitates parochiales', *Arch.Camb.* 1846, p.391.

8  BUASC Penrhyn 10.

9  BUASC Baron Hill 1276; 959.

10  Paul R. Hyams, op.cit., p.4, makes the point that there was no organised market in men.

Bond status had its restrictions and its disadvantages but it was far removed from slavery, an institution which had once existed in Wales and England but which had certainly disappeared by the twelfth century if not earlier.[11] The key to the nature of some, at least, of these transactions may lie in the wording of some of the deeds. In 1369 Dafydd Fychan ap Dafydd Llwyd paid two pounds for licence to acquire an annual rent of ten shillings from two bondmen and their heirs in Bodwrdin in Malltraeth along with half the relief and *gobrestyn* due from them, and in 1391 Angharad ferch Gruffudd, a free tenant of Tregadrod in Bodedern, conveyed a messuage in Bodedern and her rights in her bondman Madog ab Einion and his issue and four acres with her rights in Dafydd Chwith Bach to Ieuan ap Tudur Llwyd.[12] A similar grant was made in 1456 by Gruffudd ap Llywelyn ab Ieuan of Lledwigan Llys in Malltraeth when he conveyed his bondman Hywel ap Deicws ap Llywelyn ap Llywarch to William Griffith of Penrhyn with all *amobrau*, reliefs, services and customs due from him.[13] These examples suggest that the sale of a bondman really meant the sale of jurisdiction over him and the right to his labour and services. Since he was bound to the soil, if that soil were sold then that jurisdiction and that right were necessarily conveyed with it. In the 1391 transaction a piece of land was conveyed with each bondman and what this may have meant is that it was his holding that was sold. The bondman's right to his holding was protected and consequently where the tenement went, so went the tenant.[14]

In terms of social organisation a clear distinction was drawn between bond and free communities and there were several kinds of the former. First of all, there were those associated with the royal courts, of which there were five in Anglesey; these were at Aberffraw in Malltraeth, Cemais in Talybolion, Penrhosllugwy in Twrcelyn, Llan-faes in Dindaethwy and Rhosyr in Menai. There was no such community in Llifon but there was one which belonged to the bishop of Bangor at Treffos in Dindaethwy. The bondmen who lived in these *maerdrefi* were responsible for the provision of food for the court and for certain works; the *maerdref* was, in fact, the equivalent of the demesne on the English manor.[15] Examples may be found all over Wales; the *maerdref* was a bond town-

11  G.R.J. Jones, 'Post-Roman Wales', pp. 299-300, 302, where slavery is discussed. For an excellent discussion of villeinage and bond status in medieval Gwynedd see Keith Williams-Jones, ed., *The Merioneth Lay Subsidy Roll, 1292-3*, pp.xciii-xcvii.

12  NLW Llanfair and Brynodol D1129;  Sotheby 8.

13  BUASC Penrhyn 394.

14  R.R. Davies, op.cit., p.387.

15  For the *maerdref* see Dafydd Jenkins, ed., *Llyfr Colan*, 11.593, 674-8 and pp. 152, 172-4; the legal position and obligations of the bondmen are set out here. See also G.R.J. Jones, 'The distribution of medieval settlement in Anglesey', pp.81-4, T. Jones Pierce, 'Medieval settlement in Anglesey', in *Medieval Welsh Society*, pp.276-9, and William Rees, *South Wales and the March, 1284-1415*, pp.199-201.

ship but by the fourteenth century it could include several kinds of tenure. Treffos was included in the extent made of the bishop's lands in 1306; it contained two carucates or about 120 acres of land and 26 tenants paid a total of £1 12s in rent at the feast of All Saints.[16] Every week of the year they had to find nine men to do one day's work for the lord, while another group of nine tenants had to find one man to do a day's work weekly; one tenant owed half a day's work every other week. Each tenant owed heriot and *amobr* of two shillings each. The renders from the bishop's dominical bondmen were in fact very similar to those due from manorial tenants anywhere else in western Europe.[17]

The information from the secular *maerdrefi* is more abundant and a good deal more varied. An extent of the royal lands in Anglesey was taken by the king's officials in 1284.[18] In this extent the *maerdref* of Aberffraw, the traditional seat of the princes of Gwynedd, consisted of five carucates or about three hundred acres of demesne land.[19] The heaviest burden of renders and services was due from the bondmen of Aberffraw itself; here there were fifteen bond tenements, six of which were unoccupied. The community owed 8s 8d rent of assise and 300 day-works in the autumn, together with renders of wheat, oatmeal and barley meal and the nine bondmen who were actually resident owed milk, sheep, lambs, butter, eggs and hens. Each of them also owed three day-works hoeing the corn and each tenant was entitled to one loaf daily when performing them. They owed £1 10s annually for fuel and straw for the prince's court and oats for his horses and a total of 550 harrowing works were also due from the *maerdref*. Each of its dependent hamlets also owed a heavy burden of rents and services. These obligations bore heavily on the bond tenants, particularly since they were held by a tenure which involved a fixed burden of rents, renders and services, whatever the bond population might be. Those payments, described in Edward I's extents as rents of assise or, as in the case of the Aberffraw hamlet of Tref Was Padrig, as *twnc* rents, were quit-rents or rents in place of food renders which had been commuted to cash payments by the princes of Gwynedd before 1282.[20] There had been little commutation on the royal demesnes around the various courts for the very simple and practical reason that food-renders were required for the maintenance of an itinerant court and that labour services were required to work the prince's land. But after the Edwardian con-

16  *Rec. Caern.*, p.100.

17  See Georges Duby, *Rural Economy and Country Life in the Medieval West*, pp.486-7 (Normandy, lands of St Ouen of Rouen, 1291), and J.Z. Titow, *English Rural Society, 1200-1350*, pp.155-6 (Hodsock, Notts., 1324), for similar obligations, albeit in more detail.

18  Smith, 'The Extent of Anglesey, 1284', pp.93-116.

19  ibid., pp.96-9; see also G. Rex Smith, 'The manor of Aberffraw, 1284-1339', *Cambrian Medieval Celtic Studies* 60 (2010), 81-91.

20  T. Jones Pierce, 'The growth of commutation in Gwynedd during the thirteenth century', in *Medieval Welsh Society*, pp.113-16.

quest and settlement food-renders and labour services on the prince's demesne were no longer needed; consequently they were listed in the extent but their cash value, representing the quit-rents to which they were henceforth commuted, was also given.[21]

The extent of 1284 may usefully be compared with that of 1352.[22] In the hamlet of Treberfedd in 1284 nine bondmen had owed 9s 8d rent of assise together with food-renders and works valued at a total of £2 11s 1½d. In 1352 the tenants of the hamlet paid an annual rent of £3 0s 9d due in quarterly instalments. They owed suit to the prince's mill of Aberffraw and, as well as carrying timber and millstones for it, they were responsible for making the ditch, the watercourse and the roof. They also contributed to the *staurum*, an annual render for the provisioning of the local castle and to each *cylch* except that of the falconers.[23] If necessary they had to provide a man and a horse to carry for the prince at a cost of twopence a day and they paid relief and *amobr* at the bond rate of five shillings. The pattern in the other hamlets was similar; in the hamlet of Garddau there were fourteen bond tenements described as gardens which paid a total rent of £2 18s 10d and which may each have had an area of one acre.[24] Thus the first extent shows the renders and services due from the bondmen actually being replaced by cash payments, while the second shows the tenants of Aberffraw owing annual rents payable in quarterly instalments.

The demesne townships did not all develop in the same way. Llifon had none, possibly because the cantref of Aberffraw remained as an administrative unit until well into the fourteenth century. At Cemais the 1284 extent only mentions a consolidated rent for all customs and services, which probably indicates that they had already been commuted.[25] The 1352 extent has more to say about Cemais; the *maerdref* is described as being of threefold nature, having in it three kinds of tenants called *gwŷr mâl, gwŷr gwaith* and *gwŷr tir bwrdd*.[26] All these were bond tenants but the development of new forms of tenure must reflect the social and economic changes which had occurred in thirteenth-century Gwynedd. *Gwŷr mâl* or tribute or cash-paying men paid cash rents and seven tenants held ten and a quarter *gafaelion* by this tenure; they also owed suit to the prince's mill of Cemais and some contributed to the *cylch* of the

21  ibid., p.113. For a discussion of the Aberffraw section of the extent see David Stephenson, *The Governance of Gwynedd*, p.60.

22  *Extent of Anglesey*, pp.172-6.

23  The *cylchoedd* or circuits were the billetting rights of the king's stallion or war-horse, the *rhaglaw*, the falconers and the king's otter-hounds, commuted to cash-rents; for details see *Extent of Anglesey*, p.164, nn.13-17.

24  *Extent of Anglesey*, pp.175-6. G.R.J. Jones suggests that these gardens were a relic of *tir corddlan* (nucleal or infield land) ('Post Roman Wales', pp.340-3, and references cited therein).

25  Smith, 'Extent of Anglesey, 1284', p.102.

26  *Extent of Anglesey*, pp. 2, 10-5.

prince's stallion. This particular tenure may have evolved as a means of induc-
ing tenants to settle on the prince's land; the only obligation was suit of mill,
which was a common enough one for both free and bond tenants.[27] The second
category was that of the *gwŷr gwaith* or work men; they comprised seven tenants
who held fifteen and a half *gafaelion*. Each *gafael* owed an annual cash rent of
19s 9d, apart from one which owed £1 4s, and they also owed suit of mill, the
carriage of timber and stones and labour services on it and on the *maerdref*. In
addition, they had to carry for the lord as far as Penrhosllugwy if necessary
and for this they were entitled to drink but no money.[28] These may have been
the original *maerdref* tenants since the services they owed were identical with
those due elsewhere.[29] The *gwŷr tir bwrdd* were the actual demesne tenants.
They were organised in nine *gafaelion*, for each of which they paid an annual
cash rent of 12s 6d or 12s 7d and there were eleven tenants. The dependent
hamlet of Meiriogen, some miles from Cemais, was also *tir bwrdd* land for
which two tenants paid an annual rent of £1 9s. In addition to cash rents, the
*gwŷr tir bwrdd* owed suit of mill and they were required to present at the sheriff's
tourn. The term *tir bwrdd* or 'table land' was applied to the land which supplied
food for the lord, or the demesne, but these tenants did not owe any agricultural services.[30]

Thus at Cemais commutation seems to have been almost universal and the
community was diluted by the introduction of more privileged tenants who
paid cash rents. At Penrhosllugwy a similar pattern prevailed in 1352 but the
earlier extent was to have repercussions which lasted for nearly forty years and
which were to take the grievances of the bondmen as far as Parliament.[31] According to the 1284 extent there were four carucates or about 240 acres of
demesne land at Penrhosllugwy and the bondmen there owed a total of £48 9s
1¼d.[32] This sum was made up of quit-rents, billetting rights for 210 of the
prince's men and 400 horses when the need arose, renders of cereals, milk,
butter, lambs, eggs, hens and fodder and the carriage of peat and straw. These
came to a total of £27 1s 2¾d. This figure was reasonable enough but there
was also a very heavy burden of agricultural services which included no fewer
than 864 day-works in the autumn, one hundred harrowing works during Lent

27  For *gwŷr mâl* see T. Jones Pierce, 'Medieval settlement in Anglesey', p.279, and G.R.J. Jones, 'The
    distribution of medieval settlement in Anglesey', pp.41-2. The etymology of the term is discussed
    by Dafydd Jenkins, *Llyfr Colan*. p.160. According to Jones Pierce they were free men but they
    owed a bondman's relief and their daughters' virtue was valued at two shillings rather than ten.
28  They also paid *cylch rhaglaw*.
29  T. Jones Pierce, 'Medieval settlement in Anglesey', p.278.
30  *Llyfr Colan*, pp.173-4. Dr Stephenson suggests that *gwŷr tir bwrdd* were those who were leasing
    the demesne after 1282 (*Governance of Gwynedd*, p.59.)
31  For an account of this episode see Carr, 'The bondmen of Penrhosllugwy', pp.15-29.
32  Smith, 'Extent of Anglesey, 1284', pp.104-5.

and 1,620 other harrowing works. In addition, thirteen cottagers owed three day-works each and there were further harrowing and manuring works. The total value of these services was £21 7s 10½d. By any standards this was an excessive burden and it was even more so when compared with what was due from the other Anglesey *maerdrefi*.[33] Nor were the bondmen prepared to accept this new burden without question and they protested in 1305, in 1315, in 1322 and in 1327.[34] Each time they proved their point but each time attempts continued to be made to collect the extra money. What probably happened is described in their petition of 1322.[35] In this they said that their predecessors before the conquest had paid a rent of assise of £4 9s 4d for six and a half *gafaelion* along with various renders and customs for the rest of their lands and for the four carucates of demesne. After the conquest the services and customs were commuted to a total payment of £18 5s 2¾d but then Richard de Abingdon made an extent which was so burdensome that it could not be paid in full. Abingdon was supposed to make the extent with Brother Llywelyn, the prior of Bangor, but he went ahead without waiting for him; when the prior came he mae a new extent and had it enrolled along with Abingdon's.[36]

Brother Llywelyn's extent is the one which appears at the end of the Anglesey document and it probably describes the services which were commuted after the conquest. These included reaping, carrying and harrowing works and manuring while the renders had consisted of cereals, peat, milk, butter and hens. There were also some cash rents. This extent almost certainly lists the original renders and services and it shows just how unjust and oppressive the Abingdon extent was. Why such an additional burden should have been laid on Penrhosllugwy is a difficult question to answer but it may be significant that there were one or two other complaints of unjust extents from Anglesey around this time.[37] The long struggle of the bondmen of Penrhosllugwy is typical of many such episodes from all over medieval Europe which show that the unfree

---

33  The total due from Aberffraw was £38 5s 1¾d, from Cemais £36 7s 7d and from Rhosyr £35 0s 6d; the degree of urban development at Llan-faes was such that no comparison is relevant.

34  *Rec.Caern.*, p.217; *CAP*, pp.260-3, and *Rot.Parl.*, i, 308-9; *CIM*, ii, no. 563; *CCR. 1323-1327*, 304; Natalie Fryde, *List of Welsh Entries in the Memoranda Rolls. 1282-1343.* no. 67. A schedule attached to the original roll of the extent states that an error of £14 5s 4¾d was remedied after the bondmens' petition to parliament in Hilary Term, 1305.

35  *CIM* ii, no. 563; see also F.Seebohm, *The Tribal System in Wales* (London, 2nd edn., 1904), App., pp.27-31.

36  Smith, 'Extent of Anglesey, 1284', pp.114-6.

37  Among the Kennington petitions of 1305 was one from the bishop of Bangor asking that his bondmen of Moelfre be not compelled to fish for the prince's bailiffs nor to look after the *rhaglaw* of Penrhosllugwy's horse (*Rec.Caern.*, p.214), and the petitions also include one from the four sons of Gruffudd ab Iorwerth of the cantref of Aberffraw complaining of a false extent made of their lands in the time of Roger de Pulesdon (ibid.), while the prince's bondmen of Rhosyr complained about an additional rent of assise (ibid., p.217).

tenant was very far from being a slave and was both ready and able to stand up for what he considered to be his rights.[38] He might not always be successful but he was ready to make the effort. How far this extent was part of that oppressive government for which the sheriff of Anglesey, Roger de Pulesdon, was hanged by the rebels in 1294 is not known but such extortion and injustice were undoubtedly among the grievances which led to Madog ap Llywelyn's revolt.[39]

At Penrhosllugwy in 1352 the six *gwŷr mâl gafaelion* were those which had owed cash rents and renders of corn in the earlier extent; there was no mention of any corn in 1352, but commutation may be reflected in higher rents.[40] Ten tenants owed suit of mill, some to that of Bryn Gwydded and some to that of Dulas, depending on where in the township their lands were situated, and they contributed to the *cylchoedd* of the king's stallion and the *rhaglaw*.[41] The *gwŷr gwaith* held fifteen *gafaelion* with an additional six acres; each of these paid an annual rent of 15s 5d and they all owed suit to the mill of Bryn Gwydded and work on the walls and roof of the kitchen and stable of the court. They owed carrying services within Anglesey and some labour services on the lord's mill, as did their counterparts at Cemais. The *tir bwrdd* tenants held seven and a half *gafaelion;* each paid an annual rent of 13s 4d and they all owed suit to Melin Dulas and to the tourn. By 1352 there had been some change and, indeed, dilution; four of the *gwŷr mâl* tenants had interests in *tir bwrdd gafaelion*, as had one *gŵr gwaith*.[42]

The renders due at Rhosyr in 1284 were much the same.[43] They included rent of assise, food renders, fodder and fuel and reaping, carrying and harrowing works. In 1352 Rhosyr, like Cemais and Penrhosllugwy, had three kinds of tenants but they were not described in quite the same way.[44] Here there were 'pure bondmen called *maerdref*. And other bondmen who say they are free bondmen. And others called garden men'. The first group held twelve and a half *gafaelion*, each of which paid an annual rent of 10s 11d; they owed the same labour services as did the other bondmen of the commote of Menai.[45] They

---

38  For other examples see M. Bloch, 'From the royal court to the court of Rome: the suit of the serfs of Rosny-sous-Bois' in S. Thrupp, *Change in Medieval Society: Europe north of the Alps, 1050-1500* (1965), pp.3-13, and H.J. Hewitt, *Medieval Cheshire* (1929), pp.146-8 (the villeins of Darnhall).

39  One of those responsible for Pulesdon's death was the *rhingyll* of Twrcelyn.

40  *Extent of Anglesey*, pp.229-33.

41  For a brief discussion of these tenants in Penrhosllugwy see G.R.J. Jones, 'The distribution of medieval settlement in Anglesey', pp.41-2, and T. Jones Pierce, 'Medieval settlement in Anglesey', pp.278-9.

42  This was not the case at Cemais.

43  Smith, 'Extent of Anglesey, 1284', pp.107-9.

44  *Extent of Anglesey*, pp.258-62.

45  For these see ibid., p.252, also *Llyfr Colan*, p.48.

also had to carry food for the lord and his officers and they owed relief at the unfree rate of five shillings. This tenure seems to correspond to that of the *gwŷr gwaith*. The free bondmen held eight *gafaelion*, the total rent from which came to five pounds. They owed suit of mill and paid their share of the *staurum* and they paid relief and *amobr* of ten shillings, a sign of free status. In general they resembled the *gwŷr mâl*.[46] The garden men held twelve gardens for which they paid small rents ranging from fourpence to 2s 3d. They all owed suit of mill, they paid relief and *amobr* of two shillings, the smallest sum due in Anglesey and they had to find sumpter horses for the prince's army. Like the gardens at Aberffraw, these tenements might have been part of the nucleus of the *maerdref*. Rhosyr, of course, changed considerably between 1284 and 1352 as some of it had been handed over to the former burgesses of Llan-faes to create the new borough of Newborough.

The tenure by which the original bond tenants of the *maerdref* held was called *tir cyfrif* and it comprised a fixed burden of renders and services shared equally among all the adult males.[47] Under this tenure the arable land was supposed to be redistributed with every change in the adult male population and the 1352 extent does suggest that this had happened very recently. At Cemais the *gwŷr gwaith gafael* of Madog ap Wyn included Wyn ap Madog, possibly the son of the eponym, among its tenants and at Penrhosllugwy the distribution seems to have been even more recent. Of the *gwŷr gwaith* tenants Madog ap Cynwrig was joint tenant of Gafael Madog ap Cynwrig and Madog ab Adda of Gafael Madog ab Adda. At Rhosyr the free bondmen included Dafydd Llwyd ap Dafydd ap Tegwared who held Gafael Dafydd ap Tegwared; indeed, most of these tenements were held by the sons of the eponyms. The traditional tenure had certainly been diluted; the presence of escheat lands and the differential rents paid by the *gwŷr mâl* were not consistent with the *tir cyfrif* pattern.[48] In some cases outsiders had moved into some of the *maerdref* tenements.[49] All this shows that, although the *maerdref* as a bond demesne township was changing and although new tenants and new forms of tenure had been coming in before 1282, the institution still had considerable vitality in the fourteenth century.

---

46  The free bond *gafaelion* at Rhosyr included those of the ferrymen and the porters; at Penrhosllugwy the *gwŷr mâl* holdings included those of the smiths, the porters and the herdsmen. These may suggest a freer tenure for certain specialists.

47  The tenure is defined in *Extent of Anglesey*, pp. 175 (Aberffraw), 247 (Hirdre-faig).

48  T. Jones Pierce, 'Medieval settlement in Anglesey', p.278

49  A possible example was at Rhosyr in 1352 where Gruffudd ab Iorwerth Foel held Gafael Philip Môn and had a share in Gafael y Porthorion; his father had been in the service of Edward I and had been a man of some wealth and position in Aberffraw. Also at Rhosyr the lands of Dafydd ab Ithel ab Ieuan and the land called Gwas Dewi were held by the community of the township.

*Tir cyfrif* tenure was not restricted to the *maerdref;* the 1352 extent lists seven townships held in this way, along with three others in which the tenure existed. There were also various townships, described as free in 1352 because they were held by individuals or kindred groups, but where there were also bond tenants, jurisdiction over whom had been granted to the ancestors of the free proprietors before 1282.[50] In many of these the bondmen may have been organised in *tir cyfrif* communities but in such cases the rents and services were due to the proprietor so that nothing was revealed in extents which were concerned only with what was due to the prince.[51] One example of a *tir cyfrif* township was Deri in Twrcelyn. Here in 1284 the tenants owed hens, lambs and reaping works valued at a total of 5s 3d.[52] The bondmen of the four adjacent *tir cyfrif* townships of Deri, Bodhunod, Bodednyfed and Rhosmynach were also liable for the billetting of 400 men, 200 horses and 200 dogs for one day each year, presumably when the prince was hunting in Anglesey and this had been commuted to a payment of £3 15s. In 1352 the tenants of Deri owed an annual rent of £3 1s and they owed suit to the mill of Dulas.[53] With the other *tir cyfrif* tenants of the commote they had to work on the hall, chamber, chapel and privy of the court at Penrhosllugwy and to make and repair the pantry and the buttery there at their own expense. They were also responsible for the ditch, watercourse and roof of the mill of Bryn Gwydded and they had to carry timber and millstones for it. They contributed to each *cylch* and they paid relief and *amobr* of 6s 8d. With the *maerdrefi* the *tir cyfrif* townships may well have been the most archaic forms of social and tenurial organisation in medieval Wales.[54]

Although *tir cyfrif* was probably the original form of bond tenure, it was not the only one. Although the *gwely* or landholding kindred group was originally a free institution, there were by 1352 many unfree townships held by unfree *gwelyau* in north Wales. These *tir gwelyog* townships stood somewhere between those held by *tir cyfrif* and those which were free.[55] The tenants were subject to the restrictions of bond status but they enjoyed a heritable interest in the *gwely* lands; there was no question of their shares being dependent on regular redistribution of the arable land. In Anglesey there was a number of such townships which were usually rather smaller than their free counterparts and which tended to be further from the commotal centres than were the *tir cyfrif* town-

---

50  These townships are shown in *An Atlas of Anglesey*, p.40; see also T. Jones Pierce, op.cit., pp.270-1, and G.R.J. Jones, op.cit., pp.57-8.

51  G.R.J. Jones, op.cit., pp.79-80.

52  Smith, 'Extent of Anglesey, 1284', p.107.

53  *Extent of Anglesey.* pp.226-7.

54  G.R.J. Jones, op.cit., p.55.

55  The tenure is discussed by T. Jones Pierce, op.cit., pp.274-6, and G.R.J. Jones, op.cit., pp: 56-7, 75-9.

ships.[56] These bond *gwelyau* cannot be regarded in quite the same light as free ones; in Cardiganshire it was stated in 1326 that the heirs were compelled to take up the inheritance on the death of the parent, which means that they were bound to the soil.[57] It is possible that these communities were first established on marginal land with a view to bringing it into cultivation at a time when the population was increasing. According to this argument the transplanted bondmen were granted an improvement in their status as an incentive and it may be that this was the manifestation in Gwynedd of a process of colonisation which was to be seen in many parts of twelfth-century Europe.[58]

A typical *tir gwelyog* township was Tre Feibion Meurig in Llifon. In 1284 the bond tenants here paid a total rent of assise of 19s 4½d; in addition to this they owed renders of wheat and oatmeal and the billetting of 520 men and 80 horses, the total being valued at £2 15s 8½d.[59] Every bondman who kept pigs owed one worth 1s 8d and each household owed one hen worth a penny. In 1352 four bond *gwelyau* there paid a total annual rent of £4 14s 5d. They owed suit to the prince's mill of Tre Feibion Meurig, but in 1352 they were farming the mill themselves.[60] They also owed labour services on the mill of Dindryfwl and at the court of Aberffraw, where they were responsible for part of the perimeter wall and part of the roofs of the hall and the chamber as well as making good the roof of the *rhaglaw*'s chamber against the rain and making and cleaning the lord's privy. They had to carry food and fuel for the prince, they paid each *cylch* and they owed relief, *gobrestyn* and *amobr* of 6s 8d. An addition to the extent of Tre Feibion Meurig and Bodynolwyn dated 1356 states that they owed pannage of twopence for each pig as long as the prince wished to receive it; this superseded the obligation recorded in the 1284 extent. Unlike the *tir gwelyog* tenants in other commotes, those in Menai paid the free tenants' relief, *gobrestyn* and *amobr* of ten shillings. The heaviest burden of billetting obligations or *porthiant* in 1284 fell on the bond *tir gwelyog* townships.

There are numerous references to the status of bondmen, to the various restrictions imposed on them and to the ways in which these were circumvented. At Kennington in 1305 Llywelyn Foelrhon of Cornwy in Talybolion com-

---

56  T. Jones Pierce, op.cit., p.274; G.R.J. Jones, op.cit., pp. 91, 93. They were listed in the 1352 extent and most, if not all, the townships held by ecclesiastics were probably organised in bond *gwelyau*. (T. Jones Pierce, op.cit., pp.272-3).

57  T. Jones Pierce, 'Medieval Cardiganshire: a study in social origins', *in Medieval Welsh Society*, pp.317-8.

58  G.R.J. Jones, op.cit., pp. 56-7, 62.

59  Smith, 'Extent of Anglesey, 1284', p.100.

60  *Extent of Anglesey*, pp.187-9. The farm of the mill may stem from an early fourteenth-century petition of the bondmen of Tre Feibion claiming that their ancestors had had their own mill in the township from time immemorial until Roger Mortimer, the justice, had taken it into the king's hand (*CAP*, p.241; see also TNA SC6/1229/2).

plained that the sheriff had deprived him of three of his bondmen with their children, to which the prince replied that they claimed to be free since their ancestors had come from Ireland and come into avowry and that it was up to him to prove his case in the courts.[61] The archdeacon of Anglesey asked that his bondman Gwtyn ap Tegwared who had left his land and become the prince's avowry tenant should be returned to him; he received the same answer.[62] Had more court records survived it is likely that they would reveal many cases of proprietors seeking the return of fugitive bondmen. The bondman was bound to the soil and could not leave the manor or township without his lord's consent, but this was generally obtainable on payment of a fine; in England this payment for licence to dwell away from the manor was called chevage. There are several examples from Anglesey; at the sessions held at Beaumaris on 29 May 1355 Ieuan Goch ap Rhirid made fine of five shillings to live wherever he wished, and in 1376-7 Ieuan ab Ieuan Goch of Rhosmor in Malltraeth paid two shillings, the usual rate in such cases, for a similar licence.[63] In 1441-2 Llywelyn ab Ieuan ap Dafydd, a bond tenant of the king in Hirdre-faig, paid ten shillings for licence to dwell wherever he chose to practise his trade as a mason. The medieval mason was an itinerant worker who moved from site to site and here a skilled craftsman was, to all intents and purposes, enfranchised.[64] On the other side of the coin, Meilir ap Goronwy was amerced two shillings in 1304-5 for withdrawing from the prince's villeinage at Llanllibio without licence although this may have been the equivalent of a chevage fine.[65] The payment was really a recognition by the bondman of his continued dependence on his lord and by paying it he admitted that he had no unfettered right to live away from the manor or the township.[66]

A bondman could gain his freedom, sometimes by purchase and sometimes, though rarely in the middle ages, by a Christian action on the part of a lord who sought to gain spiritual merit. Manumission had a long history and its roots lay in Roman law. In 1360-1 Dafydd ap Tegwared ap Madog, a bondman of the prince in the commote of Menai, made fine of two pounds that he and his heirs might be free and that he might have a charter showing this, and in 1441-2 Gruffudd ap Hywel ab Iorwerth ab Ieuan Goch, a former bondman of a free tenant who had been manumitted, made fine for licence to purchase

61  *Rec.Caern.*, p.216.
62  ibid., p.218.
63  NLW Peniarth 405, p.438; for a similar case two years later see ibid., p.441; TNA SC6/1150/3, m.1a. For examples of chevage elsewhere in Wales see R.R. Davies, *Lordship and Society in the March of Wales*, p.385, n.105, and William Rees, *South Wales and the March*, p.241, n.2
64  TNA SC6/11S3/5, m.13b; see also BUASC Penrhyn 1599 which records two payments of chevage by Gwilym ap Gruffudd's bondmen in Twrgarw in 1413.
65  TNA E101/120/1.
66  R.R. Davies, op.cit., p.385.

land from a free tenant in Llechylched.[67] One way in which freedom could not be obtained was by marriage; indeed, the consequences of a free tenant marrying an unfree spouse were the opposite of this since the children of such a union would be unfree. Moreover, if the marriage took place without the lord's licence the free tenement might be forfeit. The accounts of medieval officials reveal a number of cases of disparagement; in 1377-8, for example, the escheator answered for 3s 4d, the issues of land in Aberffraw formerly held by Lleucu ferch Dafydd Foel, a free tenant who married Ieuan ab Elidir, a royal bondman.[68] Nest ferch Maredudd ap Dafydd ap Hywel was a landed proprietor of some substance in Trelywarch and Caergybi, but in her case, too, the head failed to rule the heart. She married Goronwy ap Rhirid Crydd, a royal bondman of Carneddor, without licence and in 1386-7 the escheator accounted for the issues of her lands.[69] The offspring of this union would be royal bondmen and, indeed, in 1437-8 the inheritance was described as having descended to Nest's grandson, Goronwy ap Maredudd, a bond tenant.[70]

An interesting case arose in 1371; it was concerned with the right to present to a vacant prebend in the collegiate church of Caergybi or Holyhead.[71] The right belonged to the descendants of Llywarch ap Bran and Hwfa ap Cynddelw and by this time it was divided among a large number of them. The prince's attorney claimed that the prebend was in his master's gift because one of the joint heirs, Tangwystl ferch Maredudd Llwyd, whose brother Llywelyn had died without legitimate heirs, had married a bondman and her share had therefore fallen to the prince, which gave him an interest in the presentation. The heirs' answer was that according to custom the decision of the patrons was by majority vote. One tends to regard the division between free and bond as a deep social gulf but marriages across it were not at all uncommon in Wales or England.[72] It may be that in the everyday life of the local community questions of status were not always as important as one might think; nature did not always imitate art.

One restriction attached to bond status was that the bondman could not marry at all, be his spouse free or bond, without his lord's licence. Such licences were usually granted in the commote court, as in the cases of Gwenllian ferch Bleddyn ap Cyfnerth who made fine at the Malltraeth court in 1325-6 and

67  TNA SC6/1150/1, m.8b; 1153/5, m.14b. Manumission in the march is discussed briefly by R.R. Davies, op.cit., p.385.
68  TNA SC6/1150/4, m.6a.
69  TNA SC6/1151/3, m.9b.
70  TNA SC6/1153/4, m.14b.
71  TNA E315/ 166, ff 5a-b.
72  For a brief discussion of the consequences of mixed marriages in England see E. Miller and J. Hatcher, *Medieval England: Rural Society and Economic Change, 1086-1348*, pp.132-3.

Gwerfyl ferch Mab *Dummagh* who did likewise at one of the Llifon courts during the same year.[73] Mixed marriages, at least in the fifteenth century, seem to
have been dealt with at the justice's sessions. Iorwerth Tew *Tastour*, a royal
bondman, was amerced ten shillings in 1418-9 for giving his daughter Cari in
marriage to a free tenant and in 1437-8 Gwenllian ferch Deicws, a free tenant
of Dindryfwl, paid 13s 4d for licence to marry her daughter Gwerfyl, who was
free on her mother's side but not on her father's, to any free man she liked.[74]
One of the most interesting examples comes from the escheator's account for
1481-2; this was the case of Dafydd ab Ieuan Moel, a recently deceased bondman of the commote of Menai.[75] Dafydd had made a will, had married his
daughters to free men and had himself married the daughter of Meurig ap Llywelyn ap Hwlcyn of Bodeon, one of the leading free tenants in the commote
of Malltraeth, all apparently without licence. The wealth of Dafydd ab Ieuan
Moel sheds an interesting light on the economic position of some bondmen;
he was worth £26 18s 4d in goods and chattels as well as being the son-in-law
of the head of what was to become one of the leading Anglesey families.

A bondman could not make a will, nor could he take holy orders. The reason
for the first of these restrictions was that in theory his property belonged to
the lord, while the second is explained by the fact that ordination conferred
freedom, thereby depriving the lord of the bondman's services. Llywelyn ab
Ieuan ap Dafydd of Hirdre-faig paid ten shillings in 1441-2 for licence to make
two or three bondmen his executors and to leave his goods to whoever he
chose, and in the same year Ieuan ap Hywel ab Ieuan ap Madog, a bond tenant
of Hendre Rhosyr, paid 6s 8d for licence to bequeath his goods and chattels to
any royal bondman of that township related to him by blood.[76] In 1452-3 Ieuan
ap Mato ab Ieuan ab Einion of Rhosmor paid £1 10s to make a testament and
to appoint whomsoever he liked as executors; the fine suggests that his was a
fairly substantial estate.[77] Licence to take orders was also available on payment
of a fine. On 9 June 1374 the prince granted Madog ap Dafydd ab Iorwerth,
the sixth son of a royal bondman of Hirdre-faig, licence to take orders from
any bishop who would confer them, and in 1456-7 Dafydd ap Dafydd ap
Symon, otherwise known as Dafydd ap Dew Moel, chaplain and bondman of
Hendre Rhosyr, made fine of one pound for his trespass in accepting priest's

---

73  TNA SC2/215/11, mm.7, 8: the fine in the first case was 2s and in the second 1s; 1s was also paid
by a widow from Llifon. The dates cannot be any more precise because these are lists of estreats
(extracts from the court rolls).
74  TNA SC6/1152/7, m.10a; 1153/4, m.14b. For a late example of a licence to marry (in this case
a bondwoman from Cleifiog in 1502) see NLW, Llanfair and Brynodol P654.
75  TNA SC6/1155/6, m.11a.
76  TNA SC6/1153/5, mm.14b, 14a; Ieuan ap Hywel's brother paid the same sum for a similar
licence.
77  TNA SC6/1154/1, m.17b.

orders without obtaining the necessary licence.[78]

The status and the concomitant obligations of bond tenants did bring them before the courts from time to time. The question of bond status itself might be tested; in 1303 Tudur Fychan was amerced 6s 8d for not being present in court to pursue a claim that two men were his bondmen and in a case heard at Aberffraw before the deputy-justice in 1351 concerning the status of Dafydd Ffon, the prince's attorney claimed that he was a bondman but the jury found in his favour.[79] There is a similar action on the only surviving medieval plea roll from Caernarfonshire.[80] But the issue which usually brought bondmen into the courts, led them to petition and generally gave rise to grievances was that of customary rents and services. The long struggle of the bondmen of Penrhosllugwy was only the best-known of these complaints; there were many others, both from the authorities and the tenants. Goronwy Crach, the *rhingyll* of Menai, was amerced two shillings in 1304-5 for failing to summon the prince's bondmen of Treferwydd, Tre Feibion Pyll and Tregarwed to carry millstones to the new windmill at Newborough.[81] At Kennington in 1305 the bondmen of Menai complained to the prince that they were forced to perform their customary works on his mills in a different way to that to which they had been accustomed under the personal rule of Edward I and Llywelyn ap Gruffudd.[82] Some time in 1325-6 the communities of five bond townships in Talybolion were amerced at the hundred court for their failure to repair the chamber of the *rhaglaw* at Cemais, and at the Twrcelyn hundred court held around the same time the bondmen of the commote were amerced five shillings for not repairing the court buildings at Penrhosllugwy, the whole community, both free and bond, was amerced one pound for not repairing the solar and the bond tenants of the *maerdref* paid two shillings for their failure to perform their share of the work.[83] In the same year the bondmen of Rhosmynach and Deri were amerced for not repairing the king's mills.

The line of demarcation between free and bond could be a fine one. It appears that both conditions could exist within a single family. In 1390-1 the escheator accounted for 30 virgates of land and a turbary in the free township of Llysdulas in Twrcelyn which had come into his hands because Gruffudd ap Hywel ap Gwerfyl and Tangwystl ferch Ieuan ap Gwerfyl had died without direct heirs, with the result that a bondman, Einion ab Ieuan ab Einion of Pen-

78  TNA E163/24/1, m.6a; SC6/1154/2, m.19a.
79  TNA E101/119/33, m.5; SC6/1305/16, m.2a.
80  Keith Williams-Jones, op.cit., p.xcvi
81  TNA E101/120/1; *Governance of Gwynedd.*, p.61.
82  *Rec.Caern.*, p.214.
83  TNA SC2/215/11, mm.8, 9.

rhosllugwy, was the next heir.[84] Free tenants who married unfree spouses might lose their land; in the same way bond tenants might forfeit their goods and chattels. In 1418-9 those of Tudur Ddu, a bondman of Deri, who married his daughter Hoen to a free tenant of Llanllibio without licence, were valued at 6s 8d, and those of Hywel ab Ieuan ab Adda of Hendre Rhosyr, whose daughter Efa married a free tenant of St Beuno, at two shillings.[85] If a bondman died intestate or without a direct heir the lord might claim his goods; those of Dafydd ap Tegwared Ddu of Llanllibio who died without heirs in 1420-1 were valued at 5s 2d, while Hywel ap Dafydd Hir of Penrhosllugwy had property worth £5 3s in 1441-2.[86]

The bond tenant of 1450 may have been a very different creature from that of 1300. For the earlier part of this period Keith Williams-Jones's comments on the difficulties faced by bondmen are probably generally applicable and a certain stigma remained well into the sixteenth century; as late as 1551 to call a free man a villein was actionable.[87] But the world had changed and villeinage was dying out. It has been said of the institution in England that it was not abolished but withered away and that the withering began in the fourteenth century. This may also be true of Wales, although the great problem is the shortage of evidence, compared with the quantity of medieval manorial records to be found in most English county record offices.[88] The Anglesey evidence does suggest that by the fifteenth century bond status was regarded more as a means of raising revenue by collecting fines for licence to dispense with restrictions than anything else. This was true of many societies; in England, for example, there was considerable exploitation of villeinage to the benefit of the lord's pocket and its deliberate revival in the duke of Buckingham's lordships of Brecon, Hay, Huntington and Newport had the same end in view.[89] In Anglesey in 1494 the sheriff was ordered to find out who were bondmen of the prince and to send their names to the Caernarfon Exchequer and to try and remove all those who were living outside bond townships to their places of origin.[90] This shows that the authorities were trying to solve the problem of the shortfall in bond rents. They soon found that this course offered no solution and the Gordian knot was eventually cut by the series of charters granted to

84  TNA SC6/1151/6, m.9a
85  TNA SC6/1152/7, m.10a.
86  TNA SC6/1152/9, m.8b; 1153/5, m.11b. The same restriction applied in the march. (R.R. Davies, op.cit., p.386).
87  Keith Williams-Jones, op.cit., pp.xcv-xcvii; W. Ogwen Williams, *Tudor Gwynedd*, pp 44-5 and 45 n1.
88  R.H. Hilton, *The Decline of Serfdom in Medieval England* (1969), p.31
89  ibid., pp.51-5; T.B.Pugh, *The Marcher Lordships of South Wales, 1415-1536*. pp.49-50.
90  J. Beverley Smith, 'Crown and community in north Wales in the reign of Henry Tudor', 164-6.

the lordships and the principality of Wales in the next decade.[91]

Whether he was rich or poor, there were some things which distinguished the freeman from the bondman.[92] If the bondman was a 'man without ancestry', this was certainly not true of the freeman. For him ancestry was of paramount importance; it made him what he was. The free Welshman was of unblemished free descent. His place in the social order had nothing to do with his economic position; blood, not land or wealth, was the decisive factor and, however poor he might be, nothing could take this away. He was not tied to the soil but could come and go as he pleased. There was nothing to stop him making a will or taking holy orders and, as long as his partner was of free birth, he needed no man's permission to marry. His interest in the land he held came to him by inheritance. In fact, this meant that the individual proprietor had no right to his land since it came to him by virtue of his membership of the lineage and it was to the lineage that the land belonged.[93] The evidence of extents and surveys from all parts of Wales makes this clear; at Archwedlog in the commote of Uwch Aled in the lordship of Denbigh in 1334 three heirs of the stock of Gruffudd ap Maredudd held the free *gwely* of that name and at Cemlyn in Talybolion in 1352 Gwely Hwfa ap Gwion was likewise held by a number of heirs.[94]

Not only bondmen owed renders and services. By 1284 most of those due from the free townships had been commuted to rents of assise although in the cantref of Aberffraw some of this commutation was fairly recent.[95] The bishop of Bangor's free tenants owed only fealty and suit of court in addition to rents.[96] The 1352 extent is the most detailed of these documents and it shows that most free tenants owed suit to the county and hundred courts. There were some exceptions; at Heneglwys in Malltraeth, where the tenants held of the church of Heneglwys, most of them owed nothing but suit to the mill of Dindryfwl and at Llaneilian in Twrcelyn, where they held of St Eilian, they only attended the county or the hundred court if involved in an action there.[97] What many free tenants did owe was labour service on the buildings of the prince's court. At

---

91  The background to the charters is discussed in ibid., 145-71.
92  Freemen are discussed in R.R. Davies, op.cit., pp.354-78, and Keith Williams-Jones, op.cit., pp.lxxxix-cxiii; see also W. Ogwen Williams, 'The social order in Tudor Wales', pp.167-78.
93  R.R. Davies, op.cit., p.360.
94  P. Vinogradoff and F. Morgan, eds., *Survey of the Honour of Denbigh, 1334* (1914), p.203; *Extent of Anglesey*, p.206.
95  For example, there were recent commutations of food renders in Trefdraeth Wastrodion and Trefdraeth Ddisteiniaid (Smith, 'Extent of Anglesey 1284', p.101.)
96  The free tenants of Bodffyddion in Dindaethwy also owed suit of mill (*Rec. Caern.*, p.103) and others had to contribute to the repair of the lord's weir.
97  *Extent of Anglesey*, pp. 159-60, 222. Some exemptions were of very long standing as in the case of the heirs of Llywelyn ab Ednyfed in Lledwigan Llys who owed no relief or *amobr* before or after the conquest (ibid., p.161).

Trefdraeth Wastrodion the heirs of the free *gwelyau* had to build and maintain part of the lord's chamber at Aberffraw and in Llifon similar services were due from the descendants of Hwfa ap Cynddelw at Conysiog; many other free kindreds in Llifon, however, were exempt.[98] This was also the pattern in the other commotes; some kindreds owed labour services and some did not. After 1352 the tenants of the commotes of Llifon and Malltraeth each paid an annual fine of £1 10s in commutation of labour services at Aberffraw.[99] The free men of Twrcelyn paid an annual fine of three pounds for the repair of the court at Penrhosllugwy and the bondmen paid one pound.[100] There was probably a similar obligation in the other commotes; one would hardly expect the free tenants to have repaired the roof of one of the court buildings, although at the justice's sessions on 8 June 1327 tenants from the townships of Chwaen, Trefowain and Bodewran in Llifon were summoned for failing to work on the buildings at Aberffraw.[101] Nevertheless, it was highly unlikely that a man who had served the prince as *rhaglaw* or *rhingyll* would be expected to perform such works and commutation was the logical sequel, especially since there was really little use for the court buildings after 1282.

Kinship was the cement which bound the free element in society together.[102] The kindred groups which appear in the pedigrees really did exist and the 1352 extent shows their presence in different parts of Anglesey. In Twrcelyn Llysdulas was held by *gwelyau*, the eponyms of which were three sons of Carwed and four sons of his son Griffri, while the three *gwelyau* at Bodafon claimed descent from three sons of Cadrod Hardd.[103] The latter lineage was also to be found at Trefarthen in Menai and at Trefednyfed, Clegyrog and Trefadog in Talybolion.[104] In Talybolion the descendants of Rhys Goch were at Caerdegog and Cemlyn and those of Llywarch ap Bran at Trelywarch; the Llywarch lineage was also at Porthaml in Menai.[105] The most important kindred in Llifon was that of Hwfa ap Cynddelw which held Conysiog and its subsidiary hamlets. The *gwely* of Einion ap Rhodri in Cleifiog may have been descended from Rhodri ab Owain Gwynedd.[106] In Malltraeth the leading kindred was that descended from the poet Gwalchmai ap Meilir which was represented at

---

98  ibid., pp. 162-3, 179-81
99  TNA SC6/1150/3, m.1a-b.
100  *Extent of Anglesey*, p.233.
101  NLW. Peniarth 405, pp.424-5.
102  For outline genealogical tables of the main medieval lineages in Anglesey see Appendix A, Tables 1–5.
103  *Extent of Anglesey*, pp.217-21.
104  ibid., pp. 256, 192-3, 195-6, 204-6.
105  ibid., pp. 202-4, 206-7, 254-6.
106  ibid., pp. 179-81, 182-3; see also *Governance of Gwynedd.*, p.141.

Lledwigan Llys, Trefdraeth Wastrodion, Trefdraeth Ddisteiniaid and Tre-walchmai, probably as a result of royal generosity in the twelfth century, while in Menai Gwydryn, like Porthaml, may have been held by descendants of Lly-warch ap Bran.[107] The main kindreds in Dindaethwy were those of Mabon Glochydd in Porthaethwy and Cerrigtegfan, Geraint in Pentraeth and Iarddur in Penhwnllys, Twrgarw, Llanddyfnan and Tre'r Fraint; the stock of Rhys Goch was represented at Mathafarn Wion and possibly at Castell Bwlchgwyn.[108] But the most important group in Anglesey was that of Wyrion Eden, the descendants of Ednyfed Fychan. Ednyfed had been granted townships with extensive jurisdictional powers probably by Llywelyn ab Iorwerth, and from these bases at Trecastell, Erddreiniog, Penmynydd, Gwredog, Trysglwyn and Tregarnedd his descendants dominated the county in the fourteenth century.[109]

Men were still conscious of their lineage and their ancestry in the fourteenth century. The twelve prebends in the collegiate church of Holyhead, formerly the *clas* of Caergybi, were in the gift of the kindreds of Llywarch ap Bran and Hwfa ap Cynddelw. Early in the fourteenth century the two kindreds petitioned the king, reminding him that they had been patrons of Caergybi from time immemorial and asking for the investigation and recognition of their rights when the provostship next fell vacant.[110] A petition from the people of Anglesey at about the same time included a request that the descendants of Iorwerth ap Llywarch of the commote of Menai might have the Llanidan ferry as they had always had it in the time of the princes.[111] Also significant is the petition, dated 1318-9, of Llywelyn ap Gruffudd ab Iorwerth of the cantref of Aberffraw in which he said that his father and ancestors had *pencenhedlaeth* over the heirs of the lineage of Hwfa ap Cynddelw.[112] He had not been able to lay claim to the office before because of his youth and lack of power, but now he asked the king for it. This is a particularly interesting petition because it reveals the existence in post-conquest Wales of such a person as the chief of the kindred. There are other references to lineage in an action brought at the sessions at Caernarfon in September 1327.[113] A number of tenants from the cantref of Aberffraw were summoned to answer the king and the farmer of the royal mills in the cantref as to why they had not done suit. They all claimed that they had mills or shares

---

107 *Extent of Anglesey*, pp. 161-6, 171, 250.
108 ibid., pp. 245-6, 236-7, 235, 240, 244-5, 242-3, 239. The stock of Mabon Glochydd was also represented at Carnan in Menai (ibid., p.256).
109 The descendants of Ednyfed Fychan are discussed in detail in Glyn Roberts, 'Wyrion Eden', pp.179-214.
110 *CAP*, p.453
111 ibid., p.452. There was a Gwely Iorwerth ap Llywarch in Porthaml and another in Trelywarch (*Extent of Anglesey*, pp. 254, 193).
112 *CAP*, p.84. What little is known of the office is discussed *in Llyfr Colan*, pp.166-7.
113 NLW Peniarth 405, pp.418-9.

in mills of their own; six denied the obligation because they lived on the lands of the stock of Hwfa ap Cynddelw which had seven private mills and another four of the lineage of Gruffudd Sais of Llifon did the same because they had a share in the mill of Cymynod. It was also denied by members of the stock of Rhodri because they lived on the land of Einion ap Rhodri and had a share in the mill of Cleifiog.

The rights and interests of the kindreds of Hwfa ap Cynddelw and Llywarch ap Bran in particular must reflect a pattern of social, tenurial and ecclesiastical organisation that prevailed before the twelfth-century reform of the Welsh church. Later sources also suggest that these lineages went further in their reflection of an earlier social pattern. The stock of Hwfa held Conysiog and its dependent hamlets of Bodedern, Llechylched, Deubwll, Llechgynfarwy, Yr Arw, Trefangharad, Tregadrod, Bodfeddan and Treriffri.[114] This was a large area which comprised most of the commote of Llifon and it might be argued that Conysiog was originally a *maenol* or social and tenurial unit which consisted of a court and a number of dependent hamlets; Conysiog was in fact divided into two townships, Conysiog Lys and Conysiog Lan.[115] It is possible that the whole *maenol* of Conysiog with its bondmen was granted to Hwfa ap Cynddelw in the twelfth century and here, too, may lie the origin of the commote of Llifon which was unique in having no *maerdref.* Something similar may be seen in Menai with the stock of Llywarch ap Bran. According to Henry Rowlands Porthaml was once known as a *maenol* and had dependent hamlets at Llanedwen, Bodlew, Bodowyr, Myfyrian, Berw Uchaf, Cefn-poeth and Trescawen.[116] Here again there may have been a grant of a *maenol* to a prominent figure in twelfth-century Gwynedd. Aberffraw with its circle of hamlets might be regarded as a *maenol* and Dindryfwl in Malltraeth might once have been another; in 1352 it had dependent hamlets at Cerrigcafael, Grugor, Ddrudwy and Trewalchmai.[117] There may have been other such multiple estates in Anglesey; at Cemais the church of Llanbadrig was in the township of Maenol Badrig and in 1352 the *maerdref* of Cemais had a hamlet at Meiriogen.[118]

The division between free and bond was important but that between male and female was fundamental. Women at the higher levels of society certainly

---

114  *Extent of Anglesey*, p.179;  see also G.R.J. Jones, 'Post-Roman Wales', p.296.

115  The best discussion of the *maenol* is by G.R.J. Jones, op.cit., pp.298-320; see also *Llyfr Colan*, pp.161-3 and David Longley, 'Medieval settlement and landscape change on Anglesey', *Landscape History* 23 (2001), 41-3.

116  Henry Rowlands, 'Antiquitates parochiales', in *Arch.Camb.*, 1849, pp.37-41.

117  G.R.J. Jones, op.cit., pp. 297, 332. In the case of Dindryfwl the name may be significant.

118  *Extent of Anglesey*, p.215;  Longley (op.cit., 41) also suggests Llysdulas and Bodafon as other possibilities.

did not enjoy equality, partly because of that organisation of feudal society that made primogeniture necessary. It is, however, important to remember that among medieval women were such outstanding figures as Eleanor of Aquitaine, Joan of Arc, Margaret Paston and St Catherine of Siena, while Chaucer's Wife of Bath must have been more than a figment of the poet's imagination.[119] The wife of a great nobleman was certainly far from being a downtrodden chattel. In Saunders Lewis's picture of the wife of Llywelyn ab Iorwerth the imagination of the dramatist may well have come nearer that truth which the lack of contemporary sources denies the historian. It is the lack of sources which makes it difficult to say much about the position of women in medieval Wales.[120] In many ways Welsh historians are fortunate in the existence of a mass of medieval poetry but little of it is addressed to the women of Anglesey and what there is tends to be formal praise or elegy. The exception is the misadventure which befell Dafydd ap Gwilym at Newborough when a spirited and attractive girl poured his gift of wine over his messenger's head.[121] On the whole the poets do not shed much light on the position of women in society but this was not their function; they were professional entertainers.

But there are other references to women.[122] Surviving court records are few but they are a valuable source. The long list of those amerced in 1325-6 for not attending the county court includes 37 women who must have been landowners in their own right.[123] Various women were fined at the hundred courts for failing to pay rent, again an indication of land-holding and from time to time they were involved in actions of trespass or debt; being in debt may sometimes be a sign of independent economic activity.[124] One woman was amerced at the Malltraeth tourn held on 9 March 1323 for ploughing her strips in the common fields before the appointed time, which suggests that women worked their own lands; in England, where the evidence is so much more extensive, there was

---

119  For general discussions of women in the middle ages see Friedrich Heer, *The Medieval World* (trans. Janet Sondheimer, 1963), pp.317-23, and John B. Morrall, *The Medieval Imprint: the founding of the western European tradition* (1970), pp.116-29. The feudal reasons for the depression of the status of medieval women are discussed by Marc Bloch, *Feudal Society* (trans. L.A. Manyon, 1965), pp.200-1. A recent study of the part played by women in the rural economy is R.H. Hilton, 'Women in the village', in idem., *The English Peasantry in the Later Middle Ages*, pp.95-110.

120  The best discussion is by Llinos Beverley Smith, 'Towards a history of women in late medieval Wales' in Michael Roberts and Simone Clarke, eds., *Women and Gender in Early Modern Wales* (2000), pp.14-49; for the position of women in Welsh law see Dafydd Jenkins, *Cyfraith Hywel* (1970), pp.33-43, and Dafydd Jenkins and Morfydd E. Owen, eds., *The Welsh Law of Women* (1980).

121  D. Johnston et al., eds., *Cerddi Dafydd ap Gwilym* (2010) pp.340-2.

122  For women in the workforce in medieval Wales see particularly Llinos Beverley Smith, 'Towards a Welsh womens' history', pp.30-35.

123  TNA SC2/215/11, mm.1-5.

124  R.H. Hilton, op.cit., p.105.

nothing unusual in this.[125] Retail trade, especially in dairy products, was one activity in which medieval women often played a prominent part. During the period for which court rolls have survived, a few women were amerced for buying and selling outside the market although most of those punished for this offence were men.[126] In a violent age women could be as violent as their menfolk; at the Malltraeth tourn held on 20 August 1325 the wife of Hywel ap Dafydd was amerced one shilling for drawing blood and there is no lack of similar cases.[127] They also contributed their share of petty crime and at different sheriff's tourns held in 1346 women were accused of stealing a cow, sheep, corn, wool, flour and peas.[128] One of the most interesting cases came before the Twrcelyn hundred court at Penrhosllugwy on 23 June 1346 when Llywelyn ab Iorwerth ap Tegwared relinquished his sister Gwenhwyfar as a common [blank].[129] This suggests that Gwenhwyfar was declared a common prostitute; such a step could be taken in open court by a woman's kindred to avoid paying *amobr* for her.[130]

There is a good deal of evidence of women as landed proprietors and as sharers in lands held by kindred groups. Among the bishop of Bangor's free tenants in 1306 there were seven women, while among the unfree there were no fewer than 31. The 1352 extent names 24 free tenants who were women, along with seven unfree and six in Newborough. Although the 1406 list of submissions after the Glyn Dŵr revolt includes only five women, a list of amercements for non-suit to the county and hundred courts in 1410-11 names 138 from Dindaethwy, Twrcelyn, Talybolion and Llifon, a significant figure when one remembers that suit of court was an obligation attached to the free tenure of land.[131] But it is deeds that have the most to say about women as proprietors and they show very clearly that women were involved in the land market. In a large number of them women who were obviously tenants in their own right appear as sellers or purchasers.[132] They also disposed of personal property; in

125  TNA SC2/215/8, m.2a
126  TNA SC2/215/11, mm.12, 14, are examples of women trading outside the market.
127  TNA SC2/215/11, m.11; these attacks were always on other women.
128  G.P. Jones, 'Anglesey court rolls, 1346', *TAAS* 1930, pp. 34, 38; 1932, pp. 43, 45, 46.
129  ibid., 1932, p.43.
130  R.R. Davies, 'The status of women and the practice of marriage in late medieval Wales', in *The Welsh Law of Women*, pp. 111-12; in some lordships she was handed a white rod as a symbol of her status. For other examples from the hundred court of Ardudwy in Merioneth in 1325-6 see E.A. Lewis, 'The proceedings of the small hundred court of Ardudwy in the county of Merioneth from 8 October 1325 to 18 September 1326', *BBCS* 4 (1928), 160, 162.
131  NLW Llanfair and Brynodol M3; it is possible that the large number of women may be due, at least in part, to the deaths of their male kinsfolk in the revolt. The 1413 rental of the lands of Gwilym ap Gruffudd includes 17 women among his Anglesey tenants (BUASC Penrhyn 1599). An Anglesey rental of 1410-11 contains eight and one dated 1 November 1415 contains 28 (BUASC Penrhyn Further Additional rentals 1410-11 and 1 November 1415).

1429 Arddun ferch Gruffudd, the wife of Rhys ap Dafydd ap Rhys of Trehwfa
in Bodedern, left two shillings to the parish church and four yards of white
cloth to the poor and in 1433 Elen ferch Gruffudd ap Hywel Escut of Llechgynfarwy made several bequests of animals.[133] One feature of Welsh nomen-
clature in the middle ages which is sometimes puzzling to the outsider can be
explained, at least in part, by the position of women as landed proprietors. This
is the use of the matronymic in personal names; this may sometimes indicate
illegitimacy but in deeds it stems from the context. A person's name was more
than a statement of descent; it was in effect an abstract of title since it proved
his or her right to hereditary lands. Consequently if a man conveyed lands
which he had inherited through his mother, it was natural that he should de-
scribe himself by his maternal descent. The point is clearly made in some
deeds; in about 1491-2 Dafydd ap Hywel ap Gruffudd *alias* Dafydd ab Angharad ferch Gaynor ferch Ieuan ap Madog released his lands in Mathafarn Eithaf which had once been the inheritance of his aunt Margaret ferch Gaynor
and her husband to Goronwy ap Dafydd Fychan. The descent from his maternal grandmother was given in the deed because this was how the lands had
come to him.[134]

What surviving records do not reveal is the background to such things as
marriage and childbearing. According to Welsh law there were several ways in
which a woman could be bestowed or bestow herself in marriage and there
was in medieval Wales, as elsewhere in Europe, an unresolved clash between
the sacramental and contractual conceptions of marriage.[135] At the upper levels
of society marriage was a major step, often involving the alliance of two kindreds and complex questions of land and money. Existing sources do not have
very much to say about this but one late example may reflect the way in which
these things were arranged.[136] On 17 October 1539 the arbitrators in the dispute
between Robert ap Rhys ap Llywelyn ap Hwlcyn and his son Hugh and Rowland Griffith of Porthaml made their award. Hugh ap Robert had eloped with
Rowland Griffith's daughter Margery. The arbitrators ruled that he was to

132  There are 21 such deeds among the Baron Hill documents, 6 in the Penrhyn papers, 2 in the
     Plas Coch papers, 9 in the Sotheby collection and 3 in the Carreglwyd papers. The Penrhyn
     Further Additional deposit at Bangor includes a cartulary containing copies of 212 deeds
     recording acquisitions of land between 1329 and 1488; 38 of the parties are women.
133  NLW Bodewryd Correspondence 1034 (I am indebted to the Revd Dr Dafydd Wyn Wiliam for
     this reference); Sotheby 32.
134  BUASC Baron Hill 1014.
135  This is discussed by Dafydd Jenkins, *Cyfraith Hywel*, pp.33-43; also *Llyfr Colan*, pp.52-3. In
     'The significance of the law of Hywel' (*THSC* 1977, p.69) Professor Jenkins makes the point
     that although the status of women in Welsh law was higher than it was in English law, they were
     still second-class citizens. The most recent treatment of the subject is R.R. Davies, 'The status
     of women and the practice of marriage in late medieval Wales', pp.94-103.
136  NLW Sotheby 145.

marry her by the end of November and that his father was to entail his lands.
After the marriage the two families were to meet at Newborough and there the
bride and groom would ask Rowland Griffith's forgiveness, which would be
given. Hugh's father was to lease lands of the annual value of two pounds to
him, presumably to enable him to support a wife. The arbitrators also stipulated
what trousseau should be provided for Margery by her father; she was to have
three pairs of garments, one pair in time for the wedding and the rest the following May and a cap and frontlet of velvet along with sufficient beds or bed-
ding. The bride's father was also to give one hundred head of cattle to his new
son-in-law 'to be sorted after the use and custom of the countre'; they were all
to be handed over by the middle of 1541 and they were counted by the long
hundred.[137]

An elopement could be a blow to a landowner's plans for his daughter and
ill-feeling was bound to follow. Margery Griffith may have been a girl of spirit
who was determined to choose for herself but most marriages at this level of
society were probably arranged. In any case, reconciliation was easier because
bride and groom were social equals. The elopement of a free heiress with a
bondman would have been a different matter altogether, especially since it
could involve the forfeit of a free inheritance to the crown. There are some
other references to the marriage of heiresses. Madog ap Goronwy Fychan of
Gwredog in Twrcelyn, a great-grandson of Ednyfed Fychan, had one daughter,
Generys, who was his heir. Madog died in 1348 and in 1356-7 the wardship of
Generys was sold to two clerics, her kinsman Hywel ap Goronwy ap Tudur,
the archdeacon of Anglesey, and Ithel ap Roppert, later archdeacon of St Asaph
for £30. Before long she was married to another kinsman, Gruffudd ap Gwilym
ap Gruffudd, a descendant of Tudur ab Ednyfed Fychan and ancestor of the
Penrhyn family.[138] There was another marriage within this kindred group in
the next generation when Morfudd, the daughter of Goronwy ap Tudur of Penmynydd, who was drowned in 1382, became the first wife of Gruffudd ap
Gwilym's son Gwilym.[139] But marriages, however carefully arranged, did not
always last the course. In 1388, for example, Morfudd, daughter of Goronwy
ab Ieuan ap Dafydd and her husband Henry Clerk, a burgess of Beaumaris,
separated; to prevent Henry from making any claim to her inheritance in Beaumaris, Newborough and Crymlyn she quitclaimed her rights in it to two
trustees.[140]

---

137  The long hundred was 120.
138  TNA SC/1149/7, m.5a; Glyn Roberts, 'Wyrion Eden', pp.207-8.
139  Glyn Roberts, op.cit., p.208.
140  BUASC Penrhyn Further Additional, 3 May 1388; for another example of marriage breakdown
     see G.P. Jones and Hugh Owen, eds., *Caernarvon Court Rolls* (1951), pp.15-16.

The bondman and the freeman might be described as full members of society; they owed their place in it to their birth. There were others, however, who had no such birthright but had come into the community from outside, sometimes from other parts of Wales and sometimes from further afield. The incomer stood next to the bondman in the social order; he was the avowry tenant who had come into the lordship or the principality from outside and who paid a small annual fine for the lord's protection.[141] Behind this tenure lay the idea that every man should have someone to answer for him, an idea common to most societies; its roots in Wales are to be found in Welsh law in the person of the *alltud* or man from another kingdom who was under the protection of king, prince, or lord.[142] This was because he had no kindred to take responsibility for him. Avowry tenants appeared before the courts from time to time. In 1304-5 Cynddelw ap Thomas and his brother Cynwrig were each amerced one shilling for withdrawing from the prince's avowry and concealing an annual rent of two bushels of wheat for 21 years.[143] At the Mall-traeth tourn held on 5 March 1326 Madog and Dafydd ab Adda of Heneglwys each paid an avowry fine of one shilling and at the Llifon tourn on 23 February 1325 Mab Brawdfaeth was amerced one shilling for withdrawing from avowry.[144] The goods and chattels of any avowry tenant who died without heirs naturally went to the prince.[145] There was certainly no shortage of immigrants; in 1296-7 the income from avowry fines in the commote of Menai alone was 10s 8d and in 1306-7 the total from the whole county came to £3 0s 8d.[146]

For a few years after the introduction of a new system of accounting in 1350 the accounts give more details. In 1350-1 there were eleven tenants in Dindaethwy, 33 in Llifon, twenty in Talybolion and nine in Twrcelyn; they each paid an annual fine of fourpence and their heirs paid the bondman's relief of 6s 8d.[147] The profits of the Anglesey avowry were farmed by Thomas Spencer who paid two pounds a year. In 1351-2 there were another fifteen in Dindaethwy, six in Malltraeth and eleven in Twrcelyn and there were more again

---

141 Avowry tenants are discussed by William Rees, *South Wales and the March*, pp. 179, 221-2, and Arthur Jones, ed., *Flintshire Ministers' Accounts, 1301-1328*, pp.xxxi-xxxiii. See also Derrick Pratt, 'Medieval people: the advowry tenants of Bromfield and Yale', *TDHS* 36 (1987), 5-27.

142 *Llyfr Iorwerth*, pp.58-9; *Llyfr Colan*, p.38.

143 TNA E101/120/1.

144 TNA SC2/215/11, m.10; 215/9, m.7a.

145 In 1322-3 the goods and chattels of the deceased avowry tenant Einion ap Gruffudd were worth five shillings (TNA SC2/215/8, m.4a).

146 John Griffiths, 'Early accounts relating to north Wales, *temp.* Edward I', in *BBCS* 15, pp, 152-4, 16, p.122.

147 TNA SC6/1149/1, mm.1b, 4b, 5b, 6b.

in 1352-3, 1354-5 and 1355-6.[148] This large number of immigrants may be connected with the effects of the Black Death and the consequent labour shortage.
After 1355-6 the accounts are less detailed and the avowries for the whole
county were farmed at sums varying from five pounds in 1360-1 to £2 2s in
1408-9 after the Glyn Dŵr revolt.[149] Avowry tenants might provide a pool of
migrant labour; they might, on the other hand, rapidly become part of the local
community, acquiring land and consequently a stake in it. In 1351-2 Iorwerth
ap Brawdfaeth was leasing escheat lands in Llifon and in the 1352 extent
avowry tenants held escheat lands at Cleifiog, Tre'r-ddôl and Treddolffin, all
in that commote; escheat lands were an obvious way for a hard-working but
landless man to build up a landed inheritance.[150] Avowry fines were still being
collected in the fifteenth century.

The most common immigrants from outside Wales have always been English
and English names were not infrequent in medieval Anglesey. Most of their
bearers were connected with the town of Beaumaris, intended from the beginning to be an English colony. Beaumaris burgesses did buy property elsewhere
in the county and they did sometimes move into the ranks of the gentry, as did
the Bulkeleys, but they did so from an Anglesey base. The occasional Caernarfon burgess might also have Anglesey interests. The cognomen *Sais* is irrelevant
in this context. It could mean someone who could speak English, or who had
been to England, or who had an English parent, or who admired and imitated
English ways.[151] More interesting, perhaps, are such people as Cecilia Anglica
who was an alewife in Talybolion in 1324-5 or William Anglicus in Llechgynfarwy in 1321; Cecilia may have been the first of many English licensees in Anglesey.[152] One or two strange names are to be found in the ranks of those who
submitted in 1406; Wilcock ap Wathampton of Talybolion may have been the
son of the Caernarfon burgess Walter Haunton and Janyn Franc of Dindaethwy
may have been able to speak French or even have been a Frenchman who had
found his way to Anglesey after the French wars.[153]

148  TNA SC6/1149/1, mm.1, 4b, 5b, 6b;  SC6/1149/2, mm.1a, 2b, 5a;  1149/3, mm.3a, 5b;  1149/5,
     mm.3a, 3b, 4b;  1149/6, m.2a. The totals over the whole period were 42 in Dindaethwy, 64 in
     Llifon, 71 in Talybolion, 40 in Twrcelyn and 6 in Malltraeth.
149  TNA SC6/1150/1, m.2b;  1152/4, m.1a.
150  TNA SC6/1149/2, m.3b;  *Extent of Anglesey*, pp. 182, 187, 188. The entry for Carnan in Menai
     states that avowry tenants owed demesne services (ibid., p.254).
151  Melville Richards, 'Gwŷr, gwragedd a gwehelyth', *THSC* 1965, p.41.
152  TNA SC2/215/10, m.1;  215/5, m.1.
153  Keith Williams-Jones, 'Caernarvon', in Ralph A. Griffiths, ed., *Boroughs of Medieval Wales*, p.95;
     he was known in Caernarfon as Gwilym ap Wat;  Melville Richards, op.cit., p.31;  Janyn Franc
     was pardoned an amercement of sixpence at the Dindaethwy hundred court in 1382-3 because
     he had nothing (TNA SC6/1150/9, m.7a).

Anglesey's closest neighbour was Ireland. Irish links with Gwynedd were of long standing; one need only think of Gruffudd ap Cynan, of the refuge found there by various members of the Gwynedd dynasty and of the contacts reflected in the story of Branwen. The cognomen *Wyddel* was not uncommon; the ancestor of the Porthaml family was Ieuan Wyddel who flourished in the middle of the fourteenth century and whose mother was said to have been Irish.[154] The word also appears several times in the 1406 submissions which include Gruffudd ab Iorwerth ap Gwyddel, Ieuan ab Ieuan y Gwyddel and his brother Iorwerth and Llywelyn ap y Gwyddel in Llifon and Mato Wyddel in Menai. Other examples include Efa ferch Dafydd Wyddel and her nephew Gruffudd ab Iorwerth Wyddel at Bodedern in 1346 and an avowry tenant, Iorwerth ab Iorwerth Wyddel, in Llifon in 1355-6.[155] Other names also suggest Irish influence, among them the bond township of Twrllachied in Twrcelyn and Gwas Sanffraid ap Twrllach who lived in the township of Maenol Badrig in Talybolion in 1325-6.[156] In 1406 Dafydd ap Jack ap Diarmed was one of those from Dindaethwy who submitted and in 1441-2 the escheator stated that the goods of Jankyn ap Deicws ap Rhirid of Crymlyn y Mynydd, indicted for felony, were in the hands of Ieuan Teiliwr and Patrick Heyrish.[157] All these names suggest an Irish presence in medieval Anglesey which, given the facts of geography, is hardly surprising.

154 Henry Rowlands, 'Antiquitates parochiales', in *Arch.Camb.*, 1848, p.242.
155 G.P.Jones, 'Anglesey court rolls 1346', *TAAS* 1930, p.43; 1932, p.49; TNA SC6/1149/6, m.2a.
156 TNA SC2/215/11, m.14.
157 TNA SC6/1153/5, m.12a.

# 6   Rich Man, Poor Man

IF THE SOCIAL ORDER was based on personal status, wealth and position were based above all on the tenure of land. The basic division between free and bond applied to land as well as to men and free land in Wales was hereditary land or land the possession of which was vested in the kindred group rather than in the individual As far as Welsh law was concerned, the individual freeholder had only what amounted to a life interest in his inheritance. He enjoyed it by virtue of his membership of a kindred group called the *gwely*, usually translated as 'resting-place'.[1] The *gwely* bore the name of a paternal ancestor and these eponyms seem usually to have flourished in the late twelfth or early thirteenth centuries. At Porthaml in Menai in 1352, for example, two of the heirs of Gwely Iorwerth ap Llywarch were Ieuan Wyddel and Gruffudd ap Goronwy who were, according to the pedigrees, a great-great-grandson and a great-grandson of Iorwerth.[2] Each *gwely* owed a fixed annual rent, which was a commutation of former food-renders and services, to the prince; the rent was due in quarterly instalments on 1 November, 2 February, 1 May and 1 August.[3] At Llanddyfnan in Dindaethwy in 1352 the heirs of Gwely Goridyr owed a total of £2 0s 1d.[4]

Since each member of the *gwely* only enjoyed a life interest it was the right to a share rather than outright proprietorship that was passed on to the heirs and this hereditary land could not be alienated, a rule which, in the reign of Edward II, caused considerable protest in north Wales. However, if a freeholder died without heirs his or her share escheated to the lord; in 1363-4 the escheator accounted for nine virgates of arable land and three virgates of turbary in Trefdraeth Ddisteiniaid, the share of Genilles ferch Philip ab Ithel who died without heirs.[5] A share would also be escheat if its tenant died against the peace or

1 A considerable amount has been written on the *gwely*. The most recent discussion of its origins is Dafydd Jenkins, 'A lawyer looks at Welsh land law', pp.241-7; see also T. Jones Pierce, *Medieval Welsh Society*. passim. Its nature in the later middle ages is summed up by R.R. Davies, *Lordship and Society in the March of Wales, 1282-1400*, p.360.
2 *Extent of Anglesey*, p.254; Bartrum, *WG*, Llywarch ap Bran 2, 3.
3 *Extent of Anglesey*, p.160.
4 ibid., p.240.
5 TNA SC6/1150/2, m.7a.

was convicted of felony. In Gwely Wyrion Sandde in Bodafon in Twrcelyn in 1352 there were four bovates of escheat land formerly held by Dafydd Rwth ap Llywelyn Foel and according to the sheriff's account for 1317-18 these had been forfeit because Dafydd had been outlawed for homicide and had died in custody in Beaumaris castle.[6] His share of the total rent of £3 3s 8d due from the *gwely* was elevenpence; the liability to pay the rent was divided among the heirs. Those shares which came into the lord's hand would be leased out for an annual rent, in addition to which the lessee was still responsible for the holding's original contribution.

The term *gwely* originally meant the kindred group, but it came to be applied to the group's land as well. Its size could vary considerably as could the shares of individual members. Gwely Iorwerth ap Llywarch in Porthaml included six bovates or about 24 acres of escheat land in 1352 and this was reckoned to be a twenty-fourth part of the whole; if this were the case the whole *gwely* would have consisted of 576 acres, but, since measurements of land were variable, it was probably a good deal less.[7] In Gwely Cadwgan ap Llywarch in the same township half a bovate of escheat land was said to be a twentieth part which would make a total area of some 40 acres. Such a discrepancy seems a little excessive but a great deal of topographical investigation of particular townships is needed. In some cases a single *gwely* was coterminous with a township, as in the *case* of Gwely Conws in Tregornor in Malltraeth and Gwely Goronwy Foel in Trefollwyn in Menai.[8] Some figures for the size of *gwelyau* are to be found in the 1306 extent of the bishop of Bangor's lands. In Bodwylog in Dindaethwy the seven members of one *gwely* held 24 bovates or 96 acres; here, again, *gwely* and township seem to have been coterminous.[9] A similar pattern may be seen nearby at Llamel where three heirs held a *gwely* of six bovates or 24 acres, while at Nanhwrfa in Menai there was rather more congestion with fourteen heirs sharing four bovates or sixteen acres.[10] At Cornwy Lan in Talybolion, on the other hand, 33 tenants held a carucate and a half, which was approximately 90 acres and at Bodegri in the same commote eleven held two carucates or 120 acres.[11] Thus the density of settlement varied considerably in different parts of Anglesey as did the amount of land available to each individual heir.[12] Some of these would have found it difficult to subsist on their shares of arable land alone; the difference between Bodorgan in Malltraeth where six members of one *gwely*

---

6  *Extent of Anglesey*, p.220; TNA SC6/1227/14.

7  *Extent of Anglesey*, p.255.

8  ibid., pp. 167, 253.

9  *Record of Caernarvon*, p.102.

10  ibid., pp. 102, 104.

11  ibid., pp. 106, 107.

12  G.R.J. Jones, 'The distribution of medieval settlement in Anglesey', pp.40-1.

held a carucate in common and Nanhwrfa is staggering. It is, however, important to remember that this extent was made in 1306 at a time when the medieval population was probably at its highest and pressure on the land was a very real problem. The problem was to be solved by the Black Death and the subsequent drastic decline in population which went on into the fifteenth century.

Both the size of the free *gwely* and that of the individual share were therefore capable of almost infinite variation and this is confirmed by escheators' accounts. In 1311-2 Madog ab Idwal's share in Gwely Madog ap Meilir in Pentraeth amounted to fourteen bovates or 56 acres, by any standards a substantial holding.[13] At the other end of the scale in the same township Heilin *Tuth* had held two acres in the same *gwely*. Such a disparity is probably explained by the fact that the share of each member was, according to the rules of partible succession, divisible among his heirs and much therefore depended on the number of sons an individual freeholder might father. But an heir was not solely dependent on the arable land which fell to his lot. A share in the inheritance also included a share in the pasture and the waste which belonged to the *gwely* and these grazing rights could make a considerable difference. It could also include a share in the mill and its profits and many free kindreds had their own. In fact, what any heir inherited and what the lord gained by escheat has been aptly described as 'a bundle of rights and inheritance' and not the actual land. The nature of the *gwely* is probably best summed up by reference to examples in the 1352 extent. In the township of Tre Fraint in Dindaethwy there were two free *gwelyau*, those of Wyrion Iarddur and Wyrion ap Cynddelw.[14] The heirs of the former were Dafydd Llwyd, Madog ap Gruffudd and others and they owed no rent. They had their own mill called Melin Braint. The heirs of the second *gwely* were Ieuan ab Ieuan and Ieuan ab Ednyfed who likewise paid no rent and who had a share in the mill. All the heirs owed suit to the county and hundred courts and they paid the free tenants' relief, *gobrestyn* and *amobr* of ten shillings when the occasion arose. The rents due from free *gwelyau* varied a great deal, as did the services they owed. Some, like the two in Tre Fraint, owed nothing; of the others, the one owing the highest rent was Gwely Tudur ab Itgwon and *Gothlon* ab Itgwon in Trefdraeth Ddisteiniaid which paid £4 11s 2d annually, while the lowest rent was the 1s 1d due from Gwely Bleddyn ap Llywarch in the hamlet of Bodwigan in Talybolion.[15] Those who did not have their own mills owed suit of mill, although some could choose the royal mill at which it was performed. Some also owed labour services at the *maerdref* on the court buildings and some contributed to the various *cylchoedd* or commutations of

13  TNA SC6/1227/8.
14  *Extent of Anglesey*, pp.244-5.
15  ibid., pp. 165, 194.

the billetting rights of some of the prince's officers and animals.

It may have been the plague and its consequences which led to some *gwelyau* having only one heir in 1352; examples were Gwely Cynwrig ap Tegwared in Trefdraeth Wastrodion, held by Llywelyn Moel and Gwely Maredudd ab Einion in Botan in Talybolion, held by Gruffudd ap Dafydd Goch.[16] In such cases the surviving heir must have been related closely enough to those who had died to inherit their shares, but the number of holdings which did escheat to the prince or to the crown in the fourteenth century meant that there was a substantial dilution of the kindred group in many townships. Even so, the *gwely* remained as the basic unit on which the traditional rents were assessed and in which land was held, although it was often no more than a formal framework. In a list of estreats of fines for non-suit to the county and hundred courts from free tenants in Dindaethwy, Twrcelyn, Llifon and Talybolion in 1410-11 those in Mathafarn Eithaf, Mathafarn Wion, Pentraeth, Nantmawr, Bodafon and Llysdulas were listed under *gwelyau*. In Llifon those who held lands in the five Conysiog *gwelyau* which bore the names of the sons of Hwfa ap Cynddelw were not associated with any townships.[17] These *gwelyau* seem to have retained a certain importance; in 1433 Madog ab Iorwerth ap Hywel ap Gruffudd, a free tenant of Bodedern, conveyed all his share in Gwely Iorwerth ap Hwfa in that township to Dafydd ab Ieuan ap Hywel of Llysdulas.[18] A crown rental of Twrcelyn drawn up in 1549 also shows that the *gwely* still had some meaning, as, indeed, it had in some places into the seventeenth century.[19] Here again the tenements in the townships of Bodafon and Llysdulas were arranged under *gwelyau* and the rental shows just how far the process of dilution had gone. It also shows that, just as the holding of an individual tenant was usually made up of scattered strips in open fields, so was the territory of the *gwely* scattered over the township and one township might well have outliers in others, which reflected the original pattern of settlement. The lands of Gwely Wyrion Sandde in Bodafon included tenements near the churches of Penrhosllugwy, Coedana and Llanfihangel Tre'r-beirdd as well as between Maenaddwyn and Mynydd Bodafon and on the mountain itself.[20] A similar distribution can be seen in the rental of the Llysdulas *gwelyau* and had more such rentals survived for other parts of Anglesey it is likely that they would reveal much the same pattern. One must not think of an individual holding as resembling a coherent landed estate, although these had begun to make their appearance.

---

16  ibid., pp. 162, 196.
17  NLW Llanfair and Brynodol M3.
18  NLW Bodewryd 186.
19  T. Jones Pierce, 'An Anglesey crown rental of the sixteenth century', pp.87-101.
20  ibid., pp.92-3.

Although the *gwely* was the normal pattern of free tenure a number of unfree kindreds held land in the same way; this tenure was called *tir gwelyog*.[21] The members of these *gwelyau* had a heritable interest but at the same time they were subject to some of the restrictions and obligations of bond status and they were tied to the soil. The 1306 extent sheds some light on the size of unfree *gwelyau;* at Llangoed in Dindaethwy one group of five heirs held six bovates or 24 acres and another of seven twelve bovates or 48 acres.[22] In each case there were as many messuages as there were tenants; these were the homesteads. Another *gwely* in Llangoed had one member who had the whole holding of six bovates. Practically all the unfree *gwelyau* in Dindaethwy had holdings of six bovates, but the picture was very different on the bishop of Bangor's lands in other parts of Anglesey. At Conysiog Lan in Llifon four carucates or about 240 acres were held in common by 49 tenants and at Bodeon in Malltraeth one holding of two-thirds of a carucate or 40 acres was held by one man.[23] The holdings in Malltraeth, Llifon and Talybolion were measured in carucates which indicates that they were larger than those in the other three commotes; in Twrcelyn, as in Dindaethwy, they were smaller and more uniform. In Llandyfrydog five *gwelyau* held eight bovates or 32 acres each and in Moelfre four held two and a half bovates or ten acres each.[24] Thus in theory neither free nor bond tenants could claim anything more than rights in the lands which were vested in the kindred; a man's tenement was not his land but his share. Nevertheless, there was 'a strong individual consciousness of possession' and a tenant's share was normally passed on to his heirs.[25]

The middle of the fourteenth century is usually seen as the time when the individual landed proprietors began to take the place of the kindred. Even before this, however, escheators' accounts list those tenements which had come into the hands of the crown by forfeiture or by the failure of heirs and this does reveal something of the size of individual shares in the *gwelyau*. Some holdings were measured in acres, some in bovates and some in virgates; the acre was not the modern statute acre but the Welsh acre made up of five *llathenni* or yards.[26] The *llathen* was called a virgate in medieval records, but it must not he confused with the English virgate which was a unit of between twenty and thirty acres. The bovate in Gwynedd consisted of four acres and it thus corresponded to the Welsh *erw* which was the basic unit of measurement of tenements within the *gwely*. The carucate was usually 60 acres, but all these units

---

21  The tenure is discussed in the preceding chapter.
22  *Rec. Caern.*, p.100.
23  ibid., pp. 105, 104.
24  ibid., pp.107-9.
25  T. Jones Pierce, 'The *gafael* in Bangor MS. 1939', in *Medieval Welsh Society*, p.226.
26  ibid., pp.216-7.

could vary considerably in size. The holdings listed in Anglesey escheators' accounts before 1350 ranged in size from the 60 acres in Gwydryn formerly of Cynwrig Teg who was killed in the war of 1282 to the two acres in Mathafarn Eithaf formerly of Cynwrig ap Madog ap Cynwrig.[27] There are not enough tenements listed in these accounts to suggest any average size; the figures in the episcopal extent of 1306 suggest an average free holding of just under five acres but this average conceals a good deal of local variation.

Although the Black Death eased the pressure of population on the available arable land, it did not follow that more was at the disposal of individual members of the kindred since the holdings of those without heirs were escheat. The longest list of escheats is that in the great consolidated escheator's account for 1408-9 and this is the only source which provides a large enough sample to work out an average figure.[28] The average for holdings of arable land where the area is given comes to a little under nine acres and this does seem to fit in with the pattern elsewhere; it has been suggested that in the march the majority of Welsh tenants had arable holdings of ten acres or less.[29] This must lead one to ask if such a holding was enough to feed a man and his family. Historians differ about the minimum size necessary for self-sufficiency but most hold the view that the figure lay somewhere around ten acres.[30] Very many holdings were substantially less than this and some were less than an acre, but the point has already been made that holdings within the *gwely* also included grazing rights and livestock husbandry played as important a part in the medieval rural economy as did the growing of crops.

Some had already amassed sizeable holdings, sometimes within the limits of the hereditary land and sometimes by purchase. Some of these nascent estates were the result of grants, particularly to the descendants of Ednyfed Fychan, by the thirteenth-century princes. In 1352 Hywel ap Goronwy and his brother Tudur held the townships of Trecastell and Penmynydd and part of Erddreiniog in Dindaethwy and some of their kinsmen held Gwredog in Twrcelyn.[31] Other townships were also held by individuals; Llywelyn ap Dafydd Fychan held Bodffordd in Malltraeth, Hywel ap Madog ap Llywelyn, the son of the leader of the 1294-5 revolt, held Lledwigan Llan in the same commote, Meurig ap Bleddyn held Bodfardden in Talybolion and Gruffudd ap Tudur Llwyd and his brother Ieuan held Clorach in Twrcelyn.[32] But some of the most

---

27  TNA SC6/1227/7, 8.
28  TNA SC6/1233/1.
29  R.R. Davies, op.cit., p.393.
30  E. Miller and J. Hatcher, *Medieval England: Rural Society and Economic Change, 1086-1348*, pp.147-8.
31  *Extent of Anglesey*, pp. 235, 245, 227.
32  ibid., pp. 158, 162, 208, 226.

interesting accumulations appear in the 1408-9 account and their presence there shows that some promising estates had ceased to exist, largely because of the Glyn Dŵr revolt. Hywel ab Ieuan ap Cynwrig had held a total of 72 acres, most of which was in Trefowain in Llifon, and Hywel ap Gruffudd ap Hywel, who died in rebellion, had held a total of twenty bovates or 80 acres of arable, mountain and marsh in Trefieuan and Llyslew in Menai. Another victim of the revolt was Gwilym ap Gruffudd ap Tudur Llwyd, a member of a leading local family whose father and uncle had held the whole township of Clorach in 1352. In Llifon Gwilym had held five messuages and about 75 acres of arable, mountain land, marsh, meadow and turbary in Eiriannell. This may well have been his inheritance; his great-grandfather had been granted a share in Gwely Iorwerth ab Ieuan there by Edward I.[33] But he also held a considerable amount of land in Talybolion, much of which had been acquired by him. This consisted of six messuages and some 77 acres in Caerdegog, Cemlyn and Maenol Badrig along with annual rents of 18s 6d from tenants who held other lands in Maenol Badrig and Bodronyn of him on lease. Gwilym ap Gruffudd ap Tudur Llwyd may be compared with the prominent Beaumaris burgess Richard Golding who also appears in the account. He had acquired a substantial estate, largely as a result of his marriage to the daughter and heiress of another burgess, William de Cranwell. In Beaumaris itself he had 28½ burgages as well as about 300 acres in the town lands. In Pentraeth he had 29 acres and in Menai he and his wife had one-third of the township of Trefollwyn. Other lands in the commote of Malltraeth and in Caergybi were let to tenants.

As the holdings of some individual proprietors increased in size it became difficult for them to work all the lands themselves, especially when they were scattered over a number of townships. Land might therefore be leased to tenants, some of whom were anxious to acquire more but were not in a position to buy. Others might sell their patrimony to a richer and more successful neighbour who would then lease it back to them.[34] This was one development in the pattern of land-holding which gathered momentum after the Black Death and to some extent it is reflected in the 1408-9 escheator's account. The lands of Goronwy ap Tudur ap Hywel in Maenol Badrig had been seized because of his outlawry for felony in 1390-1 and in 1408-9 the escheator answered for annual rents from two of his tenants.[35] The lands of Nest ferch Maredudd ap Dafydd ap Hywel in the same commote had also been forfeit in 1390-1 because she had married a bondman; she had two tenants in Dronwy who paid annual

33  ibid., p.186.
34  For an example of this in the lordship of Chirk see A.D. Carr, 'The making of the Mostyns: the genesis of a landed family', in *THSC* 1979, p.151.
35  TNA SC6/1151/6, m.8b; 1233/1.

rents of fivepence and tenpence and Richard Golding had ten tenants in Caergybi.

By far the most interesting lists of tenants are the rentals of the lands of
Gwilym ap Gruffudd ap Gwilym, drawn up in 1410-11, 1413 and 1415.[36] In
Anglesey in 1410-11 he had 107 tenants in eighteen townships in five of the six
commotes; in Dindaethwy there were 53 tenants but only in Penmynydd and
Dinsylwy Rys. The 1413 rental only lists the Anglesey tenants in Dindaethwy.
There were 196 of them in fourteen townships and the total rent-roll came to
£53 3s 11½d (the total of rents in 1410-11 was £43 7s 7d of which £15 0s 1d
was from Dindaethwy). The total in the 1415 rental, from all six commotes,
was £65 14s ½d. The highest rent in 1410-11 was £3 13s 4d paid by two tenants
for the mill of Melin Gwna in Trefdraeth Ddisteiniaid; some others, in all the
rentals, were no more than a few pence. These rentals say little about the size
of individual holdings; in Twrgarw in 1413 Adda ab Ieuan ap Madog was paying
2s 6d for twenty virgates, while in Pentraeth Tudur ab Ieuan ab Ieuan ap Madog
paid tenpence for nine and Ieuan ap Hywel ab Iorwerth sixpence for six, but
that is all. In Penmynydd the unit of tenure was the *gafael;* a complete one was
generally arrented at fifteen shillings but some were valued at ten shillings, 16s
8d or even one pound. In Dinsylwy most tenements were arrented at 3s 8d.
Some tenants in all the rentals were described as being in the second or third
year of their tenancies. The rentals tell us little about estate management but
they do reveal the existence of one large estate with many tenants and an estate,
moreover, which was largely based on purchase rather than inheritance.[37]

Gwilym ap Gruffudd was probably the wealthiest man in Anglesey in the
early fifteenth century and he went on adding to his wealth.[38] Perhaps the most
important question posed by the many surviving deeds which record the acquisition of land and the accumulation of estates is how such purchases were
financed; in the case of Gwilym ap Gruffudd it is possible that an answer is
available. By 1400 he was a man of some standing in Anglesey, having held
various local offices, among them that of sheriff. He would later inherit a substantial amount of land from his father and he was also able to acquire properties forfeited by those who had died against the peace during the Glyn Dŵr
revolt. But these gains were overshadowed by his investments after the rebellion
and the key to these may lie in a document which forms part of a previously

36  BUASC Penrhyn 1599 (1413); Penrhyn Further Additional, rental, 12 Henry IV; Penrhyn
    Further Additional, 1 November 1415.
37  J. Rowland Jones, 'The development of the Penrhyn estate up to 1431' (University of Wales,
    unpubl. M.A. thesis, 1955), pp.165-7.
38  The career of Gwilym ap Gruffudd is discussed by A.D. Carr, 'Gwilym ap Gruffudd and the rise
    of the Penrhyn estate', *WHR* 15 (1990), 1-20.

unknown accumulation of Penrhyn documents which came to light in 1983.[39] This is a list of debts owing to Gwilym dated 14 October 1406: the total owing to him was at least £41 (not all the document is legible) and he was also owed quantities of corn and millstones. The debts included some due to him from the time when he was sheriff of Anglesey but what is particularly interesting is the range of other debts. Some owed him money for corn and others for wine. Loans of money made at various centres, among them Chester, Beaumaris, Caernarfon and even Llannerch-y-medd are recorded, which suggests mercantile activity, and many payments were due for the lease of oxen and for the hire of cows and their milk. Some entries suggest tithe-broking and it is also possible that he was farming the Anglesey millstone quarries. It is interesting to see a man of Gwilym's standing involved in so many commercial transactions and one cannot but wonder if other *uchelwyr* were as enterprising. Even before the revolt this list shows that he was a wealthy man and it may well explain how he was able to invest so much in land.

The fact that Gwilym's estate was largely the result of his activity in the land market, along with the survival of so many medieval deeds, shows how active and flourishing this market was. Since free land was vested in the lineage rather than in the individual and since the individual heir had no more than a life interest, it followed that he had no right to dispose of his inheritance and that it was to be divided equally among his heirs.[40] But it was inevitable that some whose shares were too small for subsistence might wish to dispose of them and that others who were more fortunate or more ambitious might wish to add to their lands. After 1282 there was increasing pressure for this to be permitted although the Statute of Wales made no change in Welsh land law. At Kennington in 1305 the community of north Wales asked that they might be permitted to buy and sell land; this was not granted, but in 1316 it was conceded for a period of three years.[41] Despite representations, the concession was not renewed and in theory the ban on free alienation remained.

There was one way around the prohibition. This was by means of a transaction which was provided for in Welsh law called conveyance in *tir prid*.[42] The transaction is best described as a kind of perpetual gage of the land in question;

39  BUASC Penrhyn Further Additional, 14 October 1406; the document and its significance are discussed in detail in A.D. Carr, 'The wealth of the medieval Welsh gentry: the case of Gwilym ap Gruffudd of Penrhyn' in *Proceedings of the Harvard Celtic Colloquium* 20-21 (Cambridge, Mass., 2007), 222-31; see also Carr, 'Gwilym ap Gruffudd', 7, 12-13.

40  Llinos Beverley Smith, 'The gage and the land market in late medieval Wales', in *Econ. Hist. R.*, N.S. 29 (1976), 537-41; J. Beverley Smith, 'Crown and community in the principality of north Wales in the reign of Henry Tudor', 147-9; R. R.Davies, op.cit., p.402.

41  *Rec.Caern.*, p.214; Ivor Bowen, *The Statutes of Wales*, p.29.

42  The *tir prid* conveyance is discussed in detail by Llinos Beverley Smith, op.cit.; J. Beverley Smith, op.cit., 149-51; R.R.Davies, op.cit., pp.408-10.

the gage was usually for an initial term of four years and it was renewable in-definitely for further four-year periods until it was redeemed. This did actually happen from time to time; in 1494, for example, a *prid* conveyance of a tene-ment in Llaneilian made in 1445 was redeemed by the son of the gagee.[43] Thus the money raised on the security of the land was, to all intents and purposes, the purchase price. There was considerable local variation in the pattern of the transaction and in the initial term but the essence was always the same; the gage was never redeemed and the gagor might even go so far as to quitclaim or release the reversion to the gagee.[44] In this way it was possible to dispose of or to acquire hereditary land and very many *tir prid* deeds survive. Indeed, it was one of the main ways in which an estate could be built up. There are ex-amples from all over Wales, two of the best-known being those accumulated by Tudur ab Ithel Fychan, the ancestor of the Mostyn family, in and around Whitford in Flintshire in the middle years of the fourteenth century and by Gruffudd ab Aron of Peniarth in Merioneth in the early years of the fifteenth.[45]

There is no lack of evidence of such transactions in Anglesey. The earliest surviving deed is one of about 1313 in which Hywel ab Iorwerth, a free tenant of the commote of Talybolion, conveyed all his lands and tenements in Llangefni to Sir Gruffudd ap Rhys or Gruffudd Llwyd for two pounds.[46] When Gwilym ap Gruffudd of Llaniestyn died in 1376 he left all his *tir prid* lands in Anglesey and Caernarfonshire to Gruffudd ap Gwilym ap Gruffudd, a re-minder that such lands, unlike hereditary ones, could be bequeathed since technically the gagee had an interest in the land rather than the land itself.[47] The forfeited lands of Gwilym ap Gruffudd ap Tudur Llwyd in 1408-9 included some which he had obtained in the same way in Llifon and Talybolion; there are many other examples in the same account.[48] The transaction was also used in towns; there are ten such deeds from Beaumaris among the Baron Hill pa-pers.

The *tir prid* conveyance played as important a part in the working of the late medieval land market in Anglesey as it did elsewhere in Wales. But although well over one hundred such deeds survive, there are far more ordinary con-veyances of land in fee. At first sight this may seem strange in view of the ille-gality and, indeed, the impossibility, of such conveyances. However, as with so

43  BUASC Baron Hill 1337; the original conveyance is BUASC Baron Hill 1327.
44  A number of examples drawn from different parts of Wales are discussed by Llinos Beverley Smith, '*Tir prid:* deeds of gage of land in late-medieval Wales', in *BBCS*, 27 (1977), 263-77.
45  A.D. Carr, 'The making of the Mostyns', pp.152-6; J. Beverley Smith, op.cit., 149-50.
46  BUASC Mostyn 731.
47  BUASC Penrhyn 5; Llinos Beverley Smith, 'The gage and the land-market in late medieval Wales', 549.
48  TNA SC6/1233/1.

many restrictions, the power of dispensation was often a convenient way of raising money and individuals might obtain licences to acquire lands in fee on payment of a fine.[49] The general prohibition of alienation of hereditary land might thus be overcome without any need to resort to a *tir prid* conveyance. Licences were granted at the justice's sessions and they were a useful source of profit. A number survive in collections of family papers; in 1368, for example, Dafydd Fychan ap Dafydd Llwyd of Trefeilir in Trefdraeth Ddisteiniaid made fine of £3 6s 8d for licence to acquire seventeen acres there from Llywelyn ap Dafydd Fychan.[50]

Although no medieval Anglesey plea rolls survive, fifteenth-century sheriffs' accounts contain references to many fines made for licences to acquire land; this was because such fines were paid in annual instalments, generally over three years and the sheriff had therefore to note that part was still unpaid. The large number of fines recorded again reflects the vitality of the land market. In the account for 1437-8, for example, there are ten, all made in that year, while the 1441-2 account includes instalments of four fines for licence to acquire land and four for pardon for acquiring it without licence.[51] Many of those who did seek licences and were active purchasers of land were, as one might expect, members of leading lineages; a typical example was Hywel ap Llywelyn ap Dafydd ab Ieuan of Berw in the commote of Menai, a descendant of Llywarch ap Bran. In 1421 he obtained a licence to acquire lands in Bodlew and Berw Uchaf and in 1437-8 he made fine of £3 6s 8d to acquire more in Berw Isaf and several adjacent townships. The fact that a number of different holdings are indicated suggests that he had already purchased them and that the licence was intended to be retrospective.[52] At the sessions held at the beginning of November 1438 Hywel obtained licence for further acquisitions in Rhoscolyn, Bryngwallan and Trefarthen. In the same month Llywelyn ap Tudur ap Cynwrig, a free tenant in Gwydryn, sold him land there and Sym ap Dafydd Goch of Trefarthen quitclaimed his rights in land in that township already conveyed to Hywel in *tir prid*.[53] Some of these purchases were substantial ones; in 1437-8 Hywel ap Conws ap Hywel of Trefowain in Llifon was granted a licence to acquire three tenements containing a total of 62 acres in that township and Rhodogeidio.[54] Conveyances in fee were conveyances by English law and the

49  J. Beverley Smith, op.cit., 150-1; T. Jones Pierce, 'Some tendencies in the agrarian history of Caernarfonshire during the later middle ages', in *Medieval Welsh Society.* pp.52-3.

50  NLW Llanfair and Brynodol D1129; for other examples see NLW Llanfair and Brynodol D1113, BUASC Baron Hill 1000, 1001, NLW Sotheby 7, 67, and NLW Carreglwyd i, 2352.

51  TNA SC6/1153/4, mm.16b-17a; 1153/5, mm.13b-14b.

52  NLW Llanfair and Brynodol D1113; this point about retrospective licences is made by J. Beverley Smith, op.cit., 150.

53  NLW Carreglwyd i, 2352, 2358, 2357.

54  TNA SC6/1153/4, m.16b

licence had to be followed by livery of seisin and usually a deed as evidence that the transaction had taken place before it had any force. But so many deeds have survived that they suggest that very many conveyances in fee took place without any licence at all and the fines for pardon may relate to those which were subsequently detected.

Many fines were also made at the sessions for licence to acquire lands by *cynnwys*. This was really a combination of Welsh and English procedure which served to swell the contents of the royal coffers. Under Welsh law illegitimacy was no bar to a share in the inheritance as long as a son was recognised by his father. This was changed by the Statute of Wales in which it was enacted that the Welsh law of inheritance should remain, except that illegitimate sons should no longer have a share.[55] *Cynnwys* was a legal device which was used as a way round the prohibition; to avail themselves of it those who sought free land had to obtain the licence of the lord or the prince, while the unfree had to be recognised in open court by their fathers.[56] The 1441-2 account includes ten licences to persons of illegitimate birth to acquire land by *cynnwys*, but only two of them were seeking to obtain land from their fathers; this suggests that the procedure had become one whereby any such person might acquire land.[57] The same account includes eight licences for avowry tenants to acquire land in this way. This was a natural development; as a man who came in from outside the avowry tenant had no patrimony and *cynnwys* was one way in which he could acquire hereditary land.

All these were ways in which land could be obtained. Yet another way was by leasing hereditary land which had escheated to the king or the prince for lack of heirs or because of forfeiture by the proprietor. Early fourteenth-century accounts contain details of many escheat lands which had been leased out. Thus land in Anglesey was constantly being bought and sold and this raises another question, that of price. In 1316 Madog Gloddaith paid £24 for four tenements and a share in a mill and a weir in Porthaethwy, while in 1337 Madog Ddu ap Meurig of Trysglwyn Ednyfed in Twrcelyn paid £1 4s for seven virgates there.[58] Three years later Hywel ap Goronwy ap Tudur paid two pounds for the conveyance in *tir prid* of lands in Perthgyr in Dindaethwy.[59] Later prices fluctuated a great deal; Gruffudd ap Madog Gloddaith and his son Rhys paid £40 in 1396 to Tudur ab Einion Goch ap Llywelyn, a free tenant of Porthaethwy, for all his lands in Porthaethwy, Cerrigtegfan, Castellior, Pwll-

---

55  Dafydd Jenkins and Morfydd E. Owen, eds., *The Welsh Law of Women*, pp.197-8; *Llyfr Colan*, p.147; G. P Jones, ed., *The Extent of Chirkland, 1391-1393* (1932), p.61

56  G.P. Jones, op. et. loc. cit.

57  TNA SC6 1153/5, mm.13b-14b.

58  BUASC Mostyn 716, Penrhyn 379.

59  BUASC Penrhyn 381

gwyngyll, Carnan Uchaf and Tregwŷr-rhyddion, a transaction which suggests a sizeable holding.[60] In 1466 Elen Bulkeley, the wife of William, paid twenty marks (£13 6s 8d) to Thomas ap Dafydd ap Tudur, the rector of Llanddyfnan, for the conveyance in *tir prid* of five tenements in Castell Bwlchgwyn in Dindaethwy and in the same year she paid five marks to Hywel ap Dafydd ap Tudur, presumably Thomas's brother, for five named tenements in Castell-Bwlchgwyn and four in Llanddyfnan.[61] In 1439 Madog ab Ieuan ap Hywel of Plas Coch in Porthaml paid £22 5s for lands in Gwydryn.[62] These deeds do not always state the full price but it is obvious that the cost of land was capable of almost infinite variation.

The best way to illustrate the working of the land market is to examine some of the best-documented townships. As most surviving deeds are in the archives of the larger landed families they must reflect a gradual concentration of proprietorship. Nevertheless, since the records of earlier conveyances had to be preserved as evidence of title, the whole history of changes in landownership can sometimes be traced. A good example is the township of Llanddyfnan in Dindaethwy, much of which came to form part of the Bulkeley estate; many fifteenth-century Llanddyfnan deeds survive among the Baron Hill papers. In 1415 Lleucu, the daughter of Dafydd Brytaen, conveyed Tyddyn Ieuan ap Cadwgan to Dafydd ap Tudur ap Dafydd ap Gwyn.[63] In 1421 Dafydd acquired land in Llanddyfnan from Dafydd ap Tangwystl ferch Gwenhwyfar ferch Madog and in the same year he obtained Tyddynod Mab Cynwrig Goch from Tangwystl, the daughter of Dafydd ap Madog.[64] In 1464 Dafydd's son Hywel conveyed a number of tenements in Llanddyfnan to Elen, the wife of William Bulkeley the elder, in *tir prid*. Two years later the same tenements were joined with others, among them Plas Hywel ap Dafydd ap Tudur, in a similar conveyance and this was followed in 1467 by their conveyance to William and Elen in fee.[65] It was not unusual to reconvey lands already conveyed in *tir prid* in fee as a means of strengthening title.[66]

This was not all of Dafydd ap Tudur's inheritance to find its way into the possession of the Bulkeleys. Hywel conveyed Tyddynod Mab Cynwrig Goch, acquired by his father in 1421, to William in 1466 and he disposed of more lands to William and Elen in 1468 and to Elen in 1477.[67] His brother Thomas,

---

60  BUASC Mostyn 4085.
61  BUASC Baron Hill 1098, 1097.
62  BUASC Plas Coch 2.
63  BUASC Baron Hill 1088
64  BUASC Baron Hill 1089, 1090.
65  BUASC Baron Hill 1095, 1097, 1100.
66  J.Beverley Smith, op.cit., 151.
67  BUASC Baron Hill 1099, 1103, 1111.

the rector, conveyed Tyddyn Llwyn Goronwy in Castell Bwlchgwyn to Elen in *tir prid* in 1464 and again in fee in 1468 and there were other conveyances in 1466 and 1468.[68] There were more in the next generation; with his wife Morfudd Hywel had at least two sons, Ieuan and Llywelyn. In 1470 Morfudd and Ieuan conveyed Bryn y Chwil in Llanddyfnan to Elen Bulkeley and this was followed in 1482 by a *tir prid* conveyance by Ieuan to Dafydd ap Hwlcyn ap Goronwy of Pentraeth of all his property.[69] He conveyed a messuage and lands to Edmund Bulkeley, one of William's sons, in 1488 and in 1497 he released all his lands in Llanddyfnan to Edmund.[70] Llywelyn ap Hywel ap Dafydd acquired land in the neighbouring township of Mathafarn Eithaf in 1483. He had three sons, Rhys, Thomas and Dafydd; Thomas's son Ieuan conveyed lands in Mathafarn Eithaf to his uncle Dafydd in 1523 and in the same year Dafydd conveyed all his lands and reversions in Anglesey to another of William Bulkeley's sons, Rowland.[71] Hywel ap Dafydd ap Tudur's daughter Myfanwy married her second cousin Hywel ap Dafydd ap Hywel ap Tudur and they too conveyed lands in Llanddyfnan and Castell Bwlchgwyn to the Bulkeleys in 1468, 1472 and 1473. In 1472 William and Elen Bulkeley confirmed their title to most of these acquisitions by levying two fines against Hywel and Myfanwy.[72]

A similar process can be seen in the two adjacent townships of Mathafarn Eithaf and Mathafarn Wion. In 1469 Dafydd ab Ieuan ab Iorwerth ap Hwfa conveyed a messuage in Mathafarn Wion to Ieuan ap Rhys ab Ieuan Llwyd of Llanddyfnan.[73] The following year Ieuan acquired three acres near Porthyllongdy in Mathafarn Wion from Gwerfyl ferch Lleucu ferch Dafydd Brytaen and her son Hywel and in 1473 Ieuan and his wife Mallt obtained a mansion and lands in Mathafarn Wion and Pentraeth from Tudur ap Goronwy ap Hywel ap Gruffudd Trefgoed.[74] Ieuan's son Thomas was also active in the land market and in 1489 he purchased Cnwc y Tair Lon and other lands in Mathafarn Wion.[75] This was followed in 1491 by Tyddyn Gobaith Bran and other lands in Castell Bwlchgwyn and in 1512 he obtained more lands in Mathafarn Wion from Rhys ap Tudur ap Sir Dafydd and his wife Angharad. Rhys, described as 'of Heneglwys', had acquired Hafod Grythwr and other properties in Mathafarn Wion from Goronwy ap Dafydd Fychan in 1510.[76] Goronwy had in turn

68  BUASC Baron Hill 1069, 1106, 1098, 1105.
69  BUASC Baron Hill 1108, 1118.
70  BUASC Baron Hill 1120, 1124.
71  BUASC Baron Hill 1024, 1029, 1030.
72  BUASC Baron Hill 1102, 1104, 1110, 1115, 1112.
73  BUASC Baron Hill 1005.
74  BUASC Baron Hill 1006, 1008
75  BUASC Baron Hill 1013.
76  BUASC Baron Hill 1121, 1021, 1020.

obtained lands in Mathafarn Eithaf in 1482, in the early 1490s and in 1506 from Dafydd ab Angharad ferch Gaynor, otherwise known as Dafydd ap Hywel ap Gruffudd.[77] In 1515 Thomas ab Ieuan ap Rhys conveyed all his lands in Mathafarn Wion, Castell Bwlchgwyn and Pentraeth to Rowland Bulkeley and this transaction was confirmed by a common recovery.[78]

The turnover of land in a number of other townships would repay investigation. But, although land was the basis of wealth, it is important to consider personal property as well. Extremes of wealth and poverty exist in every society and although it is the better-off who have generally left more records behind them the poor have never gone unrecorded. There were some whose only means of support was the charity of their more fortunate neighbours and who had therefore to beg for a living; this stratum of society does not appear all that often, but the few surviving records of local courts in Anglesey do reveal the existence of mendicancy. At the Malltraeth tourn held at Trefdraeth Ddisteiniaid on 12 March 1321 a case of begging was presented from Heneglwys and Bodffordd; Efa Ddu of Dindryfwl was amerced sixpence for the same offence as was a defendant from Trefednyfed at the Talybolion tourn three days later.[79] So few court records have survived that one cannot safely draw any firm conclusions; it might be pointed out that all these presentments appear in March 1321 and the previous harvest appears to have been a poor one.[80] However, begging, or, more accurately, perhaps, seeking *commortha*, was an institution long accepted in a society where the community accepted some responsibility for its less fortunate members.[81] A few indications of poverty are also to be found in accounts. In 1352-3 Dafydd Hakeney of the commote of Talybolion owed a fine of ten pounds but the sheriff stated that he had nothing on which it could be levied.[82] This is not easily explained since he was a man of some standing; in 1352 he was one of the Talybolion jurors when the new extent was drawn up and he was one of the heirs of Gwely Goronwy ab Ednyfed in Trefednyfed.[83]

---

77  BUASC Baron Hill 1009, 1014, 1015, 1019.

78  BUASC Baron Hill 1024, 1025.

79  TNA SC2/215/5, mm.1a, 2a; three others were amerced from Talybolion and there were cases from Twrcelyn as well.

80  J.M. Stratton and J. Houghton Brown, *Agricultural Records, A.D. 220-1977*, p.28.

81  The point about the lack of information about this section of society is made by R.R. Davies, op; cit., pp.397-8; he also discusses the exodus of tenants from various marcher lordships, suggests that they formed a 'pool of migrant labour' and mentions begging and *commortha*. The practice was forbidden from time to time in various lordships. For a brief discussion of rural poverty in England see J.Z. Titow, *English Rural Society, 1200-1350*, pp.93-6.

82  TNA SC6/1149/3, m.8b. In the same account Goronwy ab Ieuan was stated to have nothing on which a similar amercement could be levied but he did have lands in Crymlyn which could be taken up.

83  *Extent of Anglesey*, p.192. He was acting *rhingyll* of Talybolion in 1351-2 (TNA SC6/1149/2, m.4a).

In 1394-5 Thomelyn ap Dafydd Was and his brother Edward were unable to pay an amercement imposed on them for felony; they were both royal bondmen who had nothing except the labour of themselves and their sons and they were pardoned half the amercement.[84] The authorities do not seem, on the whole, to have been unjust in their dealings with the poor; in 1441-2 amercements on three brothers from Cemlyn who were bondmen were respited because they were poor and had been amerced through malice.[85]

One indication of poverty or, at least, of a shortage of liquid capital in rural communities is the amount of moneylending to be found there. As elsewhere in Europe, there was a good deal of money lent and borrowed in rural Wales in the middle ages, although, as Keith Williams-Jones pointed out, the professional moneylender did not exert the stranglehold which he so often had on the rural community in India or, indeed, in parts of Europe.[86] There was an increasing need for ready cash after 1284. Services and renders in kind were commuted to money payments, few could escape amercement from time to time as individuals or as members of the community and there were also the demands of royal or seigneurial tax-collectors.[87] All this meant an increasing demand for money in a society which was largely self-sufficient. Although the shortage of ready money in medieval Wales was not as great as has sometimes been suggested, the fact remains that a man whose assets amounted to a few cows or sheep and some corn might find it hard to raise the money to pay an amercement or contribute to a subsidy. A bad harvest, too, could cause a major crisis. In a world where kinship counted for so much many might have recourse to more prosperous kinsmen; otherwise they probably turned to friends and neighbours.[88] The few court rolls from the last years of Edward II's reign include some amercements for usury. At the Dindaethwy tourn on 9 March 1326 a woman from Pentraeth was presented for usury and was amerced the large sum of ten shillings and there were similar presentments at the Llifon and Taly-bolion tourns in September 1321 and at the Malltraeth tourn on 23 March 1322.[89] Four presentments from a handful of surviving court records can hardly be called an adequate sample, but the total of the amercements shows that usury, universally condemned by the medieval church, was regarded by the au-

84  TNA SC6/1152/1, m.7a.

85  TNA SC6/1153/5, m.13b.

86  Keith Williams-Jones, *The Merioneth Lay Subsidy Roll. 1292-3*, p.xxii. He discusses the general problem of liquidity in late thirteenth-century Gwynedd in pp.xx-xxiii. For usury in England see E. Miller and J. Hatcher, op.cit., p.151.

87  The point about the growing demand for cash is made by G. Duby, *Rural Economy and Country Life in the Medieval West*, pp.252-4; see also T. Jones Pierce, 'The growth of commutation in Gwynedd in the thirteenth century', pp.103-24.

88  Keith Williams-Jones, op.cit., p.xxii.

89  TNA SC2/215/11, m.1b; 215/5, mm.5b, 6a; 215/7, m.1a.

thorities as a serious offence. The fact that two of the four accused were women may reflect the part they played in economic life.

The assessment for the subsidy of 1292-3 for the commote of Malltraeth is the only such assessment from Anglesey to survive and it does shed some light on the amount of personal property owned by different members of a local community.[90] The wealthiest tenant there had livestock and corn worth £17 1s and the poorest fifteen shillings. Those whose goods were valued at less did not pay and household goods were not taxed. The goods of most taxpayers were worth between one pound and four pounds. But there is a limit to the use that can be made of an assessment of this kind. Other information may be found in the accounts of coroners and escheators, particularly the latter. One interesting account is that rendered in 1328-9 by the coroners of the borough of Beaumaris of the goods of Dafydd ap Hywel Ddu, killed by a blow on the head from Robert le Chamberlain.[91] The list shows that Dafydd was a pedlar or itinerant trader and his stock-in-trade, worth a total of £2 4s, included 60 ells of fabric, kerchiefs, gloves, purses, belts, thread, combs, needles, wax, ginger and pepper, along with numerous other items. This account does not in itself say much about Anglesey society but it does say something about local retail trade and the distribution of small but necessary household goods and personal items.

In 1377-8 the goods and chattels of Iorwerth ab Ieuan ap Cyfnerth who died intestate were valued at £1 12s 4d and those of Gruffudd Crythwr who killed Ieuan ap Dafydd ab Einion at £1 6s 8d; the value of the property of others who had either died intestate or without heirs or had been outlawed that year ranged from £1 15s in the case of Philip ab Ieuan *Dommok,* a royal bondman of Din-sylwy, to 4s 2d for Angharad, the wife of Madog Sionc.[92] In 1379-80 the possessions of two royal bond tenants were worth no more than 1s 4d.[93] The values given in these accounts were probably often under-estimated, as is suggested by the value of one shilling placed in 1391-2 on the horse which caused the death of Iorwerth ap Madog and which was therefore forfeit as a deodand.[94] Fifteenth-century accounts are, on the whole, more detailed. That for 1418-9 included five shillings in cash which had belonged to Angharad ferch Cuhelyn who died suddenly and intestate, nine shillings for the goods and chattels of Dafydd ab Einion ab Iorwerth who died intestate in his bed, 3s 4d for those of Dafydd ab Ithel, drowned in the water of Deri, 6s 8d for those of Gwenllian

90  TNA E179/242/49.
91  TNA SC6/1170/19.
92  TNA SC6/1150/4, m.6b.
93  TNA SC6/1150/6, m.6b.
94  TNA SC6/1151/7, m.9a.

ferch Ieuan Crythwr who was burned to death and two shillings for those of Gwenllian, the wife of Heilin ab Ieuan ab Iorwerth.[95] In 1420-1 the property of Edward Haryot, who killed a prominent Newborough burgess, Mato ab Ieuan Llwyd, comprised a horse and a saddle, a sword and twenty arrows, worth altogether 16s 4d.[96] Tano ferch Ieuan ab Adda who died intestate without heirs had the large sum of £3 6s 8d in cash; it had been paid to Deicws ap Cuhelyn, the prior of Beddgelert, who refused to hand it over to the escheator. Several others had livestock, which does seem generally to have had a very low value set on it; Efa ferch Madog ap Wyn, outlawed for felony, had nine affers, 51 sheep, a pan and a trivet but the total value was only fifteen shillings.

In 1424-5 the escheator accounted for sixteen shillings, the value of a book which belonged to a cleric, David Bryan, who had been drowned.[97] The account for 1437-8 must reflect an accident which befell the Porthaethwy ferry-boat on 21 March 1438.[98] Eight passengers were drowned and their property was sold very cheaply. Deicws ap Hywel ap Dafydd ap Cadwgan had two horses and a pig which fetched a total of 2s 4d and two shillings in cash. Of the other victims Ieuan ap Deicws ab Ieuan *Toger* was worth sixpence, Goronwy ab Einion ab Ieuan ap Madog 3s 10d, Jankyn ab Einion ap Tudur ten shillings, Llywelyn Pengraith £1 14s 4d, Goronwy Teiliwr four shillings, Dafydd ap Deicws ap y Gof 4s 6d and Ieuan ab Iorwerth ab Einion, the only bondman among them, fourteen shillings, which made him the second richest. Llywelyn Pengraith's goods included oatmeal, wheat, seven bullocks and two cows. The account for 1441-2 is more detailed; the richest of the four for whom the escheator accounted was a bondman, Hywel ap Dafydd Hir of Penrhosllugwy, who died without issue.[99] As well as livestock and crops he had bees, four ells of cloth, a harp, two trestles, a table and other domestic utensils; he was worth a total of £5 3s.

In 1449-50 two avowry tenants, Dafydd ab Einion Ddu of Cornwy Lys and Goronwy ap Rhys ap Goronwy Pill of Penhesgyn in Dindaethwy were worth thirteen pounds and £14 3s 4d, sums which suggest considerable prosperity.[100] The goods and chattels of Hywel ab Ieuan ap Gruffudd Ddu of Clorach, a fugitive felon, were valued at £14 12s 11d in 1471-2. A man of some substance, he had a quantity of cattle, 54 yards of woollen cloth and thread, three coverlets, three sheets, three blankets, a brass pot, a chest, bees, geese, poultry and oats.[101]

95  TNA SC6/1152/7, m.10a.
96  TNA SC6/1152/9, m.8b.
97  TNA SC6/1153/2, m.8a.
98  TNA SC6/1153/4, m.15a.
99  TNA SC6/1153/5, mm.11b-12a.
100  TNA SC6/1153/6, mm.14b-15b.
101  TNA SC6/1155/2, m.10b.

This was farming on a more substantial scale than most of those for whose goods the escheator answered and yet on 12 November 1470, at Rhosmynach, Hywel stole a cow from John ap Deicws Goch. Robert Fryser, late of Newborough, another fugitive, had owned three coverlets, five sheets, two brass pots, a trivet, two pans, eleven cheeses, a pair of sandals and a saddle; the goods of these two men reflected a higher standard of domestic comfort than usual. But the richest of all those whose goods were appraised by the escheator was Dafydd ab Ieuan Moel, a bondman of the commote of Menai, whose property was accounted for in 1481-2.[102] His livestock, goods and chattels fetched £26 18s 4d when sold. Moreover he had made a will, had married his daughters to free men and had himself married the daughter of one of the leading men in the commote of Malltraeth, all without licence. These examples cannot be regarded as a large enough sample from which any conclusions can be drawn; they are too few and too scattered. But they do shed some light on the kind of possessions that the inhabitants of medieval Anglesey might be expected to have and in this respect they are the forerunners of the probate inventories of the seventeenth and eighteenth centuries.

These accounts tell us something about the way these people lived. At the same time there are, inevitably, many gaps; we can know little about such things as houses, food and clothing. One thing is certain; the lifestyles of the inhabitants of Anglesey in the middle ages varied enormously. Goronwy ap Tudur, the constable of Beaumaris who died in 1382 and his fellow landed proprietors did not live in the same way as did the bond tenants Adda ab Adda Fawr and Gwerfyl ferch Adda whose goods in 1379-80 were worth a total of 1s 4d. Likewise prosperous Beaumaris burgesses like the Clerks in the fourteenth century or the Ingrams in the fifteenth obviously enjoyed a far higher standard of living than did most bondmen and a good many free tenants. Even among the bondmen there was a wide range of economic status and a man like Dafydd ab Ieuan Moel in the late fifteenth century must have lived like a gentleman in every sense of the word.

Few medieval houses have survived. In this respect Anglesey and Gwynedd in general are vastly different from lowland England where so many medieval timber-framed houses are not only habitable but sought after. Probably the largest house erected in the middle ages was Henblas in Beaumaris, the original home of the Bulkeleys, demolished in the nineteenth century.[103] Hafoty in Llansadwrn may date from the late fourteenth or early fifteenth century, while

102  TNA SC6/1155/6, m.11b.
103  There is a detailed description of Henblas in RCAHM *Anglesey Inventory*. pp.clviii-clxii.

the hall at Plas Bodewryd is probably a late medieval building.[104] The ruins of substantial medieval houses remain at Bodychen in Bodwrog and at Plas Berw in the parish of Llanidan.[105] At least one fifteenth-century house survives in Beaumaris and there may well be surviving medieval work in some of the other houses in the town despite the depredations wrought there in the nineteenth century.[106] But such buildings were not representative of the type of housing enjoyed by the majority of the population. There was no lack of building stone in Anglesey but most houses were probably built of mud or clay and thatched with straw.[107] Timber was not easily available and when required it had to be brought from the mainland. This is clear from the accounts of expenditure on the repair of royal mills in the first half of the fourteenth century. In 1336-7 two crucks were bought for the repair of Bodronyn mill, while at Aberalaw in 1339 straw was bought for roofing and a thatcher was paid for five days work.[108] Excavation may yet reveal medieval house-plans; at the hundred court of Ardudwy in Merioneth in 1325-6 Ieuan Fawr was sued by Ithel Foel for failing to carry out a contract to build a house 27 feet long by fifteen feet wide and this may give some indication of the size of a typical free tenant's house.[109]

As important as a roof over one's head was an adequate diet. There is no precise information about what the medieval Welshman ate or drank; according to Gerald his diet consisted largely of oats, dairy products and meat.[110] In fact, a good deal more bread must have been eaten and most people would probably have eaten much the same food as their counterparts in England. The extent of 1284 and that of the bishop of Bangor's lands of 1306 give a clear picture of the food produced in Anglesey. More oats were grown than wheat and oats were probably used to make some kind of bread or oatcake as well as for brewing and for feeding horses. The 1284 extent mentions renders of flour, butter, milk, oat and barley meal, sheep, eggs and hens at Aberffraw, while at Penrhosllugwy it refers to wheat, barley, beans, peas and rye.[111] Rye is not often

104 For Hafoty see the excellent excavation report and survey by Patricia Borne and Philip Dixon (unpubl., University of Nottingham, 1979); for a revised version see Philip Dixon, 'Hafoty, Llansadwrn, Anglesey: excavations and survey of a medieval house', *Studia Celtica* 29 (1995), 53-126. The history of the house is discussed by David Longley, 'Hafoty and its occupiers', *TAAS* 2007, pp.25-39. For Bodewryd see RCAHM *Anglesey Inventory*, p.19.

105 RCAHM *Anglesey Inventory* pp. cli, 20, 100-1; see also David Longley, 'Excavations at Plas Berw, Anglesey, 1983-4', *Arch.Camb.* 140 (1991), 102-19.

106 ibid., pp.13-4 (No. 32 Castle Street).

107 ibid., p.ci; Iorwerth Peate, *The Welsh House* (1944), pp.17-9.

108 TNA SC6/1229/3; 1229/6.

109 W.H.Waters, *The Edwardian Settlement of North Wales in its Administrative and Legal Aspects (1284-1343)*, p.184. For comparable figures from rural England see E. Miller and J. Hatcher, op.cit., pp.156-8.

110 Gerald of Wales, *The Description of Wales*. p.233.

111 Smith, 'Extent of Anglesey 1284', pp. 96-9, 105.

mentioned, which suggests that more bread was baked from wheat and barley. Fish must certainly have played an important part in the diet and since no part of Anglesey is far from the sea, as much fresh as salt fish must have been eaten. The 1306 extent includes renders from some bond townships of wheat, malt, oats, barley, hens, bread and butter. Such renders were, of course, intended for the victualling of royal and episcopal courts and may not be representative of the diet of most of the population, but on the other hand they do show what food was produced and any tenant with some land must have been in a position to produce some of these things for himself. The usual diet in rural Wales in the middle ages was probably not far removed from that described in the evidence presented to the Welsh Land Commission at the end of the nineteenth century, although the medieval diet did not, of course, include the potato.[112] The staple food was probably some kind of stirabout or *uwd* made of oatmeal and milk; cheese and eggs would also have played a part but meat may have been a rare item on most tables. A good deal of the crop might have to be sold. On the whole the diet was high in carbohydrate but low in protein.[113] The diet of the wealthier landed proprietors was a good deal more varied and contemporary poets bear witness to the wines and exotic spices which graced their tables.[114] When Maredudd ap Cynwrig of Porthaml died some time in the 1420s Rhys Goch Eryri described in his elegy how the previous day he had seen a ship laden with wine making for Gwynedd. From the shore he hailed the captain and told him to return to France; there was no profit to be had in bringing wine from Spain now that Maredudd was dead.[115] Wine was the drink of the better-off; most people drank ale and, judging by the amount of oat malt which was produced, it was generally brewed from that cereal.

Another aspect of medieval life of which little is known is health; awareness of disease and its prevention or cure tends to begin and end with the Black Death. Surviving records say little about the sick but there was one class of these who were traditionally shunned by society and cut off from it; these were the lepers. Leprosy had a long history and in Welsh law it was a recognised ground for divorce.[116] As an endemic disease it seems to have been at its worst in Britain during the thirteenth and fourteenth centuries and Anglesey refer-

112 Some of the evidence is summarised in J. Rhys and D. Brynmor Jones, *The Welsh People* (4th edn., 1906). pp.551-65.

113 E. Miller and J. Hatcher, op.cit., pp.159-61, where diet in rural England is discussed; also Keith Williams-Jones, op.cit., p.cxx, and G.R.J. Jones, 'Post-Roman Wales', p.355.

114 For a general discussion of this see W. Ambrose Bebb, *Machlud yr Oesoedd Canol* (1951), pp.19-21.

115 *Gwaith Rhys Goch Eryri* ed. Dylan Foster Evans (2007), p.45.

116 Iorwerth Peate, 'The antiquity of leprosy in Wales', in *BBCS* 26 (1975), 361-2; *Llyfr Iorwerth*, p.25, para. 45. For leprosy in Wales see Glyn Penrhyn Jones, *Newyn a Haint yng Nghymru* (1963), pp.55-61. The most recent examination of it as an endemic disease is Peter Richards, *The Medieval Leper and his Northern Heirs* (1977).

ences come from the latter. It has been estimated that there were some two hundred leper hospitals in fourteenth-century Britain.[117] There are no references to any such institutions in Anglesey or, indeed, in Gwynedd, but there were houses set aside for lepers. In Anglesey these seem to have been organised on a commotal basis; one is recorded at every *maerdref* except Penrhosllugwy. In 1381-2 the escheator accounted for two shillings, the profits of a house and three acres of land in Aberffraw which were in the king's hand because there were no lepers there; the king was the founder and places for lepers were in his gift.[118] It was occupied in 1386-7 when it was delivered to a leper, Gruffudd ap Hywel Ddu.[119] In 1390-1 the escheator answered for a house and four virgates in Rhosyr set aside for lepers because it was empty and in 1393-4 land assigned to lepers in Cemais was in the king's hand for the same reason. The great cumulative escheator's account of 1408-9 includes the income from a house for lepers in Llan-faes which was likewise unoccupied.[120] These houses may be remembered in place-names; Clafdy is three-quarters of a mile from Aberffraw on the road to Llanfaelog, Rhyd-y-clafdy is just over a mile to the east of the present village of Cemais and there is still a Ffrwd-y-cleifion in Newborough.[121] At the Dindaethwy tourn on 31 August 1321 Dafydd ab Ithel of Dinsylwy was amerced sixpence for harbouring a leper and similar amercements were imposed on two women at the Malltraeth tourn a few days later. This may have been in contravention of a local by-law because the sole statute against the harbouring of lepers was that of 1346 which only applied to London.[122] The usual emptiness of the lepers' houses suggests that the disease was not all that common, but there is not enough evidence to make a firmer statement than that.

The sick needed medical attention and examination of personal names suggests that there was no lack of physicians in Anglesey. The calling must not be confused with that of the modern medical practitioner. The medieval country doctor was probably more akin to the *gŵr hysbys* or the herbalist than to his modern counterpart and one would certainly not wish to experience the professional skills of Hwlcyn ap Dafydd ap Goronwy ap Dafydd, a surgeon in the commote of Talybolion in 1406.[123] The protest of the inhabitants of Llan-faes

117  Peter Richards, op.cit., p.11.
118  TNA SC6/1150/8, m.7b.
119  TNA SC6/1151/3, m.9a.
120  TNA SC6/1151/8, m.9a; 1151/9, m.8b; 1233/1.
121  Hugh Owen, *Hanes Plwyf Niwbwrch ym Môn* (1952), p.21. There are other Welsh references, including a house for lepers in Caernarfon in the reign of Edward III and lands in Wrexham and Hawarden; Rhyd-y-clafdy near Pwllheli may be another example of a house for lepers near a commotal centre (Glyn Penrhyn Jones, op.cit., pp.60-1).
122  TNA SC2/215/5, mm.4a, 5a; C. Creighton, *A History of Epidemics in Britain from A.D. 664 to the Extinction of Plague* (1891), p.106.
123  Keith Williams-Jones, op.cit., p.cx; Glyn Penrhyn Jones, 'Some aspects of the medical history of Caernarfonshire', *in Trans. Caerns. Hist. Soc.*, 23 (1962), 71-2

against their removal to Newborough at the beginning of the fourteenth century was led by a local physician, Master Einion. The prefix suggests that he was a cleric and an educated man, which serves as a reminder that medieval Wales was not cut off from the medical tradition of Europe.[124] Several medical manuscripts have survived and the hereditary physicians of Myddfai in Carmarthenshire are well-known.[125]

Many aspects of life in medieval Anglesey must remain a mystery. Little, for example, is known of family life. The importance of the kindred among the free has already been mentioned but nothing remains to tell us if the normal unit was the extended or the nuclear family or what the position of grandparents might have been. Recent work has laid a new emphasis on the importance of the individual in medieval England and has suggested that the normal pattern was the three-generation group.[126] It was not uncommon for the head of the family to hand over his holding or property to his son in return for an undertaking to support him and one such undertaking from Anglesey has survived; in 1458 Hywel ap Gruffudd ap Dafydd of Eiriannell granted his goods and chattels to his daughter Efa and her husband Gruffudd ap Llywelyn ab Iorwerth ap Rhys in return for his maintenance.[127] Another problem is population.[128] Medieval population estimates are not lightly attempted and any attempt is bedevilled by the nature of the sources available since the historian has no parish registers or census returns to facilitate a demographic survey. The 1292-3 subsidy assessment for the commote of Malltraeth could possibly be used in conjunction with the relevant section of the 1306 Bangor extent as the basis of a working hypothesis for the end of the thirteenth century but such an exercise would be so tentative as to be of little value; furthermore, it could not be used to consider the dynamics of the medieval population. All that can be said is that in Anglesey, as elsewhere in Europe, the population was declining steadily, at least from the middle of the fourteenth century.[129]

124  TNA E101/120/1.

125  Morfydd E. Owen, 'Functional prose: religion, science, grammar, law', in A.O.H. Jarman and Gwilym Rees Hughes, eds., *A Guide to Welsh Literature*, i (1976), pp.264-6.

126  A. Macfarlane, *The Origins of English Individualism* (1978), Chapter VI of this book is an important discussion of rural economy and society *in* England in the thirteenth and fourteenth centuries and many of the points raised are probably relevant to Wales. See also E. Miller and J. Hatcher, op.cit., p.137, and R.H. Hilton, *Bond Men Made Free* (1973), p.27.

127  NLW Sotheby 47; for a general discussion see A. Macfarlane, op.cit., pp.137-8.

128  The only discussion of the population of medieval Wales is J.C. Russell *British Medieval Population* (1948), pp.319-44, which is not entirely satisfactory.

129  The population of Merioneth at the end of the thirteenth century is discussed by Keith Williams-Jones, op.cit., pp.xxxv-lxvii; the 1292-3 subsidy roll covered the entire county.

1 The coffin of Joan, wife of Llywelyn ab Iorwerth (the Great), now in Beaumaris church.

2    Aerial view of Tal-y-llyn church; today it stands in isolation but archive evidence suggests the existence of a community of 22 households holding about 150 acres between them in 1306.

3   The site of the court complex at Rhosyr; the adjacent parish church may
originally have been associated with it. The later Edwardian borough (Newborough)
is visible in the background and the nearby crossroads may be a relic of the Welsh
settlement associated with the court.

4   Aerial view of Penmon Priory. The whitewashed building between the church and the ruins of the refectory and dormitory was the Prior's House, dating probably from the early sixteenth century.

5   The Romanesque arch in Aberffraw church. It has been suggested that this may
have been the entrance to a long-vanished west tower.

6 Aerial view of Aberffraw; the court buildings lie beneath the present village.

7 Aerial view of Newborough: the street plan of the medieval town is clearly visible.

8  The site of the town of Llan-faes in relation to Beaumaris; the nucleus of the town was probably around the church.

9  Beaumaris castle from the north; the concentric plan can be clearly seen.

10 Possibly the earliest surviving Anglesey deed,
recording the conveyance in *tir prid* of land in Llangefni
to Sir Gruffudd ap Rhys (Sir Gruffudd Llwyd), 1313.

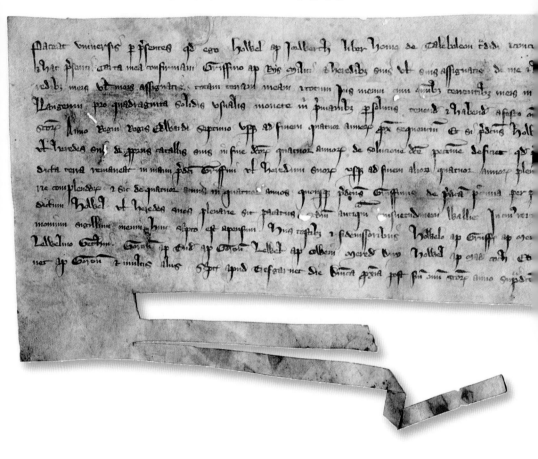

11 A page from the 1352 extent of Anglesey showing the
entries for the townships of Dinsylwy Rys, Penhwnllys,
Trecastell and Twrgarw in the commote of Dindaethwy.
It is also an excellent example of the distinctive hand-
writing of William de Cranwell.

# Commotus de Vuodmho

Extenta eiusdem commoti facta apud Bellum ex[tra]iudicium cor[a]m [pre]fato Ioh[anne] ten[ore] d[i]e [...]
... post f[estu]m ... anno sup[radic]to p[er] sacr[amentu]m ... examinatorum c[or]am f[ac]ta ten[ore]
eiusdem commoti tam liber[o]rum [com]un[ati]on[um] ... et postea expe[n]ditur p[er] sacr[amentu]m ... liber[o]rum eiusd[e]m
c[om]moti [...]

- Dauid l[ow]r
- Dauid Brytogu[n]
- [...] ap Gruff[ud]
- D[auid] ap Bes
- W[ill]i ap Ma[d]
- ...s ap [...]
- Gron ap It
- Io[ha]n ap ...s
- Io[ha]n ap G[...]
- Io[ha]n gooh
- Gru[ffu]n Velt
- Ten l[ow]r

**Consulteles Teres:** M[...]re eiusdem ville est in manu Dos ap Gruff[ud] Et nichil inde d[i]c[itu]r [p]rim[o] [p]er annum ... p[er] sacr[amentu]m ad com[mune] Et d[icitu]r q[uo]d ipse [et] [villa]ni fui[deb]nt fac[ere] c[er]ta ad duos ... tern[a] uic[ibus] p[er] annum Et h[ab]et [...] in molend[in]o de [...] Et alia medietas eiusd[e]m
ville est in manu Gr[on] ap Io[ha]n Dauid ap ...s [et] alior[um] [villa]t[orum] Et est de nat[iv]a ... [...] Et [...] inde [...] ... [p]er annum . xix d q [...] p[er] annum [...]
Et fac[iunt] c[er]ta ad molend[in]u[m] d[omi]ni de [...] Et fac[iunt] eiusdem [...] Et fac[iunt] [...] eiusd[e]m mol[endini]
Et fac[iunt] [...] [...] eiusd[e]m m[...] com[...] Anglor[um] c[us]tubil[is] ... Et [...]
[...] [...] [...] [...] Et [...] q[uo]d [...] Et fac[iunt] [...] d[omi]ni de [...]
[...] [...] et c[...] et [...] d[omi]ni volu[er]int fore [et] c[on]o c[...] p[...]e . ij d

**Denburultes:** In eadem [villa] est c[er]ta Vele t[...] Vele t[i]ld[e] ap ...s[?] Et om[n]es ind[e] [...]
[...] ap Gruff[ud] Dauid ap Bes [et] al[ii] Et nichil inde d[e]b[e]t d[omin]o [p]rim[o] de [...] de
[...] n[e]c [...] [...] c[er]ta ad com[mune] [...] [...] Et h[ab]et mol[endinum] [...] uel [...] t[i]ld[e]
Et [villa]ni [...] [...] [...] [...] [...] in anno ad duos ... ter[na] uic[ibus]

**Tresulttel:** E[adem] [villa] l[ib]ata est Et om[n]es d[omi]no ten[...] Kolkott ap Gron a t[i]ld[e] A[...] om[n]es Et
nichil inde [...] d[i]c[itu]r [p]rim[o] p[er] annum de [...] n[e]c [...] n[e]c amot[us] [...] c[er]ta ad com[mune]
Et u[nu]s de nat[iv]a istius ville [...] de nat[iv]o de Gr[on] Gr[on] [ib]i in guer[r]a d[omi]n[i] p[er]
[...] s[angui]ne ipsius Gr[on] ad c[us]tod[iam] sua[m] [pro]pria[m] m[...] m[...] Walt [...] c[us]tod[iam] d[omi]n[i]
Et ip[s]i a [villa]ni s[u]i [...] fac[iunt] c[er]ta ad duos ... ter[na] uic[ibus] uic[es] p[er] annum

**Gourgarel:** In eadem [villa] est u[nu]m Vele uoc[atum] Vele t[i]ld[e] ap ...s[?] Et om[n]es ind[e] [...] Dauid
ap Bes Dauid Bet[?] a t[i]ld[e] Et nichil inde [...] d[i]c[itu]r [p]rim[o] p[er] annum [...] c[er]ta ad
com[mune] a h[...] Et h[ab]et molend[inum] [...] uel [...] t[i]ld[e] Et ip[s]i a [villa]ni s[u]i
fac[iunt] c[er]ta ad duos ... ter[na] uic[ibus] uic[es] p[er] annum

152

12 & 13  The birth of the Penrhyn estate: the will of Gwilym ap Gruffudd ap Tudur, proved in 1376, and the fine relief of St Iestyn in Llaniestyn church given by his widow Gwenllian ferch Madog and his nephew and heir Gruffudd ap Gwilym ap Gruffudd in his memory. It is a product of the same workshop that produced the images of Pabo Post Prydain in Llanbabo church and of Efa, Gwilym's sister, in Bangor Cathedral.

The inscription on the relief reads in translation:

'Here lies St Iestyn to whom Gwenllian ferch Madog and Gruffudd ap Gwilym offered this image for the salvation of their souls.'

14 & 15  Tudor prehistory : the tomb of Goronwy ap Tudur (*d.*1382) and his wife
Myfanwy ferch Iorwerth Ddu, now in Penmynydd church and a deed recording
the conveyance in *tir prid* of lands in Anglesey to Goronwy's brother Maredudd,
the great-grandfather of Henry VII, 1389.

16 Part of a roll recording debts due to Gwilym ap Gruffudd of Penmynydd and later of Penrhyn, 1406. This document sheds light on the origins of the wealth of one of the greatest families in north Wales in the fifteenth century.

156

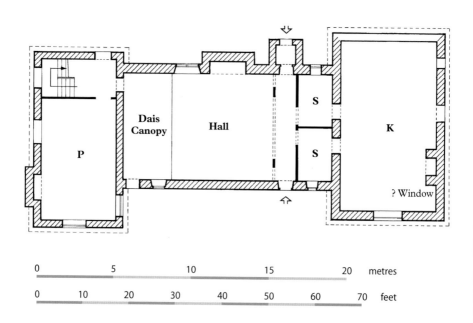

17 **A house for Mr Bulkeley**: the conveyance to William Bulkeley the elder of the burgage in Beaumaris where he built his new house, Henblas, 1474, and a plan of the house. On the plan **P** stands for parlour, **K** for kitchen and **S** for service rooms.

18   Henblas, Beaumaris, prior to its demolition in 1869.
The drawing is based on J. J. Dodd's watercolour, 1838.

19   Hafoty, Llansadwrn, begun in the fifteenth century and probably
the best surviving example of a medieval house in Anglesey.

20   The late fifteenth-century east window of Llangadwaladr church, the gift
of Meurig ap Llywelyn of Bodeon and his son Owain ap Meurig and their wives.

# 7 *The Making of the Gentry*

THE RISE OF THE GENTRY has often been seen as a sixteenth-century phenomenon. This was the period of their apotheosis when they emerged as the rulers of the county community. In Wales it was the Acts of Union which saw the seal of royal approval placed on that local leadership and social influence which they had already exercised for several centuries. There is no doubt that the Tudor age was one of great importance in the development of this class. Detailed local or regional studies of the rise of such families during the middle ages, however, are rare and the approach to such studies of English counties tends to emphasise the political and military dimensions. The examination of the leadership of local society demands a more detailed analysis.[1]

The rise of individual families was based on three factors; these were the dominant position of particular lineages in particular areas, the holding of local offices under the native princes before 1282 and under the crown afterwards and the acquisition of land as a market developed from the fourteenth century onwards. In medieval and post-medieval pedigrees much emphasis was laid on membership of the leading kindreds and the poet-genealogists of the sixteenth century devised the concepts of the five royal tribes of Wales and the fifteen noble tribes of Gwynedd.[2] The eponyms of these tribes probably lived in the twelfth century and together they formed a kind of procrustean bed into which the various families of *uchelwyr* were fitted. Of the royal tribes the only one represented in Anglesey was that of Gruffudd ap Cynan, the royal house of Gwynedd, a number of cadet branches of which held land there in the later middle ages.[3] Of the noble tribes, those of Llywarch ap Bran, Hwfa ap Cynddelw and Gweirydd ap Rhys Goch were almost exclusively connected with An-

1 The significance of the medieval *uchelwyr* is discussed by R.R. Davies, *The Revolt of Owain Glyn Dŵr* (1995), pp.49-57.
2 The five royal tribes are listed in Edmund Hyde Hall, *A Description of Caernarvonshire (1809-11)*, (ed. Emyr Gwynne Jones, 1952), pp.162-4, and the fifteen noble tribes in ibid., pp.113-5. See also Francis Jones, 'The heraldry of Gwynedd', in *TCHS* 24 (1963), 43-5.
3 In 1352 a descendant of Gruffudd ap Cynan held Gwely Cynwrig ap Tegwared in Trefdraeth Wastrodion (*Extent of Anglesey*, p.162: Bartrum, *WG*, Gruffudd ap Cynan 9). Land in Bodynolwyn and Llanfigel which had belonged to Maredudd Benhir, a great-grandson of Hywel ab Owain Gwynedd, was escheat in 1352 (*Extent of Anglesey*, pp. 190,197; Bartrum, *WG*, Gruffudd ap Cynan 10).

glesey and the stock of Marchudd ap Cynan was represented there. The other leading Anglesey kindreds were those of Cadrod Hardd, Carwed, Gwalchmai, Geraint and Iarddur. Most of the descendants of Llywarch ap Bran were to be found in Menai and Talybolion, those of Hwfa ap Cynddelw in Llifon and Malltraeth and those of Gweirydd ap Rhys Goch in Talybolion.[4]

Thus each kindred group had what may be described as a sphere of influence, but the roots of landed families did not always lie in the same soil, nor did every family rise in the same way. Those who were men of standing in the late thirteenth and early fourteenth centuries were not necessarily the ancestors of those families which emerged in the fifteenth and sixteenth. There are several lists which reveal who the leading men of the county were in the first half of the fourteenth century. Soon after Edward of Caernarfon was created prince of Wales in 1301 he visited his new principality to receive the homage and fealty of its leaders.[5] A number from Anglesey can be identified; they included at least two members of what was undoubtedly the most important kindred in Gwynedd at this time, the descendants of Ednyfed Fychan of the stock of Marchudd ap Cynan. At the head of the list stood Sir Gruffudd ap Rhys or Gruffudd Llwyd of Tregarnedd in Menai. One of the descendants of Ednyfed Fychan, he had already been knighted by the time Edward of Caernarfon became prince and he had a long career in the service of the crown; in fact he was the leader of the Welshmen of north Wales during the reigns of the first two Edwards.[6] Tudur ap Goronwy, the next on the list, was the head of the main line of the descendants of Ednyfed.[7] His father had been Llywelyn ap Gruffudd's seneschal until his death in 1268 and Tudur himself was Madog ap Llywelyn's steward during the latter's revolt. Of the other names in the list six were of the lineage of Llywarch ap Bran; Tudur ap Gruffudd was granted the raglotry of Talybolion in 1282 as a reward for his good service and Maredudd ap Goronwy, also known as Maredudd Ddu, was *rhaglaw* of Menai between 1306 and 1308.[8] Two of those in the list were members of the stock of Hwfa ap Cynddelw, one of that of Cadrod Hardd, one of that of Gwalchmai and one of the line of Iarddur. This last was Tudur Fychan who in 1284 had been granted the township of Nantmawr in Twrcelyn; between at least 1303 and 1308 he was

---

4  These are discussed briefly in Chapter 5; for outline genealogical tables see Appendix A, Tables 1 (Wyrion Eden), 2 (Llywarch ap Bran), 3 (Hwfa ap Cynddelw), 4 (Iarddur) and 5 (Carwed).

5  The Anglesey names on the list are *in CPR 1343-1345*, 228-9, 232.

6  The career of Sir Gruffudd Llwyd is described in detail by J.G. Edwards, 'Sir Gruffudd Llwyd', in *EHR* 30 (1915), 589-601, and in *Y Bywgrafiiadur Cymreig*. p.299; more information is in J. Beverley Smith, 'Gruffudd Llwyd and the Celtic alliance, 1315-6', *BBCS* 26 (1976), 364-78, and 'Edward II and the allegiance of Wales', *WHR* 8 (1976), 39-71.

7  For Tudur see Glyn Roberts, 'Wyrion Eden', pp.186-8.

8  *CAP*, pp.454-5; TNA SC6/1170/5; 1227/7. Maredudd Ddu was the ancestor of the Porthaml family.

*rhaglaw* of that commote.[9]

In 1327 representatives from the north Wales counties were summoned to the parliament at which Edward II was deposed.[10] Again some of the Anglesey men and their sureties can be identified; Hywel ap Gruffudd was one of four brothers of the lineage of Hwfa ap Cynddelw and was also known as Hywel y Pedolau. He was almost certainly the Hywel ap Gruffudd who was *rhaglaw* of the cantref of Aberffraw in 1316-7 and 1328-9 and who had been an esquire of the king's household.[11] Another representative, Tudur ap Llywelyn, was a descendant of Ednyfed Fychan whose lands were in the township of Trysglwyn Ednyfed in Twrcelyn; he was *rhingyll* of that commote between 1308 and 1316.[12] The sureties included Gwilym ap Philip, a burgess of Newborough, Hywel Lipa of Llysdulas of the stock of Carwed who was elected one of the coroners of the county in 1346, John de Ereswell, farmer of the Anglesey avowries and *rhingyll* of Twrcelyn in 1328-9 and Einion ab Ieuan, a prominent burgess of Beaumaris and former sheriff.[13] On 26 October 1327 Roger Mortimer, the justice of north Wales, was ordered to release a number of men from imprisonment in Caernarfon castle and to take sureties or hostages for them.[14] Their imprisonment was probably connected with their support for Edward II; in fact they may have been the leaders of that north Wales plot to rescue Edward from Berkeley castle, the discovery of which led to the decision to eliminate him.[15] Their leader was Sir Gruffudd Llwyd; they also included Madog Llwyd, a former sheriff of Anglesey, the brothers Hywel and Iorwerth ap Gruffudd of the line of Hwfa, Hywel Lipa and Gwilym ap Philip. And when Hywel ap Gruffudd brought an action in the King's Bench against Mortimer's lieutenant William de Shalford in 1331, accusing him of having encompassed the king's death, his sureties included his brother Iorwerth, Sir Gruffudd Llwyd, Goronwy ap Tudur of Penmynydd and Gwilym ap Gruffudd ap Tudur of Llaniestyn, all well-known figures.[16]

9  *CChancRVar*, 288; TNA SC6/1227/5, 7.

10  F. Palgrave, ed., *Parliamentary Writs and Writs of Military Summons (Edward I – Edward II)* (1834), ii, 364.

11  TNA SC6/1227/13;  1229/1;  J. Beverley Smith, 'Edward II and the allegiance of Wales', 170, n.171.

12  Tudur ap Llywelyn was described in 1337 as lord of a tenant in Trysglwyn Ednyfed (BUASC Penrhyn 379); TNA SC6/1170/6; 1227/11.

13  Gwilym ap Philip had ceased to hold land in Newborough in 1352 (*Extent of Anglesey*, p.266). For the election of Hywel Lipa see G.P. Jones, 'Anglesey court rolls, 1346', *TAAS* 1933, p.48; TNA SC6/1229/1.

14  *CCR 1327-1330*, 182.

15  J. Beverley Smith, 'Edward II and the allegiance of Wales', 166-7.

16  This affair is discussed and the documents printed by T.F. Tout, 'The captivity and death of Edward of Caernarvon', in *Collected Papers*, iii (1934), pp.175-88

Perhaps the most interesting of these fourteenth-century lists is that of the Anglesey men who did fealty to the Black Prince's representatives after he became prince of Wales in 1343.[17] First on the list came Rhys ap Gruffudd, a man better known in south Wales than in Gwynedd although he was a descendant of Ednyfed Fychan.[18] But the fact that he did fealty with the men of Anglesey suggests that he was there at the time and he certainly held land in the county.[19] The second name was that of Ieuan Wyddel of Porthaml, a descendant of Llywarch ap Bran and ancestor of the Berw family.[20] At least seven of those who did fealty were of the stock of Hwfa ap Cynddelw and two were of the royal lineage of Gruffudd ap Cynan; one of these was Hywel ap Madog ap Llywelyn, one of the sons of the leader of the 1294-5 revolt.[21] Two belonged to the line of Carwed; one of them, Hywel ap Cynwrig of Llysdulas, was three times *rhaglaw* of Twrcelyn and the other was Hywel Lipa.[22] The only descendant of Ednyfed Fychan was Madog ap Tudur, probably the son of Tudur ap Llywelyn, who held part of Trysglwyn in 1352. There were at least four descendants of Llywarch ap Bran and one of the stock of Iarddur, Gwilym ap Gruffudd ap Tudur, who died in 1376. A number of others on the list remain unidentified.

These lists have been discussed in some detail because these were the men who counted in Anglesey between 1300 and 1350. These were also the men who might be summoned by name by the crown for military service against the Scots or the French. Sir Gruffudd Llwyd frequently led the troops levied from north Wales and men from Anglesey were led more than once by Iorwerth ap Gruffudd. Others involved in the campaigns of Edward II and Edward III included Iorwerth's son Hywel Ddu, his brother Hywel and Hywel's son Gruffudd, Tudur ap Llywelyn, Goronwy ap Tudur of Penmynydd and his son Tudur and Gwilym ap Gruffudd ap Tudur.[23] Here were the leading members of free kindreds who dominated their localities and from some of whom the gentry were descended. From the second half of the fourteenth century their

---

17 The list is printed in *Arch.Camb. Original Documents*, p.clii.
18 The details of his life and career are set out in Ralph A. Griffiths, *The Principality of Wales in the Later Middle Ages* i: *South Wales, 1277-1536*, pp.99-102.
19 He held half the township of Dinsylwy in Dindaethwy in 1352 (*Extent of Anglesey*, p.234); after his death in 1356 it passed to the Penmynydd line of the descendants of Ednyfed
20 In 1352 Ieuan Wyddel held land in Ysgeifiog and in Gwely Iorwerth ap Llywarch in Porthaml, both in Menai (*Extent of Anglesey*, pp. 248, 254).
21 Hywel ap Madog ap Llywelyn held the township of Lledwigan Llan in Malltraeth in 1352 by a very free tenure (*Extent of Anglesey*, p.162); he was also the heir of Gwely Philip ab Owain in Tregwehelyth although he had conveyed it in *tir prid* to Robert de Hambury (ibid., p.184; see also NLW Thorne 265).
22 TNA SC6/1229/3, 7; 1149/3, m.6b; Bartrum, *WG*, Carwed 2. In 1360-1 Hywel ap Cynwrig was one of the farmers of the tolls of Llannerch-y-medd fair (TNA SC6/1150/1, m.5a).
23 Military service is discussed by A.D. Carr, 'Anglesey and war in the later middle ages', *TAAS* 1984, pp.24-30.

descendants were to start building up landed estates as the old tenurial system gradually broke up and as the emphasis came increasingly to be on the landed proprietor rather than on the kindred group.

Some had been rewarded by the princes before 1282. In the twelfth and thirteenth centuries grants, especially of bond townships, seem to have been made to individuals who enjoyed exemption from secular service and rent along with the delegation of royal authority over the communities concerned.[24] These grants had stemmed from the need to create and reward a bureaucracy which contained a strong lay element, as well as from the need to recognise good service and to provide a secure basis for military recruitment. The most important of these grants were the ones made to Ednyfed Fychan, presumably by Llywelyn ab Iorwerth and subsequently held by his descendants. Several of these townships were held by military service and they, together with the offices their proprietors held, were the basis of the power and influence of Wyrion Eden, the descendants of Ednyfed.[25] For these accommodation with the new order came very soon after the death of Llywelyn ap Gruffudd; indeed, in many cases it probably came before and some of Ednyfed's descendants fought for Edward I in 1282.[26] Even those who remained loyal to Llywelyn to the end do not seem to have suffered in any way and they retained their lands, their position and their influence.

For most of the fourteenth century the descendants of Ednyfed held local offices and they were probably the most influential people in the county. Tudur ap Goronwy or Tudur Hen was *rhaglaw* of Dindaethwy in 1302-3; the Hywel ap Tudur who held the same office in 1306-7 may have been his son and the Goronwy ap Tudur who held it in the 1320s certainly was and succeeded him as head of the senior line of the family which is usually associated with Penmynydd.[27] Goronwy died in 1331; his son Tudur was *rhaglaw* in 1336 and probably held the office until his death in 1367.[28] One of Tudur's sons, Rhys, was farming the office in 1372-3 and another, Goronwy, was doing the same in 1374-5.[29] Goronwy, the son of Tudur Hen, was *rhaglaw* of the cantref of Aberffraw in 1311-2 and Gwilym ap Tudur, a brother of Rhys and the younger Goronwy, farmed the township of Nantmawr in 1387-8.[30] Rhys ap Tudur was

---

24  This is discussed by Stephenson, *Governance of Gwynedd*, pp.95-135, especially pp.130-135.

25  The townships held by military service were Penmynydd, Erddreiniog and Trecastell in Dindaethwy, Gwredog and Trysglwyn in Twrcelyn and Tregarnedd in Menai.

26  The attitude of the leading families in Gwynedd before and after 1282 is discussed by Glyn Roberts, 'Wales and England: antipathy and sympathy, 1282-1485', in *Aspects of Welsh History*, pp.300-5; see also 'Wyrion Eden', pp.184-5.

27  TNA SC6/1227/4; 1170/5; 1228/5.

28  TNA SC6/1229/3; 1150/2, m.4a.

29  TNA E163/24/1; mm.1a-b.

30  TNA SC6/1227/8; 1151/4, m.6a.

escheator of Anglesey in 1374-5 and 1381-2 and joint escheator in 1383-4 and yet another brother, Maredudd, held the same office in 1388-9; Maredudd was also *rhaglaw* of Malltraeth between 1387 and 1395.[31] The most important Anglesey office attained by any of the family was the shrievalty, which was held by Rhys in 1374-5.[32]

Tudur ap Goronwy, who died in 1367, had five sons, Goronwy, Ednyfed, Gwilym, Rhys and Maredudd. His brother Hywel was a cleric and he answered at the *Quo Warranto* proceedings of 1348 for Penmynydd, Trecastell and Erddreiniog where he claimed a number of jurisdictional privileges.[33] During the fourteenth century the family was among the most important patrons of the poets and Iolo Goch and the Talybolion poet Gruffudd ap Maredudd ap Dafydd seem to have enjoyed a special relationship.[34] In a *cywydd* addressed to four of Tudur's sons Iolo associated Goronwy with Penmynydd, Ednyfed with Trecastell, Rhys with Erddreiniog and Gwilym with Clorach in Twrcelyn.[35] Goronwy ap Tudur was a man of considerable standing. He had probably served in the French wars and was steward of the bishop of Bangor's lands in Anglesey. In 1382 he was appointed constable of Beaumaris castle but he died by drowning, apparently in Kent, only four days after his appointment.[36] His son and heir Tudur was under age. Tudur seems to have died about 1400 and his lands were inherited by his sister Morfudd. She was the first wife of Gwilym ap Gruffudd ap Gwilym whose father had married Generys, the daughter and heiress of another of the line of Ednyfed, Madog ap Goronwy Fychan of Gwredog. Gwilym was the founder of the great house of Penrhyn which was to dominate Gwynedd for the next century and a half, but the Penrhyn lands passed to his son with his second wife Jonet Stanley. With Morfudd he had one son, Tudur Fychan and it was to him and his descendants that the remains of the Penmynydd inheritance eventually passed. In the sixteenth and seventeenth centuries the family of Tudor or Owen Tudor of Penmynydd was a line of small squires, a far cry from the greatness of the house of Ednyfed Fychan or of their kinsmen who had snatched the most glittering prize of all in 1485.[37]

---

31 TNA E163/24/1, m.1b; SC6/1150/8, m.7a; 1150/10, m.9a; 1151/5, m.9a; 1151/4, m.1b; 1152/1, m.1a.

32 TNA E163/24/1, m.1b.

33 *Rec.Caern.*, p.150

34 Glyn Roberts, 'Wyrion Eden', pp.191-9; 'Teulu Penmynydd' in *Aspects of Welsh History*, pp.250-1. See also D. Myrddin Lloyd, 'The later Gogynfeirdd', in A.O.H. Jarman and Gwilym Rees Hughes, eds., *A Guide to Welsh Literature*, II (1979), pp.50-1.

35 D.R. Johnston (ed.), *Gwaith Iolo Goch* (1988), pp.22-4.

36 For Goronwy see Glyn Roberts, 'Wyrion Eden', pp.199-201, where his impressive alabaster tomb, now in Penmynydd church, is also discussed.

37 For the later history of the family from Morfudd onwards see Glyn Roberts, 'Teulu Penmynydd', pp.254-74.

Ednyfed ap Tudur also died in 1382 leaving two daughters, Myfanwy, who married Rhys ap Cynwrig ap Roppert of Llaneurgain in Flintshire and Angharad, the wife of Ieuan ab Adda of Pengwern in Nanheudwy, an ancestor of the Mostyn family.[38] For Gwilym the pedigrees name neither wife nor children. He and Rhys were retained in the service of Richard II in 1398 and they were both deeply implicated in the revolt of their cousin Owain Glyn Dŵr.[39] In fact Gwilym was responsible for one of the most audacious exploits in the history of medieval warfare, the capture of Conwy castle on Good Friday 1401.[40] When the men of Anglesey made their peace with Henry IV in 1406 Gwilym, Rhys and Maredudd were still in rebellion and Gwilym seems to have been still unreconciled in 1408-9; according to some sources he was executed for his part in the revolt but there is nothing to confirm this.[41] Rhys was also one of the leaders of the revolt in Anglesey in 1400. He was probably executed at Chester in 1411; some of his lands were inherited by his daughter Gwerfyl who married Madog ab Ieuan of Bron-y-foel in Eifionydd and from them was descended the family of Tregaian.[42] Nothing is known of the lands or the fate of Maredudd although he did acquire some land in Newborough in 1389.[43] Iolo Goch did not mention him in his *cywydd* to the brothers. A possible explanation may be found in the pedigrees which state that Maredudd was the son of Tudur ap Goronwy's second marriage; if this were so he would have been a good deal younger than his brothers.[44] Even if he did not survive the revolt his son did. Owain ap Maredudd, otherwise known as Owen Tudor, found his way to England and the rest of the story needs no repetition. But all this happened a long way from Anglesey and after the Glyn Dŵr revolt the family of Penmynydd counted for little and gained nothing from its royal connections. Others made their peace and lost little or nothing but for the family which had dominated Gwynedd in the fourteenth century the glory had departed.

Yet not all the descendants of Ednyfed Fychan were losers and out of the wreckage a new family emerged. The man who picked up the pieces was Gwilym ap Gruffudd ap Gwilym, the son-in-law of Goronwy ap Tudur and a descendant of Tudur ab Ednyfed Fychan. His rise had already started before

---

38  A.D. Carr, 'The Mostyn family and estate, 1200-1642' (unpubl. Ph.D. thesis, University of Wales, 1975), p.57.

39  *CPR 1396-1399*, 400.

40  The outstanding account of this event is that by Keith Williams-Jones, 'The taking of Conwy castle, 1401', *TCHS* 39 (1978), 7-43.

41  Glyn Roberts, 'The Anglesey submissions of 1406', 59.

42  TNA SC6/1233/1; Glyn Roberts, 'Teulu Penmynydd', p.254.

43  BUASC Mostyn 774; see also Glyn Roberts, 'Wyrion Eden', pp 199 and 211-2, and 'Teulu Penmynydd', pp.252-3.

44  Bartrum, *WG*, Marchudd 13; I am indebted to Professor G.Aled Williams for drawing my attention to this reference

the revolt; his family became established in Anglesey by a marriage and a
legacy.[45] The marriage was into a family whose lands lay around Llaniestyn in
Dindaethwy. In June 1310 Hywel ap Tudur and Gruffudd and Madog ap
Dafydd ap Tudur released to Gwilym ap Gruffudd ap Tudur the lands in var-
ious townships held by his father Gruffudd ap Tudur at his death including
Penhwnllys.[46] Gruffudd ap Tudur was the son of Tudur ap Madog of the line
of Iarddur and the brother of Tudur Fychan who was granted Nantmawr by
Edward I in 1284. The standing of the family is reflected by some of the wit-
nesses to this deed; they included Sir Gruffudd Llwyd, Goronwy Fychan and
Robert ap Gruffudd, all of them descendants of Ednyfed Fychan.

Gwilym ap Gruffudd ap Tudur had no children. His sister Efa married
Gwilym ap Gruffudd ap Heilin of Nant in Flintshire, a descendant of Tudur
ab Ednyfed Fychan and when Gwilym of Llaniestyn died in 1376 he left most
of his property to his sister's son Gruffudd ap Gwilym ap Gruffudd. This was
the foundation of the family's fortunes but they were to improve even more
dramatically.[47] Gwilym ap Gruffudd ap Tudur had also held lands in Caernarfonshire, Flintshire and Dyffryn Clwyd and in his will he left all his *tir prid*
lands in Anglesey and Caernarfonshire to his nephew; he also left him all his
bondmen and their issue and the residue of his goods.[48] By his marriage to the
daughter of Madog ap Goronwy Fychan, Gruffudd acquired part of Gwredog
and land in the Caernarfonshire township of Cororion; his son Gwilym was
therefore the heir to a substantial estate. Gruffudd died in 1405 but Gwilym
was already an established figure. In 1394-5 he was joint *rhingyll* of Dindaethwy
and he farmed the office in his own right the following year.[49] From 1392 he
farmed the township of Nantmawr, in 1390-1 he was steward of the commote
of Menai and in 1396 he was sheriff of Anglesey.[50] In 1389 his father had conveyed all his lands in Anglesey and Caernarfonshire to him and his brother
Robin, the ancestor of the Cochwillan family.[51] When the Glyn Dŵr revolt
broke out in 1400 his wife's uncles were involved from the start but Gwilym

45  Gwilym's family background and career are discussed in detail in Carr, 'Gwilym ap Gruffudd'.
46  BUASC Penrhyn 405.
47  The standard account of the early history of the Penrhyn family is J. Rowland Jones, 'The
    development of the Penrhyn estate to 1431'; see also the article by Glyn Roberts on the family
    of Griffith of Penrhyn in *Y Bywgraffiadur Cymreig: Atodiad*, pp.95-8, 'Wyrion Eden', pp.206-13,
    and 'Teulu Penmynydd', pp.253-8 and Carr, 'Gwilym ap Gruffudd'.
48  BUASC Penrhyn 5. Gwilym's lands in Dyffryn Clwyd were divided between his two first cousins
    and three first cousins once removed (R.R. Davies, *Lordship and Society in the March of Wales,
    1282-1400*, p.424n); however, in 1377 several kinsmen in Dyffryn Clwyd quitclaimed all their
    rights to lands in Llangynhafal to Gruffudd ap Gwilym ap Gruffudd (BUASC Penrhyn Further
    Additional, 4 May 1377).
49  TNA SC6/1152/1, m.4a; 1152/2, m.4a.
50  TNA SC6/1151/8, m.6a; 1151/6, m.4b; 1152/3, m.8a.
51  *Y Bywgraffiadur Cymreig*, Atodiad, p.95.

bided his time. His own father and uncle were to die against the peace but he did not join until 1402, by which time family pressure probably left him little choice. When the men of Anglesey submitted in 1406 he and his brother were described as still being in rebellion. In fact they had submitted in the summer of 1405, being perspicacious enough to see that the revolt had passed its peak and that nothing could be lost by changing sides at the right time.[52] By 1408 he was *rhaglaw* of Dindaethwy and he retained the office for the rest of his life.[53]

But Gwilym's real gains were in land; if anyone profited from the misfortunes of his Tudor kinsmen he did. In March 1407 the Prince of Wales had granted his lands with those of 27 other named rebels in Dindaethwy, Talybolion, Twrcelyn and Menai to his chamberlain, Hugh Mortimer. Eight months later he obtained licence to acquire all these lands from Mortimer.[54] This was followed in 1410 by the lands once held by Gwilym ap Tudur ap Goronwy.[55] Thus Gwilym ap Gruffudd may be said to have gone a long way towards re-assembling the Tudor inheritance. The combination of inherited lands, lands acquired by marriage and the fruits of his instinct for survival had made Gwilym a wealthy man.[56] Rentals of his Anglesey lands made between 1410 and 1415 show that his annual income from rents there, quite apart from any lands which he may have kept in his own hands, was substantial.[57] A conveyance made in 1413 in which he conveyed bondmen and land in 32 townships indicates the extent of his Anglesey property at that time; between 1413 and his death in 1431 38 deeds record further purchases in Anglesey and Caernarfonshire.[58]

His first wife Morfudd died early in the fifteenth century and some time after 1405 he married Joan or Jonet Stanley, a daughter of Sir William Stanley of Hooton in Cheshire and probably the widow of Robert Parys, the former constable of Caernarfon.[59] With her he had several children and the marriage meant the temporary disinheritance of Tudur Fychan, his son with Morfudd; it also meant the beginning of a long and advantageous connection with the great house of Stanley. Gwilym died in 1431 and in his will he desired to be

---

52 For Gwilym's part in the revolt see ibid., p.69, and Glyn Roberts, 'Wyrion Eden', pp.209-11, and 'Teulu Penmynydd', p.255. In fact he and his brother had submitted in August 1405 (R.R. Davies, 'Owain Glyn Dŵr and the Welsh squirearchy', in *THSC* 1968, p.155, n.20).

53 TNA SC6/1152/4, m.4b; 1153/2, m.1a. From 1419 to 1421 he was joint *rhingyll* (SC6/1152/8, m.1a).

54 *Calendar of Ancient Deeds*, v, A13604 (4, 1).

55 BUASC Penrhyn 10.

56 There is some discussion of his wealth and its sources in Chapter 6 above.

57 BUASC Penrhyn 1599; Penrhyn Further Additional, rentals, 1410-11 and 1 November 1415.

58 BUASC Penrhyn 386. The conveyance was probably connected with creating an entail to secure the position of his heirs; he had obtained licence to do this (BUASC Penrhyn 11).

59 Glyn Roberts, 'Wyrion Eden', p.209.

buried in the parish church of Penmynydd or that of Llandygái or in the friary of Llan-faes. His daughters Elizabeth and Eleanor were to have enough money for their maintenance and he left money to pay for masses for his soul for twenty years and for a trental.[60] Everything else was left to his widow and his son William who was under age; six days after the will William's wardship was granted to his mother and two of her kinsmen.[61] Thus Gwilym ap Gruffudd had laid the foundations of what was to be the greatest landed family in Gwynedd in the fifteenth and early sixteenth centuries and he owed his good fortune to Gwilym ap Gruffudd ap Tudur's lack of a male heir, his own first marriage and a sharp eye for the way the wind was blowing during the Glyn Dŵr revolt.

Although William or Gwilym Fychan bore his father's name he often appears in deeds as Gwilym ap Gruffudd and by the middle of the century he had anglicised his name to William Griffith. With him the family's centre of gravity moved from Anglesey. His father probably lived at Penmynydd; deeds associate him with it and it was there that he made his will. But Gwilym Fychan crossed the Menai Straits and established himself in Gafael Goronwy ab Ednyfed in the township of Cororion near Bangor. Here was built Penrhyn, the house which was henceforth associated with the family.[62] It may have been the move to Penrhyn that led to the return of Penmynydd to the descendants of Tudur Fychan. But the link with Anglesey was not broken; before the rise of the Bulkeleys of Beaumaris the Griffiths of Penrhyn were probably the leading landowners in the county. Gwilym Fychan was farming the manor of Gafrogwy between 1456 and 1459 and his son, the future chamberlain of north Wales, was *rhaglaw* of Twrcelyn between 1480 and 1482.[63] He died in 1483 and was succeeded by his son William who was appointed chamberlain in that year and who was knighted in 1489. The family's influence declined in the second half of the sixteenth century after much of the inheritance had been divided among co-heiresses. It was the activities of the spendthrift Piers Griffith, the last of the direct male line, that finally brought the greatness of Penrhyn to an end.

As well as buying land on an even larger scale than his father (a cartulary contains details of some 212 deeds, almost all of them recording acquisitions by him in Anglesey and Caernarfonshire) Gwilym Fychan was responsible for the foundation of another Anglesey family, that of Plas Newydd in the township of Porthaml in Menai.[64] This was an estate based entirely on the purchase of

60  BUASC Penrhyn 14.
61  BUASC Penrhyn 17-18.
62  For the subsequent history of the family see *Y Bywgraffiadur Cymreig, Atodiad*, pp.95-8.
63  TNA SC6/1154/2, m.14a; 1155/5, m.6a; 1155/6, m.6a.
64  BUASC Penrhyn Further Additional, cartulary, 1329-1488.

land outside the kindred. Porthaml was originally held by descendants of Lly-warch ap Bran; among them at the end of the fourteenth century was Hwlcyn ap Dafydd ab Ieuan Wyddel who was killed in the Glyn Dŵr revolt.[65] Hwlcyn had four sons, Madog, Llywelyn, Goronwy and Maredudd. According to the pedigrees none of the brothers had any sons and Llywelyn is said to have sold the lands that became the nucleus of the Plas Newydd estate to Gwilym Fy-chan ap Gwilym ap Gruffudd about 1475; other sources suggest that all the brothers had sold their shares to Gwilym ap Gruffudd.[66] These statements are not entirely correct but there is a grain of truth in them which suggests that men remembered something about the origins of the estate. In 1476 Hywel ap Robin ap Gruffudd had quitclaimed all the former lands of Maredudd ap Hwl-cyn in Porthaml to William Griffith and four years later Gwenhwyfar, the wife of Hywel ab Iorwerth Fychan and the daughter and executrix of Llywelyn ap Hwlcyn did the same with the lands which her father had acquired in *tir prid* from Goronwy Llwyd.[67] In 1482 Ieuan ap Madog ap Hwlcyn conveyed all his property in Porthaml to William.[68]

These were not the only lands bought by Gwilym Fychan in Porthaml; he had been acquiring property there since 1465 at least.[69] This property was not intended as an addition to the main Penrhyn estate. Gwilym Fychan's first wife was Alice, the daughter and heiress of Sir Richard Dalton of Apthorpe in Northamptonshire and this marriage probably explains his petition of 1442 for a grant of denizenship (the legal status of an Englishman).[70] Some pedigrees name his second wife as Gwenllian, daughter of Iorwerth ap Dafydd, with whom he had three sons, Robert, Edmund and William. But these sons were not born in wedlock. On 7 February 1479 William Griffith granted lands in Maenol Bangor to his sons Robert, Edmund and William by *cynnwys;* their il-legitimacy is made perfectly clear in the deed which describes them as bas-tards.[71] The estate was intended as an inheritance for Robert and this probably explains a series of transactions between 1477 and 1479, the result of which was to convey lands in Porthaml and several adjacent townships to him.[72]

65  TNA SC6/1233/1

66  Bartrum, *WG*, Llywarch ap Bran 4; Henry Rowlands, op.cit., 1848, p.243; J. E.Griffith, *Pedigrees of Anglesey and Caernarvonshire Families* (1914), p.56.

67  NLW Llanfair and Brynodol D15, D26.

68  NLW Llanfair and Brynodol D30; this proves that Madog ap Hwlcyn did, after all, have a son.

69  NLW Llanfair and Brynodol D31, D9, D11, D28, D20, D29, D13.

70  *Y Bywgraffiadur Cymreig*, Atodiad, p.94; *CAP*, p.38; *CPR 1441-1446*, 164. His father had petitioned in similar terms but his petition is incorrectly dated to 1439-42 in *CAP* since he died in 1431.

71  NLW Llanfair and Brynodol D24.

72  NLW Llanfair and Brynodol D22, D27, D18. Robert was also the founder of the family of Llanfair-is-gaer across the Menai Straits.

A later document suggests that there was some ill-feeling between Robert and his neighbours in Porthaml; on 31 October 1499 an award was made by arbitrators in the dispute between him and Maredudd ap Thomas ap Maredudd which had led to his 'hurtyng and maymyng'.[73] The estate, sometimes known as Plas Newydd and sometimes as Porthaml, was sold by Maurice Griffith to Sir Henry Bagnall at the end of the sixteenth century.[74]

A number of families in the commote of Menai claimed descent from Llywarch ap Bran. A leading member of the kindred was Maredudd Ddu of the line of Iorwerth ap Llywarch, who lived at the beginning of the fourteenth century; he had two sons, Cynwrig and Ieuan Wyddel. Cynwrig had at least six sons; two of them, Tudur and Deicws, held some local offices but they were overshadowed by another brother, Maredudd. As early as 1378-9 he was farming the Llannerch-y-medd tolls and the manor of Rhosyr; he was *rhingyll* of Menai from 1390-1 until the revolt in which he played an active part.[75] He and his brothers submitted in November 1406 and the quality of his contribution to the cause of Owain Glyn Dŵr may be reflected in the fine he had to pay for forgiveness. This was the large sum of five pounds, the third highest fine imposed in Anglesey.[76] But the authorities needed men like him since with his experience he was one of those on whom the royal administration had to depend. By 1408-9 he was farming the manors of Cemais and Penrhosllugwy and the Llannerch-y-medd tolls as well as being steward of the borough of Newborough, an approver of the manor of Rhosyr and under-sheriff of the county. In the same year he acquired escheat lands in Malltraeth, Talybolion, Menai and Newborough.[77] He was still farming Penrhosllugwy in 1413-4 as well as the Llanidan ferry, several mills and escheat lands in Menai and in 1421-2 he was farmer of Rhosyr, joint steward of Menai with his brothers and farmer of Newborough.[78] As one might expect, he was a prominent figure in Newborough and in deeds of 1418 and 1426 he was described as alderman of the borough; in 1417 he was appointed the king's serjeant-at-arms in Anglesey.[79] He was dead by 1428 and was succeeded by his son Thomas and the line ended with Thomas's great-grand-daughter Elen ferch Richard ap Maredudd ap

---

73  NLW Llanfair and Brynodol D38, for another dispute in which he was involved in 1490 with Rowland Bulkeley, see NLW Llanfair and Brynodol D11.

74  BUASC Plas Newydd, v, 1434;  Griffith, *Pedigrees*, p.56.

75  TNA SC6/1150/5, mm.3a, 4b;  1151/4, m.4b;  1151/6, m.4b.

76  Of his brothers Deicws paid £1 10s, Tudur £1 and Llywelyn 10s. (Glyn Roberts, 'The Anglesey submissions of 1406', 57).

77  TNA SC6/1152/4, mm.2a, 3b, 5a, 5b, 6a;  1233/1.

78  TNA SC6/1152/5, mm.2a, 4a;  1153/1, mm.7b, 6b.

79  NLW Carreglwyd, i, 1754; E.A. Lewis, *The Mediaeval Boroughs of Snowdonia* (1912), pp.297-8; *CPR 1416-1422*,101.

Thomas who married William, the second son of Rowland Bulkeley. The family of Bulkeley of Porthaml came to an end in 1714, having in 1707 absorbed what was left of the Penmynydd estate.[80]

Maredudd ap Cynwrig is an interesting figure.[81] His career shows just how rapid rehabilitation could be for an experienced administrator after the Glyn Dŵr revolt and it also shows how a leading member of a local lineage could dominate his community. Although no surviving deeds show him acquiring land, he must have held a considerable amount in and around Porthaml. And his was not the only family whose roots lay in that township. The Plas Newydd estate originated in the inheritance of the four sons of Hwlcyn ap Dafydd ab Ieuan Wyddel and from Dafydd's other son Llywelyn was descended the Berw family. Llywelyn ap Dafydd was *rhaglaw* of Menai between 1388 and 1391 and *rhingyll* on three occasions between 1377 and 1382.[82] Of his two sons Rhys inherited Bodowyr and Hywel Berw; Hywel held several offices in the early fifteenth century, including the ringildry in 1418-9 and again in 1421-2 and during the century he added to his inherited lands by purchase as his father had done.[83] His son Ithel was also a man of substance who was *rhingyll* of the commote in 1437-8 and one of the approvers of it in 1449-50 and 1456-7.[84] Ithel ap Hywel had at least one son, Owain and his son John Owen, a cleric, sold the Berw estate to Owen Holland in 1521.[85] According to the family history, Ithel had a daughter who married Owen Holland's father.[86] It may have been Ithel ap Hywel who towards the end of the fifteenth century built the house at Berw, now in ruins, which adjoins the house built by Sir Thomas Holland in the seventeenth century.[87]

It was not only the descendants of Iorwerth ap Llywarch who founded landed estates. Between Porthaml and Plas Newydd stands one of the most impressive sixteenth-century houses in Anglesey, Plas Coch, built by Hugh Hughes in the reign of Elizabeth I. The Plas Coch family was descended from Cadwgan ap Llywarch ap Bran; Hywel ap Gwyn ab Iorwerth was one of the

---

80  In a rental of Newborough made in 1428 his son Thomas held a number of plots but there were none in his name (NLW Llanfair and Brynodol M4). Griffith, *Pedigrees*, p.12; Glyn Roberts, 'Teulu Penmynydd', p.274.

81  For Maredudd's career see A.D. Carr, 'Maredudd ap Cynwrig: a medieval public person', *TAAS* 1998, pp.13-21.

82  TNA SC6/1151/5, m.4b; 1151/6, m.4b; 1150/4, m.3b; 1150/6, m.4a; 1150/8, m.4a.

83  TNA SC6/1152/7, m.4a; 1153/1, m.6a; NLW Carreglwyd i, 2362, 2351, 2352, 2358. For purchases by his father see NLW Carreglwyd i, 2355, 2359.

84  TNA SC6/1153/4, m.7a; he was joint farmer with Madog ap Hwlcyn ap Dafydd. SC6/1153/6, m.7a; 1154/2, m.8a.

85  NLW Carreglwyd i, 2338, 2041.

86  John Williams, *The History of Berw*, 1861 (1915), pp.7-8.

87  ibid., pp.6-7. The house is described in RCAHM *Anglesey Inventory*, pp.100b-101a.

heirs of Gwely Cadwgan ap Llywarch in Porthaml in 1352.[88] Hywel's grandson
Madog ab Ieuan ap Hywel was still in rebellion in 1408-9 but he must have
made his peace soon afterwards; he purchased land in 1438 and 1439 and he
died in 1447.[89] In his will he described himself as a parishioner of the church
of Llanedwen and desired to be buried there; all his lands were left to his sons
Ieuan and Llywelyn and his goods to Ieuan.[90] Neither Madog nor Ieuan held
any offices, which suggests that they were not among the more eminent of the
descendants of Llywarch ap Bran. Ieuan died in 1483; his son Llywelyn was
one of the approvers of Menai in 1479 and between 1476 and 1495 he acquired
a substantial amount of land.[91] He was probably dead by 1500 and his lands
were inherited by his son Hugh who went on adding to his inheritance in
Porthaml in the early years of the sixteenth century. The families of Plas
Newydd, Porthaml, Berw and Plas Coch are among the few Anglesey houses
for which some medieval documents have survived and they are also interesting
because they all emerged in the township which had been the cradle of the lineage of Llywarch ap Bran.

The commote of Llifon was dominated by the descendants of Hwfa ap Cynddelw. The leading families which emerged there were those of Prysaeddfed,
Chwaen, Bodychen and Treiorwerth and these were all descended from Iorwerth Ddu ab Iorwerth ap Gruffudd ab Iorwerth of the line of Matusalem ap
Hwfa. Although a layman, Iorwerth Ddu was one of the prebendaries of the
collegiate church of Caergybi and he was dead by 1391.[92] He had one son,
Hywel, who in 1371 was one of those who claimed the right to present to one
of the Caergybi prebends.[93] Between 1372 and 1375 he was *rhaglaw* of Llifon
and in 1381-2 he farmed the townships of Cleifiog and Llanllibio.[94] There is
no mention of him in connection with the Glyn Dŵr revolt although he was
alive at that time, but his son Hwlcyn, *rhingyll* of Talybolion between 1392 and
1395 and again in 1397-8, died in rebellion.[95] The rise of these families really
began with Hwlcyn's son Llywelyn who certainly does not seem to have suffered in any way despite his father's fate. He was among the men of Talybolion
who made their peace with the king in 1406 when he must have been very

---

88  In 1317 Gwyn ab Iorwerth ap Cadwgan conveyed land in Porthaml to Maredudd Ddu (Henry
    Rowlands, op.cit., 1849, p.105). *Extent ol Anglesey*, p.255.

89  TNA SC6/1233/1; BUASC Plas Coch 1, 2.

90  BUASC Plas Coch 3.

91  BUASC Plas Coch 17, 11. The lands Llywelyn acquired were in Porthaml and Tre'r-beirdd
    (BUASC Plas Coch 9, 10, 13, 16, 18, 20, 22).

92  *CPR 1388-1392*, 400.

93  TNA E315/166, f.5a.

94  TNA E163/24/1, mm.1a-b; SC6/1150/8, m.1b.

95  He was among the witnesses to a deed in 1408 (BUASC Penrhyn 384). TNA SC6/1151/8, m.2a;
    1152/1, m.2a; NLW Llanfair and Brynodol M2; TNA SC6/1233/1.

young and in 1419-20 he was *rhaglaw* of Llifon.[96] In 1421-2 he was *rhingyll* of Talybolion as well as being one of the farmers of Cleifiog and Llanllibio and in 1437-8 he farmed the manor of Cemais.[97] He was again *rhingyll* of Talybolion between 1448 and 1454 and farmer of Cemais in 1453-4. In the latter year lead was supplied by him for the king's works and the last reference to him is in a deed of 1460.[98]

Of Llywelyn's sons, Huw, or Huw Lewis as he is generally known, inherited Prysaeddfed and was the founder of that family. He was *rhaglaw* of Malltraeth in 1471-2 and in 1480-1 he farmed the raglotries of Malltraeth, Llifon and Talybolion.[99] From 1464 onwards he farmed various escheat lands and he may at one time have held some office at court.[100] Rhys ap Llywelyn ap Hwlcyn founded the family of Bodychen in Bodwrog; by way of reward for his service at Bosworth he was appointed sheriff of Anglesey in 1485 and granted denizenship in 1486.[101] Gruffudd ap Llywelyn ap Hwlcyn was the ancestor of the family of Chwaen, while Meurig established the house of Bodeon in Malltraeth. The fine east window in Llangadwaladr church was either erected by him or by his son Owain in his memory.[102] Another Llifon family was that of Treiorwerth which was descended from Llywelyn, the brother of Hwlcyn ap Hywel, who made his peace with the crown in 1406 and held various farms in Llifon and Talybolion, both before and after the revolt.[103] His son Hywel, known as Hywel y Farf, was *rhingyll* of Llifon in 1424-5 and had four sons.[104] These were not the only land-owning families to emerge in Llifon but it was the lineage of Hwfa ap Cynddelw that was particularly associated with that commote.

In Twrcelyn the dominant lineage was that of Carwed and the most important family to emerge from it was that of Llwydiarth and Llysdulas. The line really began with Hywel ap Cynwrig ab Iorwerth Fychan, one of the heirs of Gwely Tegerin ap Carwed in Llysdulas in 1352.[105] His grandfather Iorwerth Fychan had been *rhaglaw* of Twrcelyn in 1302-3; Hywel was *rhaglaw* between

96  Glyn Roberts, 'The Anglesey submissions of 1406', p.50; TNA SC6/1152/8, m.2b.

97  TNA SC6/1153/1, mm.3a, 4a; 1153/4, m.11a.

98  TNA SC6/1216/7; 1217/2; NLW Sotheby 51.

99  TNA SC6/1155/2, m.2b; 1155/5, m.2a.

100  TNA SC6/1154/5, m.4b; 1155/2, m.3b; Eurys I. Rowlands, ed., *Gwaith Lewys Môn* (1975), p.14.

101  *Gwaith Lewys Môn*, p.391; H.T.Evans, *Wales and the Wars of the Roses* (1915), p.223; Dafydd Wyn Wiliam, 'Llys Bodychen', *TAAS* 1966, pp.50-70.

102  There is a detailed description of the iconography of the Llangadwaladr east window by Richard B. White, 'The Llangadwaladr east window – an examination of the inscription and its personae', *TAAS* 1969-70, pp.80-110.

103  Glyn Roberts, op.cit., p.48; he paid a fine of £3 6s 8d, which suggests that he was among the leading rebels.

104  TNA SC6/1153/2, m.3a.

105  *Extent of Anglesey*, p.217.

1336 and 1340, in 1343-4 and again between 1351 and 1353.[106] He had three sons, Ieuan, Cynwrig and Llywelyn; Ieuan was *rhaglaw* in 1388-9 and again in 1394-5 and *rhingyll* between 1391 and 1395 and like many other members of this class he died in rebellion.[107] His son Dafydd made his peace in 1406; it was not uncommon for the father to be killed or unreconciled and for the son to submit.[108] Dafydd's career was long and not undistinguished; from 1418 to 1425 he was both *rhaglaw* and *rhingyll* of Twrcelyn and he was still *rhingyll* in 1441-2.[109] In 1437-8 he farmed the Llannerch-y-medd tolls and the manor of Penrhosllugwy and the latter was still in his hands in 1449-50.[110] According to tradition he met his end in an affray in Beaumaris. His heir was his son Gwilym who was farming Penrhosllugwy in 1452-3. Gwilym was followed by his son Dafydd who held the ringildry in 1472-3 as well as farming Penrhosllugwy and Nantmawr and the escheat lands in Amlwch which his grandfather had farmed more than fifty years before.[111] Dafydd ap Gwilym ap Dafydd had at least six sons, Rhys, Thomas, Nicholas, Huw, William and Dafydd; Rhys inherited Llwydiarth and Thomas Llysdulas and they proceeded to build up their estates. The Twrcelyn crown rental of 1549 shows how much they held and it also shows how the system of land tenure based on kindred had gradually disintegrated.[112] It also shows how long a process was the accumulation of a coherent landed estate. Thomas Lloyd of Llysdulas held no fewer than 49 parcels scattered over the commote, while Dafydd ap Rhys ap Dafydd ap Gwilym of Llwydiarth had 25 different parcels. As Llysdulas and Bodafon were large and diffuse townships this kind of scatter was probably inevitable.

The power and wealth of the Penrhyn family was the consequence of a combination of pre-conquest privilege, office, inheritance and purchase. The other great Anglesey family, the Bulkeleys of Beaumaris, who were to dominate the county from the sixteenth century to the nineteenth, began with an immigrant from Cheshire and a strategic marriage.[113] The family came originally from Cheadle and the first to settle in Beaumaris was William Bulkeley the elder who was born in 1418. William was not a poor man; when he first came to Beaumaris he was heir to an estate in Cheshire worth £40 a year.[114] But what

---

106  TNA SC6/1227/4; 1229/3; 1229/7, m.2a; 1149/2, m.5a; 1149/3, m.6b.

107  TNA SC6/1151/5, m.3b; 1152/1, m.3b; 1151/7, m.3a; 1152/1, m.3a; 1233/1.

108  Glyn Roberts, op.cit., p.52.

109  TNA SC6/1152/7, m.7a; 1153/2, m.2a; 1153/5, m.7a.

110  TNA SC6/1153/4, mm.7a, 10a; 1153/6, m.12a.

111  TNA SC6/1154/1, m.12a; 1155/3, mm.7a, 8b; 1155/2, m 6b,

112  T. Jones Pierce, 'An Anglesey crown rental of the sixteenth century', pp.87-101.

113  D. Cyril Jones, 'The Bulkeleys of Baron Hill, 1440-1621' (unpubl. M.A. thesis, University of Wales, 1958), summarised in D. Cyril Jones, 'The Bulkeleys of Beaumaris, 1440-1547', *TAAS* 1961, pp.1-20.

114  D. Cyril Jones, 'The Bulkeleys of Beaumaris, 1440-1547', pp.1-2.

really established him in Gwynedd was his marriage to Elen or Eleanor, a daughter of Gwilym ap Gruffudd.[115] He was certainly in Beaumaris by 1444 when the burgesses petitioned parliament for the enforcement of the penal laws against Welshmen; they asked for the exception of William 'which is English of Fader and Moder, and in England born, which hath wedded a woman of half blood Welsh'.[116] He also petitioned to be allowed to hold office in Wales notwithstanding the statute which disqualified any Englishman with a Welsh wife, pointing out, not altogether correctly, that his late father-in-law had been loyal to the king throughout the Glyn Dŵr revolt.[117] The marriage undoubtedly locked him into local society. In 1448 he was appointed the king's serjeant-at-arms in Anglesey and north Wales and by 1452-3 he was deputy-constable of Beaumaris castle, an office which, more than any other, gave him status and influence in the town since the constable was generally an absentee and under the terms of the 1296 charter the deputy-constable was therefore to all intents and purposes mayor.[118] From 1473 to 1489 he was alderman of the borough and he also had interests outside it; in 1456-7 he was farming Cleifiog and Llanllibio and the Llannerch-y-medd tolls, both of which farms he retained for many years, and others later came into his hands.[119] He was a member of various commissions which were appointed from time to time.[120]

All this shows that William Bulkeley was a substantial figure. The way to the top in the fifteenth century was through patronage and he had no lack of that. The position in north Wales is shown very clearly by the events which surrounded the landing of Richard, duke of York, at Beaumaris on his return from Ireland in September 1450.[121] The key element here was the Stanley connection; William's mother-in-law Jonet Stanley was the daughter of Sir William Stanley of Hooton and Sir Thomas Stanley of Alderley had been chamberlain of north Wales since 1439, joint justice of Chester and north Wales from 1443

115  ibid., pp.2-3. Mr Jones suggested that this marriage may have been part of a system of alliances. Gwilym ap Gruffudd's widow Jonet Stanley had married John Pykemere of Caernarfon after Gwilym's death and in 1437 Pykemere's daughter Leticia married the Conwy burgess Bartholomew de Bolde; Bolde's daughter Alice was to marry William Bulkeley's eldest son William.
116  *Rot. Parl.*, v, 104.
117  *CAP*, pp.146-7.
118  *CPR 1446-1452*, 129; TNA SC6/1217/1.
119  Colin M. Evans, 'The medieval borough of Beaumaris and the commote of Dindaethwy, 1200-1600' (unpubl. M.A. thesis, University of Wales, 1949), App., p.108. TNA SC6/1154/2, mm.12b, 13b. From 1459-60 he was farming the manor of Gafrogwy, from 1465 to 1473 he was joint farmer of Cemais and in 1483-4 he was farming Aberffraw (TNA SC6/1217/3; 1154/6, m.7a; 1155/3, m.5a; 1217/7).
120  *CPR 1461-1467*, 529; *CPR 1467-1477*, 524.
121  Ralph A. Griffiths, 'Richard, duke of York and the royal household in Wales, 1449-1450', *WHR* 8 (1976), 14-25.

to 1450 and sole justice after the murder of the duke of Suffolk in 1450.[122] Two of William's sons were to marry daughters of Sir Thomas and the son and heir of Gwilym Fychan of Penrhyn was to marry a grand-daughter.[123] In these circumstances it is not difficult to attribute William's rise to his membership of that network of Cheshire families which played so prominent a part in the affairs of the fourteenth and fifteenth-century principality.

But it was not only office and patronage that contributed to the rise of the Bulkeleys. Like all such families, their power and influence were in the last resort based on the acquisition and tenure of land. The centre of Bulkeley power was the town of Beaumaris itself; the first reference to William acquiring a stake there is a conveyance dated 20 March 1450 to him by John Bate of a burgage adjoining the burgage of the chapel of St Mary.[124] The next acquisition was on 8 August 1451 and from then on there was a steady stream of conveyances.[125] Altogether there are 35 conveyances of burgages, lands and rent-charges between 1450 and 1490.[126] William Bulkeley became the leading proprietor in the town and it was in the last quarter of the fifteenth century that he built the house near the church, Henblas, which was the family's principal seat until they moved to Baron Hill in the early seventeenth century.[127] Land was bought in other parts of Anglesey and Caernarfonshire and the Anglesey estate soon began to grow. The earliest purchase outside Beaumaris was of lands in Cemlyn by Elen between 1449 and 1451, while the first purchases on a large scale were in Llanddyfnan and Castell Bwlchgwyn where between 1462 and 1476 there were no fewer than twenty separate transactions by which William, or his wife, or both of them acquired property.[128] Between them William and Elen must have made a formidable team; the foundations of the greatest Anglesey estate, which was to overshadow and outlive Penrhyn, had now been laid.

William Bulkeley the elder died in 1490. In his will he left money for masses and prayers and for books and vestments for Beaumaris church; twenty pounds were to be spent on a tomb for him alongside his wife.[129] His sons Richard, Edmund and Rowland were to be maintained out of his estate, as was his son

---

122  ibid., p.16.
123  ibid., p.18.
124  BUASC Baron Hill 465.
125  BUASC Baron Hill 467.
126  These break down as follows: 1450: 1;  1451-60: 16;  1461-70: 9;  1471-80: 5;  1481-90: 4.
127  D. Cyril Jones, 'The Bulkeleys of Beaumaris, 1440-1547', pp.4-5; the site came into his hands in 1474 (BUASC Baron Hill 510).
128  BUASC Baron Hill 1494-6, 1094-1113; 1115-6; the growth of the estate is also discussed by D. Cyril Jones, 'The Bulkeleys of Baron Hill, 1440-1621'.
129  BUASC Baron Hill 4;  Mr D. Cyril Jones argues that this tomb is the alabaster one still to be seen in Beaumaris church ("The Bulkeleys of Beaumaris, 1440-1547', p.18, n.38). I am grateful to Dr Madeleine Gray for discussing the dating of the tomb with me.

Hugh should he lose the office of deputy-constable of Conwy castle. Richard was a cleric and by 1490 he was archdeacon of Merioneth and a prebendary of Caergybi; if he should gain further preferment or should any of the other sons get on in the world their share of the income would go to their less fortunate brothers. The residue of the estate was to go to the eldest son William, as long as he was of sound mind; if not, it was to go to the others in order of seniority. William did, in fact, inherit, but there is no further mention of him until his death in 1516.[130] He had certainly bought land in Beaumaris and elsewhere before 1490 and between 1462 and 1473 he was alderman.[131] He had married Alice, the daughter and heiress of the wealthy Conwy burgess Bartholomew de Bolde and this marriage brought the Bolde inheritance in the Conwy valley into the possession of the Bulkeleys.[132] William's brothers Edmund, Richard and Rowland also obtained a considerable amount of property and the steady stream already mentioned was to become a torrent after 1500. The younger William had at least one son but he must have predeceased him as the main line was to descend through his brother Rowland.[133] The dominant figure in this generation, however, was Richard who, being a cleric, was unable to found a dynasty; he was one of the bailiffs of Beaumaris in 1483-4 and he succeeded his father as alderman in 1489.[134] Rowland, after succeeding his father as deputy-constable of Beaumaris castle, eventually became constable, an appointment which recognised the position of the Bulkeleys in the town.[135]

One of the principal social and cultural functions of the leaders of local society was the patronage and sustenance of the bardic tradition.[136] The tradition in medieval Anglesey awaits its chronicler and there are many questions that have yet to be answered about patronage, especially about its economic background. To what extent, for example, did poetry reflect the economic standing of a patron and to what extent was patronage a form of conspicuous consumption? Most professional poets were themselves members of the same social class as their patrons and several came from Anglesey; of the poets who sang to the princes, Meilir, his son Gwalchmai and Gwalchmai's sons Einion and

130  D. Cyril Jones, op.cit., p.6.

131  BUASC Baron Hill 499, 506, 508, 1331, 1333, 1434;  Colin M. Evans, op.cit., App., p.108.

132  D. Cyril Jones, op.cit., p.3; the marriage agreement is BUASC Baron Hill 1. Bolde died in 1453; for details of his lands see T. Jones Pierce, 'The *gafael* in Bangor MS. 1939', pp.195-228, and C.A.Gresham, 'The Bolde rental (Bangor MS. 1939)', *TCHS* 26 (1965), 31-49.

133  The younger William had a son Bartholomew who was living in 1470 (BUASC Bangor 1920 (i)).

134  TNA SC6/1217/7 Colin M. Evans, op.cit., App., p.108.

135  D. Cyril Jones, op.cit., p.7.

136  For an encyclopaedic study of the bardic tradition in a single parish see Dafydd Wyn Wiliam, 'Y traddodiad barddol ym mhlwyf Bodedern, Môn', *TAAS* 1969-70, pp.39-79; 1971-2, pp.52-97; 1973, pp.55-110; 1974, pp.41-77; 1975, pp.24-68.

possibly Elidir Sais held lands there and Dafydd Benfras came from Cornwy in the north-west corner of the island.[137] Gruffudd ap Maredudd ap Dafydd held lands in Dronwy, Aberalaw and Carneddor in 1352 and was *rhaglaw* of Talybolion between 1372 and 1375, while Gruffudd Gryg was the tenant of lands at Tregwehelyth in Llifon and may be the Gruffudd *Grek* who was *rhingyll* of Malltraeth in 1357-8.[138] Gwilym ap Sefnyn had lands in Llwydiarth Esgob early in the next century and one of the most eminent poets of the late fifteenth and early sixteenth centuries was Lewys Môn, whose roots may have been in Llifon.[139]

There are few poems to those not of royal blood among the surviving works of thirteenth-century poets, but Bleddyn Fardd sang to Gruffudd ab Iorwerth ap Maredudd of the line of Hwfa ap Cynddelw.[140] The greatest Anglesey patrons of the fourteenth century were the descendants of Ednyfed Fychan and a substantial body of poetry addressed to them survives. One poet, Gruffudd ap Maredudd ap Dafydd, was particularly associated with them; he composed at least seven poems to Tudur ap Goronwy who died in 1367, to his brother Hywel and to his son Goronwy.[141] Other poets who sang to different members of the family included Gruffudd Fychan ap Gruffudd ab Ednyfed, Gruffudd Gryg, Llywelyn Goch ap Meurig Hen and Rhisierdyn.[142] The other poet particularly associated with the family was Iolo Goch who mourned Tudur ap Goronwy and two of his sons, Goronwy and Ednyfed and who, in another poem, warned four of Tudur's sons of an impending visit to each of their houses.[143] Gruffudd Gryg sought reconciliation with the seven sons of Iorwerth ap Gruffudd of the stock of Hwfa ap Cynddelw. What he had done to bring down their wrath upon him we shall never know, but he said that they hated him 'like an Englishman' and he protested his innocence.[144] Rhisierdyn sang to another member of the lineage of Hwfa, that Hwlcyn ap Hywel ab Iorwerth

137  For Dafydd Benfras see Dafydd Wyn Wiliam, 'Dafydd Benfras a'i ddisgynyddion', *TAAS* 1980, pp.33-5.
138  A.D.Carr, 'Rhai beirdd ym Môn', *BBCS*, 28 (1980), 599.
139  ibid; *Gwaith Lewys Môn*. pp.xi-xvii.
140  Dafydd Wyn Wiliam, 'Y traddodiad barddol...', *TAAS* 1969-70. pp.44-6;  Rhian M. Andrews, 'Gwaith Bleddyn Fardd' in Rhian M. Andrews et al., eds., *Gwaith Bleddyn Fardd a beirdd eraill ail hanner y drydedd ganrif ar ddeg* (Cyfres Beirdd y Tywysogion vii, 1996), pp.634-40.
141  Barry J. Lewis, ed., *Gwaith Gruffudd ap Maredudd (i):canu i deulu Penmynydd* (2003). the most recent appraisal of Gruffudd's work is that in D. Myrddin Lloyd, op.cit., pp.49-54.
142  Nerys Ann Jones and Erwain Haf Rheinallt, *Gwaith Sefnyn, Rhisierdyn, Gruffudd Fychan ap Gruffudd ab Ednyfed a Llywarch Bentwrch* (1995), pp.137-44;  Barry J. Lewis and Eurig Salisbury, eds. *Gwaith Gruffudd Gryg* (2010), pp.44-9;  Dafydd Johnston, ed., *Gwaith Llywelyn Goch ap Meurig Hen* (1998), pp.30-35;  *Gwaith Sefnyn*, pp.52-64.
143  *Gwaith Iolo Goch*, pp.16-32. This poetry is discussed briefly by Eurys I. Rowlands, 'Nodiadau ar y traddodiad moliant a'r cywydd', *Llên Cymru*, 7 (1963), 234-5.
144  *Gwaith Gruffudd Gryg*, pp.38-43.

Ddu who was killed in the Glyn Dŵr revolt.[145] The descendants of Hwlcyn inspired more surviving poetry than any other fifteenth-century Anglesey family. His five grandsons, the sons of Llywelyn ap Hwlcyn, were particularly generous patrons and three poets, Hywel Cilan, Guto'r Glyn and Rhys Goch Glyndyfrdwy, sang to all five. Some of the leading poets of the day sang to individual brothers, among them Tudur Penllyn, Lewys Glyn Cothi, Lewys Môn, Guto'r Glyn, Ieuan Deulwyn, Hywel Rheinallt and Tudur Aled.[146] Tudur Penllyn laid particular stress on the good table kept by Huw Lewys at Prysaeddfed and Lewys Glyn Cothi and Lewys Môn mourned the death of his wife Sioned or Joan, the daughter of William Bulkeley the elder.[147]

But the sons of Llywelyn ap Hwlcyn were not the only patrons in the county. Dafydd ab Edmwnd and Hywel Cilan mourned the death of Dafydd ab Ieuan ap Hywel of Llwydiarth, traditionally killed in a brawl in Beaumaris.[148] According to the story Dafydd's wife Angharad died of shock when she heard of her husband's death and they were buried together in the friary at Llan-faes, a point confirmed by Hywel Cilan.[149] Guto'r Glyn and Tudur Penllyn praised Dafydd's grandson Dafydd ap Gwilym and he, too, was mourned by Lewis Glyn Cothi.[150] It is hardly surprising that more poetry was addressed to Anglesey patrons by Lewys Môn than by any other poet. The families he praised included those of Chwaen, Erddreiniog, Trefeilir, Bodewryd, Penmynydd and Porthaml.[151] Among Tudur Aled's patrons were Sir Nicholas ab Elis, the parson of Llaneilian and John Ingram, prior of Penmon.[152] Rhys Goch Eryri had mourned the death of Maredudd ap Cynwrig of Porthaml and Dafydd ab Edmwnd composed several poems to Rhys Wyn ap Llywelyn ap Tudur of Bodffordd, in one of which he advised him against marrying an Englishwoman.[153] He also praised Elen ferch Llywelyn ap Hwlcyn of Llwydiarth and her fourth

---

145 *Gwaith Sefnyn*, pp.78-83.

146 These poems are discussed in ibid., pp.55-70.

147 Thomas Roberts, ed., *Gwaith Tudur Penllyn ac Ieuan ap Tudur Penllyn* (1958), pp.16-18; Dafydd Johnston, ed., *Gwaith Lewys Glyn Cothi* (1995), pp.496-7; *Gwaith Lewys Môn*, pp.10-12.

148 Thomas Roberts, *ed.*, *Gwaith Dafydd ab Edmwnd* (1914), pp.76-8; Islwyn Jones, ed., *Gwaith Hywel Cilan* (1963), pp.55-70.

149 Saunders Lewis, 'Dafydd ab Edmwnd', in J.E. Caerwyn Williams, ed., *Ysgrifau Beirniadol*, 10 (1977), pp.221-2.

150 *Gwaith Guto'r Glyn*, pp.96-7; *Gwaith Tudur Penllyn*, pp.38-40; *Gwaith Lewys Glyn Cothi*, pp.493-5.

151 *Gwaith Lewys Môn*, pp. 24-7, 78-80, 81-3, 91-4, 99-101, 105-8; these are not Lewys's only poems to Anglesey patrons.

152 T. Gwynn Jones, ed., *Gwaith Tudur Aled* (1926), pp. 342-5, 399-402.

153 *Gwaith Rhys Goch Eryri*, pp.45-8; *Gwaith Dafydd ab Edmwnd*, pp.89-101; Saunders Lewis, op.cit., pp.224-8. Mr Lewis suggested that these poems are by way of being an exhortation to Rhys to remain true to his inheritance and not to let himself be anglicised. Rhys held no office but he appears in a deed of 1481 (BUASC Baron Hill 1600); he also made fine for acquiring land in Heneglwys without licence in 1456-7 (TNA SC6/1154/2, m.19a).

husband Cynwrig ap Dafydd ab Ithel Fychan. Other poets sang to other patrons and many of their poems have yet to be published.

One aspect of this class which merits particular attention is its marriages.[154]
At this level of society marriage had nothing to do with romantic attachment
or the whims of young people. This is not to say that romantic love did not
exist in medieval Wales; the love poetry of contemporary poets cannot all be
dismissed as a literary convention. But marriage involved the alliance of two
families and many interests were involved. Unfortunately no medieval marriage
settlements have survived so we know nothing of such things as dowries or
portions, although they were provided for in Welsh law.[155] But we do know that
the sons of *uchelwyr* generally married the daughters of *uchelwyr;* the class has
been well described as 'an integrated, closely intermarried group of men'.[156] A
well-planned marriage could do much for both families and could affect the
local balance of power; it was not so much the material gains which counted
as influence and status. Free landed proprietors and bond tenants might sometimes intermarry but for the leading families of the county such alliances could
only mean disparagement. So romantic love, passion and the union of two
hearts generally took second place to land, influence and possibly eugenic con-
siderations.

Any discussion of marriage should begin with the descendants of Ednyfed
Fychan; marriage was eventually to bring them a crown. By virtue of Ednyfed's
marriage to a daughter of the Lord Rhys his descendants held some scattered
lands in Cardiganshire and Carmarthenshire by the tenure known as Welsh
barony.[157] This tenure was peculiar to those descendants of Welsh royal houses
who had managed to retain part of their patrimony after 1282. These fragments
of the former kingdom of Deheubarth were not much but they were enough
to elevate the heirs of Ednyfed to the ranks of the native aristocracy and most
of the marriages of the heads of the kindred were within this class until they
lost their baronial status in the second half of the fourteenth century. Sir
Gruffudd Llwyd married Gwenllian, a daughter of Cynan ap Maredudd of the
royal line of Deheubarth. Goronwy ap Tudur, who died in 1331, was the husband of Gwerfyl, daughter of Madog ap Gruffudd of Hendwr in Edeirnion,
one of the barons of that commote and a descendant of the royal house of
Powys. According to some pedigrees Madog ap Gruffudd had married one of
Sir Gruffudd Llwyd's daughters, which may explain how lands in Tregarnedd

---

154  The most important marriages are noted in the notes to the genealogical tables in Appendix A.
155  R.R. Davies, 'The status of women and the practice of marriage in late medieval Wales', pp.93-
      114.
156  R.R. Davies, 'Owain Glyn Dŵr and the Welsh squirearchy', p.164.
157  A.D. Carr, 'An aristocracy in decline: the native Welsh lords after the Edwardian conquest',
      *WHR* 5 (1970), 112-3.

came to be in the possession of the Hendwr family at the end of the fourteenth century.[158] Tudur ap Goronwy, who died in 1367, was the second husband of Margaret, daughter and co-heiress of Owain ap Thomas ap Llywelyn of the commote of Is Coed in Cardiganshire, the last male member of the Deheubarth dynasty. Her first husband was William de la Pole, lord of Mawddwy and her sister Elen married Gruffudd Fychan, lord of Glyndyfrdwy and Cynllaith Owain and was therefore the mother of Owain Glyn Dŵr. These marriages made Tudur's sons the first cousins of Owain.[159]

The family's status changed with Tudur's death and this seems to be reflected in his sons' marriages. The links with Gwynedd Is Conwy continued; Tudur's grandfather Tudur Hen had married Angharad, a daughter of Ithel Fychan ab Ithel Gam of Tegeingl in north-east Wales.[160] Goronwy ap Tudur, who died in 1382, married Myfanwy, the daughter of Iorwerth Ddu ab Ednyfed Gam of Pengwern near Llangollen, one of the Mostyn family's many ancestors; her effigy lies beside his on the tomb now in Penmynydd church. The wife of Rhys ap Tudur ap Goronwy was Efa ferch Gruffudd Goch from Ceri in mid-Wales, while Ednyfed married Gwenllian, daughter of Dafydd ap Bleddyn Fychan from Tegeingl; her sister married John or Jenkin Hanmer, the brother-in-law of Owain Glyn Dŵr. Maredudd ap Tudur ap Goronwy found a wife in Anglesey in the person of Margaret, one of the daughters of Dafydd Fychan ap Dafydd Llwyd of Trefeilir in Malltraeth, so Queen Elizabeth II can rank Hwfa ap Cynddelw among her ancestors.[161] It was only to be expected that a kindred as eminent as that of Ednyfed Fychan should find its wives and husbands in many parts of Wales. Tudur ap Goronwy's daughter Angharad, for example, married twice, her first husband being Maredudd Ddu ap Gruffudd of Arwystli and her second Gruffudd Hanmer, another brother-in-law of Owain Glyn Dŵr.

Lesser men did not usually look so far afield. Maredudd Ddu of Porthaml was one who did; his first wife is said to have been a daughter of Ithel Fychan ab Ithel Gam while his second was Irish.[162] Maredudd's heir Cynwrig married Angharad, daughter of Madog ap Gruffudd Fychan of the line of Hwfa ap Cynddelw who was one of the heirs of Gwely Matusalem ap Hwfa in Conysiog in 1352.[163] One of Maredudd's daughters, Arddun, married within the kindred;

---

158 ibid., 122-3; Ralph A. Griffiths, *The Principality of Wales in the Later Middle Ages*, i, p.10; A.D. Carr, 'The Mostyn family and estate, 1200-1642', pp.145-6. The devolution of lands in Tregarnedd is discussed by A.D. Carr, 'Tregarnedd', *TAAS* 1992, pp.20-50.
159 Carr, 'An aristocracy in decline', 123-4.
160 Bartrum, *WG*, Marchudd 12.
161 ibid., Marchudd 13.
162 ibid., Llywarch ap Bran 3.
163 ibid.; *Extent of Anglesey*, p.179.

her husband was Hywel ap Gwyn ab Iorwerth of Plas Coch.[164] The best known of the sons of Cynwrig ap Maredudd, Maredudd, is said to have married Annes, daughter of Robert Puleston of Maelor Saesneg, while one daughter, Nest, was the wife of Hwlcyn Llwyd of Glynllifon who died defending Caernarfon castle against Owain Glyn Dŵr's men in 1404.[165] Maredudd's son and heir Thomas married Angharad, daughter of Hywel y Farf of Treiorwerth and Thomas's cousin Mallt ferch Cynwrig Fychan married Morgan ap Maredudd ap Dafydd, another descendant of Hwfa ap Cynddelw; Mallt was the mother of Hugh Morgan who was dean of Bangor in 1468.[166] A similar pattern may be seen among the other descendants of Maredudd Ddu; Madog ap Hwlcyn ap Dafydd had three daughters, one of whom, Mallt, married Ieuan ap Madog of Plas Coch, also of the stock of Llywarch and two whose names are unknown married Hywel ab Ieuan ap Cynwrig of the line of Hwfa and Llywelyn ap Hwlcyn ap Llywelyn Moel of Trefdraeth Wastrodion, a member of the stock of Gruffudd ap Cynan who was a figure of some importance in the commote of Malltraeth.[167] The family of Berw was descended from Hywel ap Llywelyn ap Dafydd ab Ieuan Wyddel; Hywel's wife was Nest, one of the daughters of Ithel Fychan ap Madog ap Hywel who was killed in the Glyn Dŵr revolt.[168] Their son and heir was a little more adventurous; he married a daughter of Hywel Fychan ab Ieuan of Gesail Gyfarch in Eifionydd.

The marriages of the descendants of Hwfa ap Cynddelw in Llifon followed much the same pattern. Iorwerth Ddu ab Iorwerth married Gwenllian, daughter and heiress of Maredudd Benhir of Talybolion of the stock of Gruffudd ap Cynan.[169] The wife of Iorwerth Ddu's son and heir Hywel was Angharad ferch Hywel ap Cynwrig Fychan from Is Aled and their son Hwlcyn married Erddylad ferch Dafydd ab Iorwerth, a member of that branch of the Llywarch ap Bran kindred which was settled in Twrcelyn. Hwlcyn's son Llywelyn, the ancestor of so many of the leading families in the commote, was twice married. His first wife was Mali ferch Ieuan Llwyd ap Gruffudd of Gorddinog near Llanfairfechan and his second was Angharad, daughter of Dafydd ap Cynwrig ap Goronwy, also of the stock of Hwfa, who was *rhingyll* of Talybolion in 1413-4.[170] Of Llywelyn's five sons, Meurig of Bodeon married Margaret, daughter

164  Bartrum, *WG*, Llywarch ap Bran 3.
165  ibid. The Puleston pedigree, however, requires critical examination. For Hwlcyn Llwyd see Glyn Roberts, 'The Glynnes and the Wynns of Glynllifon', in *Aspects of Welsh History*, p.162.
166  Bartrum, *WG*, Llywarch ap Bran 3; J. Le Neve, *Fasti* 11, p.6.
167  Bartrum, *WG*, Llywarch ap Bran 4; Llywelyn ap Hwlcyn ap Llywelyn Moel was *rhaglaw* of Malltraeth in 1408-9 and between 1413 and 1425 (TNA SC6/1152/4, m.3a; 1152/5, m.3a; 1153/2, m.3b).
168  Bartrum, *WG*, Llywarch ap Bran 4.
169  ibid., Hwfa 8, Gruffudd ap Cynan 10.
170  ibid., Hwfa 8; TNA SC6/1152/5, m.2a.

of Ieuan Fychan ab Ieuan ab Adda of Pengwern, an alliance with a house which owed a good deal to judicious marriages. Huw Lewis of Prysaeddfed married Joan or Sioned, one of the daughters of William Bulkeley the elder of Beaumaris; this again was an alliance of two rising families and in a way marked the acceptance of the Cheshire Bulkeleys into the ranks of the Anglesey *uchelwyr*. Rhys of Bodychen was the husband of Margaret, daughter of Rhys ap Cynwrig ap Roppert from Tegeingl and grand-daughter of Ednyfed ap Tudur of Trecastell. In the next generation the increasing wealth and prestige of the house of Prysaeddfed is shown by the marriage of Huw Lewis's son and heir John to Elizabeth, daughter of Watcyn Fychan of Hergest in Herefordshire.[171]

One family whose marriages are one of the best examples of the way in which a close-knit network of relationships developed was that of Trefeilir. Dafydd Fychan ap Dafydd Llwyd flourished in the second half of the fourteenth century. Between 1350 and 1364 he was *rhingyll* of Llifon, an office in which he was succeeded by his son Cynwrig; in 1363-4 he was joint escheator of Anglesey and in 1372-3 *rhaglaw* of Malltraeth.[172] His first wife was Angharad ferch Gruffudd ap Dafydd ap Tudur of the line of Iarddur; his second, Nest, came from Eifionydd. His heir was his son Conws or Cynwrig who married Mallt, daughter of Gruffudd ap Madog Gloddaith of Gloddaith and Tregarnedd and with her he had three daughters, Gwerfyl, who married Conws ap Hywel ab Iorwerth Ddu, the brother of Hwlcyn ap Hywel of Prysaeddfed, Mallt, who inherited Trefeilir and married Llywelyn ap Dafydd Coch of Mawddwy and Gwenhwyfar, who married Hwfa ab Iorwerth ap Hwfa of Eiriannell in Llifon. Dafydd Fychan also had seven daughters; Gwerfyl married Rhys ap Gruffudd ap Madog Gloddaith, the brother of Mallt who married her brother Conws. This is an interesting pair of marriages which probably formed a single transaction; such alliances were not at all uncommon. Gwenhwyfar was twice married, her first husband being Madog ap Hywel Gymen of the line of Hwfa and her second Gruffudd ab Ieuan ap Gruffudd, a nephew of Sir Hywel y Fwyall, the Eifionydd knight and hero of the French wars. This was also a double marriage since Gruffudd's sister Nest was Dafydd Fychan's second wife. Gwladus married Llywelyn Fychan ap Llywelyn of the stock of Hwfa and Morfudd married Ieuan ap Hywel ap Cynwrig of Llysdulas and Llwydiarth of the Carwed lineage. Margaret, a daughter of Dafydd's second wife, was the wife of Maredudd ap Tudur ap Goronwy. Altogether Dafydd's seven daughters contracted eight marriages and six of these were with Anglesey *uchelwyr* or people with Anglesey connections.

---

171  Dafydd Wyn Wiliam, 'Y traddodiad barddol ...', *TAAS* 1971-2, pp.53-4.
172  Bartrum, *WG*, Hwfa 3; TNA SC6/1149/1, m.4a; 1150/2, m.1b; 1150/3, m.1b; 1150/2, m.7a; E163/24/1, m.1a.

   This discussion of marriages reads like a catalogue, but it is important because it shows the extent to which these families tended to marry within Anglesey and because it shows how many links there were between them over successive generations. It was these marriages which made them such a close-knit group; it has been rightly said of them that '...the ties of marriage served to extend the circle of kinship, to bind one lineage to another and to involve the individual in a further web of obligations'.[173] The marriages of this class could well be analysed in greater detail but enough has been said here to make the point. Marriage was important and men took the greatest care in the selection of suitable partners for their sons and daughters. Sometimes alliances could extend over several generations and with every generation the bonds became stronger and the group more closely knit.

173  R.R. Davies, 'Owain Glyn Dŵr and the Welsh squirearchy', pp.162-4.

# 8 The Towns

THERE WERE TWO BOROUGHS in medieval Anglesey, Beaumaris and Newborough. Beaumaris was founded by Edward I but Newborough was not entirely new; it was the pre-conquest town of Llan-faes transplanted, with the less than whole-hearted enthusiasm of its inhabitants, to a new site. Llan-faes was the centre of the commote of Dindaethwy and urban settlements developed at several such centres during the thirteenth century; there were others at Nefyn, Pwllheli, Caernarfon and Tywyn.[1] But Llan-faes was undoubtedly the most important of them and there is evidence to suggest that the princes granted it certain privileges. In 1284 a total sum of £8 8s 5¾d was due in what were specifically described as burgage rents. Moreover, the foundation of a house of Franciscan friars there by Llywelyn ab Iorwerth in memory of his wife also points to the existence of an urban community since the mendicant orders generally settled in towns.[2] By 1254 Llan-faes was the richest church in Anglesey.[3]

Detailed evidence of urban development and commercial enterprise comes from the period immediately after the Edwardian conquest and is to be found in the records of the new royal administration, in particular the extent of the county made in 1284 and an Anglesey sheriff's account for 1291-2.[4] The extent of Anglesey was made on 13 March 1284. The lands of the manor comprised about 780 acres, valued at sixpence an acre, which meant that it was land of good quality.[5] A duty of tenpence was levied on each tun of wine or ale carried from the port to the town, which indicates that the latter was some distance from the shore. A considerable income from duties on herrings landed and sold is a reminder that fishing played an important part in the economy of medieval Anglesey. Dues of fourpence were collected from each ship calling at the

1 T. Jones Pierce, 'The growth of commutation in Gwynedd during the thirteenth century', pp.122-3.

2 *CAP*, pp.82-3; *Brut y Tywysogyon* (Peniarth 20 version), p.104. The other friaries founded in north Wales in the thirteenth century were likewise in towns at Rhuddlan, Bangor and Denbigh.

3 W.E. Lunt, ed., *The Valuation of Norwich* (1926), p.195.

4 Smith, 'Extent of Anglesey 1284', pp.79-92; an English translation follows on pp.93-116. John Griffiths, 'Two early ministers' accounts for north Wales', 64-5.

5 G.R.J. Jones, 'The distribution of medieval settlement in Anglesey', p.41.

port; as the total value was assessed at £1 6s 8d this suggests that about 80 ships called each year.[6] Tolls were levied on cloth, ale, mead, butchers, bakers and shoemakers as well as on the carriers mentioned in the earlier account. The amount of toll collected from the brewers suggests an annual output of nearly 3000 gallons of ale. The tenants owed certain agricultural services, which suggests again that the town's origins lay in a bond community which was not completely enfranchised.[7] The total issues of the whole town, including the demesne, amounted to £78 5s 11¾d. At Llan-faes, therefore, there were bur-gages, a port, fairs and a court, all of which combined to make a thriving com-mercial centre. This gives the lie to the old and oft-repeated statement that urban life held no attraction for Welshmen.[8]

In 1291-2 the burgage rents due from the tenants of Llan-faes still amounted to £8 8s 5¾d. The account also mentions a ferry across the Menai Straits, dues from ships calling at the port and from a herring fishery, customs on ale and mead and tolls levied on carriers taking horses, pigs and hides from the fairs. Other receipts came from fair tolls, customs on shoemakers and butchers, two trades which reflect the town's agricultural hinterland, the carriage of wine and mead, the issues of the communal oven owned by the prince and the profits of grazing on the borough lands. The total income came to £17 18s 9d. It is clear from this figure that Llan-faes was the commercial centre of Gwynedd and it has been suggested that some 70 per cent of the trade of the principality passed through the port; the discovery there in 1992 of a large quantity of twelfth and thirteenth-century coins underlines its significance.[9] It was the main centre for the import of wine, which implied trading contacts with France and in 1283-4 wine was shipped from there to Conwy and Caernarfon.[10] It is not difficult to account for this prosperity; Llan-faes was conveniently sited, it had a good har-bour and the fact that it was a *maerdref* or royal manor meant that the waste belonged to the prince and that a new kind of tenure could therefore develop. Later legal texts recognised a tenant called *gŵr y farchnad* (lit. market man) who corresponded, more or less, to a burgess.[11] The *maerdref* was, of course, a bond township inhabited and cultivated by bondmen and it is possible that the

---

6  The 1291-2 account allowed for 30 ships.

7  T. Jones Pierce, 'Medieval settlement in Anglesey', p.280; Stephenson, *Governance of Gwynedd*, pp.58-9.

8  Keith Williams-Jones, *The Merioneth Lay Subsidy Roll. 1292-3*, pp.lx-lxi. The population of the borough has been estimated at between 400 and 600 and the number of tenements at about 120 (Colin M. Evans, 'The medieval borough of Beaumaris and the commote of Dindaethwy, 1200-1600', p.35; T. Jones Pierce, 'Medieval settlement in Anglesey', p.279).

9  E. Besly, 'Short cross and other medieval coins from Llanfaes, Anglesey', *British Numismatic Journal* 65 (1995), 46-82.

10  A.J. Taylor, *The King's Works in Wales, 1277-1330*, p.395.

11  T. Jones Pierce, 'The old borough of Nefyn, 1355-1882', *TCHS* 18 (1957), 40.

burgesses of Llan-faes were originally its unfree tenants and their burgages bond tenements.[12]

But Llan-faes was nearing the end of its life. In September 1294 the revolt led in north Wales by Madog ap Llywelyn broke out and in the course of this revolt the rebels burned the church and probably the town as well.[13] Although Edward I spent some time there during his suppression of the rebellion, as he had done in 1283, there was to be no future for the commercial centre of Gwynedd.[14] Once the king had decided to build a new castle and create a borough only a mile from the existing town, its fate was sealed; to have two towns, one Welsh and one English, almost within a stone's throw of each other, made neither political nor economic sense.[15] Llan-faes was not rebuilt; it was deliberately run down. About 1296 the burgesses petitioned the king.[16] In the first of two petitions they complained that they were English by blood and nationality as their ancestors had been; as a result they had suffered greatly during the revolt at the hands of the Welsh, but since they lived in Wales and among the Welsh they were treated as such by the English and consequently had the worst of both worlds. If this claim were true it would suggest that the town had already attracted settlers from outside and that the trade of Gwynedd was to some considerable degree in English hands, but the burgesses of Newborough, legatees of Llan-faes, were Welsh to a man as were those inhabitants of Llan-faes who for some years refused to leave. One can only assume that they were trying to appeal to Edward's generosity and protesting their loyalty. The second petition suggests that they were suffering in the interests of Beaumaris.[17] They had been deprived of the liberties granted them by the charters of the princes. They were not allowed to trade, nor were ships allowed to use the port and they had not been compensated for their houses which had been taken to Beaumaris for the use of the new borough; they were also forbidden to pasture their animals. The justice was ordered to explain why they had not been compensated for their houses, but that was all. Their borough had, to all intents and purposes, been extinguished. On 23 November 1295 the king ordered that the market previously held every Saturday at Llan-faes should in future be held on the same day at Beaumaris and that two fairs should be held there on the eve, day and morrow of the feast of the Assumption and the five following days

12  T. Jones Pierce, 'Medieval settlement in Anglesey', pp.279-81.

13  CCR 1318-1322, 70-1.

14  CPR 1281-1292, 72; CPR 1292-1301, 133-5.

15  Gwilym Usher, 'The foundation of an Edwardian borough; the Beaumaris charter, 1296', TAAS 1967, p.2.

16  CAP, pp.82-3.

17  This petition is printed in full in E.A. Lewis, The Mediaeval Boroughs of Snowdonia, p.295; it must date from this period rather than 1318 as suggested by Professor Rees.

and for a similar period at the feast of the Nativity of the Virgin Mary (7-14 September).[18] The last reference to the port had been in April 1295 when a safe conduct was issued to the master of a ship which had loaded goods there.[19]

Having established Beaumaris and suppressed Llan-faes, Edward was faced with the problem of what to do with the latter's burgesses. The eventual decision was to transfer the borough in its entirety to another site. The site chosen was another *maerdref*, that of Rhosyr, the commotal centre of Menai, about twelve miles away. A borough was founded there and every attempt was made to do justice to the men of Llan-faes; the total burgage rent was exactly the same as before, as was the area of the borough.[20] The first charter was granted on 24 April 1303 under the name of the New Borough and Newborough it has been ever since.[21] But the Llan-faes burgesses were reluctant to move to their new home. Led by a local physician, Master Einion, a number of them refused to leave and more than 30 were amerced for their unreasonable delay in doing so; in 1304-5 Einion and 22 of his fellows had still not paid their amercements and may not have moved.[22] They do not, however, seem to have suffered; the 1352 extent of Newborough mentions several tenements there which some of them had held.

Thus the borough of Llan-faes, a community which bad grown up under the princes and which had reflected the degree of economic change in thirteenth-century Gwynedd, vanished from the face of the earth. Before long it was as if it had never been; the very houses had been dismantled and moved to Beaumaris. As early as 1300-1 the sheriff of Anglesey was accounting for various decayed rents formerly due from Llan-faes, among them a waste plot in the market place, several burgages and two crofts next to the court.[23] The ferry was still there but a year later it had been moved to Beaumaris, where it was to remain.[24] The yield from brewing was down to £1 5s 'because there are not now so many brewers as there used to be' and the bakehouse had been demolished.[25] The town rents and court perquisites were still being farmed in 1302 but in 1303 the sheriff accounted for nothing. The prince's prison was

18  *CCR 1296-1302*, 1. In fact the first fair was held at the feast of the Ascension, not the Assumption (E.A. Lewis, op.cit., p.171).

19  *CPR 1292-1301*, 134.

20  M. Beresford, *New Towns of the Middle Ages* (1967), p.535; Colin M. Evans, op.cit., pp. 31, 95-6.

21  *CPR 1321-1324*, 407; it is printed in E.A. Lewis, op.cit., p.283.

22  M. Beresford, op.cit., p.49; TNA E101/120/1. Master Einion was amerced 3s 4d and the others either 6d or 1s each.

23  TNA SC6/1227/3; the rents included one of 2s 3d from the tenement of Einion the physician, described here as a burgess of Beaumaris, while the burgages had belonged to Einion Ddu, Gwenllian ferch Ieuan, Henry Crach and Richard le Mercer who held three.

24  TNA SC6/1227/4.

25  H.R. Davies, *The Conway and the Menai Ferries*, p.23.

still there in 1304-5, when one Robert ab Ithel was imprisoned there in error when he should have been taken to Beaumaris castle.[26] It was some time before all the burgesses were finally satisfied; in 1305 two of them petitioned the prince for compensation for the lands taken from them.[27]

All that was left was the Franciscan friary near the shore and the parish church. The church was faced with a major problem because of the evaporation of its urban hinterland. It had been the richest church in Anglesey and it went on being taxed as such despite representations.[28] An inquiry was eventually held and on 22 May 1319 it was ordered that the dean and chapter of Bangor, as collectors of the clerical subsidy due from the diocese in 1318, be quit of the tax due from Llan-faes.[29] This was the last episode in the town's history. The church remained in the prince's gift like those on the other royal manors and in 1394 the churches of Llan-faes and Penrhosllugwy were granted to Penmon priory in view of the poverty of that house.[30] When a new extent of Anglesey and Caernarfonshire was made in 1352 all that remained at Llan-faes was the mill.[31] As no remains survive above ground, even the location of the town is uncertain. The reference in 1284 to wine being carried from the port to the town suggests that it lay some distance from the shore. The original centre of the manor must have been on the site of the house called Henllys and the town might therefore have been situated between there and the church. Indeed, the present pattern of roads around the church looks very like a nucleus of urban development. The *maerdref* community would have been the natural nucleus for any growth and the centres of Nefyn, Pwllheli and Tywyn are all some distance from the shore.[32]

The revolt of Madog ap Llywelyn showed Edward I that the defensive system he had devised for Gwynedd at such great cost was incomplete. The decision to plug the gap by building a castle at Beaumaris seems to have been taken in November 1294 and its construction was followed by the establishment of a borough.[33] The purpose of the castle boroughs of north Wales was the pro-

---

26  TNA E101/120/1.

27  *Rec. Caern.*, p.217; one of the petitioners was Master Einion.

28  ibid., p.269; *CAP*, p.138.

29  *CIM* ii, no. 327; *CCR 1318-1323*, 70-1. See also Natalie Fryde, *List of Welsh Entries in the Memoranda Rolls, 1282-1343*, no.420.

30  *CPR 1391-1396*, 504.

31  *Extent of Anglesey*, p.246.

32  This view challenges that put forward by C.J. Delaney and I.N. Soulsby, 'The archaeological implications of redevelopment in the historic towns of Ynys Môn – Isle of Anglesey' (1975), para. 4.2.3. H.R. Davies, op.cit., p.21, also argued for the town being around the church. In 1974 an area near the former Cammell Laird factory was examined during excavations for the Shell pipeline and a ditch was uncovered but no conclusions could be drawn (Richard B. White, 'Rhosgoch to Stanlow Shell Oil pipeline', *BBCS* 27 (1977), 486-7).

33  A.J. Taylor, op.cit., p.396. The construction of the castle is discussed in ibid., pp.396-408.

vision of secure supply bases for the garrisons. If these depended on the hinterland for their food supplies they could easily be cut off; a borough, inhabited
by English settlers, could control local trade and provide additional manpower
for the castle in an emergency. The charters, apart from that of Bala, did not
restrict municipal privileges to Englishmen, but other documents make it abundantly clear that in the castle boroughs this was the intention. In this they resembled the fortified towns established in Gascony by John, Henry III and
Edward I. They were new towns and their street-plans show that they were the
product of the drawing-board rather than of organic municipal growth.[34]

The rights and privileges of these boroughs were contained in their charters
of incorporation. For many towns such liberties were the fruit of long and often
bitter struggles, but for the Edwardian boroughs they were the free gift of the
king.[35] These charters have been compared to company prospectuses; the object was to attract people from all over England to settle in a remote and re-
cently-conquered territory.[36] The Beaumaris charter was granted on 15
September 1296; its terms were identical with those contained in the charters
of the other boroughs. The constable of the castle was mayor *ex-officio;* the effective officers were the two bailiffs elected in the borough court at Michaelmas.[37] The borough was to have a free prison and a merchant guild. The sheriff
was excluded and no Jews were allowed to live there.[38] Any bondman who
managed to remain there for a year and a day would obtain his freedom. The
burgesses were entitled to collect various dues and their liberties, like those of
the other north Wales boroughs, were based on those of Hereford.

The charter gave the borough its legal framework; the next stage was to attract settlers. These would enjoy their lands rent-free for the first ten years and
would thereafter pay an annual rent of one shilling for each burgage. The earliest rental dates from 1305; surnames suggest that the burgesses' places of origin included Lancaster, St Albans, Crosby and Ludlow.[39] There was later a
strong Cheshire element in the town with names like Bunbury, Sandbach,
Macclesfield and, of course, Bulkeley. The building of the castle and the town
led to the displacement of some of the tenants of the township of Cerrig-
gwyddyl which adjoined the Llan-faes demesnes and they were compensated

---

34  The standard work on planned towns is M. Beresford, op.cit.; see also Colin and Rose Bell, *City
Fathers: the early history of town-planning in Britain* (1972), pp.35-61.

35  Gwilym Usher, op.cit., p.1.

36  ibid., pp.1-2.

37  *CChartR.* ii, 465; a full translation and commentary is in Gwilym Usher, op.cit., pp.4-16

38  In fact, all Jews had been expelled from the kingdom in 1290 but there was one in
Carmarthenshire in 1386-7 (William Rees, *South Wales and the March, 1284-1415.* p.222n).

39  *Arch.Camb. Original Documents.* pp.xiv-xviii.

with lands elsewhere in Anglesey.[40] In 1305 there were 132¼ burgages in Beau-maris. Between 1307 and 1316 there were 141½ and in the latter year the num-ber went up to 148. From 1317 there were 154¼ and there the total remained. This made Beaumaris the largest of the castle boroughs. In the second half of the fourteenth century there were 61 burgages in Caernarfon and in 1316, when the various issues of Conwy ceased to be accounted for separately, there were 124 there.[41] There were 77 holders of burgages in 1305, of whom nine were non-resident; the latter included Master James of St George, the Savoyard re-sponsible for Edward's castles in north Wales, who held six and Sir Thomas Danvers, sheriff of Anglesey from 1295 to 1300, who held eleven. Of the resi-dent burgesses the best-endowed was a Welshman, Dafydd ab Einion, who held six burgages; he was the richest man in the town since he also had 162 acres in the borough lands and in the adjacent townships of Llan-faes and Bodgylched.[42]

The borough lands contained 1,486½ acres of which 1,333 acres were arable and 104½ acres were pasture; some was attached to the castle as demesne land. The burgesses held their lands in scattered strips and the size of their shares varied considerably. Next to Dafydd ab Einion the largest share was held by William de Felton, the first constable, who had 53 acres as well as five burgages. The holdings of the other burgesses ranged in size from the 50 acres of Danvers and another former sheriff, Walter de Winchester, to a number of four-acre shares. Thirty burgesses had no land at all and there were four tenants who had land but no burgages. Each burgage plot measured 80 feet by 40 feet. The fact that a plot of land was a burgage did not necessarily mean that it was built on and there was often a good deal of empty space in a medieval town.[43] The topography of medieval Beaumaris is reasonably straightforward; the two main streets were Castle Street and Church Street and they retain their names to this day. The High Cross or market cross was at their intersection. The sea came right up to the castle and it also reached the edge of the town itself where several burgages were lost to it during the fourteenth century. The very name

---

40 E.A. Lewis, 'The decay of tribalism in north Wales', p.62. The lands were in Perthgyr, Castellior, Bodynwy, Dinsylwy, Lledwigan Llys, Trewalchmai and Eiriannell. 22 acres of Cerrig-gwyddyl remained in the hands of the tenants and there were three there in 1352 (*Extent of Anglesey*, pp.238-9).

41 E.A. Lewis, *The Mediaeval Boroughs of Snowdonia*, p.66.

42 Dafydd had been a prominent burgess of Llan-faes; in 1286 he had supplied ropes for the works at Harlech castle (A.J. Taylor, op.cit., p.1034). He also held lands in Conwy and was a bailiff and coroner of Beaumaris in 1303-4 (Keith Williams-Jones, op.cit., p.lxi. and n. which makes the point that he may have served Llywelyn ap Gruffudd before 1282; TNA SC6/1227/5). His son Ieuan was a bailiff in 1316-7 (TNA SC6/1170/11)

43 E.A. Lewis, op.cit., p.63. For an overview of the topography of the town see Richard Hayman, 'Architecture and the development of Beaumaris in the nineteenth century', *Arch.Camb.* 153 (2004), 105-24.

of the borough is a reminder that both town and castle were built on reclaimed marshland. Unlike Caernarfon and Conwy, Beaumaris was not provided with a town wall; this was not erected until after the Glyn Dŵr revolt.

Much of the early history of Beaumaris is revealed in the petitions submitted by the burgesses to the king and the prince of Wales. At his manor of Kennington between 1301 and 1305 Edward of Caernarfon, Edward I's son, received and replied to a large number of petitions from north Wales. The burgesses complained about the failure of the inhabitants of Anglesey to trade in the borough and that of ships coming to the island to use the port.[44] They asked for the farm of the castle demesne lands and this was eventually granted to them in 1314.[45] Some time after 1315 they asked that the bishop of Bangor be instructed to consecrate the chapel which they had built because the parish church (Llandegfan) was some distance away and they could not go there in bad weather. Around the same time they asked for the erection of a wall.[46] The petitions of individuals were entirely to do with land, two of them being from non-residents; the communal petitions show the burgesses strident in defence of their commercial privileges which were being not so much flouted as ignored by the people of the hinterland.

Nevertheless, Beaumaris was intended to be a trading centre and it became the main one in Gwynedd. The earliest statistics available are those for 1304-5 when the fair tolls were £3 13s 4d and the market tolls fourteen shillings; in 1306-7 the former were £4 7s 5d and the latter 10s 11d.[47] A comparison of these figures with those for Newborough indicates that at that time there was more trade there than at Beaumaris and in 1305 the burgesses complained that the inhabitants of the commotes of Dindaethwy, Twrcelyn and Talybolion were taking their goods to Newborough for sale rather than to Beaumaris as they were supposed to do.[48] The fair tolls at Caernarfon and Harlech were also more than those of Beaumaris in 1304-5. But trade was not restricted to markets and fairs. Although all the Edwardian boroughs were ports Beaumaris was undoubtedly the most important; it was the commercial centre of Gwynedd after 1282 as Llan-faes had been before, being the main port of entry and centre for distribution. Although the burgesses complained in 1305 that ships were calling at other Anglesey ports when they should have called there, Beaumaris certainly had a considerable foreign trade. During the reign of Edward II they

---

44  *Rec.Caern.*, p.223.

45  ibid.; *CAP*, p.295; *CCharR*. iii, 272.

46  *CAP*, p.471. The first petition obviously relates to the building of the present parish church.

47  E.A. Lewis, 'The account roll of the chamberlain of the principality of north Wales from Michaelmas 1304 to Michaelmas 1305', 260; TNA SC6/1170/5.

48  *Rec.Caern.*, p.223; in 1304-5 the Newborough fair tolls were £4 4s 9½d and the market tolls £2 2s 1½d.

asked for the construction of a quay and the repair of the quay between the castle and the sea was ordered in 1322.[49] One burgess who was active in the first half of the fourteenth century was Adam Sandbach, a Liverpool merchant. He was one of the bailiffs in 1315-6, 1323-4 and 1331-2 and in 1325 he owned one ship of 60 tons in the port.[50] In 1317-8 he supplied beans for the castle and in the same year his fellow-burgess, the Welshman Einion ab Ieuan, supplied a large quantity of iron.[51] Wine was bought for the castle in 1328-9 from the burgess Edward Friend and much of it was shipped to Caernarfon, Conwy and Cricieth.[52] In fact wine was one of the principal imports, not only to victual the castle but also to grace the tables of English burgesses and Welsh *uchelwyr*. By the early sixteenth century such goods as canvas, iron, hops and ginger were also coming in and the main exports were wool, cloth and hides.[53] The needs of the castle stimulated local trade; without it there would have been no borough and no need to supply Conwy or Caernarfon. To that extent the town might be described as parasitic but Beaumaris handled the trade that had previously gone through Llan-faes and this probably did more than the presence of the castle to encourage commercial activity.

The borough's executive officers were the two bailiffs. In their accounts they answered for the burgage rents, the fair and market tolls and the profits of justice. As in the other north Wales boroughs there were three courts, the borough court held every three weeks, the court leet or view of frank-pledge held twice a year at Easter and Michaelmas and the court of pie-powder, a commercial court held in conjunction with the markets and fairs.[54] The bailiffs also answered for the income from burgages and lands which were in the prince's hands because of the non-residence of their tenants. The Beaumaris ferry was also farmed by the burgesses and the accounts sometimes record the loss of the boat or damage to it.[55] Market and fair tolls fluctuated considerably; the highest figure for the former was 15s 8¾d in 1335-6 and the lowest 1s 6d in 1352-3, while for the latter the highest figure was £4 2s 5d in 1306-7 and the lowest

49  *CAP*, p.117; *CCR 1318-1323*, 415.

50  Colin M. Evans, op.cit., p.267; TNA SC6/1170/10; NLW Pitchford Hall 452; TNA SC6/1213/10; *CAC*, p.219.

51  Colin M. Evans, op. et loc. cit.

52  TNA SC6/1213/6; Edward Friend was a bailiff in 1322-3, 1335-6 and 1339-40 and in 1323 he supplied 160 gallons of Spanish honey for the castle (TNA SC6/1213/1).

53  E.A. Lewis, 'A contribution to the commercial history of medieval Wales', 108-20, 128-31, 170-1; the maritime trade of Beaumaris is also discussed in Chapter 4 above. Trade with Chester is discussed briefly in Laughton, *Life in a Late Medieval City*, pp.176-7.

54  The courts in the north Wales boroughs are discussed by E.A. Lewis, *The Mediaeval Boroughs of Snowdonia*, pp.127-35. For the working of courts in one borough see G.P. Jones and Hugh Owen, *Caernarvon Court Rolls, 1361-1402* (1951).

55  TNA SC6/1170/7. In 1324-5 the bailiffs reported that the boat was entirely destroyed on account of old age and could not be repaired (TNA SC6/1170/16); H.R. Davies, op.cit., p.29.

£1 5s 8d, again in 1352-3.[56] After 1350-1 the accounts are more detailed; in that year the total rents from the borough were £22 17s 6½d. The rest of the income included customs revenue, tolls, profits of justice and the bailiffs accounted for the decay of thirteen burgages inundated by the sea in 1346-7.[57] After 1358 the bailiffs ceased to account separately for these different items since in that year the burgesses began to farm the ferry, profits of justice and tolls for an annual lump sum and they went on doing so for the rest of the medieval period; the initial farm was for ten years at an annual rent of ten marks (£6 13s 4d).[58]

There follows a gap in the accounts until 1376-7, by which time the Black Prince had granted the burgesses the neighbouring township of Bodynwy at an annual rent of six pounds.[59] By 1379-80 there were 21¼ vacant burgages for which no rent had been paid. These had been empty for the last four years, which suggests that the borough was going through a period of decline.[60] Yet another fell vacant the following year and three more in 1381-2 although one of these had been lost to the sea.[61] Some time after Michaelmas 1381 the ferry-boat was sunk in a storm and the catalogue of disasters continued. Four more burgages were vacant in 1384-5, one of which had been burned by the Scots who had attacked the town in 1381, while another belonged to a burgess, Thomas le Kempe, who had been kidnapped by them.[62] The 1385-6 account reported that two others had been destroyed by the Scots and a third by the sea and in 1387-8 Thomas Clerk, bailiff in 1381-2, was pardoned twelve pounds of the arrears of his term of office because the Scots had robbed and despoiled him.[63] The burgesses were excused payment of all the rents due from them for one year from Easter 1389 in the hope that they would be able to pay the full rent in future.[64] This suggests severe economic problems in the town during the reign of Richard II and this seems to have been generally true of north Wales.[65] There was a further respite of rents in 1391-2 because the bailiffs did not know where the money could be raised and the king pardoned the burgesses payment of half the annual rents for five years from Michaelmas 1395.[66]

56  These figures are tabulated in E.A. Lewis, op.cit., p.304.
57  TNA SC6/1149/1, m.7a;  the earliest reference to a burgage swallowed up by the sea is in 1308-9 (SC6/1170/6).
58  TNA SC6/1149/9, m.5b.
59  TNASC6/1150/3, m.4a;  the grant was made on 10 October 1366.
60  TNA SC6/1150/6, m.4b.
61  TNA SC6/1150/7, mm.4b-5a;  1150/8, m.4a-b.
62  TNA SC6/1150/ 10, m.6a-b;  1151/1, mm.6b-7a;  E.A. Lewis, op.cit., p.245.
63  TNA SC6/1151/2, mm.5b-6;  1151/4, m.5a.
64  TNA SC6/1151/5, m.5a.
65  The same was true of Caernarfon and the other boroughs of north Wales (Keith Williams-Jones, 'Caernarvon', p.84).
66  TNA SC6/1151/7, m.5b;  1152/3, m.5b.

In 1400 Owain Glyn Dŵr rose in revolt and, like every other town in Wales, Beaumaris was affected. On his first circuit through north Wales Henry IV stopped there and destroyed the friary at Llan-faes. The castle was later besieged by the rebels and it appears have fallen to them for a time.[67] The besiegers had some Scottish help; the escheator later accounted for some of the debris the Scots had left behind and they had also burned down several houses in the town.[68] After the revolt the burgesses claimed that they had lost goods and chattels worth 2,000 marks and that the rebels had burned down two houses, causing twenty pounds worth of damage; this suggests that Beaumaris suffered far less than did Conwy or Caernarfon.[69] But the revolt did have one very obvious result for the town. In 1407 the burgesses were granted ten pounds towards the cost of making a town ditch and in their account for 1413-4 the bailiffs reported that 30 burgages had been destroyed because a new stone wall had been built.[70] Thus, at long last, Beaumaris got its wall, although it did nothing to arrest the town's decline; in addition to the burgages extinguished by its erection another nine had been submerged by the sea, which brought the total number destroyed in this way since 1346 to at least 23. In 1421-2 the arrears were still considerable and though they were reduced over the next few years, a sum of £10 11s 1d was written off in 1424-5 for reasons described as lack of tenants and the destitution caused by the rebellion.[71] A cumulative list in the 1437-8 account included 48 burgages and a substantial amount of land laid waste by the sea or by lack of tenants and this figure may underestimate the extent of urban decay in fifteenth-century Beaumaris, since among the burgages were the thirty destroyed by the building of the wall.[72] Some burgesses seem either to have died without heirs or to have left the borough, like John Goodhew who returned to England because of his poverty.

Apart from the bailiffs' accounts there is little information about the government of medieval Beaumaris. The main governing body was probably the court leet or view of frankpledge but the only surviving court record is a list of fines and amercements imposed at the borough courts in 1301-2 and this contains little more than names.[73] These are not, however, to be despised and they include many wives amerced for breaches of the assise of ale, among them the wives of five men who had been or who were to be bailiffs. In time some kind

67  William Owen, *Hanes Owain Glandwr, Blaenor y Cymry mewn Rhyfel* (1833), p.37. The course of the revolt in Anglesey is discussed in Chapter 10 below.
68  TNA SC6/1233/1; 1152/4, m.4a.
69  TNA E163/6/38.
70  TNA SC6/1216/2; 1152/5, m.4b; TNA SC6/1151/5, m.5a.
71  TNA SC6/1153/1, m.7a; 1153/2, m.5a.
72  TNA SC6/1153/4, m.12a-b.
73  TNA SC2/215/1.

of town council or common council probably developed; in 1386-7 one Henry Kernyther was selling ale at Holyhead without a licence, having been appointed by the community of the town of Beaumaris.[74] The community mentioned here was probably the town council or some similar assembly of the leading burgesses.[75] The bailiffs were not the only officials. Early accounts include several references to a coroner and there was another official who was not mentioned in the charter although he also existed in the other north Wales boroughs. This was the alderman; the earliest reference to this office in Beaumaris is in 1327 when it was held by Peter Russell.[76] The alderman may have acted as a kind of substitute mayor since the mayoral office was held by the constable of the castle who must often have been an absentee.[77] The office may have had its origin in the gild merchant granted to the burgesses by their charter; in the fifteenth century the alderman was elected at the borough court and the status was much sought after by the wealthier burgesses.[78] Another municipal office may have been that of town clerk, possibly held in the mid-fifteenth century by one John Forrest, described as a notary public. No fewer than 38 deeds between 1446 and 1474 are in a hand which may be his and these include a conveyance by the borough community.[79]

Like the other castle boroughs, Beaumaris was intended as an English colony, but unlike Caernarfon and Conwy there was a considerable Welsh element there in the early years in spite of Edward I's ordinance that 'no Welshman should stay or hold burgages in the walled towns'.[80] There was a good reason for this Welsh presence; these Welshmen were probably former burgesses of Llan-faes who had chosen or who had been allowed to settle in Beaumaris instead of moving to Newborough. Dafydd ab Einion, the wealthiest burgess in 1305, had formerly been associated with Llan-faes and it is possible that it was the richer inhabitants of that town who had been permitted to remain. At least four Welshmen held office as bailiffs of Beaumaris; the 1305 rental listed four Welsh burgesses and three were among those from the town who did fealty to the Black Prince in 1343.[81] Other names appear in deeds; one burgess, Roger de Burton, had either married a Welsh wife or had so much adapted to Welsh

74  TNA SC6/1151/3,m.5b.
75  Keith Williams-Jones, op.cit., p.86;  Colin M. Evans, op.cit., pp.123-4.
76  NLW Pitchford Hall 590.
77  Keith Williams-Jones, op.cit., p.86.
78  E.A. Lewis, op.cit., pp. 155, 159;  Colin Platt, *The English Medieval Town* (1979), pp. 157, 161-2, where Ipswich and Leicester are cited as examples where this was the case.
79  This is discussed by A.D. Carr, '"This my act and deed": the writing of private deeds in late medieval north Wales' in Huw Pryce, ed., *Literacy in Medieval Celtic Societies* (1998), pp.229-30; BUASC Baron Hill 500.
80  *Rec.Caern.*, p.132.
81  TNA SC6/1227/5; 1211/3; 1170/7,11; 1213/8; *Arch.Camb. Original Documents*, pp. xiv-xviii, clii.

ways as to name his daughter Gwerfyl and in 1325 land was conveyed by a burgess called Philip ap Robyn.[82] In 1301-2 the wife of another burgess, Henry de Trim, was called Angharad and in September 1327 six Welshmen were among a number of burgesses who were parties to an action at the justice's sessions.[83]

The leading member of this body of Welsh burgesses was Einion ab Ieuan or Einion Bach. He was a bailiff three times, in 1309-10, 1311-2 and 1343-4.[84] In 1316 he was appointed sheriff of Anglesey and he was still in office in 1327. During all the troubles of Edward II's reign he remained loyal to the king, even when the English sheriffs of Caernarfonshire and Merioneth had gone over to the baronial opposition.[85] He appears to have suffered some persecution, possibly either because of his support for Edward II or because he was a Welshman in a world increasingly dominated by the English burgesses of north Wales. He was imprisoned several times, once, ironically, with William de Shalford, the right-hand man of Roger Mortimer; on that occasion his loyal conduct was put on record.[86] In 1327 he was granted a licence to build a windmill on the Mill Hill by Beaumaris.[87]

Thus the first half of the fourteenth century was a period when Welshmen were not only welcome in Beaumaris but were active and prominent there; if Llan-faes was dead, its spirit lived on. When Hywel ap Gruffudd of Anglesey brought an action in 1330 against Roger Mortimer's former lieutenant William de Shalford claiming that he had caused the death of Edward II by warning Mortimer of a plot to rescue him, not one Beaumaris burgess was among Shalford's sureties.[88] Since these sureties included burgesses of Caernarfon, Conwy, Harlech and Bala, this may reflect the strength of the Welsh element in the town. But this situation was not entirely acceptable to the authorities and about 1345 action was taken against the Welsh burgesses.[89] It was stated that most of the burgesses were now Welsh although the town and its privileges were intended for Englishmen. The liberties of the borough were therefore suspended

---

82  NLW Pitchford Hall 461, 1365.
83  TNA SC2/215/1; NLW Peniarth 405, p.417.
84  He held one burgage in 1305.
85  W.H.Waters, *The Edwardian Settlement of North Wales in its Administrative and Legal Aspects, 1284-1343*, pp. 172, 68.
86  *CAC*, pp.183-4. His conduct and loyalty were investigated as were certain charges brought against him as sheriff in 1320-1 (TNA C143/145/20). He was also in trouble over arrears at the audit of 1330-1 (Natalie Fryde, op.cit., no.679).
87  *CPR 1327-1330*, 194.
88  T.F.Tout, 'The captivity and death of Edward of Caernarvon', pp.186-8. In fact one of Hywel's sureties was called Madog ap Dafydd and a Madog ap Dafydd was a burgess of Beaumaris (NLW Peniarth 405, p.432).
89  TNA E315/166, f.8a.

and a number of burgesses, including, oddly enough, Einion ab Ieuan, made fine for the restoration of their liberties until the next sessions. The formal result of the action was not recorded but the implications were clear enough; Welshmen were not welcome as burgesses in a castle borough.[90]

There are some references to this removal of foreign bodies. Several burgesses applied for burgages left vacant by the departure of Welshmen.[91] There may be some significance in the fact that the burgesses of Newborough in 1352 included two who had been burgesses of Beaumaris; perhaps they had gone at last to the place prepared for them.[92] It is possible that action was taken against the Welsh burgesses after the assassination of Henry de Shalford, the royal attorney in north Wales, in 1345. It is certainly interesting that the men of Beaumaris did not write a hysterical letter to the prince after that event as did their fellows of Denbigh, Caernarfon, Rhuddlan and Conwy.[93] This was the end of the Welsh stake in Beaumaris and the town now took on an almost exclusively English character. The men of Llan-faes and their sons had been tenacious but they had lost in the end; even so, their record shows that the Welsh urban tradition in this part of Anglesey was a strong one.

But the Welsh never seem to have been excluded completely. An inquisition taken in 1408 found that Robert Salmon and other burgesses had leased lands and burgages by *prid* to Deio ap Tudur and other Welshmen and in 1418-9 the escheator accounted for land in the franchises of Beaumaris conveyed by a burgess to a Welshman 'against the statute and ordinance of the king'.[94] This not only suggests that Welshmen were still trying to settle; it also makes it clear that some burgesses, at least, were willing for them to do so. Robert Salmon may, indeed, have had a foot in both camps since a William Roberson Salmon was among those still in rebellion in 1406.[95] In 1415 a burgage was described as adjoining that of Gwenllian de Llŷn.[96] A figure of some standing in the town in the second half of the fifteenth century was John Moyle, whose name suggests that he was Welsh; in 1463 he was deputy-constable of the castle and his interests extended all over Anglesey.[97] When he was outlawed for treason in

90  Three burgages in Cricieth were taken into the king's hand in 1337 because they were held by Welshmen (E.A. Lewis, op.cit., p.196n). The same was true of the two castle boroughs of Flintshire, Flint and Rhuddlan (C.R. Williams, *The History of Flintshire*, i (1961), p.93).

91  NLW Peniarth 405, pp. 432, 437; TNA SC6/1149/1, m.7a.

92  *Extent of Anglesey*, pp. 268, 271.

93  Keith Williams-Jones, *The Merioneth Lay Subsidy Roll, 1292-3*, p.lxii; *CAC*, pp. 230-2, 234-5.

94  BL Add. MS. 33372, p.49; I owe this reference to Keith Williams-Jones; TNA SC6/1152/7, m.10a.

95  Glyn Roberts, 'The Anglesey submissions of 1406', 59.

96  BUASC Baron Hill 458.

97  According to one pedigree he was the son of Goronwy ap Hywel Foel of Talybolion of the stock of Cadrod Hardd (Bartrurn, *WG*, Cadrod Hardd 1); BUASC Baron Hill 462; Colin M. Evans, op.cit., pp.14-34; E.A. Lewis, op.cit., p.81; TNA SC6/1154/5, m.,1b.

1488 he had two burgages and 18½ acres in Beaumaris.[98] But on the whole the Welsh were not popular in the towns and the burgesses were not popular in the hinterland. The tradition survived of a famous affray in the town, 'Y Ffrae Ddu yn y Biwmares', in which Dafydd ab Ieuan ap Hywel of Llwydiarth in Twrcelyn was killed.[99] In 1442 the English burgesses of north Wales petitioned parliament for the renewal of Edward I's ordinances which excluded Welshmen from the boroughs and this was granted in 1444 and confirmed in 1447.[100]

By far the greater part of the population was English although there was probably always some kind of Welsh substratum or proletariat. Although the town had no industry to speak of, it had the normal complement of tradesmen, as surnames show. In the early fourteenth century the burgesses included a butcher, several bakers and mercers, a shoemaker, a shearman, a tailor and millers and tanners and many of these, with their shares in the borough lands, were also farmers. Obviously, as in any borough, some burgesses were richer and more influential than others. Perhaps it is an exaggeration to speak of a municipal patriciate in so small a town but there emerged a local élite, a group of burgesses who generally held the borough offices and who appear as witnesses to deeds. As the fourteenth century progressed some of them held office at county level and in the next century some were to move out of the town and into the ranks of the landowners. The composition of this group may be determined from those who held office as bailiff and from attestations to deeds and the list of those who did fealty to the Black Prince in 1343 reveals who the principal burgesses were at that time.[101] Apart from the borough officers, 22 did fealty and of this number ten had held or were to hold the office of bailiff.

One of the leading figures in Beaumaris at this time was Peter Russell. As well as being alderman, Russell was a bailiff four times between 1306 and 1312 and he was a bailiff of Conwy in 1321-2, a fact which reminds us that many of these early burgesses had interests in more than one town.[102] In 1330 he endowed a chantry.[103] The office of bailiff was obviously restricted to an inner circle of burgesses and already some families were becoming particularly influential; one of the best examples is the Clerk family. A Henry Clerk was bailiff in 1301-2, 1303-4 and 1306-7 and another in 1378-9, 1386-7 and 1394-6.[104]

98  Colin M. Evans, op. cit., p.243
99  E.A. Lewis, op. cit., pp.263-4; William Williams, 'Historia Bellomarisci', in *Arch.Camb. Supplement* (1917), p.288; Saunders Lewis, 'Dafydd ab Edmwnd', pp.221-2.
100  E.A. Lewis, op. cit., pp.264-5.
101  *Arch.Camb. Original Documents*, pp.clii.
102  TNA SC6/1170/5, 6; 1211/3, 5; 1212/7. For a similar example see Keith Williams-Jones, 'Caernarvon', p.83.
103  *CPR 1327-1330*, 549.
104  TNA SC6/1227/4, 5; 1170/5; 1150/5, m.4a; 1151/3, m.5b; 1152/1, m.4b; 1152/2, m.4b.

Thomas Clerk was bailiff in 1381-2, Adam in 1385-6 and Robert in 1397-8.[105] The family continued to play an active part after the revolt; the office was held by John in 1414-5 and 1418-9, Hugh in 1449-50, 1463-4 and 1467 and William in 1473-4.[106] For a burgess family the Clerks seem to have lasted a long time; as a rule these civic dynasties rarely lasted long and there is evidence from many towns of a consistent failure of heirs among the leading families.[107] The part played by the Clerks in local commercial life may be reflected in the appointment of Adam, Nicholas and Richard to supply the castle with provisions in 1384.[108] In 1384-5 Adam took up the farm of Penrhosllugwy and in 1388 he became sheriff of Anglesey, an office which he held until his death in 1395. Henry became escheator of the county in 1391.[109]

The Ingrams were another family which was to be influential in the town for many years. Peter Ingram was bailiff in 1374-5, 1379-80, 1387-8, 1388-9 and 1407-8, while William Ingram held the same office in 1415-6 and 1448-9, John Ingram the elder in 1454-5 and John the younger in 1455-6 and in 1465-6.[110] William Ingram was alderman between 1457 and 1462 and in 1452 he endowed an almshouse beside the West Gate for blind or lame men and women and those in most need, but the foundation does not seem to have survived very long.[111] In 1468 a John Ingram became prior of Penmon, a house which had a close relationship with the town and there were still Ingrams in Beaumaris in 1614.[112] The Salmons were also old-established; William Salmon and Peter Russell represented the town in the parliament held in 1327 for the formal deposition of Edward II and William was bailiff in 1329-30.[113] Nicholas was bailiff in 1324-5 and 1331-2, Roger in 1363-4 and Robert in 1392-3 and 1396-7; after the revolt the office was held by Henry in 1424-5 and 1437-8.[114] Other families came to prominence in the fifteenth century, among them the Godfreys and

105  TNA SC6/1150/8, m.4a;  1151/2, m.5b;  NLW Llanfair and Brynodol M2.
106  TNA SC6/1152/6, m.7b;  1152/7, m.5a;  1153/6, m.13a;  NLW Llanfair and Brynodol M7; TNA SC6/1217/6;  1155/4, m.9a.
107  Colin Platt, op.cit., p.119;  Keith Williams-Jones, 'Caernarvon', p.83. According to Fritz Rörig, *The Medieval Town* (1967), pp 114-5, the same thing happened to burgess dynasties in German towns and this persisted, as witness Thomas Mann's novel *Buddenbrooks*.
108  *CPR 1381-1385*, 471.
109  TNA 526/1151/1, m.5b;  1151/5, m.8a;  1152/1, m.7a;  1151/7, m.8a.
110  TNA E163/24/1, m.1b;  SC6/1150/6, m.4b;  1151/4, m.4b;  1151/5, m.8a;  1152/4, m.4a; BUASC Baron Hill 458;  TNA SC6/1216/7;  BUASC Baron Hill 472, 474, 499.
111  For William Ingram as alderman see BUASC Baron Hill 473, 477;  NLW Lleweni 227. For the almshouse see BUASC Bangor 26331 which is a photographic copy of a survey of Beaumaris made in 1563 now at Bodorgan I am grateful to the late Sir George Meyrick for the temporary deposit of this volume in the Library of the then UCNW where I was able to examine it.
112  *CPR 1467-1477*, 165;  Flintshire Record Office, Hawarden, D/NH460.
113  F. Palgrave, ed., *The Parliamentary Writs and Writs of Military Summons*, ii, 364;  TNA SC6/1213/8.
114  TNA SC6/1213/1,10;  1150/2, m.5a;  1151/8, m.4b;  1152/3, m.5b;  1153/2, m.5a;  1153/4, m.12a.

the Strettons. A Thomas Godfrey was bailiff in 1448-9 and 1466-7 and William in 1472-3, 1480-1 and 1481-2; another Thomas was prior of Penmon until his death in 1452 and the last prior was John Godfrey.[115] William Stretton was bailiff in 1421-2, Roger in 1458-9 and Hugh in 1463-4 and 1468-9.[116] An interesting fourteenth century family was that of the Helpstons who probably came originally from Northamptonshire. They were master-masons in Cheshire and later burgesses of Ruthin. Their trade also brought them to Caernarfon and some found their way to Beaumaris where Thomas de Helpston was bailiff six times between 1336 and 1358 and Robert in 1340-1.[117] Thomas was one of the town coroners in 1343 and a John de Helpston was presented to the living of Llan-faes in 1334.[118] In the fifteenth century such Caernarfon families as the Scarisbricks had interests in Beaumaris.[119]

A market in land had developed among the burgesses from early in the fourteenth century. In 1316 the justice was ordered to release a burgage in the town which had been confiscated because it had been acquired from Sir Thomas Danvers without licence, which suggests that non-resident burgesses with large holdings regarded them as an investment.[120] Some were already building up their holdings; between 1317 and 1327 John Lagan and his wife Alice acquired a number of properties.[121] These were only strips in the borough fields but they show that even then some burgesses were more enterprising than others. On 8 July 1355 the prince granted the mills of Llan-faes and Cefn-coch, never farmed by the burgesses but an integral part of the local economy, to William de Cranwell and Thomas de Nesse for ever; Cranwell was also allowed to build a new mill on his land in Beaumaris.[122] As well as being a burgess Cranwell was the clerk to the chamberlain of north Wales and he may well have been responsible for drawing up the 1352 extent of Anglesey and Caernarfonshire. Nesse was bailiff in 1355-6.[123]

This was the beginning of a substantial estate. Cranwell died in 1396 leaving a daughter Katherine who married Richard Golding, sheriff of Anglesey be-

115  TNA SC6/1216/7; 1155/1, m.9a; 1155/3, m.10a; 1155/5, m.9a; 1155/6, m.9a; *CPR 1446-1452*, 527; *Letters and Papers. Henry VIII*, ix (1538), no.866.
116  TNA SC6/1153/1, m.7a; 1154/4, m.12a; NLW Llanfair and Brynodol M7.
117  R.R. Davies, 'Colonial Wales', in *Past and Present*, 65 (1974), 7; Keith Williams-Jones, 'Caernarvon', p.83.
118  *Arch. Camb. Original Documents*, p.clii; *CPR 1330-1334*, 488.
119  In 1488 Thomas Bickerstaff *alias* Jenkinson, tailor, of Beaumaris conveyed a burgage to Thomas Scarisbrick of Caernarfon (BUASC Baron Hill 526).
120  *CCR 1313-1318*, 288.
121  NLW Pitchford Hall 216, 452, 461, 516, 590, 1365.
122  TNA SC6/1149/5, m.4b.
123  Colin M. Evans, op.cit., p.135; A.D.Carr, 'The Black Death in Caernarfonshire', *TCHS* 61 (2000), 15-16; TNA SC6/1149/6, m.4b.

tween 1385 and 1387 and alderman in 1406; Golding had twice been bailiff and was clerk to the justice of north Wales.[124] During the Glyn Dŵr revolt Golding was unable to collect his rents and on his death in 1406 or 1407 his lands were seized by the crown.[125] In Beaumaris itself he held 29 burgages, all of which had been rented out. He also had nearly three hundred acres in the borough lands and property in Dindaethwy, Menai, Malltraeth and Llifon, including one-third of the township of Trefollwyn and land and rents in Holyhead.[126] In 1407 his widow conveyed all her property to Sir John Kyghley; the grant also included the advowson of the chantry of St Mary in Beaumaris church and property in Bangor, Conwy and Rhuddlan.[127] After Kyghley's death the lands passed to Sir Thomas Norreys, an incomer from Lancashire who was alderman between 1447 and 1456 and captain of the town. They came eventually to Lady Eleanor Stanley, the sister of the earl of Warwick and they remained in the possession of the earls of Derby until 1527 when they were exchanged with Sir William Griffith of Penrhyn for the Lancashire manor of Bispham.[128] This was the beginning of the Griffith interest in the borough which was to contribute to the bitter struggle between the Bulkeleys and the constable of the castle, Sir Rowland Vielville and the Griffiths in the 1520s.[129]

The existence of a flourishing land market in the fifteenth century is borne out by the wealth of deeds in the Baron Hill archive.[130] They include several conveyances in *tir prid;* in the fifteenth century this transaction was coming to be used by English burgesses as well as by Welsh proprietors as a means of securing title.[131] But, above all, the Baron Hill deeds tell the story of the rise of one family, the Bulkeleys, to power and influence, not only in Beaumaris but also in Anglesey. William Bulkeley the elder, the founder of the family fortunes, came from Cheadle in Cheshire and he seems to have arrived in Beaumaris by 1444.[132] His first acquisition of land in the town was in 1450 when he pur-

124  Colin M. Evans, op.cit., p.137; TNA SC6/1152/2, m.8a; 1151/3, m.8a BUASC Baron Hill 457; Ralph A. Griffiths, 'The Glyndŵr rebellion in north Wales through the eyes of an Englishman', in *BBCS* 22 (1967), 141.

125  Colin M. Evans, op.cit., p.137.

126  TNA SC6/1233/1.

127  *CCR 1409-1413*, 213. The name Kyghley (Cichle) survives in two place-names in the area.

128  Colin M. Evans, op.cit., pp.137-42; E.A. Lewis, op.cit., pp.81-2; TNA SC6/1152/6, m.5a; BUASC Nannau 3083; *CPR 1461-1467*, 428.

129  This is discussed by D. Cyril Jones, 'The Bulkeleys of Beaumaris, 1440-1547', pp.7-10.

130  These deeds and their background are briefly discussed by Carr, "This my act and deed":, pp.223-37.

131  BUASC Baron Hill 467 (1451), 473 (1457), 485 (1459), 489 (1462), 501 (1470), 509 (1463) are examples; Llinos Beverley Smith, 'The gage and the land market in late medieval Wales', p.547.

132  The rise of the Bulkeleys is briefly discussed in Chapter 7; see also D. Cyril Jones, op.cit., and 'The Bulkeleys of Baron Hill, 1440-1621'.

chased a burgage from John Bate and his subsequent activities are reflected in a quantity of deeds, many of which were conveyances by long-established local families. Among the vendors are names like Salmon, Godfrey and Clerk.[133] Between 1450 and his death in 1490 he obtained 18¾ burgages and some time after 1470 he built the house in Church Street, later known as Henblas, on the sites of several of the burgages he had acquired; it was demolished in 1869.[134] Between 1473 and 1489 he was alderman; his eldest son William had preceded him in the office between 1462 and 1473 and he was followed in it by another son, Richard. With William the Bulkeley ascendancy in the town began and the special relationship remains to this day.

Like the other Edwardian boroughs of Gwynedd. Beaumaris was dominated by the castle. Although the history of Beaumaris castle is less than dramatic it is not without interest. It was frequently used as a prison; between 1318 and 1328 three prisoners, Patrick mac Coter, Stephen mac Steffan and Andrew mac Orlot, described sometimes as Manxmen and sometimes as Scots, were held there.[135] In 1395 a number of Lollard prisoners were sent to Beaumaris; three of them were fellows of Merton College, Oxford and one was a canon lawyer of some standing but their theological views were obviously too unorthodox or speculative for the authorities.[136] According to some sources Beaumaris was visited by Richard II between his return from Ireland and his arrival at Conwy in 1399.[137] The castle may have fallen to the rebels during the Glyn Dŵr revolt and the garrison was reinforced from time to time during the fifteenth century, as it was in 1447.[138] This increase in the establishment was authorised, it was said, because the people of Wales were more riotous than they had been, because Scots, Bretons and other enemies were given to landing in Anglesey and because the castle was the island's only defence.

It was at this time that Beaumaris received its most famous prisoner; this was Eleanor Cobham, by now the widow of Henry VI's uncle, Humphrey, duke

133  BUASC Baron Hill 467, 473, 476, 483 (Rees Salmon); 484 (Henry Salmon); 489, 492-3, 509 (Thomas Godfrey); 503 (Hugh Clerk); 504 (Margaret Clark).

134  D. Cyril Jones, 'The Bulkeleys of Beaumaris, 1440-1547', pp.4-5; Colin M. Evans, op.cit., pp.147-50. Henblas is discussed in RCAHM *Anglesey Inventury*, pp.clviii-clxii. BUASC Baron Hill 510 may be the original conveyance of the site to William.

135  TNA SC6/1212/2; 1213/3; they were each allowed threepence daily. They were no longer there in 1328-9 which suggests that they may have been released as a result of the Anglo-Scottish Treaty of Northampton of 1329. See also *CCR 1318-1323*, 656, and *CCR 1323-1327*, 3, where the justice was ordered to receive ransoms from Scots lately captured in Anglesey.

136  TNA SC6/1215/7; ten pounds were spent on their maintenance for which Adam Clerk was reimbursed. They are named in *CCR 1392-1396*, 344; for details see A.B. Emden, *A Biographical Register of the University of Oxford to A.D. 1500* (3 vols., 1957-9)

137  James Sherborne, 'Richard II's return to Wales, July 1399', in *WHR* 7 (1975), 395, 400.

138  TNA SC6/1216/7, m.7; Ralph A. Griffiths, 'Richard, duke of York and the royal household in Wales', pp23-4.

of Gloucester, who had been condemned to life imprisonment for witchcraft in 1441.[139] For some years she was in custody in the Isle of Man but she was transferred to Beaumaris in March 1449. On 7 July 1452 she died there and was buried, presumably in the parish church. The constable was paid one hundred marks for the expense incurred by him in her burial.[140] It has been suggested that it was the presence there of the widow of Duke Humphrey, a figure around whom a political cult was already growing, that led Richard, duke of York, to land at Beaumaris on his return from Ireland in September 1450, a return which could be described as the beginning of a sequence of events which was to lead to the Wars of the Roses.[141] Although the castle had never been completed, a good deal of money was spent on its upkeep. In 1321-2, for example, £130 11s 1¼d was spent on repairs and in 1347 extensive work was carried out on the prison.[142] Money was still being spent on the defence of Beaumaris in the second half of the fifteenth century and the castle was not the town's only safeguard; in 1439 Thomas Norreys was granted the captaincy of the town with a force of five men.[143]

The church was as active in the castle boroughs as it was elsewhere in the medieval world. Beaumaris was in the parish of Llandegfan, a church valued in 1254 at only 13s 4d. The growth of the town is reflected in the fact that in 1535 the gross annual value of the living of Llandegfan was twenty pounds and only one living in the deanery of Dindaethwy and Twrcelyn was worth more.[144] Most of Beaumaris church dates from the early fourteenth century, while the chancel was rebuilt about 1500 when the town was entering its most prosperous period as a port and when much work was being done on town churches.[145] Many burgesses remembered the church when they died. John Lagan left three-quarters of a burgage for masses for his soul and Agnes, the widow of Nicholas le Barber, left a burgage for the same reason; the chaplain answered for them in 1350.[146] There were also chantries; Peter Russell was granted a licence to provide for a chaplain to say mass daily for his soul and those of his ancestors in 1330 and in 1418-9 the escheator answered for property in the town given without licence to the chantry of St Mary for the celebration of divine service.[147] In his will in 1490 William Bulkeley endowed two chaplains,

139 For the story of Eleanor Cobham see Ralph A. Griffiths, op.cit., 22-3; TNA SC6/1216/7, m.9.
140 TNA SC6/1217/1, m.11.
141 Ralph A. Griffiths, op.cit., 14-25.
142 TNA SC6/1212/7; 1229/8.
143 *CPR 1436-1441*, 301.
144 *Valuation of Norwich*, p.195; *Valor Ecclesiasticus*. iv, 431.
145 RCAHM *Anglesey Inventory*, pp.3-8; Colin Platt, op.cit., pp 207-9; Glanmor Williams, *The Welsh Church from Conquest to Reformation* (1962), pp.429-33.
146 NLW Peniarth 405, p.432.
147 *CPR 1327-1330*, 529; TNA SC6/1152/7, m.10a.

one to say mass in the church of Beaumaris for the souls of himself, his wife
and his parents for two years and another to say mass and pray daily for the
soul of his sister for one year.[148] He also left money for the purchase of serv-
ice-books and vestments. This kind of bequest was probably typical of the wills
of wealthy burgesses and the chaplain was one of his executors. In 1425 the
archdeacon of Anglesey was a burgess, as was the chaplain of the church of St
Tegfan and chapel of Beaumaris, William Forde, in 1452.[149] Forde also conveyed some of his glebe lands to William Bulkeley the elder in 1463 and four
years later the borough authorities granted land near the church to the chaplain, John Audlem.[150] These transactions show local clergy playing their part
in the life of the town.

The third Anglesey borough was Newborough. It was intended as a reincar-
nation of Llan-faes, transplanted to the *maerdref* of Rhosyr in the commote of
Menai. Rhosyr seems already to have been a trading centre; in 1254 the church
was valued at £1 13s 4d, less than those of the other commotal centres but still
among the richer churches of the island.[151] In 1296-7 the fair tolls came to £1
14s 3½d and the market tolls to ten shillings and in 1302-3 the tolls on beer,
mead, leather and other merchandise sold at the market of Rhosyr were farmed
by Roger of Rhosyr for eight pounds.[152] In view of the existence of the market
and fair it is possible that the men of Rhosyr were less than enthusiastic about
the plantation of a new community which took over all their trading rights in
their midst and this, as much as the opposition of the men of Llan-faes to their
removal, may explain the seven-year delay between the foundation of Beaumaris and the incorporation of Newborough.[153] But most of the Llan-faes
burgesses did eventually move and the new borough was designed to compen-
sate them as precisely as possible.[154] The burgesses were given just over 90
acres of the Rhosyr demesne which consisted of more than 600 acres.

Among the petitions submitted by the burgesses at Kennington in 1305 was
one in which they asked for the name of their borough to be changed from
Rhosyr to Newborough and for the liberties of Rhuddlan 'word for word'.[155]
The request was granted, but with the liberties of Caerwys rather than those
of Rhuddlan. Yet they had received a charter from the prince on 3 May 1303 in

148  BUASC Baron Hill 4.
149  BUASC Baron Hill 459, 468.
150  BUASC Baron Hill 491, 500.
151  *Valuation of Norwich*, p.192; Aberffraw and Cemais (Llanbadrig) were valued at £2 13s 4d, Llan-
     faes at £9 5s 8d and Penrhosllugwy at £1 15s 6d.
152  John Griffiths, 'Early accounts relating to north Wales, *temp.* Edward I', 152; TNA SC6/1227/4.
153  M. Beresford, op.cit. p.535.
154  ibid.; Colin M. Evans, op.cit., pp.31-2; E.A. Lewis, op.cit., p.52.
155  *Rec. Caern.*, p.220.

which they had been granted the liberties of Rhuddlan.[156] This charter is brief and to the point; the liberties are not enumerated and when the burgesses attended the 1348 *Quo Warranto* proceedings to defend their privileges they brought with them a copy of the Rhuddlan charter as well as their own.[157] As there was no castle there was no constable to serve as mayor and in 1305 the burgesses asked that the office should be held by the constable of Beaumaris. They were told that it would be held by the constable of Caernarfon who could appoint a deputy if the duties were too onerous.[158] In 1348 they stated that the office was held by the steward of the manor of Rhosyr and the commote of Menai and offered five pounds for the right to elect a mayor from among themselves.[159] This was granted, as long as he should be an Englishman; in their petition they had said that the borough had been intended for Englishmen.[160] This episode poses a chronological problem; the *Quo Warranto* proceedings are generally regarded as having been held in 1348 but on 12 December 1347 the chamberlain was ordered to make letters patent for the burgesses in accordance with the grant.[161]

The burgesses also asked at Kennington for the consolidation of their lands and the removal of Rhosyr bondmen from them. They sought the farm of the whole of the Rhosyr demesne but there is no evidence of their ever having held it.[162] The borough's form of government was the same as that of the other Edwardian boroughs, the executive officers being the two bailiffs. In 1303-4, when they accounted for the first time, the borough court yielded £2 1s 5d, the court leet 15s 3d and the market and fair courts 2s 6d; thus, not only were the proceeds of the markets and fairs more than at Beaumaris at this time, but the profits of justice were also higher. This suggests that of the two boroughs Newborough had the greater population in the early years of the fourteenth century. In 1304-5 a new windmill, perhaps one of the first of its kind in Anglesey, and a town cross were built at a total cost of £20 12s 2½d.[163] The burgesses had asked at Kennington for an annual fair on the feast of Saints Peter and Paul (29 June). The Newborough fairs were subsequently held on that day and at Martinmas (11 November) and the market was held on Tuesdays.[164]

---

156  The text of the foundation charter only exists in a later confirmation; it is printed in E.A. Lewis, op.cit. p.283.
157  *Rec.Caern.*, pp.177-81.
158  ibid., p.218.
159  ibid., p.181
160  E. A.Lewis, op.cit., pp. 42, 157, where similar examples elsewhere are discussed.
161  *BPR*, i, 155. In 1350-1 the burgesses made fine of £1 for the confirmation of certain letters (TNA SC6/1149/1, m.8b).
162  *Rec.Caern.*, p.218.
163  TNA SC6/1170/3.
164  *Record of Caernarvon*, p.218; E.A. Lewis, op.cit., p.171.

As Newborough, with the rest of the commote of Menai, had been granted by Edward II to his wife Isabella of France it did not reappear in the accounts until after her death in 1358. By this time the issues of the town, including the mill, the borough lands and the Southcrook or Abermenai ferry were being farmed. In 1359-60 William ap Madog and Ieuan Llwyd were farming these issues for £19 13s 4d and the profits of justice for £15 10s.[165] In subsequent years the farm was sometimes accounted for by the farmers and sometimes by the town bailiffs. By 1376-7 the farm of the borough stood at twenty pounds and that of the profits of justice, the tolls and the ferry at £17 6s.[166] The farm in the eighties and nineties of the fourteenth century followed the general trend downwards; by 1396-7 there was a single consolidated farm of £24 9s 3d.[167]

Anglesey in general and Newborough in particular were hard hit by the revolt and when the escheator came to compile his account in 1408-9 it was made clear just how much damage there had been.[168] Nineteen burgesses were named as rebels and of these thirteen had been killed. Nineteen burgages had been burned and were therefore valueless, which gives some indication of the impact of the revolt on the town. The victims included some of the leading inhabitants; Gwilym ab Einion had held six burgages and Gruffudd ab Einion ap Hywel had been a bailiff in 1384-5.[169] Rebels who survived included Ieuan ab Ednyfed, bailiff in 1381-2 and farmer in 1383-4 and 1390-1 and Rhys ab Ieuan ab Einion, who held four burgages.[170] There are some inaccuracies in the record, as one would expect under the chaotic circumstances of the revolt and its aftermath. Deicws ab Ieuan ap Tegwared was described as having died in rebellion and yet one of that name submitted in 1406 and was one of the farmers of the town in 1418-9.[171] Most burgages were valued in the account at 3s 4d but some ranged in value from one shilling to seven shillings

On the whole the fifteenth century was a period of decline. In some ways this was inevitable; Newborough had never really recovered from the disaster which struck the town on 6 December 1330 when 183 acres of the borough lands had been overwhelmed by sea and sand after a storm.[172] On the same day the same fate had befallen eleven cottages and 28 acres in Rhosyr.[173] For a borough to lose so much of its land was nothing short of a catastrophe. Nev-

165  TNA SC6/1149/9, m.6b.
166  TNA SC6/1150/3, m.5a.
167  TNA SC6/1152/3, m.6b. In 1397-8 the farm was £30 3s 4d. (NLW Llanfair and Brynodol M2).
168  TNA SC6/1233/1.
169  TNA SC6/1151/1, m.7b.
170  TNA SC6/1150/8, m.5a; 1150/10, m.7a; 1151/6, m.5b.
171  TNA SC6/1152/7, m.4b; he was still a burgess in 1428 (NLW Llanfair and Brynodol M4).
172  CIM ii, no.1275.
173  ibid., no. 1328.

ertheless, there was some return to normality after the revolt. In 1408-9 there was no farmer but the total issues of the town came to £19 14s 4d.[174] In the Rhosyr account it was stated that the township had been completely devastated, not only by the rebels but also by the royal forces and this must inevitably have affected Newborough as well.[175] By 1413-4 the borough was being farmed for twenty pounds but the fact that some burgages were still in the hands of the escheator suggests that recovery was still not complete.[176] The farm was up to £27 2s, including Rhosyr mill, in 1437-8 but this was followed by a steady decline; in 1467-8 it was £11 13s 4d and in 1483-4 £10 6s 8d.[177] In 1458-9, when the borough was not let at farm, the total issues, including burgage rents, profits of justice and tolls were only £11 13s.[178]

Of all the boroughs of Gwynedd Newborough was the only one included in the 1352 extent.[179] There were 54 tenants who held 145 properties, the former owners of which were all named; some of these had been burgesses of Llanfaes. Tenements were described as plots (*placea*) and lands. The former may have been burgages; the term was certainly used in the fortified towns founded by thirteenth-century English kings in Gascony.[180] There were 99 of these holdings; the ones described as lands were probably strips or allotments in the borough fields. By 1352 there was a good deal of consolidation of ownership. A number of burgesses held more than one plot, which indicates that some were more successful than others. Gruffudd ab Iorwerth Foel, whose father had served Edward I in his wars, held eight plots; the largest of these was the one formerly of Einion Goch Ffisigwr, possibly that Master Einion who had led the men of Llan-faes in their protest. Ieuan ab Iorwerth Llwyd also had eight plots, inherited from his father and Gwilym ap Madog Crythwr had four plots formerly held by David le Barker, a man of some standing in the town whose tombstone is still to be seen in the church.[181] There was no standard burgage rent; the rents of plots ranged from a halfpenny to 2s 6d, with most tenants paying threepence, fourpence or sixpence. The former tenants included several Englishmen, among them two Beaumaris burgesses, Henry Clerk and Alan de Macclesfield and a Caernarfon burgess, Robert de Parys. Possibly the expulsion of Welshmen from Beaumaris had led to the departure of Englishmen from Newborough. The extent suggests that Newborough, too, had its inner

---

174  TNA SC6/1152/4, m.5a.
175  ibid., m.5b.
176  TNA SC6/1152/5, m.4a.
177  TNA SC6/1153/4, m.7b; 1217/6, m.1; 1217/7, m.1.
178  TNA SC6/1154/4, m.11b.
179  *Extent of Anglesey*, pp.262-72.
180  T.F. Tout, 'Medieval town planning', in *Collected Papers*, iii, p.78.
181  RCAHM *Anglesey Inventory*, p.118.

circle of burgesses; at least six past or present inhabitants had held or would hold the office of bailiff, four were farmers of the borough and one was *rhingyll* of Menai.

Among those who were burgesses in the last years of the fourteenth century were three of the sons of Tudur ap Goronwy of Penmynydd. Among the rebels listed in the 1408-9 account were Rhys and Gwilym ap Tudur, while Maredudd acquired land in the town in 1389 and was one of the farmers in 1395-6 and 1397-8.[182] This suggests that a foothold in Newborough was sought by members of leading local families in the same way as Flintshire *uchelwyr* acquired burgages in Caerwys.[183] The town was certainly almost entirely Welsh. It was not alone in this, of course; the same was true of Pwllheli and Nefyn and the municipal liberties granted to the two Llŷn towns in 1355 were based on those of Newborough.[184] Unlike the English boroughs, poets were welcome here and two of Dafydd ap Gwilym's poems are connected with the town. In one he described the misfortune that befell his servant whom he had sent with a gift of wine to a girl who had attracted his attention and in the other he praised Newborough, its wine and its people.[185]

After the Glyn Dŵr revolt the town, like the rest of the commote of Menai, was dominated by Maredudd ap Cynwrig of Porthaml. There exists a rental, compiled in 1428, which lists about 184 tenements and which, like the 1352 extent, describes many as plots and names previous tenants.[186] Maredudd was dead by this time and his son Thomas held a number of plots. Other burgesses included Hywel ap Llywelyn ap Dafydd ab Ieuan of Berw, at least four women, one of whom, Elen, the daughter of Gwilym ap Madog, held several plots and Richard del Wode, a former escheator of the county. One of the leading burgesses was Thomas Kent, a burgess of Beaumaris, who was one of the bailiffs of that borough in 1424-5 and 1454-5.[187] Maredudd ap Cynwrig had been alderman; he is the only holder of that office whose name is recorded.[188] Neither the 1428 rental nor the 1352 extent reveal anything of the town's topography, but its shape is clear enough. The nucleus was the crossroads in the middle of the present village where the town cross must have stood. The bor-

182 TNA SC6/1233/1; BUASC Mostyn 774; TNA SC6/1152/2, m.5b; NLW Llanfair and Brynodol M2.

183 A.D. Carr, 'The making of the Mostyns: the genesis of a landed family', p.153.

184 E.A. Lewis, op.cit., pp.40-1.

185 Dafydd Johnston et al., eds., *Cerddi Dafydd ap Gwilym* (2010), pp. 306-9, 84-5. She poured the wine over the messenger's head.

186 NLW Llanfair and Brynodol M4. Most of the rents range from 3*d* to 1*s*; the document is much faded.

187 TNA SC6/1153/2, m.5a; BUASC Baron Hill 472.

188 BL Add.Chart. 8642, printed in E.A. Lewis, op.cit., pp.297-8 and n.2; the document is the admission of a burgess and it bears the borough seal.

ough boundaries were described in detail in the eighteenth century and some of the boundary stones remain to this day.[189] The burgage plots are clearly visible on a modern large-scale map, but, apart from the church and the site of the Rhosyr court complex, there are no medieval remains to be seen.

Enough deeds survive to testify to the existence of a market in land in medieval Newborough and the attestations to two of them include the names of the then stewards of Menai who were the mayors before 1348.[190] One deed of 1396 is a grant by a Beaumaris burgess of a plot and garden; the witnesses were three burgesses of Newborough and two of Beaumaris and had more deeds survived they might shed more light on relations between the two boroughs.[191] The witnesses to a conveyance in 1497 include the mayor, Robert Botell, by his name an Englishman in accordance with the 1347 grant.[192] Newborough was the commercial centre of the commote of Menai but its history after the early fourteenth century seems to have been one of stagnation and decline. There may have been some revival in the early sixteenth century; from 1507 to 1549 it was the county town and as such it returned a member of parliament from 1536. But in 1549 the county court was returned to Beaumaris and Newborough's moment of glory ended.[193] There is little there now, apart from the street plan, to remind the visitor of its history.

189  Henry Rowlands, 'Antiquitates parochiales', in *Arch. Camb.*, 1846, pp.310-1.
190  BUASC Penrhyn 380 (1337); Mostyn 751(1339).
191  BUASC Penrhyn 383.
192  BUASC Mostyn 752.
193  E.A. Lewis, op.cit., p.209. Hugh Owen, *Hanes Plwyf Niwbwrch ym Môn* (1952), pp.26-7.

# 9 *The Church*

IN THE TWELFTH AND THIRTEENTH CENTURIES the church in Wales was brought into line with its counterparts elsewhere and given a territorial framework of diocese, archdeaconry, rural deanery and parish.[1] There was a bishop of Bangor from at least 1120 and there were archdeacons and rural deans in the diocese by 1254. Territorial parishes may have taken rather longer to emerge in Wales, as they did in the upland parts of England. The mother church and its subsidiaries had probably been responsible for the cure of souls over a wide area but no clear delimitation of ecclesiastical authority was possible since the subsidiary churches of one mother church might be scattered among those of another. Anglesey was a natural unit for an archdeaconry and in 1254 it contained two deaneries, those of Cantref, which comprised the commotes of Menai, Malltraeth and Llifon and Dindaethwy and Twrcelyn, which included Talybolion.[2] As for the parishes, they developed from moribund mother churches and their daughters and from private foundations, but the process was a long one.[3] It was probably complete by the time of the 1379 clerical subsidy; the Warham return of 1504 lists incumbents and curates while the 1535 *Valor Ecclesiasticus* is certainly arranged by parishes.[4]

The earliest list of Anglesey churches is that in the *Valuation of Norwich* of 1254; many of these do not bear their present names but those of the townships in which they were situated. The *Valuation* lists 72 churches of which 29 bear *Llan* prefixes; four have not been identified. Some are missing, the chief among them being the great church of Caergybi and its three chapels. Other absentees include Llannerch-y-medd and Llanddwyn, although the former may have been included in Amlwch or Llanbeulan. There are also some changes of name, although the printed text does not inspire confidence; for example, Llanddeu-

---

1 J. Conway Davies, *Episcopal Acts relating to Welsh Dioceses, 1066-1272*, ii (1948), pp. 448-57, 597-601; Glanmor Williams, *The Welsh Church from Conquest to Reformation*, pp.15-18.

2 *The Valuation of Norwich*, pp.192-6. The division between the two deaneries seems to correspond with the division of Anglesey between Llywelyn ap Gruffudd and his brother Owain in 1246 and with the territories of the two coroners after 1284.

3 J. Conway Davies, op.cit., pp.455-7; Glanmor Williams, op.cit., p.154; see also John Godfrey, *The English Parish, 600-1300* (1969), pp.46-61.

4 For the Warham return see A. Ivor Pryce, *The Diocese of Bangor in the Sixteenth Century* (1923), pp.82-3

sant appears as Llanfaelog (the present Llanfaelog being under the name of
Conysiog) because the church was in the township of Tre Feibion Maelog. But
these questions of ecclesiastical toponymy cannot be pursued here; it is enough
to state that parishes did emerge during the middle ages and the clergy were
certainly described as rectors and vicars in 1379.[5]

Thus a territorial pattern of ecclesiastical organisation gradually developed.
There are few references to the church as an institution or to individual
churches before 1282. On his deathbed Gruffudd ap Cynan left money to the
*clasau* at Penmon and Caergybi, while Earl Hugh of Shrewsbury is said to have
kennelled his dogs in the church of Llandyfrydog in 1098 and the churches of
St Peter and St Mary (possibly Rhosyr and Llanfair-yn-y-cwmwd) were sacked
by the Normans in 1157. In the thirteenth century Penmon became a house of
Augustinian canons and the Franciscan friary at Llan-faes was founded by Llywelyn ab Iorwerth in memory of his wife. In 1261 one of the provisions of the
concordat which settled various disputes between Llywelyn ap Gruffudd and
bishop Richard of Bangor was that those who had committed sacrilege by fighting in the churches of Rhosyr and Talybolion should be punished.[6] Edward II
confirmed a charter of Llywelyn ab Iorwerth to the Hospitallers of Dolgynwal
in 1316; one of the witnesses to the original charter was Master Instructus,
archpriest of Caergybi.[7] There are also a few references to friars of Llan-faes,
either as witnesses to acts or as messengers. Among those paid compensation
by the king for damage sustained in the war of 1282 were the archdeacon of
Anglesey, the friary of Llan-faes and the prior of Penmon but none of the
churches seem to have suffered.[8]

The most valuable churches in 1254 were Llan-faes, valued at £9 6s 8d and
the priory of Penmon, valued at £6 13s 4d. Amlwch, valued at four pounds,
came next and Llanddyfnan and Penmynydd were each worth two pounds. Of
the *maerdref* churches Aberffraw and Llanbadrig were worth £2 13s 4d, Rhosyr
£1 13s 4d and Penrhosllugwy £1 15s 6d. The values of most churches lay between
6s 8d and £1 6s 8d, while thirteen were worth less than the lower figure; the lowest figure of all was the 2s 3d recorded for Llanfigel. The values given here were
those of the spiritualities, that is, tithes, oblations and the income from the glebe.
The figures have been analysed by Professor Glanville Jones who has correlated
the value of each church with the acreage of the later parish and this bears out
his conclusions on the siting of centres of settlement on the best soils.[9]

5  TNA E179/3/5, 2.

6  *Acts of Welsh Rulers*, no.345.

7  ibid., no.256. The authenticity of this charter is, however, open to question, as is pointed out here.

8  *Littere Wallie*, pp. 135, 65, 81-2.

9  G.R.J. Jones, 'The distribution of medieval settlement *in* Anglesey', pp.50-3; see also the map
   facing p.37.

The papal taxation of 1291 is far less informative since it only included churches of the annual value of four pounds or more.[10] Only two churches in Dindaethwy, those of Llan-faes and Llanddyfnan, qualified; they had been the two wealthiest in the commote in 1254. Talybolion and Twrcelyn formed a single deanery and here Llaneilian, Amlwch and Llanfechell contributed as did three un-named churches, one of which was probably Llanfairynghornwy.[11] The deanery of Cantref included Llifon and Malltraeth and here six churches were included. Chief among them was Caergybi, where the provost's share was worth £26 and the portions of three chaplains or prebendaries £16. The others were Aberffraw and Rhoscolyn and three which cannot be identified, although one may have been Llanbeulan, which one would expect to have been fairly valuable as it included Llannerch-y-medd and another Llantrisant.[12]

But the church was more than a collector of tithes and oblations. Apart from its spiritual functions, it was also a great landowner and much of medieval Anglesey was in its possession. The greatest ecclesiastical landlord was the bishop of Bangor and most of his lands had probably been in his possession for a very long time. They were concentrated in Dindaethwy, particularly along the Menai Straits, in Twrcelyn and in the north-west although he held townships elsewhere in the island; at the end of the thirteenth century he had 40.[13] The Dindaethwy lands were organised in the manor of Treffos; this was not a consolidated territory but a complex of free and bond settlements dependent on a central court. In other words, Treffos was a *maenol* of the same kind as existed at Bangor.[14] In 1291 the total value of the bishop's lands in Anglesey, including rents, mills and the profits of justice, was £42 15s 2d. The most recent addition to his property had been the townships of Tref Ieuan ab Iddon and Bodychen in Llifon, granted to him by Edward I in 1284 in compensation for the loss of tithe from lands in Anglesey granted to the Cistercian abbey of Aberconwy.[15]

By far the most detailed extent of the bishop's lands is that made in 1306; it has often been misdated to 1335 or 1348 but internal evidence makes it clear that 1306 is the correct date.[16] Like the great royal extent of 1352 this is a most

---

10  *Taxatio Nich.IV*, pp.290-1.

11  This is described as the rectory of Laurence ab Ithon in the church of St Mary.

12  The church of Trefowain listed in the *Taxation* with its chapels was probably Llantrisant of which living Trefowain was later a chapel.

13  The bishop's lands are briefly discussed by T. Jones Pierce, 'Medieval settlement in Anglesey', p.273; 15 townships were in Dindaethwy, 4 in Menai, 5 in Malltraeth, 3 in Llifon and 5 each in Talybolion and Twrcelyn.

14  G.R.J. Jones, 'The tribal system in Wales: a re-assessment in the light of settlement studies', pp.129-30; idem., 'Post-Roman Wales', pp.299-308.

15  *CChancRVar*, 292.

16  Among the guilty I must count myself (*Extent of Anglesey*, p.154). The Anglesey section of the extent is in *Rec.Caern.*, pp.100-9.

valuable source for the social and economic history of medieval Anglesey, giving details of rents, renders and services. From his tenants the bishop received rents in cash, works, food-renders, military service and suit of court; the total income from Anglesey was £47 15s 6½d. Two other fourteenth-century documents relate to the bishop's estates. In 1366, when the see was vacant following the death of Thomas de Ringstead, the dean answered on behalf of himself and the chapter for the income and in 1398-9 the dean rendered account after the death of John Swaffham.[17] The bishop also enjoyed various jurisdictional privileges in his lands and he defended them at the 1348 *Quo Warranto* proceedings.[18] He had a ferry across the Menai Straits at Porthesgob and he claimed the right to use his boat to carry goods wherever he wished. Amercements imposed on his tenants by the justice of north Wales were paid over to him and from time to time he appointed stewards for his Anglesey lands.[19] The last medieval information about his Anglesey estates is contained in the *Valor Ecclesiasticus*, a survey made by the crown in 1535 of all church property in England and Wales. The manor of Treffos had been leased to Sir Richard Bulkeley and his brother William at an annual rent of twelve pounds and the rest of the Anglesey income was £40 2s 8d.[20] In August 1535 bishop John Salcot leased all his property in Anglesey to William Bulkeley for twenty years at an annual rent of £20 0s 8d.[21] Such leases were very much a sign of the times; a regular income was far more use to a bishop, especially one who might well be an absentee, than was a perpetual struggle with the problems of estate management.

Next to the bishop stood the abbot of Aberconwy. This was one of the best-endowed of the Welsh Cistercian houses; in 1535 only Tintern, Valle Crucis and Margam had higher incomes.[22] The Anglesey lands of Aberconwy fell into two groups, those which were mentioned in the 1199 charter attributed to Llywelyn ab Iorwerth and those which were granted to the abbey by Edward I in 1284 as part of the compensation for the removal of the abbey from Conwy to Maenan. In fact, the earliest charter was granted to the abbey by Gruffudd ap Cynan ab Owain Gwynedd some time between 1188 and 1199; in this the monks were granted Gelliniog and Rhuddgaer in Menai.[23] This grant was re-

17  TNA SC6/1143/25; *Rec.Caern.*, pp.233-5.

18  *Rec.Caern.*, p.133; the privileges are discussed in Chapter 3.

19  In 1390-1 a total of £1 1s 2d was paid over to the bishop (TNA SC6/1151/6, m.7a). In 1382 John Martyn, the dean of Bangor, was appointed steward in succession to Goronwy ap Tudur (*CPR 1381-1385*, 422). For the Porthesgob ferry see H.R. Davies, *The Conway and the Menai Ferries*, pp.59-63.

20  *Valor Ecclesiasticus*, iv, 415.

21  BUASC Baron Hill 1956.

22  Glanmor Williams, op.cit., pp.560-1.

23  *Acts of Welsh Rulers*, no.206; the charter is also discussed by Rhys W. Hays, *The History of the Abbey of Aberconway, 1186-1537*, p.6.

peated in Llywelyn's alleged charter, along with the township of Bodgedwydd near Aberffraw; this charter gives the boundaries of all the abbey's possessions.[24] Some time between 1246 and 1265 Llywelyn ap Gruffudd granted the monks the church of Llanbadrig, the *maerdref* church of Cemais. The Cistercians had originally set their faces firmly against the impropriation of rectories but their ideals had become rather diluted by the thirteenth century.[25]

On 22 October 1284 Edward I granted the manor of Cornwy Lys, the hamlets of Ucheldref and Gwaunydog and the township of Tre Feibion Maelog in Talybolion and half the township of Penmynydd in Dindaethwy to the abbey; the Talybolion lands were valued at £21 5s 2½d, which made them a substantial addition to the house's possessions.[26] In 1291 the Anglesey lands of the abbey were worth £33. Gelliniog and Bodgedwydd were described as granges but the new lands could not be worked in the same way. The abbey took over tenants, rents and services and became a landlord and once again the Cistercians compromised their principles. By 1535 the Anglesey lands were valued at £35 11s 2d and Llanbadrig rectory was worth £15 2s 2d.[27] Under the terms of his charter the abbot had extensive jurisdictional privileges which were exercised in his court and he defended them in 1348.[28]

The former *clas* of Penmon or Priestholm had become an Augustinian priory by the early thirteenth century. The nucleus of the Penmon lands was the *abadaeth* or landed endowment of the former community and six thirteenth-century charters which relate to this land have survived.[29] They were granted between 1221 and 1248 by Llywelyn ab Iorwerth, Dafydd ap Llywelyn and Llywelyn and Owain ap Gruffudd and they conveyed the nearby townships of Bancenyn and Crymlyn as well as the original *abadaeth* to the house. The canons also held the churches and therefore the tithes of Llanddona, Llangwyllog and Bodewryd as well as Penmon. In 1291 the possessions of the priory were valued at £9 12s 10½d, including sheep, cattle and the income from rabbit skins.[30] A valuation of the house's lands was made by the prior and tenants in February 1374. The lands included both free and bond tenements and the tenants owed rents of assise, corn-renders and ploughing and reaping services

24  This charter survives in a confirmation of 1332 (*CChartR.* iv, 269); the full text is printed in *Acts of Welsh Rulers*, no.218. As is indicated in the discussion here, it cannot be accepted as authentic; see also C.Insley, 'Fact and fiction in thirteenth-century Gwynedd: the Aberconwy charters', *Studia Celtica* 33 (1999), 235-50. The topographical material is discussed by Colin Gresham, 'The Aberconway charter', 140-4.

25  *CChartR*, iv, 269; Dr Hays suggests that the grant was made before 1254 (op.cit., pp.116-17).

26  *CChancRVar*, 292.

27  *Valor Ecclesiasticus*, iv, 441-2.

28  *Rec.Caern.* pp.144-50.

29  For the texts of these charters see *Acts of the Welsh Rulers*, nos. 250, 272, 286, 288, 313, 320.

30  *Taxatio Nich.IV*, p.293.

which appear to have been commuted.[31] Rents and other income were valued
at £31 12s 10½d in 1379.[32] The priory had another source of income; this was
a quarry which produced some of the millstones for which Anglesey was famous as well as good building stone which was used for Beaumaris castle,
among other places. In 1518 the prior exhibited a bill in the Court of Requests
against one John Irlam who claimed to be the farmer of all the stone quarries
in north Wales.[33] The depositions reveal that the priory undoubtedly had a
quarry and that nobody had ever hindered the prior in working it. The churches
of Penrhosllugwy and Llan-faes were granted to the priory in 1394 because of
the smallness of its original endowment, the incompetence of previous priors
and the damage wrought by Scottish raids.[34] This property is described in some
detail in the *Valor Ecclesiasticus;* the total net income of the house in 1535 was
£40, which made it the poorest of the Welsh Augustinian houses and the poorest monastery in Gwynedd.[35] The temporalities including a mill and the profits
of justice, amounted to £14 8s 7½d, while the yield from the priory's six
churches was £33 6s 8d.[36]

The priory of Beddgelert was another Augustinian house which had grown
out of a Celtic monastic community. In Anglesey the priory held the township
of Tre'r-beirdd and the hamlet of Berw Isaf in Menai and the churches of
Llanidan, Llanedwen, Llanfair-yn-y-cwmwd and Llanddaniel.[37] Tre'r-beirdd
had been granted to the canons by Owain ap Gruffudd, the brother of Llywelyn; it is not mentioned in any extent but two deeds have survived.[38] How
Llanidan and its chapels came into the possession of this distant community
we shall never know, but it may not be without significance that the churches
of Llanfair-is-gaer and Llanddeiniolen on the opposite side of the Menai Straits
were also held by Beddgelert.[39] Land in Anglesey was also held by another former Caernarfonshire *clas.* Like Caergybi, Clynnog Fawr had become a collegiate church served by a chapter of secular canons rather than a monastic

31  *Rec.Caern.* pp.249-51; A.D. Carr, 'The Penmon valor, 1374' *TAAS* 2005, pp.13-19.
32  TNA E179/3/5.
33  TNA Req 2/6/214. The prior cited Llywelyn ab Iorwerth's charter of 1237; see also TNA
    E315/21, p.107.
34  *CPR 1391-1396,*504; another burden on the community was the constant demand for hospitality
    from 'the king's lieges coming to and fro between England and Ireland'.
35  Glanmor Williams, op.cit., pp.560-1. A few Welsh houses were poorer, among them the
    Cistercian ones of Grace-Dieu and Cwm-hir.
36  *Valor Ecclesiasticus,* iv, 429-30.
37  Henry Rowlands, 'Antiquitates parochiales', in *Arch.Camb.* 1848, pp.164-8.
38  *Rec.Caern.*, p.166; in 1348 the prior produced a charter of Edward I confirming the grant.
    BUASC Baron Hill 1647 is a lease by the prior of land in Tre'r-beirdd in 1372 and another deed
    was printed by Henry Rowlands, op.cit., p.165.
39  The only discussion of the priory is a brief one in Colin Gresham, 'The parish of Beddgelert', in
    *TCHS* 30 (1969), 21-4.

community. At one time it had been a very rich foundation; during the reign of Edward IV a charter was granted to its provost Geoffrey Trefnant which confirmed its possession of many named lands.[40] According to this charter a king called Tegwared gave the church Porthaml, Idwal gave Clynnog Fechan and Aber Braint and Rhodri Mawr gave Penrhos in Twrcelyn; the Trefriw given by Gruffudd ap Llywelyn may possibly be Tre'r-dryw in Llanidan. Porthaml and Penrhosllugwy were certainly not held by Clynnog in the later middle ages. In fact, the church had no land at all in 1535 and it has been suggested that it was all sold in the late fifteenth century to raise money for the rebuilding that made the church the finest in Gwynedd.[41]

Nevertheless Clynnog had lands in Anglesey. In Menai it held the township of Clynnog Fechan, half that of Dwyran, known as Dwyran Beuno and Tre'r-dryw and in Talybolion it seems to have had some interest in the township of Alaw'r-beirdd. In addition it held the churches of Llangeinwen and Llangaffo. No individual properties are mentioned in 1291 and only Alaw'r-beirdd appears in the 1352 extent; two *gwelyau* there held of St Beuno and their members were described as 'tenants and abbots'.[42] A few deeds relate to Tre'r-dryw; one in 1471 refers to one tenant as 'father of the tenants of St Beuno in the township' and in 1412 the sheriff ordered the royal officials in Menai not to molest the tenants of Beuno there contrary to the saint's liberties.[43] Clynnog Fechan was one of the prebends of the collegiate church, and in 1535 Llangeinwen and Llangaffo were valued at £19 14s 4d.[44] When the composer John Gwynedd brought an action over his right to the provostship of Clynnog in 1550-1 the vicar stated that he had never known of any lands belonging to the church but that the wardens had an annual sum of £1 5s from Tre'r-dryw and Alaw'r-beirdd; this must have been the last relic of Beuno's Anglesey possessions.[45]

The former *clas* of Llaneilian became an ordinary parish church. Some time in the thirteenth century Hwfa ap Madog ap Dafydd, clerk, with the assent of his three brothers, conveyed all his rights in the *abadaeth* of Llaneilian to Henry, the rector of the church.[46] The boundaries were probably those set out in an earlier charter which was confirmed in 1465 and which poses a number of

---

40  *Rec.Caern.* pp.257-8. The charter is discussed by Patrick Sims-Williams, 'Edward IV's confirmation charter for Clynnog Fawr' in Colin Richmond and Isobel Harvey, eds., *Recognitions: essays presented to Edmund Fryde* (1996), pp.229-41.

41  Colin Gresham, 'A further episode in the history of Clynnog Fawr', in *THSC* 1966, pp.300-1.

42  *Extent of Anglesey*, pp. 208-9 and n.41.

43  Henry Rowlands, op.cit., 57-8; the justice had announced that one of these liberties was that the tenants of Tre'r-dryw did not owe suit of court.

44  In 1436 Hugh Alcock, later dean of Bangor, received ratification of his estate in the prebend along with the two churches annexed to it (*CPR 1429-1436*, 595); *Valor Ecclesiasticus*, iv, 421.

45  Colin Gresham, op.cit., p.314.

46  NLW Bodewryd 187.

problems which have yet to be solved.[47] The thirteenth-century grant may well reflect the transfer of kindred rights to the incumbent of the parish and thus mark the final extinction of the *clas* community.[48] In 1352 the township of Llaneilian was held of St Eilian and tenants there were generally described as tenants of the saint.[49] The same was true of several other Anglesey churches and some of these may once have been the seats of monastic communities; the most likely examples are Llanfechell and Eglwys Ail or Llangadwaladr.[50] According to tradition the heads of the churches of Caergybi and Penmon, the successors of Cybi and Seiriol and the archdeacon were the three spiritual lords of Anglesey.[51] Caergybi seems to have had no land in the middle ages; its income came entirely from tithes and offerings. In 1291 it was worth £42 and in 1535 the income came to £48 14s 6d of which £24 was divided among the twelve canons.[52]

Certain churches and their profits had been annexed to some of the cathedral dignities. The kind of prebendal estates that were associated with so many English cathedral dignities did not exist in Wales; where named prebends existed the income came from the tithes and other spiritualities of the churches concerned. In 1535 the dean of Bangor held the rectory of Llanfihangel Ysgeifiog with its chapel of Llanffinan. The archdeacon of Anglesey had the rectory of Amlwch with the chapels of Llanysgallog and Llanwenllwyfo and the rectory of Llangristiolus with Cerrigceinwen, while the prebendary of Penmynydd had the rectory of that name.[53] One other Anglesey rectory was connected with the cathedral. This was Llaniestyn with Llangoed and Llanfihangel Dinsylwy which formed the endowment of the chantry of St Katherine there founded by Richard Kyffin who was dean from 1480 to 1502.[54]

The quality of the clergy in any medieval diocese depended to a great extent on the pattern of patronage. Too many rich prebends and livings could mean too much royal interference since these could be used to reward royal servants

---

47  The text of the charter is printed in *Cambrian Journal*, 1863, p.319. The church and its topographical background are discussed in David Longley, *St Eilian's Church, Llaneilian* (GAT Report 559, Bangor, 2004, revised 2005).

48  The transformation of the Aberdaron *clas* is discussed by T. Jones Pierce, 'Bardsey – a study in monastic origins', in *Medieval Welsh Society*, pp.391-407.

49  *Extent of Anglesey*, p.222; see, for example, BUASC Baron Hill 1330 (1470).

50  For Heneglwys, Eglwys Ail and Llanfechell see *Extent of Anglesey*, pp. 159, 166, 209, and for Llangefni *Arch.Camb.* 1849, pp.261-3; for examples of tenants TNA SC6/1153/5, m.13b (St Mechell, 1441-2), 1154/2, m.19a (St Cadwaladr, 1456-7), *Arch Camb.* 1849, p.262 (St Cyngar, Llangefni).

51  NLW Peniarth 177, p.56.

52  *Taxatio Nich.IV*, p.290; *Valor Ecclesiasticus.* iv, 428.

53  *Valor Ecclesiasticus*, iv, 416, 417, 418.

54  M.L. Clarke, *Bangor Cathedral* (1969), p.53. For an account of Dean Kyffin see Glanmor Williams, op.cit., pp.319-20; *Valor Ecclesiasticus.* iv, 418.

and clerks and this was bound to have a bad effect on the morale of the local clergy. A certain amount of patronage, usually the right to present to some livings, was always in the hands of the crown and bishops were often open to persuasion over benefices in their gift. It is well-known that the appointment of royal servants to Welsh benefices contributed to that bitterness among the clergy which led so many of them to support Owain Glyn Dŵr.[55] In Bangor little patronage was actually controlled by the crown but an active interest was taken in appointments to cathedral dignities, prebends and canonries. Most Anglesey livings were in the bishop's gift. The office of provost of Caergybi was in the gift of the crown but the right to present to canonries there was vested in two local kindreds, the stocks of Hwfa ap Cynddelw and Llywarch ap Bran. The churches attached to royal courts were all originally in the prince's gift although three were later granted to monasteries which appointed vicars as they did to the other churches which they held. The bishop's patronage was controlled by the crown whenever the see was vacant. The most valuable benefice in Anglesey in 1535 was Llanddyfnan, valued at £40; next came the archdeacon's rectory of Amlwch, worth £33 6s 8d and Llantrisant with its five chapels, worth £26 13s 4d.[56]

There were some disputes over patronage; at least three of these in the fourteenth century were over one which has long ceased to exist, namely Llanddwyn.[57] Llanddwyn was a valuable benefice; it was valued at £33, a very large sum for the time and place, which probably reflects its popularity as a place of pilgrimage. In 1379 the rector contributed ten shillings to the clerical poll-tax, the same sum as the archdeacon, the provost of Caergybi and the prior of Penmon, rather than the two shillings paid by the other Anglesey clergy.[58] The prince claimed the right to present to the living but he was vigorously resisted by the bishop. His case would seem to be rather doubtful but there was constant pressure on the church at this time. There was also a dispute in 1394 over the right to present to Eglwys Ail on the grounds that the church was a royal chapel since Cadwaladr, once prince of Wales, had his court within the township.[59]

But the most interesting example of patronage in Anglesey was Caergybi or Holyhead, which had become a collegiate church with a chapter consisting of a provost and twelve canons. The right of presentation was vested in the kin-

---

55  Glanmor Williams, op.cit., pp.137-9.

56  *Valor Ecclesiasticus*, iv, 417, 429, 431.

57  TNA E315/166, ff. 9a, 4b, 5b (1348, 1370, 1379). In 1348 the church had been granted by the prince; in 1370 it was argued that it should have been in the prince's gift because of the vacancy of the see.

58  The only other exceptions were the rector of Llanddyfnan who paid 5s and Brother Einion, canon of Beddgelert, who paid 3s 4d.

59  TNA E315/166, ff. 7a, 1a-b.

dreds of Hwfa ap Cynddelw and Llywarch ap Bran which dominated that part of Anglesey. This was a relic of the pre-Norman pattern in which lay and ecclesiastical property rights were inextricably mixed and local kindreds often had what amounted to proprietary rights in the mother churches.[60] It has been suggested that Hwfa and Llywarch themselves had held the lands from which tithes were due to Caergybi and that they may have been the re-founders and re-builders of the church in the twelfth century.[61] Their sons gave their names to *gwelyau* and according to two fifteenth-century documents the descendants of three sons of Llywarch presented to two canonries each and those of five sons of Hwfa to one each; the last one was shared by the descendants of two of the five.[62] By that time the right to present in each case was divided among a large number of heirs since it was, like any other advowson, a piece of real property.[63]

An action was brought by the prince in 1371 against 35 individuals over the right to present to a vacant prebend.[64] The prince claimed a share because one of the heirs had disparaged herself by marrying a bondman; their defence was that her status was immaterial and that the decision was that of the majority. Both before and after 1282 the head of the community was appointed by the prince and a number of presentations are recorded. There were also royal presentations to prebends from time to time; fifteen were made between 1284 and 1414 and the 1371 case may show how this came about when the right belonged to the two kindreds. The prince must have acquired various shares by escheat or forfeiture and then used his interest to provide more preferment for his servants.

Adam de Wettenhall, later chamberlain of north Wales, was appointed provost in 1288 but few, if any, of his successors seem to have had any Welsh connections.[65] They were royal clerks, civil servants, for whom preferment all over England and Wales was their reward. The only exception was Ralph of Windsor, appointed in 1313 at the age of fourteen; he probably owed his promotion to the influence of his kinsman, the archbishop of Canterbury.[66] In 1423 the office was granted to Jean Tiphaine, a Norman cleric who was Queen Katherine's physician and who was later to treat Joan of Arc during her im-

---

60  It was this kind of situation that scandalised Gerald of Wales at Llanbadarn Fawr in 1188 (*Journey through Wales*, pp.180-1).

61  A.N. Palmer, 'The portionary churches of medieval north Wales', in *Arch.Camb.*, 1886, pp.182-3. This discussion has yet to be superseded.

62  *Rec.Caern.*, pp.246-8.

63  In 1352 the former tenant of escheat lands in Trefadog was described as having had a share in the election to two prebends in Caergybi (*Extent of Anglesey*, pp.193-4).

64  TNA E315/166, ff. 5a-b.

65  *CAC*, p.136.

66  *CPR 1307-1313*, 557; Glanmor Williams, op.cit., p.63.

prisonment.[67] Stephen de Kettelbergh, presented in 1320, was an Oxford doctor of civil law.[68] He had the grace to acknowledge his limitations; in 1336 he petitioned the pope for permission to hold another benefice as Caergybi was of little value to him because of its distance and his ignorance of Welsh. Richard Medford, presented in 1384, was a Cambridge graduate who was also the king's secretary and who in 1388 became bishop first of Chichester and later of Salisbury.[69] His brother Walter, who was presented in 1413, was later papal nuncio or ambassador to England and Richard Clifford, presented in 1394, was successively bishop of Worcester and London and ambassador at the Council of Constance.[70] These were all important men who obtained high preferment but they contributed nothing to the church in Anglesey.

In 1379 there were seven canons, all but one of whom had local connections,[71] John Martyn, dean of Bangor, was presented in 1384 and another dean, Nigel Bondeby, in 1423.[72] Others were also members of the Bangor chapter and Thomas Sparkford, presented in 1392, eventually became bishop of Waterford and Lismore in Ireland.[73] Robert Hallum, who obtained his canonry in 1393, became bishop of Salisbury and was one of the English delegation at the Councils of Pisa and Constance.[74] Such presentations show that the crown had taken a hand in the filling of vacancies at Caergybi in its never-ending quest for preferment for its servants. Some local canons remained but they were now joined by absentee royal clerks and pluralists. Thomas Ardern, rector of Llanfechell, was presented by 34 patrons in 1415 in place of a member of a leading local family, Dafydd ab Ieuan ap Tudur Llwyd of Eiriannell, who had been there since before 1379.[75] The two lists in the *Record of Caernarvon* name the canons, the prebends and the patrons and seem to date from about the same time. In the sixteenth century the canonries appear to have been filled by their proper patrons as in 1518 and possibly in 1515.[76] The patrons seem to have presented for the last time in 1534; there were several more presentations

67 C.T. Allmand, 'Wales and the Hundred Years War: a French provost of Holyhead', *TAAS* 1964, pp.1-4.

68 *CPR 1317-1321*, 445; A.B. Emden, *Biographical Register of the University of Oxford to 1500*, iii, 1043.

69 *CPR 1381-1385*, 302; A.B. Emden, Biographical *Register of the University of Cambridge to 1500* (1963), pp.398-9.

70 *CPR 1413-1416*, 64; *CPR 1391-1396*, 482; Emden, *Oxford*, 1252-3, 440-1

71 TNA E179/3/2.

72 *CPR 1381-1385*. 443; *CPL 1417-1431*, 277.

73 *CPR 1391-1396*, 44.

74 ibid., p.345; Emden, *Oxford*, 854-5.

75 A. Ivor Pryce, 'The register of Benedict, bishop of Bangor, 1408-1417', *Arch.Camb.*, 1922, p.100.

76 *Rec.Caern.*, pp.246-8; the second list can be dated from internal evidence to between 1436 and 1451; A. Ivor Pryce, *The Diocese of Bangor in the Sixteenth Century*, pp. 3, 4.

before the dissolution of all colleges and chantries in 1548 but they were all by the bishop.[77] This may be connected with a deed of 1537 in which the patrons of all the canonries conveyed the next presentation to a local gentleman, Thomas ap Rhys Wyn and four clerics. This transaction could possibly indicate the surrender of their rights by the heirs of the two kindreds.[78] Caergybi is an interesting example of the patronage of local kindreds and the preferment of royal clerks existing side-by-side; there certainly seems to have been no such thing as a community and the chapter can never have met. The provostship was undoubtedly in demand; in 1353 the bishop of St Asaph had tried to obtain the advowson from the crown and had offered all his temporalities in the lordship of Denbigh in exchange.[79]

The *maerdref* churches were far less profitable, which may explain why two of them were granted to Penmon. However, the crown did present when they fell vacant; between 1308 and 1340 there were six presentations to Aberffraw, six to Llan-faes, four to Rhosyr and four to Penrhosllugwy.[80] Only one of these was Welsh.[81] Most held their cures for a very short time and it is unlikely that many ever actually set foot in their churches; for example, Benedict de Burnedish was presented to Aberffraw in 1318, Richard of Worcester in 1319, Roger de Scales in 1321 and William de Werdale in 1322.[82] The Black Prince used benefices in his gift to reward his servants and clerks of his were presented to Aberffraw and Llan-faes in 1347.[83]

The last quarter of the fourteenth century showed a marked increase in royal presentations to other benefices. There was no vacancy in the see of Bangor between 1376 and 1398 to justify the appropriation of so much of the bishop's patronage but twice presentations were made to livings on the grounds that the see was vacant when it was not.[84] Some presentations are hard to explain, like that of John Waterford to the less than profitable benefice of Llanddeusant with Llanbabo in 1388. On the other hand, five different incumbents of Llanddyfnan, probably the richest Anglesey living after Caergybi, are named on the patent rolls during this period.[85] Of the sixteen clerics named, at least eight

---

77  ibid., p.7, the patrons were named as Edmund Griffith and others.
78  *Calendar of Ancient Deeds.* v, A13268. Rights had from time to time been conveyed by individuals (e.g. BUASC Baron Hill 1670 (1506)).
79  *BPR*, iii, 128.
80  *CPR 1307-1313*, 95, 122, 271, 520; *1313-1317*, 451; *1317-1321*, 62, 106, 111, 271, 525; *1321-1324*, 2, 138; *1324-1327*, 50, 81,103, 253; *1330-1334*, 10, 107, 488; *1334-1338*, 456.
81  This was Einion, archdeacon of Anglesey, presented to Llan-faes in 1317 (*CPR 1317-1321*, 62).
82  William de Werdale was a royal clerk (*CPR 1321-1324*, 138).
83  *BPR*, i, 47, 138. The presentation of royal clerks is discussed by Glanmor Williams, op.cit., pp.137-8.
84  *CPR 1381-1385*, 302 (Penmynydd); *1388-1392*, 373 (Llaneugrad).
85  *CPR 1377-1381*, 393; *1381-1385*, 477; *1385-1389*, 278; *1396-1399*, 201, 354.

were Welsh. In December 1399 Master David Lygadbrith was presented to Llanddyfnan.[86] He was a Welsh clerk at Oxford who in 1402 was one of those indicted by a jury there for plotting on behalf of Owain Glyn Dŵr.[87] There were further presentations in the fifteenth century, several being to Llanddwyn and others to Llaneilian and Llanddyfnan. John Silcock was collated by the archbishop of Canterbury to Llanddyfnan in 1417 because the living had been vacant for so long and Richard Praty, presented to Llanddwyn in 1414, later became bishop of Chichester and was present at the trial of Joan of Arc.[88] All this suggests that although the crown did not have much patronage in Anglesey it exploited what it had to the limit and on occasion encroached on livings in the bishop's gift.

These royal clerks and chaplains probably never actually exercised the cure of souls. Even a Welshman like David Lygadbrith was presented not for the sake of the parishioners but so that he would have an income while at the university. The graduate parson was a rarity in the middle ages; when a priest obtained leave of absence to go and study, that was probably the last his parish saw or heard of him. An occasional royal presentation might be of a Welshman, but these do not seem to have been graduates and, indeed, there were really two kinds of clergy in the middle ages. On the one hand there were the educated men from whose ranks were drawn bishops and greater dignitaries as well as lawyers and administrators and on the other hand there were those who, although not always unlettered and uncultured, had not had any university training and who held all but the most valuable benefices.[89] In Wales there was a further division between those who were of good family and who led much the same kind of life as their *uchelwr* kinsmen and the ordinary incumbents and unbeneficed priests.[90]

The former group were often generous patrons of the poets. In Anglesey their ranks included Hugh Clement, rector of Llanfechell and Llangefni in 1504, to whom Lewys Môn sang and Nicholas ab Elis, rector of Llaneilian, whose elegy was sung by Tudur Aled.[91] One of the best examples of an upper-class Anglesey cleric who did not obtain any great preferment was Hywel ab Adda Grwn. His father was one of the Welsh burgesses of Beaumaris in 1327 and he had two brothers, Ieuan and Madog.[92] In 1379 he was the collector of

86 *CPR 1399-1401*, 147.
87 Ralph A. Griffiths, 'Some partisans of Owain Glyndŵr at Oxford', in *BBCS*, 20 (1963), 283 and n.289.
88 *Reg. Chichele*, i (1943), 160-1; *CPR 1413-1416*, 247; Emden, *Oxford*, s.n.
89 Glanmor Williams, op.cit., pp.325-4.
90 ibid., pp.327-8.
91 *Gwaith Lewys Môn*, pp.63-5; *Gwaith Tudur Aled*, pp.342-5
92 NLW Peniarth 405, pp.417, 435; TNA E315/ 166, f.7a.

the clerical poll tax in the archdeaconry and rector of Llaneugrad and Llanallgo and in 1385 he exchanged his living for that of Llanddwyn.[93] The fact that his father was a Welsh burgess of Beaumaris suggests a Newborough connection and in 1385-6 Hywel was one of the bailiffs there.[94] From 1386 to 1390 he was one of the farmers of the borough and in 1395-6 he was farming it again with Maredudd ap Tudur ap Goronwy.[95] These references show a cleric of good family playing an active part as a burgess and with enough behind him to undertake the farm of Newborough. Other clerics were not only of land-owning stock but were themselves landowners. Thomas ap Dafydd ap Tudur, the parson of Llanddyfnan, conveyed lands there to William and Elen Bulkeley between 1464 and 1468 and in 1451 William ap Llywelyn ab Ieuan ap Tudur Llwyd of Eiriannell paid relief and *gobrestyn* to take up the lands of his dead brother Hywel, a cleric.[96]

It is not easy to ascertain how many beneficed clergy there were in Anglesey at any given time. There were certainly not as many as there were later parishes since many churches were then no more than chapels-of-ease. Llanallgo, for example, was always held with Llaneugrad and Llandysilio with Llanfair Pwllgwyngyll although each church was rated separately in 1254. The 1379 subsidy lists 40 beneficed clergymen, along with the provost and canons of Caergybi, the prior of Penmon, a canon of Beddgelert and eleven unbeneficed chaplains, most of whom were attached to particular churches.[97] In 1406 twenty beneficed clergymen had either made their peace with the king or were still in rebellion. These included the parsons of Aberffraw and Newborough, who were presumably royal appointments, Eglwys Ail, Llangefni, Amlwch, Penmynydd and Llanddyfnan.[98] There were also two canons of Caergybi and sixteen unbeneficed clerics; the names reflect the involvement of the clergy in the revolt.

On the death of bishop Pigot in 1504 the archbishop of Canterbury, William Warham, conducted a metropolitical visitation of the diocese of Bangor.[99] A return was made of the beneficed clergy and their curates but it does not include the non-resident canons of Caergybi, only the provost, Richard Bromfield, being named. There were 23 incumbents including the provost, the

93  TNA E179/3/5, 2; *CPR 1381-1385*, 520.
94  TNA SC6/1151/2, m.6b.
95  TNA SC6/1151/3, m.4b; 1152/2, m.5b. In 1396 he witnessed a gift of land in Newborough (Flintshire R.O., Hawarden, D/MT 1).
96  BUASC Baron Hill 1096, 1098, 1106, 1105; NLW Sotheby 45.
97  TNA E179/3/2. There were chaplains at Llanddwyn, Newborough, Eglwys Ail, Caergybi, Llandrygarn, Bodedern and Rhoscolyn; a Brother Dafydd ap Bleddyn may have been connected with Llan-faes.
98  Glyn Roberts, 'The Anglesey submissions of 1406', 42-60.
99  A. Ivor Pryce, *The Diocese of Bangor in the Sixteenth Century*, pp.82-3.

dean of Bangor and the archdeacon; apart from these there were five graduates, at Newborough, Penmynydd, Llanfaethlu, Llanrhuddlad and Llaneilian. Hugh Elis, the rector of Llaneilian, was chancellor of Bangor cathedral and Richard Vaughan of Penmynydd was a canon.[100] Morgan Newborough, rector of Rhoscolyn, was provost of Clynnog Fawr about this time and Dafydd Trefor, rector of Llaneugrad with Llanallgo, was a poet of some standing who was later a prebendary of Bangor.[101] Most of the beneficed clergy seem to have been Welsh and they all had Welsh curates. This was a necessity when each incumbent was responsible for several churches and only eight had none.

In 1535 there were 26 incumbents, apart from the dean, the archdeacon, the abbot of Aberconwy and the prior of Penmon.[102] Some of those named in 1504 were still in the same parishes while others had moved to other Anglesey livings. Eleven of the 26 were graduates, a good proportion, considering that the ideal of a graduate clergy was not generally accepted until the late sixteenth century. Dr Arthur Bulkeley, the rector of Llanddeusant with Llanbabo and Llanfair-ynghornwy, was later to be bishop of Bangor and two other Bulkeleys had cures in the county, Hugh at Llanfechell and Thomas at Llangefni.

All these lists show that there were always some members of leading local families in the ranks of the Anglesey clergy. It is not possible to say very much about the lives of these men but some of the poetry of the fifteenth century makes it abundantly clear that the way of life of a parson of good family could be very secular indeed.[103] Most of the parish clergy were undoubtedly married men with families. The earliest reference to such canonical irregularity comes from 1305 when the archdeacon petitioned the prince for licence to give lands to his daughter, only to be told that as a cleric he had no business to have any children.[104] Gruffudd Trefgoed, prebendary of Bangor and canon of Caergybi, who died in 1389, had a son, Gwilym and personal names sometimes offer clues; among those who made their peace in 1406 were Madog ap Dafydd Offeiriad of Menai, Iorwerth ap Madog Offeiriad of Talybolion and Tudur ap Madog Offeiriad of Malltraeth.[105] Because of the lack of information one searches in vain for clerical dynasties like that which spanned the Reformation at Whitford in Flintshire, but this is not to say that such dynasties did not exist in Anglesey.[106]

100  *Fasti* 11, pp. 7, 17.
101  C.N. Johns, 'The Celtic monasteries of north Wales', *TCHS* 21 (1960), 43; *Fasti* 11, p.15; *Y Bywgraffiadur Cymreig*, pp.95-6; Glanmor Williams, op.cit., pp. 341, 425-6.
102  *Valor Ecclesiasticus*, vi, xvii.
103  Glanmor Williams, op.cit., pp. 261-3, 282.
104  *Rec. Caern.*, p.222.
105  Glyn Roberts, op.cit., 46, 48, 52.
106  Glanmor Williams, op.cit., p.282.

The lack of episcopal registers means that little more can be said about the Anglesey clergy in the middle ages but a few scattered references do exist. A man of illegitimate birth could not be ordained to the priesthood without a dispensation. In 1336 such a dispensation was granted by the pope to Gruffudd ap Meurig of the commote of Menai and in 1432 Hywel ap Dafydd, described as rector of Llangeinwen, a graduate who had already been permitted to take orders, was allowed to hold a benefice with cure of souls.[107] Another bar to ordination was bond status, unless the consent of the lord was obtained, but there were few restrictions which could not be relaxed on payment of a fine. In 1374 Madog, the sixth son of Dafydd ab Iorwerth, a royal bondman of Hirdre-faig, was granted a licence to take holy orders from any bishop who would confer them, and in 1456-7 Dafydd ap Dafydd ap Sym, a bondman of Hendre Rhosyr, paid an amercement of one pound for being ordained without licence.[108] The clergy as a class were hit particularly hard by the Black Death and one might argue that this high rate of mortality was a sign that most of them were carrying out their pastoral responsibilities.[109] A number of inquisitions taken at Beaumaris on 5 November 1349 relate to the goods of deceased clergy, among them the incumbents of Eglwys Ail, Llanynghenedl, Llanfaelog, Penmynydd, Llechgynfarwy and Llanbeulan and the date suggests that these were victims of the plague.[110]

Anglesey had only two religious houses, the Augustinian priory of Penmon and the Franciscan friary nearby at Llan-faes. Penmon or Priestholm was one of the holiest places in Anglesey, traditionally founded in the sixth century by Cynlas for his brother Seiriol, one of the island's two patron saints.[111] It consisted of a monastic settlement on Ynys Lannog or Priestholm, now usually known as Puffin Island and another settlement on the mainland at Penmon. The foundation developed as a *clas* or monastic community of secular canons under an abbot and like other communities it held the surrounding territory as its *abadaeth* or endowment. On the island are the remains of several cells within a rectangular enclosure and a church.[112] On his deathbed Gruffudd ap Cynan left the community ten shillings, the same sum as he gave to Caergybi, Clynnog, Enlli and various other *clasau*.[113] According to Gerald no woman was

---

107  *CPL 1305-1342*, 583;  *1427-1447*, 444.

108  TNA E163/24/1, m.6a; SC6/1154/2, m.19a.

109  Glanmor Williams, op.cit., pp.146-9.

110  TNA E315/166, ff. 20b-21a.

111  RCAHM *Anglesey Inventory*, p.119;  A.D. Carr, 'The priory of Penmon', *Journal of Welsh Ecclesiastical History* 3 (1986), 18-30;  see also *Hist. Wales*, p.133.

112  RCAHM *Anglesey Inventory*, pp.141-3; the church was built in the twelfth century with a central tower which still stands.

113  *Historia Gruffud vab Kenan*, pp. 31, 105n.

allowed on the island and he also claimed that whenever there was any dispute within the community mice would appear and devour its food.[114]

The priory church of Penmon dates from the twelfth century.[115] Such a building must reflect a period of peace and prosperity after Gruffudd ap Cynan had successfully withstood the Norman threat and his sons had extended the borders of Gwynedd. In 1199 the prior of Ynys Lannog was one of those instructed by the pope to decide on Llywelyn ab Iorwerth's petition to marry the daughter of the Manx king, who had previously been betrothed to his uncle.[116] The texts of six thirteenth-century charters have survived in a later confirmation; the most important may be that of 1237 because it was granted to the prior and canons, indicating that Penmon had by now became a regular house of Augustinian canons.[117] This was the fate of more than one *clas* in Gwynedd; the same thing happened to Beddgelert and Enlli. As the ideals of continental monasticism reached Wales this was a natural development and the Augustinians or Black Canons were the most appropriate order.[118] The extension of the church may date from this time as do the monastic buildings, the remains of which are still to be seen.[119] The cloisters were probably between these and the church, a site later occupied by the sixteenth-century prior's house. The buildings suggest that it was never a large house and this is borne out by its later history.

Little is known of the day-to-day history of the priory. Occasionally the patent rolls record the death or resignation of a prior and the sheriff sometimes accounted for the revenue of the house and its lands during a vacancy.[120] In his account for 1306-7 the sheriff answered for the issues during the vacancy caused by the removal of Iorwerth the prior in August 1306. This must be connected with an entry in the register of Robert Winchelsey, archbishop of Canterbury from 1295 to 1313, concerning the complaints of two canons against the prior, accusing him of waste, incontinence and irregularity.[121] Two petitions have survived, both of them against the sheriff of Anglesey over breaches of

---

114  *The Journey through Wales*, p.190.

115  RCAHM *Anglesey Inventory*, pp.119-21.

116  *CPL 1198-1304*, 8.

117  *CChartR*, ii, 459-60 i *Acts of Welsh Rulers* nos. 250, 272, 286, 288, 313, 320.

118  J.C. Dickinson, *The Origins of the Austin Canons and their Introduction into England* (1950), pp. 228-9, 231 ff., where the author discusses the institution of regular canons in collegiate churches in Cornwall and south-west England. He also points out that many argued that regular canons were not monks and that they did, in fact, rank with the secular clergy (pp.198-200).

119  RCAHM *Anglesey Inventory*. pp.122-3. The most recent discussion of the priory and of its topographical context is David Longley, *St Seiriol's Church and Prior's House, Penmon* (GAT Report 648, Bangor, 2006).

120  *CPR 1292-1301*, 48 (1294); *1307-1313*, 273, 279 (1310), and *1317-1321*, 4 (1317).

121  TNA SC6/1227/5; *Reg. Winchelsey*, p.77b.

the community's liberties.[122] The prior was the collector of the clerical subsidy in Anglesey on at least two occasions.[123] The foundation was never a wealthy one; in 1310 the justice was ordered to assent to the election of a new prior 'in compassion for the poverty of the house' and one of the reasons for the grant of the rectories of Llan-faes and Penrhosllugwy in 1395 was the community's poverty.[124]

Apart from a prior called John in 1380-1 there is no mention of any head of the house between Einion ap Goronwy, elected in 1335 and John Castell who resigned in 1414.[125] Nor is there any mention of the priory in connection with the Glyn Dŵr revolt. All the known priors before 1335 were Welsh, while all those after 1400 bore English names and this may reflect an anglicisation which may in turn explain why there was no involvement in the rebellion. The fifteenth-century priory seems to have been closely connected with the town of Beaumaris. A burgage belonging to the prior was in decay in 1413-4 and in 1452 another was described in a deed as being next to that of Thomas Godfrey, prior of Penmon.[126] Prior Godfrey belonged to a prominent Beaumaris family; he may have been the Thomas Godfrey, clerk and burgess, who in 1433 conveyed a burgage to a fellow-burgess, John Bate.[127] John Ingram, who succeeded William Ardescote in 1468, must also have had Beaumaris connections; like the Godfreys the Ingrams were an important burgess family and his tenure of the priory seems to have been a long one.[128] In 1504 he and two of the canons were accused by Archbishop Warham's visitors of keeping concubines.[129] He also inspired the only poem connected with the house; Tudur Aled asked a patron on his behalf for a horse and in doing so praised his attainments.[130] There is a hint in this poem that he added to the buildings; the chancel of the church was rebuilt in the fifteenth century and the kitchen, warming-house and prior's house were built in the early sixteenth.[131] Having provided a comfortable residence, Ingram may have chosen to live there rather than in Beaumaris. The last prior was John Godfrey, a name which again reflects the Beaumaris connection. Penmon seems by then to have been little more than a monastic annexe to the town.[132]

122  *CAP*, p.403; *Rec.Caern.*, p.221.
123  Natalie Fryde, *List of Welsh Entries in the Memoranda Rolls, 1282-1343*, no.945 (1332); TNA SC6/1150/3, m.6a (1380-1).
124  *CCW*, 319.
125  *CPR1334-1338*, 129; *1413-1416*, 184.
126  TNA SC6/1152/5, m.5a; BUASC Baron Hill 468.
127  BUASC Baron Hill 460. In 1416 a clerk called Thomas Godfrey acquired land in Llaneilian (NLW Sotheby 21).
128  *CPR 1467-1477*, 122.
129  Glanmor Williams, op cit., p.399. A.Ivor Pryce, op.cit., p.xviii calls him Richard.
130  *Gwaith Tudur Aled*, pp.399-401.
131  RCAHM *Anglesey Inventory*, pp. 120, 122-3.
132  *Letters and Papers, Henry VIII*, i, no.438.

The priory had lasted for nearly a thousand years but its life was now drawing to a close. The shape of things to come was already to be seen; in 1522 Prior Godfrey leased the chapel of Llangwyllog to Richard Bulkeley for a hundred years at an annual rent of one pound.[133] The lease was signed by the community which consisted of the prior and two canons. There are many aspects of Penmon's history of which we know nothing. We know the extent of its endowment and its income but we know nothing of the canons themselves. The registers of some bishops of Hereford before the dissolution record several ordinations to titles provided by Penmon. Ssome of these were during vacancies at Bangor, as in the case of William Ardescote in 1435 and Rowland Geffrey in 1505, but others may have been titles provided for clerks who were not members of the community.[134] Nor do we know anything of the nature and strength of the house's spiritual life; on the evidence available it must be suspected that Penmon in the years before its dissolution was not a centre of spiritual endeavour. One has the impression that the prior and canons lived off their rents and enjoyed a moderately comfortable bachelor existence.

The mendicant orders had one house in Anglesey, at Llan-faes. It was founded by Llywelyn ab Iorwerth in memory of his wife Joan and she was buried there.[135] Friars invariably settled in towns; not only were they the best centres for preaching but the alms on which they had to live were more readily available. Llywelyn was a patron of both mendicant orders and he and his successors made good use of the Franciscans of Llan-faes and of the Dominicans of Bangor and Rhuddlan. In 1261 the arbitrators who settled a boundary dispute between Llywelyn ap Gruffudd and the bishop of Bangor included two Llan-faes friars and two years later two of them were among the arbitrators when Gruffudd ap Gwenwynwyn of Powys submitted to the prince.[136] In 1279 Friar William, the guardian or head of the house, was Llywelyn's messenger to Edward I and he was later to write to the king on the prince's behalf.[137] Another princess of Wales had found her last resting-place in the friary in 1282; at the height of the final crisis in Anglo-Welsh relations Llywelyn ap Gruffudd's wife Eleanor de Montfort died in childbirth and was buried there.[138] There were other burials in that year; the annihilation of the royal army which had tried to

133  BUASC Baron Hill 1575.
134  *Reg. Spofford*, p.321; *Reg. Mayew.* p.241; see also *Reg. Myllyng*, pp.157-8; *Reg. Bothe*, pp. 313, 316, 318, 319, 321, 325, 329, 330; all those in the latter, ordained between 1522 and 1533, were Welsh. For letters testimonial for Edmund ap Geoffrey, dated 10 August 1524, see M. Helen Davies, 'A deed of Penmon Priory', in *NLW Journal*, 21 (1979), 111.
135  *Brut y Tywysogyon* (Peniarth 20 version), p.104.
136  Glyn Roberts, 'The Dominican friary of Bangor', in *Aspects of Welsh History*, p.220.
137  *CAC*, pp. 62, 99.
138  *Hist. Wales*, p.763.

cross the Menai Straits on a bridge of boats meant that it was the final resting-place of a number of eminent casualties.[139]

The friary's glory really departed after 1282. It was no longer at the centre of affairs, nor did the friars serve again as ambassadors or arbitrators. Their patrons in future were to be the rising landowning gentry of north Wales. They obtained a plot adjoining the friary for its enlargement in 1316 and a Beaumaris burgess, John de Housom, later gave them another five acres.[140] In 1352 they received a grant from the Black Prince which allowed them to keep whatever they might be given for their maintenance, to buy whatever they needed in the markets and fairs of the principality and to have free passage on all the ferries.[141] The Franciscans seem to have been deeply implicated in the Glyn Dŵr revolt and those of Llan-faes were involved at a very early stage. Soon after the outbreak of the revolt Henry IV himself led a force as far as Anglesey and devastated the eastern side of the island. The friars resisted him, the house was despoiled and some captive members of the community were handed over to the minister of the order.[142] An enquiry held at the order's request in January 1401 found that the house was deserted, the friars dispersed as rebels and their goods seized.[143] Some were still at large and in rebellion in 1406 but the revolt came to an end and things gradually returned to normal.[144] The king took steps for the reconstitution of the community in 1414; in the letters patent it was stated that there should in future be eight friars, two of whom would be Welsh.[145] The foundation seems to have been entirely Welsh before the revolt.

After this the records are again silent about the Grey Friars of Llan-faes. They certainly enjoyed some prestige among the laity and their church, like other friary churches, was a popular place of burial. In 1376 Gwilym ap Gruffudd ap Tudur of Llaniestyn left them two pounds as well as giving instructions for his burial among them and in 1431 Gwilym ap Gruffudd of Penmynydd expressed a wish to be buried there or at Penmynydd or Llandygái.[146] Many of the leaders of Anglesey society were laid to rest there, including Goronwy ap Tudur of Penmynydd, drowned in 1382 and his wife Myfanwy

---

139  Glyn Roberts, op.cit., p.225.
140  *CPR 1313-1317*, 388; TNA SC6/1149/2, m.6a.
141  TNA SC6/1149/2, m.7a.
142  J. E. Lloyd, *Owen Glendower* (1931), p.34; F. S. Haydon, ed., *Eulogium Historiarum* iii (1863), p.388.
143  *CPR 1399-1401*, 418.
144  Glyn Roberts, 'The Anglesey submissions of 1406', 59. Their names were Tudur Cayr, Tegwared ap Bleddyn, Madog Dewi, Gruffudd Nannau, William Conwy and Goronwy ap Dafydd ab Ithel.
145  *CPR 1413-1416*, 224.
146  BUASC Penrhyn 5, 14.

and probably many Beaumaris burgesses.[147] Also buried there were Dafydd ab
Ieuan ap Hywel of Llwydiarth, traditionally the victim of the 'Ffrae Ddu' in
Beaumaris and his wife Angharad, the daughter of Gwilym ap Gruffudd.[148]
And people remembered Llan-faes in their wills; in 1435 bishop John Cliderow
left a pound each to the friars of Llan-faes and Bangor and five years earlier
Cynwrig ab Ieuan ap Llywelyn of Rhosyr had left the same houses two shillings
each.[149] In 1491 Hugh Stretton of Beaumaris left the friars a cow and three
years later they had 6s 8d from Lleucu ferch Iolyn of Llanfair Dyffryn Clwyd.[150]
These legacies suggest that the hostility shown by some poets to the mendicant
orders was not typical of society as a whole. Part of the tombstone of a Llan-
faes friar buried among the Dominicans of Bangor has survived and a small
thirteenth-century manuscript of the Vulgate once belonged to the community
and was lent to a Bangor friar some time before 1300.[151]

Thus the monastic history of Anglesey is not particularly distinguished. But
there was more to medieval religion than land, income, patronage and monastic
property although the flavour and quality of religious life in Anglesey must necessarily elude us. Religion also involved shrines, pilgrimages and a vast inter-
national thaumaturgic apparatus. Pilgrimage could be a spontaneous act of
piety and devotion; it could also be an opportunity to travel in the way immortalised by Chaucer or it could be a survival from pagan times. All these ele-
ments could be present and Anglesey had its share of shrines. The most notable
was that of Dwynwen at Llanddwyn. Dwynwen's reputation as the patron of
lovers was more than local and pilgrims came to her well from all over Wales.[152]
In the fourteenth century Llanddwyn was one of the richest churches in Anglesey, thanks to its popularity as a place of pilgrimage and in 1535 the tithes
of the parish, which contained far more sand than soil, amounted to less than
a pound while 'offerynges of charitable peple to the Saynt in tymes past' came
to £12 6s 8d.[153] It was probably this income that was responsible for the litiga-
tion over the advowson in the fourteenth century and the rectory of Llanddwyn
contributed much to the wealth of Richard Kyffin, dean of Bangor, at the end

147  Glyn Roberts, 'Wyrion Eden', p.201.
148  *Gwaith Hywel Cilan*, p.35.
149  Glyn Roberts, 'The Dominican friary of Bangor', p.233; NLW Sotheby 26.
150  Glanmor Williams, op.cit., pp.562-6, where bequests to Welsh houses in PCC wills are
     tabulated; they include twelve legacies to Llan-faes, among them 10s from Robert ap Rhys and
     £1 6s 8d from Sir Rowland Vielville.
151  Glyn Roberts, op.cit., pp.229-30.
152  Glanmor Williams, op.cit., pp. 488, 493; the legend of Dwynwen is in G. Hartwell Jones, *Celtic
     Britain and the Pilgrim Movement* (1912), pp.322-3, although there was never a Benedictine
     house there; Francis Jones, *The Holy Wells of Wales* (1954), pp. 50, 102.
153  *Valor Ecclesiasticus*. vi, xxiv.

of the fifteenth.[154] Another famous well was that at Llaneilian and the wells of Dwynwen and Eilian continued to attract devotees long after the Reformation.[155] In the church of Newborough there was a famous statue of St Peter which attracted many pilgrims and which was commemorated by Lewis Daron.[156] Other Anglesey churches, like Penmon and Caergybi, also had their share of pilgrims; at the latter offerings on the patronal feast and other days of offering amounted to £8 14s 6d in 1535.[157]

In their wills men and women usually remembered their parish churches and often left instructions for their burial there. In 1376 Gwilym ap Gruffudd ap Tudur left ten shillings to Llaniestyn church and 2s 6d to the parson; his widow Gwenllian ferch Madog and his nephew and heir Gruffudd ap Gwilym ap Gruffudd gave the effigy of St Iestyn which is still to be seen in the church.[158] In 1429 Arddun ferch Gruffudd, the wife of Rhys ap Dafydd ap Rhys of Bodedern, left two shillings to the church and Cynwrig ab Ieuan ap Llywelyn left one shilling to Newborough church in 1430.[159] Ieuan ap Madog ab Ieuan ap Hywel left 6s 8d to the parish church of Llanedwen in 1483 and William Bulkeley the elder made a particularly generous bequest to Beaumaris in 1490.[160] There were also bequests for more immediate spiritual needs; Cynwrig ab Ieuan ap Llywelyn left ten shillings for a trental of masses for the souls of himself and his wife.

Churches reflected the prosperity of the communities which built them and Anglesey, though prosperous by the standards of Gwynedd, has nothing comparable with the glories of East Anglia or the Cotswolds. Nevertheless; much medieval work remains, despite the efforts of nineteenth-century restorers.[161] In addition to the priory church at Penmon, the tower of Llaneilian, the nave and the chancel arch at Llanfairynghornwy, most of Llanbabo and Llaneugrad and the naves of Llanbeulan, Llanfechell, Llangeinwen and Llanrhwydrys date from the twelfth century.[162] But most Anglesey churches date largely from the fourteenth and fifteenth centuries, although the evidence of many earlier fonts

154  Glanmor Williams, op.cit., p.319; for Sir Dafydd Trefor's *cywydd* to Dwynwen see Rhiannon Ifans, *Gwaith Syr Dafydd Trefor* (2005), pp.67-9.
155  Francis Jones, op cit., p.50; Glanmor Williams, op.cit., pp.431-2.
156  Glanmor Williams, op.cit., p.489; the poem is in G. Hartwell Jones, op.cit., pp.320-1.
157  *Valor Ecclesiasticus*. iv, 428.
158  BUASC Penrhyn 5; the memorial is discussed by Colin Gresham, *Medieval Stone Carving in North Wales* (1968), no. 209.
159  NLW Bodewryd Correspondence 1034; Sotheby 26.
160  BUASC Plas Coch 17; Baron Hill 4; see also NLW Sotheby 32 and BUASC Plas Coch 3.
161  E. Tyrrell-Green, 'The ecclesiology of Anglesey', *Y Cymmrodor*, 40 (1929), 45-117.
162  RCAHM *Anglesey Inventory* pp. 119-22, 59-60, 74-5, 34-5, 62, 40, 77, 91 and 108. The ruined Capel Llugwy at Penrhosllugwy is a chapel-of-ease of the kind of which many existed but have long disappeared. Churches are also described in R. Haslam, J. Orbach and A. Voelcker, *The Buildings of Wales : Gwynedd* (2009).

as well as that of the *Valuation of Norwich* shows that they replaced earlier build-ings in the same places, if not on the same sites.[163] The one new church built on a new site after the conquest was Beaumaris which is in style an English town church rather than a Welsh one. Unfortunately the rebuilding of Llan-faes in the nineteenth century has left us without an example of a Welsh town church. Holyhead and most of Llaneilian date from the late fifteenth and early sixteenth centuries, as does the finest of all the churches of Gwynedd at Clynnog Fawr; it is possible that the same masons worked on all three churches.[164] The rebuilding of Llaneilian seems to have been the work of the parson, Nicholas ab Elis.[165] There remain, too, a number of medieval fittings and effigies like the choir-stalls at Beaumaris and the alabaster tomb of Goronwy ap Tudur and his wife Myfanwy at Penmynydd, moved there from Llan-faes at the dissolution.

The story of the medieval church really comes to an end with the Reforma-tion. In the diocese of Bangor its progress was caught up in the rivalry of two of the leading local families, the Glyns of Glynllifon, represented by Dr William Glyn, archdeacon of Bangor and vicar-general of the diocese and the Bulkeleys of Beaumaris.[166] In 1535 the commissioners investigating the monasteries were on their rounds and on 21 November Sir Richard Bulkeley wrote to Thomas Cromwell seeking his favour for John Godfrey, the prior of Penmon, who had been instructed by the commissioners to show the foundation of the house to Cromwell or to them.[167] The documents were in Bulkeley's possession and the prior offered a total of 40 marks for Cromwell's goodwill and to be left alone. The house supported the prior, two canons, a priest and twelve or sixteen oth-ers and the Bulkeleys had long been its stewards. The fact that he had the deeds shows that the close relationship of priory and borough persisted and that the Bulkeleys had what amounted to a stranglehold. On 25 February 1537 Sir Richard asked for the farm of the priory if it was to be suppressed 'for it lieth hard at my nose and I and my elders have ever been stewards of the said place'.[168]

In 1535-6 the priory's possessions were accounted for by its former bailiff.[169] In Penmon there were twelve tenants-at-will and in Bancenyn six held by deed and two at will; the total value of rents and demesne was £15 2s 5½d. The im-

---

163   For details of individual fonts see RCAHM *Anglesey Inventory, passim.*

164   Glanmor Williams, op.cit., pp.431-2.

165   ibid., pp.453-4. Nicholas's work is described by Tudur Aled in his elegy.

166   Glanmor Williams, 'The Reformation in sixteenth-century Caernarvonshire', *TCHS* 27 (1966), esp.38-50.

167   *Letters and Papers, Henry VIII*, ix, no.866.

168   *Letters and Papers, Henry VIII*, xii (i), no.507.

169   TNA SC6/Hen. VIII/4705.

propriate churches were all held by the prior with the exceptions of Llan-faes, held by Thomas Bulkeley and Llangwyllog, held by Sir Richard. An action which came before the Court of Augmentations in 1552 reveals a little more about the last days of Penmon.[170] One deponent stated that when the commissioners came to suppress the house the livestock kept at Crymlyn was 'privily conveyed away'. By the end the priory was evidently more akin to John Godfrey's landed estate than to a monastery. And when that end came its fate, in view of the power of the Bulkeleys, was inevitable

The smaller monastic houses were suppressed in 1536; the turn of the friars came two years later. In August 1538 the commissioners came to Llan-faes and on 19 August the house was surrendered by its four friars, not one of whom seems to have been Welsh.[171] The inventory shows that for a small house of friars whose distinguishing mark was poverty Llan-faes was not badly appointed.[172] The fittings of the church included two printed mass-books and among the possessions of the house was a feather bed; there were also 22 sheep and standing corn worth £1 6s.[173] Over the years the friars had acquired some land which brought in £3 1s 10d in rent; the total value of their goods was £8 3s 10d. After dissolution came disposal; Richard Bulkeley offered Cromwell 100 marks for the friary which he wished to make into a house.[174] The church survived until the nineteenth century as a barn; the rest of the buildings did not long survive, the stone being carried to Beaumaris and used for the repair of the town wall and the quay.[175]

Of the protests and disturbances associated with the Reformation there is no Anglesey evidence to speak of, although the county produced a prominent Counter-Reformation figure in Owen Lewis, bishop of Cassano in southern Italy and a native of Llangadwaladr, as well as Siôn Dafydd Rhys of Llanfaethlu in whom Renaissance, Reformation and Counter-Reformation met. When the Catholic reaction came under Mary only five Anglesey incumbents and the archdeacon were deprived of their benefices as married men.[176] Only one protest is recorded; on the Sunday before All Saints, 1538, Sir Reynold Griffith, the curate, was publishing the king's injunctions in Llangefni church when one

---

170  TNA E315/122; E.A. Lewis and J. Conway Davies, *Records of the Court of Augmentations relating to Wales* (1954), p.8. The action was over a lease granted by Prior Godfrey in 1533.

171  *Letters and Papers. Henry VIII.* xiii (i), no.138.

172  *Arch. Camb. Original Documents* (1877), p.xliii.

173  Arthur Jones, 'The property of the Welsh friaries at the Dissolution', *Arch. Camb.* 1936, p.43.

174  *Letters and Papers, Henry VIII.* xiii (ii), no. 892. The site was granted to Thomas Bulkeley the elder of Beaumaris (TNA E326/7201).

175  H. Longueville Jones, 'Mona Medieva' XVI, in *Arch. Camb.*, 1855, pp.77-9;  Edward Owen, 'The fate of the structures of Conway abbey and Bangor and Beaumaris friaries', *Y Cymmrodor*, 27 (1917), 93, 101-7, 109, 112-3.

176  A. Ivor Pryce. *The Diocese of Bangor in the Sixteenth Century*, pp.12-3.

Richard Hale declared that 'they were sinister injunctions and that they were clean gone out of the faith'.[177] The clerk bade him hold his tongue and his imprisonment was ordered. And with that protest the story of the medieval church in Anglesey comes to an end.

177 *Letters and Papers. Henry VIII*, xiii (ii), no. 1037 (2)

# 10 *Plague, Slump & Revolt*

THE FOURTEENTH CENTURY was a period of crisis and its consequences lasted well into the next century if not later. It is generally seen as the result of a combination of factors, among them climatic deterioration from the end of the thirteenth century which led to longer and colder winters and shorter and wetter summers. This led in turn to more frequent failure of the harvest and increased mortality in a population which earlier favourable conditions had driven beyond its optimum level.[1] The first blow was the great famine of 1315-7 when the harvest failed in three successive years. It does not need the exercise of much imagination to realise what this meant in a society entirely dependent on agriculture; with little food and no seed-corn for the following year many communities faced disaster.[2] And this was only the beginning; it was followed in Britain by a series of livestock epidemics and a steady decline in agricultural prices and then, in 1348, came the greatest blow of all in the shape of the Black Death.

Where records survive, the effect of the famine on the individual community can be seen. Manorial records in England are particularly rich but in much of Wales and particularly in Gwynedd the manor did not exist, although something similar existed in some townships. For Anglesey, indeed, for the whole of Gwynedd, there are only a few isolated references and the historian has to proceed by silences. But the famine must have hit north Wales; it certainly affected Scotland and Ireland.[3] In February 1316 the justice of north Wales was ordered to permit the men of Caernarfon to buy corn and other victuals and the following month a safe-conduct was issued to a burgess of Conwy 'going in his little ship called *le Mariot* of Conwy' to buy corn and other foodstuffs

---

1 The general crisis of the fourteenth century is discussed by Georges Duby, *Rural Economy and Country Life in the Medieval West*, pp. 294-8, 305-11; Léopold Genicot, 'Crisis: from the middle ages to modern times', in *Camb.Econ.Hist.* i, pp.661-77. See also M.M. Postan, 'Economic foundations of medieval society', in *Essays on Medieval Agriculture and General Problems of the Medieval Economy*, pp.5-16.

2 The best discussion of the famine in England is Ian Kershaw, 'The Great Famine and agrarian crisis in England, 1315-1322', in R.H. Hilton, ed., *Peasants, Knights and Heretics* (1976), pp.85-132; see also William Chester Jordan, *The Great Famine: northern Europe in the early fourteenth century* (1996).

3 Ian Kershaw, op.cit., p.92, n.46.

for the castles and towns of Conwy, Caernarfon and Beaumaris.[4] Although this evidence suggests little more than that food had to be brought in to supply the castles and the garrison towns, it is hard to believe that the famine could have passed Gwynedd by. The subsidy levied in north Wales in 1318 yielded £929 12s 9½d, considerably less than the total of £1,333 6s 8d collected from the three counties in 1300; the reduction may well reflect contemporary problems.[5] Famine could certainly add to the tax-collector's troubles; in 1327 the sum of £50 was allowed to Edmund Dynieton, the collector for north Wales, whose expenses had been heavy 'because of the great dearth of victuals which was then in those parts'.[6]

But famine was not the only blow to fall on the agricultural community during these years. More than one chronicler mentioned the onslaught of murrain, a term which probably covers any kind of livestock epidemic, be it foot-and-mouth disease, rinderpest, liver-fluke, or any other disease which struck at animals. Of course, disease was always present; in 1291-2 the sheriff of Anglesey accounted for the sale of the hides of four oxen dead of murrain at Llan-faes.[7] However this was one of the hazards of normal life, not a plague. The great famine was accompanied and followed in England by a succession of livestock epidemics. Between 1315 and 1317 much of Britain was affected by a sheep murrain and this was followed from 1319 onwards by a cattle plague which ravaged England, Scotland, Ireland and, presumably, Wales.[8] About 1320 the bishop of Bangor petitioned the king; he had been much impoverished by bad years and was now suffering because of the murrain, as well as by having to stay in Bangor in accordance with the king's instructions.[9] Most of his lands were in Anglesey and Caernarfonshire. In 1322 the bondmen of Penrhosllugwy petitioned the king as part of their long-drawn-out struggle against the unjust extent of the *maerdref* and in their petition they said that they, too, had been impoverished by going in the king's service against his enemies, probably during the troubles of that year and by the losses caused by the murrain.[10] In 1328 Dafydd ap Hywel, the farmer of the royal mills in Anglesey, asked if he could pay off the arrears of his farm in instalments because of the losses he had suffered by murrain of cattle and a further epidemic, at least in Llŷn, is indicated

4  *CPR 1373-1317*, 387, 439.
5  Natalie Fryde, *List of Welsh Entries in the Memoranda Rolls, 1282-1343*, p.xix; the 1300 demand was for a lump sum. The 1318 figure for Merioneth was less than half that collected in 1292-3 (Keith Williams-Jones, *The Merioneth Lay Subsidy Roll, 1292-3*, p.96).
6  Natalie Fryde, op.cit., no.565.
7  John Griffiths, 'Two early ministers' accounts for north Wales', 64.
8  Ian Kershaw, op.cit., pp. 96, 102-11.
9  *CAP*, pp.499-500.
10 Seebohm, *The Tribal System in Wales*, App., p.27; Carr, 'The bondmen of Penrhosllugwy', pp.16-17.

by the petition some time between 1331 and 1337 of the *rhingyll* of Cafflogion, who asked for time to pay off his arrears for the same reason.[11]

Climatic deterioration may help to explain the natural disasters which struck part of the commote of Menai in the fourteenth century. On 6 December 1330 a storm wrought havoc at Newborough and Rhosyr.[12] At the former 183 acres of the borough lands were overwhelmed by the sea and the sand and at the latter eleven cottages and 28 acres suffered the same fate. This part of Anglesey has always been at risk from sand and even today it is probably only the Forestry Commission which holds the dunes at bay. A rise in rainfall during this period seems to have caused changes in sea level in some places and this in turn affected the coast. There were also sandstorms in other coastal regions of northern Europe during the early fourteenth century, so here again Anglesey can be seen as a victim of the disasters of the time.[13]

For the greatest of the fourteenth-century crises there is rather more Anglesey evidence. The Black Death was more than a European catastrophe; it ploughed its furrow through the known world. Starting in Central Asia, it made its way east to China and west to Europe.[14] Its first appearance in Britain was in Dorset in August 1348; from there it spread rapidly and it seems to have come into Wales by way of the lower Severn valley. It was in the lordship of Abergavenny by March 1349; by June it had reached Ruthin.[15] There is evidence of its depredations in Flintshire and the lordship of Denbigh and it was no more merciful in the principality. Almost all the bond tenants of the *maerdref* of Degannwy perished and many died in Llŷn.[16] In Anglesey in 1350-1 the *rhingyll* of Malltraeth accounted for the value of the grazing on various bond lands in Trefdraeth Ddisteiniaid, Trefiddon and Rhosmor which were in the prince's hand, presumably for lack of tenants. He also answered for decayed rents from lands formerly held by 33 named tenants in those three townships.[17] These were also let for grazing since the other tenants there could not afford to rent them. Thus in Malltraeth a band of territory across the southern part of the commote seems to have been the area worst affected by the plague; there is no mention in this account of any other community having suffered.

---

11  *CAP*, p.255. In a very badly damaged petition (ibid., p.187) several individuals from the cantref of Aberffraw sought similar relief but the petition cannot be dated with any accuracy

12  *CIM* ii, nos. 1275, 1328; G.R.J. Jones, 'Rural settlement in Anglesey', pp.225-7.

13  Colin Platt, *Medieval England: a social history and archaeology from the conquest to A.D. 1600* (1978), pp.94-5; G.R.J. Jones, op.cit., p.226.

14  For a recent general discussion of the Black Death throughout Europe see Ole Benedictow, *The Black Death 1346-1353; a general history* (2004).

15  William Rees, 'The Black Death in Wales' in R.W. Southern, ed., *Essays in Medieval History* (1968), pp.181-6.

16  ibid., pp.186-7; Carr, 'The Black Death in Caernarfonshire', 11, 13-14, 17.

17  TNA SC6/1149/1, m.3b. For an overview of the plague in Anglesey, A.D. Carr, 'The Black Death in Anglesey', *TAAS* 2010, 26-42.

In Llifon the situation was similar. Here, too, lands were in the prince's hand for lack of tenants; the bondmen who survived could not afford to rent them, nor could any tenants be found for some escheat lands of long standing.[18] The townships and hamlets affected were Treddolffin, Tre'r-ddôl, Trefeddygon and Bodynolwyn; they were not particularly close together but it was not uncommon for one community to be decimated by the plague while an adjacent one might not lose a single member. The Llifon account also includes 4s 7d, the issues of the land of Adda Was for the best part of two years because no heirs had come forward to claim the inheritance; this is a further comment on the effects of the plague. Some of the lands of the ten dead tenants named in the account had been let to others; the rest was let for grazing. The *rhingyll* of Taly-bolion accounted for grazing from various old-established escheat lands in Llanfigel, Trefadog, Caerdegog and Cnwchdyrnog, all of which were now unlet.[19] The lands of four bond tenants in Aberalaw were in the prince's hand because their surviving heirs could not afford the rent and the same was true of the lands of five bondmen in Carneddor, six in Llanol, two in Bodronyn, one in Meiriogen and one in Cafnan. The total rent due from these lands had been £5 7s 5d but they now only yielded £2 14s 4d for the grazing, while the other escheat lands, once worth £4 8s 10½d, now brought in only £1 15s 6d. Again the affected townships were scattered over the commote.

Twrcelyn also suffered; the entire bond hamlet of Twrllachied in Llysdulas was without tenants.[20] £2 13s 4d of the rent due from the *tir cyfrif* township of Bodhunod had to be written off because the five surviving tenants there could hardly pay the balance of £4 0s 2d, let alone find the full sum as they were supposed to under the terms of the tenure. In Bodednyfed only two tenants were left, one being an avowry tenant and the other being unable to find more than six shillings of the 17s 9d he had once paid; the vacant land in the township was being let for grazing. The substantial lands in Llysdulas which had once been the inheritance of Iorwerth ap Philip Goch could no longer be let as a single unit. Small parcels were now being let to various bondmen and the total income was £1 10s 6d as opposed to the £3 15s 6d which it had formerly yielded. In Dindaethwy the increment or additional rent from the Porthaethwy ferry had fallen from £1 16s 8d to 16s 8d because of the plague.[21] There is no evidence from Menai because it was among the lands held by the king's mother; nor is there any from Beaumaris, although here the market tolls for

18  TNA SC6/1149/1, m.4b.
19  TNA SC6/1149/1, m.5b. The Talybolion poet Gruffudd ap Maredudd ap Dafydd described the effects of the plague in a series of *englynion* (Barry J. Lewis, ed., *Gwaith Gruffudd ap Maredudd* (ii): *Cerddi Crefyddol* (2005), pp.68-70.
20  TNA SC6/1149/1, m.6b.
21  TNA SC6/1149/1, m.1a; no farmers could be found for the mills of Llan-faes or Cefn-coch.

the year amounted to no more than 2s 1d and the fair tolls to 40 shillings while only two foreign ships had called.[22] If the accounts for 1349-50 had survived they would probably have been far more informative as there must have been some measure of recovery, however small, during the year after the pestilence.

The plague is still reflected in the following year's accounts. In Llifon in 1351-2 the *rhingyll* was pardoned part of the rent from a tenement in Chwaen for the past two years and rents from other untenanted lands which had now been let for grazing were respited.[23] Some lands were still without tenants a year later; the *rhingyll* of Talybolion accounted for the decay of 17s 10d from escheat lands in Dronwy and the lands of Iorwerth ap Philip Goch in and around Amlwch were also untenanted.[24] The 1353-4 accounts say nothing, which suggests that most of the vacant lands had now been let.

The 1352 extent also sheds some light on the effects of the Black Death. In Malltraeth two carucates or 120 acres of land in Trefdraeth Ddisteiniaid were in the prince's hand and at Dindryfwl a whole *gwely* was farmed by the community because it was waste.[25] In Aberffraw seven of the fourteen bond tenements or gardens in the hamlet of Garddau had no tenants and other lands were unoccupied in Trefdraeth Wastrodion, Cerrigcafael and Trewalchmai.[26] A quarter of the demesne land at Cleifiog in Llifon was waste and escheat land there was let to avowry tenants, as were the hamlets of Tre'r-ddôl and Treddolffin.[27] One of the worst-hit townships in Anglesey was Bodynolwyn; of eight unfree *gwelyau* there, three and two halves were waste.[28] A similar state of affairs can be seen in Talybolion. There were no takers for a third share of the mill of Botan and at Llanfigel one-sixth of the mill and 44 acres of escheat land were without tenants.[29] More escheat land was waste in Trelywarch, Trefadog, Caerdegog and Dronwy, as were many of the *gafaelion in* the commotal centre of Cemais.[30] All this land had fallen to the prince or the crown by escheat before the plague. When the population was pressing on the available land there would be competition for leases of escheat lands but the very fact that so much was now unlet points to a drastic fall in population. The same pattern appears in Twrcelyn. There seems to have been less untenanted escheat land in Dindaethwy, which may suggest that the plague had less effect here than anywhere

---

22  TNA SC6/1149/1, m.7a.
23  TNA SC6/1149/2, m.3b; see also *Extent of Anglesey*, p.185.
24  TNA SC6/1149/3, mm.5b, 6b.
25  *Extent of Anglesey*, pp. 166, 169.
26  ibid., pp. 176, 163, 169, 171.
27  ibid., pp. 182-3, 187, 188.
28  ibid., pp. 189-91.
29  ibid., pp. 194-8.
30  ibid., pp. 193-6, 200-1, 203-4, 211-5.

else in Anglesey; in Menai a *gwely* in Gwydryn and another in Treferwydd were in the prince's hand.[31] There are also signs of a decline in population at New-borough, the only borough to appear in the 1352 extent.[32] Here there were more tenements than tenants and many individuals held several; this may, how-ever, have been a result of the disaster of 1330 rather than of the plague. But all the foregoing evidence does suggest that, although the impact of the Black Death on Anglesey varied from commote to commote, the island was seriously affected.

One possible consequence of the plague in other parts of north Wales may be the large number of avowry tenants moving into Anglesey at this time. Be-tween 1350-1 and 1355-6 32 new avowry tenants were recorded in Dindaethwy, twelve in Malltraeth, 64 in Llifon, 82 in Talybolion and 29 in Twrcelyn; there are no figures for Menai.[33] This suggests a flow of population into Anglesey. Many kinds of men must have been included in their ranks, some being fugi-tives from justice, some itinerant workers or traders and some squatters.[34] A great deal of migrant labour moved from lordship to lordship in the march and even over the borders, particularly at harvest time, but one would not really expect migrant workers to travel all the way from Dyffryn Clwyd or Bromfield and Yale to Anglesey, nor would they come into avowry, a status which involved permanent settlement.[35] In most parts of Europe the plague was followed by much movement due in part to the general feeling of restlessness and disori-entation which it generated and in part to the shortage of labour and conse-quent higher wages which followed it. Men were ready to travel to obtain the best return for their labour and Anglesey, hard hit by the plague, beckoned them. And it offered more than work; there was escheat land available and as early as 1352 avowry tenants were taking it up. If enterprise and hard work could lift a man into the ranks of the landed proprietors, then there was a very good reason for coming to Anglesey. With so much land on their hands the au-thorities would welcome any tenant.[36]

Thus the impact of the Black Death on Anglesey was little different from

31  ibid., pp.250-1.

32  ibid., pp.258-72.

33  TNA SC6/1149/1, mm.1b, 4b, 5b, 6; 1149/2, mm.1a, 2b, 5a; 1149/3, mm.3a, 4b, 5b; 1149/5, mm.3a, 4a-b; 1149/6, m.2a. A similar pattern may be seen in Caernarfonshire (Carr, 'The Black Death in Caernarfonshire', 14-15).

34  R.R. Davies, *Lordship and Society in The March of Wales. 1282-1400.* pp.138-9, discusses avowry tenants briefly. The names of those coming into Anglesey shed little or no light on their origins or occupations.

35  ibid., p.398.

36  ibid., pp.434-6, where Professor Davies discusses movement in search of better land on more favourable terms after the plague. In the lordship of Clun a man who took land ceased to be in avowry and became an ordinary tenant since his relationship with the lord had changed (ibid., p.139).

its impact elsewhere. As with so many aspects of medieval society in Wales the researcher is hampered by the fact that the manor as a tenurial, social, or economic concept did not exist in the principality. As a result Welsh historians lack the embarrassment of riches to be found in the quantities of manorial court rolls and accounts which exist in most English counties and which, more than anything else, reveal the effect of the plague on the local community. But there is no doubt of the mortality; in the Caernarfonshire commote of Nantconwy there had been 149 bond tenants before the plague but there were only 47 afterwards.[37] In one major study of bubonic plague in the British Isles it has been suggested that it could not have been the plague that wrought such havoc in such regions as north Wales because the conditions in upland areas of scattered settlement were not conducive to its spread, but this thesis has certainly not met with universal acceptance.[38] However, bubonic plague or not, the fact remains that very many people died and that as a result there were serious social and economic problems.

The most commonly quoted results of the plague are its effects on labour and on the land market. With the loss of so many bondmen the survivors were in a seller's market and as a result they began to move in search of higher wages which employers, desperate for workers, were ready to pay. It was not long before the authorities responded; in England the Statute of Labourers of 1351 laid down that prices and wages should remain at the level where they had been before the plague and labourers were forbidden to move.[39] Prosecutions and convictions for asking for excessive wages were not uncommon in the march and the position was probably much the same in the principality. At the sessions held at Beaumaris on 29 May 1355 Dyddgu ferch Iorwerth ab Adda Ddu of Pentraeth and Tegwared le Swan were amerced for taking more for their labour than the statute allowed and the following year Madog ap Madog ab Einion Amlwch was amerced for the same offence.[40] These references, copied by the seventeenth-century antiquary Robert Vaughan of Hengwrt from plea rolls which no longer exist, are no more than the tip of the iceberg; there may well have been as many cases in Anglesey as there were in other places where records have survived.

---

37  E.A. Lewis, 'The decay of tribalism in north Wales', p.45.

38  J.F.D. Shrewsbury, *A History of Bubonic Plague in the British Isles* (1970). His thesis was challenged in a review by Christopher Morris, 'Plague in Britain', in Local Population Studies, *The Plague Reconsidered: a new look at its origins and effects in 16th and 17th-century England* (1977), pp.37-47; see also Jim Bolton, 'The world turned upside down' in M.Ormrod and P.Lindley, eds., *The Black Death in England* (1996), pp.24-6 and Benedict Gummer, *The Scourging Angel: the Black Death in the British Isles* (2009), pp.417-20.

39  D.L. Evans, 'Some notes on the history of the principality of Wales in the time of the Black Prince (1343-1376)', *THSC* 1925-6, pp.79-82.

40  R.R. Davies, op.cit., pp.434-5; NLW Peniarth 405, pp.438, 441.

It is very difficult to assess the degree and pace of recovery. One communal render which was badly affected by the plague was the *staurum principis*, an annual render from the bondmen and avowry tenants of each commote towards the victualling of the local castle. Each Anglesey commote, with the exception of Menai, normally paid 16*s* 8*d* but in 1350-1 Malltraeth and Dindaethwy could only pay five shillings and 6*s* 8*d* respectively; between 1353 and 1364 the payment was suspended because of the effects of the plague.[41] As late as 1360-1 escheat lands at Trysglwyn in Twrcelyn were still unlet, having been so for the past eleven years, although other such lands seem to have been let by this time.[42]

What little evidence there is for the period between the plague and the Glyn Dŵr revolt does not point to any real recovery; indeed, some of it suggests the opposite. To what extent the farms offered and accepted for offices and mills are a reliable indicator of the economic situation is an open question but one which merits some attention. There were various fluctuations in the farms offered for commotal offices but on the whole the trend was downwards.[43] Before the Black Death there was very little change from year to year. The ringildry of Dindaethwy had been farmed at £6 16*s* 8*d*. In 1350-1 it was down to £4 10*s*; by 1356-7 it was £8 16*s* 8*d*, which must reflect some temporary recovery, but in 1359-60 it was down to seven pounds and it went on falling until it reached one pound in 1388-9. There was a rise to £3 11*s* in 1391-2 but in 1394-5 it had fallen to £1 6*s* 8*d*.[44] The pattern is not altogether consistent and it does vary from commote to commote but an overall trend can certainly be seen. In Menai in 1363-4 the raglotry was worth ten pounds and the ringildry seven. In 1372-3 the former office was farmed at two pounds and the latter at ten, but again there was a gradual decline; the raglotry stood at eight pounds in 1376-7 and six in 1380-1. It went up to seven pounds in 1390-1 but by 1393-4 it was down to three. The ringildry was £10 13*s* 4*d* in 1376-7 and eleven pounds in 1378-9; in 1380-1 it was £4 10*s* and it went on falling throughout the 1380s, reaching its lowest point in 1386-7 when it was 13*s* 4*d*. It recovered to sixteen shillings in 1390-1 and again to two pounds in 1392-3, but by 1394-5 it was down to one pound. The farm of the profits of justice in Menai went down gradually from £41 in 1376-7 to £24 in 1392-3 and it remained at that figure until the revolt. Much the same pattern can be seen in the other commotes; the fall was particularly pronounced during the 1380s. The farms of commotal

---

41  *Extent of Anglesey*, p.164, n.13; William Rees, op.cit., p.197 and n.1.

42  TNA SC6/1150/1, m.5a.

43  There is a gap in the accounts between 1363-4 and 1376-7 although some details are available for 1372-4 (TNA E163/24/1).

44  All these figures are taken from the series of ministers' accounts, TNA SC6/1149/1-9, 1150/1-10, 1151/1-9, 1152/1-3.

offices in Caernarfonshire between 1376-7 and 1393-4 show nothing like the same fluctuation although there was a certain decline; however, only four commotes there have a series of figures covering the whole period.[45]

Other farms show a similar pattern. In 1350-1 Aberffraw was let for twenty pounds and the following year the farm had gone up to £30. In 1359-60 it was down to £10 13s 4d but this was because of other grants to the farmer, Sir John de St Peter and had nothing to do with economic circumstances.[46] In 1376-7 the farm was £43 16s 8d, in 1377-8 £45 6s 8d and in 1382-3 it was down to £40 10s. There followed a sharp decline for the rest of the century, reaching £30 in 1392-3. The farms of Penrhosllugwy and Cemais also declined, although the fall in the value of the former was less pronounced, while that of the latter showed some recovery in the 1390s. The same trend can be seen very clearly at Newborough. In 1359-60 the farm of the profits of justice was £15 10s and that of the borough £19 13s 4d. By 1376-7 the former, with the Abermenai ferry, was worth £17 6s and the latter twenty pounds; they were both twenty pounds in 1377-78. By 1381-2 they were down to fifteen pounds; there was a slight improvement to £15 1s 8d in 1380-1 and there they remained until the end of the century. There is also evidence of a similar decline at Beaumaris; many burgages were vacant and heavy arrears led in 1389 to the burgesses being excused all the rents due from them for one year in an attempt to bring them up to date. It was a vain hope; in 1395 they had to be pardoned half the annual rents for the next five years.[47] Conwy and Caernarfon had similar problems in the 1390s.[48]

The farm of the mill of Hirdre-faig in Menai was four pounds in 1359-60; by 1394-5 it had fallen to £1 6s 8d, and Melin Newydd, another royal mill in the same commote, had gone down from five pounds in 1359-60 to £2 6s in 1381-2. The townships of Cleifiog and Llanllibio in Llifon were worth £18 13s 4d in 1376-7 and the farm went up to £19 1s 7d in the following year. By 1387-8 it was down to fourteen pounds; there was a slight improvement in the last decade of the century and in 1394-5 it stood at £16 6s 8d. An identical trend can be seen in the farm of the township of Nantmawr in Twrcelyn. It was worth eighteen pounds in 1376-7 and £12 6s 8d in 1388-9 and it had recovered to £14 16s in 1394-5.

All these figures point to a steady decline in the second half of the fourteenth century, with a particularly bad period in the 1380s and a slight recovery in the 1390s. The evidence is crude but it is compelling. One may ask how and why

45 TNA SC6/1172/5-11, 1173/1-9, 1174/1-4.
46 TNA SC6/1149/8, m.2b; see also SC6/1305/16, m.2b, for the grant to him of Anglesey rents.
47 This is discussed in Chapter 8 above.
48 Keith Williams-Jones, 'Caernarvon', p.84.

this came about, but with the lack of record evidence it is very difficult to offer an answer. It may have been the cumulative effect of three visitations of the plague in 1349, 1361 and 1369; a fall in the population would probably have made many of these farms less profitable. There is some other evidence which may strengthen the argument, in particular the large number of fines, amercements and other payments respited in the 1380s. A list of respites appeared for the first time in the sheriff's account for 1379-80; many of those amerced had no goods in the commote where the amercements were imposed.[49] In 1380-1 the list included Ieuan Ddu ap Hwfa who could not afford to pay his amercement and in 1382-3 two free tenants in Dindaethwy could not pay the fines necessary to take up their inheritances which were consequently taken into the lord's hand.[50] Many respites may have been recorded because fines were generally paid in instalments, but during the 1380s an increasing number of complete fines were excused.[51] It is clear that many just did not have the means to pay; in 1387-8 the lands of nine tenants in Malltraeth were taken into the lord's hand, possibly for that very reason.[52]

The effects of the crises of the fourteenth century were not only social and economic. The political restlessness of the period can be seen all over Europe and it was already manifest in Gwynedd before the plague, but there can be no doubt that the fruits of the Black Death included that discontent and disorientation which contributed to the series of popular revolts which broke out all over Europe over the next hundred years. Sometimes these movements were religious and sometimes they were social. Sometimes, too, they could be political and used by political leaders for their own ends and it is tempting to see the Anglesey Tudors, the descendants of Ednyfed Fychan, as the leaders of disaffection in north Wales. They were involved in the assassination of the prince's attorney, Henry de Shalford, in Bangor in 1345 and there is reason to suspect them of involvement in the movement which was plotting to restore Owain ap Thomas ap Rhodri, otherwise known as Owain Lawgoch or Owain of Wales, the last heir of the house of Gwynedd, to the throne of his fathers.[53] One prominent descendant of Ednyfed in north-east Wales was certainly involved and two of his sons were with Owain in France.[54]

There has been a tendency to play down the importance of Owain Lawgoch

49  TNA SC6/1150/6, m.5b.
50  TNA SC6/1150/7, m.6b; 1150/9, m.7a.
51  There are further lists in TNA SC6/1150/10, m.8b (1383-4); 1151/1, m.9b (1384-5); 1152/2, m.8b (1385-6); 1151/3, m.8b (1386-7); 1151/5, m.7b (1388-9).
52  TNA SC6/1151/4, m.7a.
53  Eurys I. Rowlands, 'Nodiadau ar y traddodiad moliant a'r cywydd', 234-5; Gruffudd ap Maredudd ap Dafydd, sang to both the Tudors and to Owain. Owain Lawgoch is discussed by A.D. Carr, *Owen of Wales: the end of the house of Gwynedd* (1991).
54  A.D. Carr, 'Rhys ap Roppert', 163-7.

and to dismiss him as 'a pawn in the Anglo-French struggle', but the surviving evidence suggests that there was a good deal more to his movement than that. In 1370 an Anglesey free tenant called Gruffudd Sais was convicted before the justice at Conwy of treason as a supporter of Owain Lawgoch, 'enemy and traitor of the lord prince'; his lands in Trelywarch and Dronwy in Talybolion and Porthaml in Menai were taken into the prince's hand.[55] He subsequently made fine of 100 marks (£66 13s 4d) before the king's council for the restoration of his lands.[56] He seems to have died before the fine was paid; an inquisition taken on 22 October 1461 found that he had died at Trelywarch on 21 May 1380 and that his lands had been taken into the king's hand pending payment in full.[57] The great-grandsons of his brother Maredudd sought their return. In this inquisition he was described as Gruffudd ap Dafydd ap Hywel and according to the pedigrees he was a descendant of Iorwerth ap Hwfa ap Cynddelw. His brother Hywel was *rhingyll* of Menai in 1363-4 and a Gruffudd ap Dafydd ap Hywel had been joint *deputy-rhingyll* of Talybolion in 1351-2 and 1355-6.[58] Thus, if the identification is correct, he belonged to a family which was not unaccustomed to holding local office and if Owain Lawgoch had the support of members of this class his movement was a serious one. The poet Gruffudd ap Maredudd ap Dafydd, who sang to Owain Lawgoch, also held lands in Dronwy.[59]

The names of two Anglesey men appear in an inquisition taken at Flint on 25 September 1374 which lists men known to be in France in the company of Owain ap Thomas ap Rhodri and Ieuan ap Rhys ap Roppert; these were Hywel ap Llywelyn ap Gwyn of the commote of Menai and Tegwared ap Goronwy.[60] The only Hywel ap Llywelyn ap Gwyn to be found in the pedigrees was a descendant of Rhodri ab Owain Gwynedd who was connected with the commote of Twrcelyn, but in 1387-8 the escheator accounted for two acres and part of a house in Llanddyfnan formerly the property of Tegwared ap Goronwy ap *Sildrig* who had been outlawed for felony.[61] Tegwared ap Goronwy remained in French service after the assassination of Owain Lawgoch in 1378 and was a member of one of the three small Welsh companies present at the siege of Ventadour in 1389.[62] Owain Lawgoch's death was mourned by Llywelyn ap Cyn-

55  *Rec.Caern.*, p.133; TNA SC6/1150/4, m.6a.
56  TNA SC6/1150/7, m.6a.
57  TNA SC6/1154/6, m.10b.
58  Bartrum, *WG*, Hwfa ap Cynddelw 1; TNA SC6/1150/2, m.4b; 1149/2, m.4a; 1149/6, m.3a.
59  *Extent of Anglesey*, p.200.
60  TNA CHES 25/24, m.10b.
61  Bartrum, *WG*, Gruffudd ap Cynan 12; TNA SC6/1151/4, m.8b.
62  Carr, *Owen of Wales*, p.63. His name also appears in early muster rolls, including that of Owain's company taken at Limoges on 8 September 1377 and Ieuan Wyn's company taken at Bourgneuf on 1 May 1381 (ibid., p.45).

wrig Ddu o Fôn who referred in his elegy to people watching the shore and
buying horses in preparation for Owain's coming.[63]

Owain ap Thomas ap Rhodri obviously appealed to many influential Welshmen who may have begun to think again of the dynasty of Aberffraw and as a
candidate he had everything to recommend him. He was a direct descendant
of Llywelyn ab Iorwerth and a distinguished soldier who could bring with him
active French support. But an assassin's dagger put an end to any hopes of the
return of the line of Owain Gwynedd and it was left to a later Owain to take
up the challenge. The culmination and, in a way, the resolution of the tensions
of the fourteenth century came in Wales with the outbreak of the revolt of
Owain Glyn Dŵr in 1400.[64] The revolt was many things. It was a feudal con-
spiracy, a social and agrarian rebellion of the kind which broke out all over Europe at this time' a civil war, a messianic movement and a national rising. One
of the most interesting features is the significance of family links; many of its
leaders were related to Owain himself and many more were related to each
other.[65] The Anglesey leaders of the revolt fit into this category; they were,
above all, the Penmynydd family, the senior line of the descendants of Ednyfed
Fychan. All three surviving sons of Tudur ap Goronwy were implicated and
two of them were Owain's first cousins, their mothers having been sisters.[66] It
has been suggested more than once that the Tudor brothers were the power
behind Owain; indeed, one historian has gone so far as to suggest that 'Joan of
Arc ... heard voices from heaven; Owain Glyn Dŵr may have heard voices from
Anglesey'.[67] This may be open to question but there is no doubt about the
brothers' involvement. Rhys and Gwilym ap Tudur had been in the service of
Richard II and on 27 July 1398 each was granted an annual pension of ten
pounds, being retained to stay for life with the king.[68] But the revolt cannot really be connected with the cause of the deposed king; Richard's power-base
lay in Cheshire rather than in north Wales.

The revolt began with the proclamation of Owain as prince of Wales at
Glyndyfrdwy on 16 September 1400. This was followed by an attack on Ruthin
and attacks on some of the other towns of north Wales, among them Denbigh,
Rhuddlan and Flint.[69] At the same time a revolt seems to have broken out in

---

63  Edward Owen, 'Owain Lawgoch – Yeuain de Galles', in *THSC* 1899-1900, pp.94-6.
64  The most detailed local study of the revolt is J.E. Messham, 'The county of Flint and the rebellion
    of Owen Glyndwr in the records of the earldom of Chester', in *Journ. Flints. Hist. Soc.*, 23 (1967-
    8), 1-34. The standard work on the revolt as a whole and its background is R.R. Davies, *The
    Revolt of Owain Glyn Dŵr* (1995).
65  R.R. Davies, 'Owain Glyn Dŵr and the Welsh squirearchy', especially pp.161-3.
66  Glyn Roberts, 'Wyrion Eden', p.198.
67  Gwyn A. Williams, 'Owain Glyn Dŵr', in A.J. Roderick, ed., *Wales through the Ages* i (1959), p.179.
68  *CPR 1396-1399*, 400.
69  Lloyd, *Owen Glendower*, pp.31-2.

Anglesey, led by Gwilym and Rhys ap Tudur. Henry IV was on his way back from Scotland when he heard of the revolt. He raised an army and moved rapidly through north Wales to the island. The men of Anglesey, under the leadership of Rhys ap Tudur, awaited him on Rhos Fawr. The king led his army to Beaumaris, despoiled that side of the island, burned the friary of Llan-faes and killed the friars, ordered the depopulation of Anglesey from shore to shore and then went through it with fire and sword to Rhos Fawr where he was met by the inhabitants and chased back to Beaumaris.[70] This is William Owen's version of events and some of it is confirmed elsewhere; on 28 January 1401 a commission under the great seal was issued by the king at the request of the minister and friars of the order of Minors in England.[71] This stated that the house at Llan-faes had been deserted because the friars were dispersed as rebels and that all the goods of the house had been seized by the king's forces on his last ride into Wales; the king might see to their restitution for the sustenance of the friary. A contemporary chronicler also referred to the sacking of Llan-faes; the *Eulogium Historiarum* states that the friars resisted Henry IV and that they were killed or seized and the house despoiled.[72] The king handed the captured friars over to the minister of the order and ordered the restitution of the house and its future occupation by Englishmen.

This was the first phase of the revolt. The king's circuit through north Wales restored order and the justice, Henry Percy, did his best to reduce the tension. A general pardon was issued on 10 March 1401 to the men of Anglesey, Caernarfonshire, Merioneth and the lordship of Denbigh, with the exception of Owain himself, Rhys and Gwilym ap Tudur, those in custody and those still in rebellion.[73] It may have been the exclusion of Rhys and Gwilym from the pardon that led to their capture of Conwy castle on the following Good Friday; this episode was followed by a further pardon on 8 July 1401 to Gwilym ap Tudur and a number of others.[74] No more seems to have been heard of the rising in Gwynedd until 1403 when a barge and 60 men were sent from Chester

---

70  The king came at the head of an army of 6,000 men according to William Owen, *Hanes Owain Glandwr, Blaenor y Cymry mewn Rhyfel* (1833), pp.13-4. This pamphlet is discussed in some detail by J.E. Lloyd, op.cit., pp.157-8; the point is made that, for all its faults, Owen's work contains material not available elsewhere which has the ring of authenticity and which is unlikely to have been invented by a nineteenth-century antiquary. His reference to a history of Owain Glyn Dŵr written in Welsh by David Bulkeley, physician, of Beaumaris, in 1520 may be significant although the manuscript, which Owen claimed to have in his possession, cannot now be traced.

71  *CPR 1399-1401*, 418.

72  F.S. Haydon, ed., *Eulogium Historiarum* iii, 388.

73  *CPR 1399-1401*, 451.

74  The capture of Conwy castle in 1401 is described in detail by Keith Williams-Jones, 'The taking of Conwy castle, 1401'; *CPR 1399-1401*, 447; they are discussed by Keith Williams-Jones, op.cit., 29-37. Apart from Gwilym ap Tudur none of those involved can be identified conclusively as Anglesey men.

to patrol the coast of Anglesey.[75] In the same year Percy, otherwise known as Hotspur, rebelled on his own account and made common cause with Owain, only to be defeated and killed at Shrewsbury a few weeks later. One of Percy's right-hand men in north Wales was the Yorkshireman Thomas Barneby, who had been his receiver in Anglesey and who was later to be chamberlain of north Wales.[76] In 1414 Barneby's conduct was investigated by a royal commission, possibly as a consequence of charges made against him by the county communities of north Wales; he already appears to have been under suspicion. As a servant of Percy he joined his master in rebellion and in 1414 the Beaumaris jurors made a number of accusations against him.[77] Just after Hotspur declared his rebellion on 10 July 1403 Barneby came to Anglesey; on 16 July he addressed the assembled community and urged them to back the revolt, hinting that an Anglo-Welsh peace would also be involved. It was in connection with these activities that Barneby came into contact with some of the leading Anglesey rebels. During the week preceding Hotspur's rebellion he met Rhys ap Tudur ap Goronwy several times in Bangor and they ate and drank together. In return for guarantees of support Barneby released Hywel ap Rhys ap Tudur, who may have been Rhys's son, from his imprisonment in Beaumaris castle; this was on the day before the battle of Shrewsbury.

This was not Barneby's only offence; he even seems to have been prepared to profit from his master's misfortune.[78] Hotspur had left much of his property at Beaumaris in Barneby's charge; after his defeat and death at Shrewsbury Barneby kept it and concealed it from the king. John Scalby, a former receiver of Anglesey, had been killed in the battle; he had consigned his property, worth about 2,000 marks, to the care of his mistress Gwenllian Wen but Barneby had seized both mistress and property for himself. Yet, in spite of all this, he had not suffered in any way. In 1404 he had become chamberlain of Chester, in 1406 chamberlain of north Wales and in 1410 constable of Caernarfon.[79] But his activities continued to be highly suspect; in 1404 one Rhys, the foster-brother of Rhys ap Tudur, had been arrested on the instructions of the constable of Beaumaris for trying to incite the burgesses and the garrison. In October 1405 he was released by Barneby from Caernarfon castle. He was even prepared to release supplies to the Welsh rebels; in September 1406 they were supplied at Bangor with twenty marks worth of food and goods, including iron

---

75  Davies, *Revolt of Owain Glyn Dŵr*, p.254.

76  The deplorable career of Thomas Barneby is discussed in detail by Ralph A. Griffiths, 'The Glyndŵr rebellion in north Wales through the eyes of an Englishman', *BBCS* 22 (1967), 151-68; the original source is TNA Ancient Indictments, KB9/204/K18-26.

77  Ralph A. Griffiths, op.cit., 155-6.

78  ibid., 156-7.

79  ibid., 157.

and sand, in return for which he received five pounds and a goshawk.[80] It is obvious that Barneby's actions were dictated, not by any sympathy with the cause of Owain Glyn Dŵr but by a wish to make the greatest possible profit for himself.[81] There can be no doubt that the unsettled circumstances of the revolt were an ideal opportunity for him to line his pockets and he went on lining them until his fall in 1414.[82]

The first surviving account for the period of the revolt is that of the chamberlain, Robert de Parys, from 29 September 1401 to 9 December 1402.[83] It includes expenditure on bows and arrows for resisting the rebels in Anglesey. In November 1403 the mayor and community of the city of Chester were pardoned for their treason with Henry Percy on payment of a fine of three hundred marks and on condition that they provided ships 'for the rescue of the castle of Beaumaris and victuals for the same'.[84] This is clear evidence of the siege of Beaumaris and possibly of its fall to the rebels. In their attack on the town they had some help from the Scots who burned several houses there.[85] But there is no firm evidence of the taking of the castle although one Anglesey rebel was later reported as having been killed at its relief. In a letter dated by its editor to 21 January 1405 William Venables of Kinderton reported to the king that a week previously the sheriff, Maredudd ap Cynwrig, had gone out from Beaumaris with his clerk and his servants to collect debts and levy distraints. A force of some 200 Welshmen and Frenchmen had ambushed him; he had been badly wounded and taken prisoner and his whole company of 50 or 60 men, including an escort of twelve archers, had been killed.[86] The castle was in great danger, especially since the constable, Thomas Bold, was away. However, the editor's dating of this letter is unacceptable. Maredudd ap Cynwrig was definitely in rebellion by the beginning of 1405, although he had still been loyal to the king at the time of Venables's letter. On 19 January of that year Owain's chancellor Gruffudd Young and William Fychan, prebendary of Llanddwyn, had appointed him one of their proctors to collect the income from that church.[87] His adhesion to the rebel cause may have been even earlier;

80  ibid., 157-8.
81  ibid., 160-1.
82  In fact, his fall was more apparent than real. He retained the constableship of Caernarfon until his death in 1427, by which time he was also constable of Bordeaux (ibid., 167-8). In 1402 he had obtained the living of Llanddwyn (*CPR 1401-1405*, 60).
83  TNA SC6/1216/1.
84  *CPR 1401-1405*, 330.
85  TNA SC6/1152/4, m.4a.
86  F.C. Hingeston, ed., *Royal and Historical Letters during the Reign of Henry IV*, (ii) (*1405-1413*), 13. This is a particularly bad edition and must be used with care. Maredudd was never sheriff, although he may have been the deputy.
87  Henry Rowlands, 'Antiquitates parochiales', in *Arch.Camb.*, 1846, p.131.

he had borrowed money from Gwilym ap Gruffudd at Machynlleth, which may be an indication of his presence at the parliament held there by Owain in 1404.[88] This suggests a date of late 1403 or early 1404 for the ambush; having married Owain's niece, Maredudd would hardly have been able to stand aside

In his pamphlet William Owen stated that in June 1405 an Irish army commanded by Stephen Scrope, deputy-lieutenant of Ireland, landed at Holyhead and did great damage in Anglesey. Thousands of local people met them at Rhosmeirch but they were put to flight because there were six times as many Irishmen. The force went on to Beaumaris and recaptured the castle and the town from the Welsh, killing the rebel garrison in the course of the campaign. Many fled to the mountains with their livestock. The Irish left after devastating the whole island; they took the shrine of St Cybi from Holyhead and put it in Christ Church cathedral in Dublin.[89]

These losses could not but be a blow to the rebels who had previously been in control of Anglesey and the events of 1405 may have led to those of 1406; according to William Owen the inhabitants had suffered so much from the Irish that they had no choice but to submit and pay fines.[90] There certainly does seem to have been a determination in early 1406 to recapture Anglesey and this renewed effort may lie behind the submission of the county community the following November.[91] The list of those who submitted contains 2,121 names from the six commotes and the total fine imposed was £537 7s.[92] Not everyone living in Anglesey at that time appears in the list and some appear more than once, but it may represent a common fine rather than individual pardons; the submissions probably mark the effective end of the revolt in Anglesey.[93] The names in this list merit attention, although payment may not of necessity indicate wholehearted and committed backing for Owain. One who contributed was Dafydd Goch ap Gruffudd who had been *rhingyll* of Malltraeth from 1376 to 1381, from 1384 to 1388 and from 1393 to 1395 and farmer of Aberffraw from 1383 to 1388; another from the same commote was Ieuan ab Einion Bodfeurig who was to be *rhingyll* in 1414-5.[94] Similar examples are to be found in other commotes. In Dindaethwy in 1406-7 the ringildry was shared by Ieuan ap Dafydd ap Goronwy of Mathafarn Wion and Gruffudd ab

---

88  Carr, 'Maredudd ap Cynwrig', p.17.

89  William Owen, op.cit., p.37; J.E. Lloyd, op.cit., p.99. The Irish force and the removal of the shrine are also mentioned by J.H. Wylie, *History of England under Henry the Fourth* (1884), ii, p.46.

90  William Owen, op.cit., p.41.

91  Davies, *Revolt of Owain Glyn Dŵr*, pp.122-3.

92  Glyn Roberts, 'The Anglesey submissions of 1406', 39-61.

93  Davies, op.cit., pp.305-6.

94  TNA SC6/1150/3, m.1a; 1150/7, m.1a; 1150/10, m.1a; 1151/1, m.1a; 1151/4, m.1a; 1151/9, m.1a; 1152/1, m.1a; 1152/6, m.3b.

Einion Tew of Pentraeth and in Menai in the same year the same office was shared by Gruffudd ap Madog ap Goronwy and Llywelyn ab Ieuan ab Iorwerth.[95] These men all had one thing in common; they had all submitted to the king in 1406. Thus support for Glyn Dŵr seems to have had no effect on a man's hopes of holding local office.

One class which was well represented in the 1406 list was the clergy. Sixteen beneficed clerics submitted and another three were still in rebellion. If the title 'Offeiriad' in a personal name indicates a man in priest's orders there were also fifteen unbeneficed clergy together with four canons of Caergybi, six Franciscan friars from Llan-faes and the archdeacon of Anglesey; two of the canons, the friars and the archdeacon had not submitted. This bears out the argument that the revolt was also a clerical protest.

A more interesting list is that of those whose names were contained in a writ of exigent dated 1405-6 and who were therefore considered to be in rebellion.[96] They include Rhys, Gwilym and Maredudd ap Tudur ap Goronwy and the two daughters of their brother Ednyfed with their husbands, as well as Owain himself. The name of their kinsman Gwilym ap Gruffudd ap Gwilym, the founder of the fortunes of the Penrhyn family, is also there, although he had probably already made his peace the previous year. The writ was read for the first time at the Anglesey county court held at Beaumaris on 26 December 1406 which indicates that things had returned to normal by then.

Another valuable source for the impact of the revolt on Anglesey is a detailed escheator's account for 1408-9.[97] This records various arrears for the period before the revolt but it also contains a great deal more information about the revolt itself. The escheator accounted for various tenements in Bodffordd, Trefdraeth Wastrodion and Heneglwys which had been acquired by Rhys ap Tudur ap Goronwy by *prid;* they had all been delivered to Thomas Barneby. Escheats also included the lands of Gwilym ap Gruffudd ap Tudur Llwyd of Eiriannell. In 1352 Gwilym's father had held land there and at Clorach in Twrcelyn; he was acting *rhingyll* of Talybolion in 1355-6, deputy-*rhaglaw* in 1354-5 and *rhaglaw* from 1356 to 1361 and farmer of the Anglesey avowries in 1360-1.[98] His uncle Ieuan was even more active, being *rhingyll* of Talybolion from 1356 to at least 1360 and again from 1386 to 1389, *rhaglaw* of Llifon from 1381 to

---

95  TNA SC6/1216/2.

96  Tomos Roberts, ' "An ancient faer Record"? Anglesey adherents of Owain Glyndŵr', *BBCS* 38 (1991), 129-33. This is an exemplification of this writ from BUASC Penrhyn Further Additional; a copy made by Robert Vaughan was published by Glyn Roberts, op.cit., 58-60. The names of Henry Percy the younger and his uncle Thomas Percy, earl of Worcester are included in the writ although the former was killed at Shrewsbury in 1403 and the latter executed after the battle.

97  TNA SC6/1233/1.

98  *Extent of Anglesey*, pp. 186, 226; TNA SC6/1149/5, m.3a; 1149/6, m.2a; 1149/7, m.3a; 1150/1, m.3b, 3a.

1389, joint escheator of Anglesey in 1363-4 and escheator from 1384 to 1388, joint farmer of Cemais in 1388-9 and farmer in 1390-1, joint farmer of Pen-rhosllugwy from 1392 to 1395 and farmer in 1395-6 and farmer of Cleifiog and Llanllibio in 1390-1.[99] Ieuan's son Llywelyn was *rhingyll* of Llifon from 1394 to 1396 and *rhaglaw* in 1420-1 and another son, Dafydd, was a canon of Caer-gybi.[100] It was on families like this that the authorities depended for effective local government and now Gwilym's lands were forfeit because of his treason. They included lands in Eiriannell in Llifon and in Caerdegog, Llanddygfael, Maenol Badrig, Bodronyn and Cemlyn in Talybolion; in the Talybolion account he was described as having been killed in rebellion at the relief of Beaumaris. In Llifon the escheator also accounted for the dower lands of his wife Nest.

Another Talybolion official, Madog ap Dafydd ap Hywel, who was *rhingyll* in 1402, lost his land in Maenol Badrig because of his flight for treason.[101] This entry, however, shows that the escheator was not always sure of his facts. Madog had, in fact, submitted in 1406 and in 1408-9 he was farming Bodronyn mill; he was still farming it in 1421-2 and he was farming the mill of Cemais in 1437-8.[102] In 1419-20 he was joint *rhingyll* of the commote.[103] Other prominent victims of the revolt were Hywel ab Ieuan ab Ednyfed of Caerdegog, *rhingyll* of Talybolion from 1395 to 1397 and Ieuan ap Hywel ap Cynwrig of Bodafon, *rhingyll* of Twrcelyn from 1391 to 1395 and *rhaglaw in* 1388-9 and 1394-5; they both died in rebellion.[104] In Twrcelyn the property for which the escheator ac-counted included lands and a watermill in Clorach and the whole township of Trysglwyn which had been held by Gwilym ap Tudur ap Goronwy, the leader of the attack on Conwy castle. Gwilym also held land in Llanddyfnan, Math-afarn Wion, Mathafarn Eithaf, Pentraeth and Treforion and half the township of Crymlyn in Dindaethwy. One of those still in rebellion in Menai was Cyn-wrig Fychan of Porthaml, the brother of Maredudd ap Cynwrig, and his wife Elen. Some 159 rebels from Anglesey are named in the account; of these 102 had been killed and 47 were still unreconciled. The largest number of victims was in Llifon where 32 had died. Of the rebels named nineteen were women and nine of these had been killed.

99  TNA SC6/1149/7, m.2b; 1149/9, m.3a; 1150/2, m.7a; 1150/8, m.1b; 1151/1, m.10a; 1151/3, m.2b; 1151/4, m.8a; 1151/5, m.2a; 1151/6, m.1b; 1151/6, m.2a; 1151/8, m.3b; 1152/1, m.3b; 1152/2, m.3b. Gwilym himself had been *rhingyll* of Talybolion from 1383 to 1386 and *rhaglaw* in 1391-2 (TNA SC6/1150/10, m.3a; 1151/2, m.2b; 1151/7, m.3a).
100  TNA, SC6/1152/1, m.1b; 1152/2, m.1b; 1152/9, m.4b; Glyn Roberts op.cit., 43.
101  NLW Sotheby 13.
102  TNA SC6/1152/4, m.2b; 1153/1, m.3b; 1153/4, m.6a.
103  TNA SC6/1152/8, m.5a.
104  TNA SC6/1151/5, m.3b; 1151/7, m.3a; 1152/1, m.3a; 1152/1, m.3b; 1152/2, m.2a; 1152/3, m.2b.

The first account rendered by a royal official as the tide of revolt ebbed was that of Thomas Barneby as chamberlain of north Wales, for 1407-10.[105] By this time the administration had returned to something approaching normality and offices were again being farmed, but much of Caernarfonshire was still unpacified and there were no profits from avowries in Anglesey. Fines for rebellion made in Anglesey in November and December 1406 amounted to £359 8s 7d. John Mainwaring, captain of the island of Anglesey, was paid £232 2s for the wages of 22 men-at-arms and 80 archers who made up the Anglesey garrison for the quarter from 1 February 1407. He was also paid £36 10s 9d owed him by the prince for the wages of eight men-at-arms and archers, along with seamen used by him to guard Anglesey and the Menai Straits. Thomas Bold had two men-at-arms and twenty archers in Beaumaris castle but the garrison seems to have been halved from August 1407. Ten marks were paid to John Salghall to reimburse him for his expenses in seizing boats and ensuring the safe keeping of the Menai Straits and the burgesses of Beaumaris were granted ten pounds towards the cost of making a ditch around the town.

The next chamberlain's account is the one for 1417-8; this included 100 marks, an instalment of a fine of 800 marks from the community of the county of Anglesey to obtain a charter of pardon.[106] Another 100 marks was paid towards a fine of 600 marks for the restoration of those rights and liberties lost as a result of the rebellion. The first pardon was granted on 30 November 1413 and it included all debts and arrears due to Richard II, Henry IV and Henry V incurred before 5 November 1411.[107] But grants to others of the lands and goods of rebels were still valid and a second pardon granted on 18 May 1414 restored the commonalty of Anglesey to all their lands and possessions as they had held them before the revolt in return for 600 marks.[108] The wives of deceased rebels were to have their dower but the pardon did not apply to lands in royal hands before the outbreak of the revolt.

The lack of sources makes it difficult to know to what extent there were reprisals although Rhys ap Tudur was probably executed in Chester in 1411. Gwilym ap Tudur seems to have been pardoned in 1413, but Maredudd disappeared without trace, his line reappearing in the shape of his son Owain and then going on to conquer new worlds.[109] The revolt marked the end of the greatness of the house of Penmynydd, although other families had gone down with them; even so, the descendants of Ednyfed Fychan were not all down-

105 TNA SC6/1216/2.
106 TNA SC6/1216/3.
107 *CPR1413-1416*, 137.
108 ibid., 195.
109 Glyn Roberts, 'Wyrion Eden', pp. 203-4, 199; 'Teulu Penmynydd', pp.252-3.

and-out. Gwilym ap Gruffudd had acquired extensive lands in Anglesey and Caernarfonshire and had held various offices in the former county before 1400 and then, like so many of his class, he had joined the revolt.[110] It has been suggested that he had no choice in the matter. He certainly made his peace with the king in time to profit greatly from the downfall of his Penmynydd kinsmen and his appreciation of the right time to change sides brought its reward. Not only did he recover the Penmynydd inheritance which he had originally acquired by his marriage to the heiress of Goronwy ap Tudur who died in 1382; he also obtained the forfeited lands of a number of other rebels in various parts of Anglesey, including Gwilym ap Tudur.[111]

Recovery was a slow process; indeed, in some ways there was none. This may clearly be seen in the accounts. The first account of the various Anglesey officials after the revolt is that for 1408-9.[112] As the chamberlain's account also suggests, things were returning to normal. The mills of Aberalaw and Cemais were not let at their former value because of the revolt; the farm had gone down from £8 3s 4d to £3. But in 1394-5 the *rhingyll* of Talybolion had reported that even then the two mills were derelict.[113] The tolls of Llannerch-y-medd fair were farmed by the ubiquitous Maredudd ap Cynwrig at one pound; in 1395-6 the farm had been £5 3s 4d.[114] The farms of offices had also slumped, even in comparison with their decline in the 1380s; in 1395-6 the ringildry of Talybolion had been worth eight pounds and that of Twrcelyn ten, but now they were down to ten shillings and 13s 4d.[115] In Beaumaris ten and a half burgages were in decay, having been burned and destroyed by the Welsh rebels and the Scots. The Porthaethwy, Llanidan and Abermenai ferries yielded nothing and the town of Newborough had suffered considerably. At Rhosyr the rents were down because the township had been devastated, not only by the rebels but also by the coming of Lord Talbot and John Mainwaring and their men during the revolt.

Subsequent accounts reveal little improvement in many places. That for 1413-4 reveals that there was no ferry at Porthaethwy during the revolt. In the same year the raglotry of Menai was only worth £1 8s because of the damage wrought in the area.[116] Mills in the commote had also suffered; that of Hirdrefaig was let at £1 6s 8d on condition that the lessees repaired it, Melin Newydd was let to Maredudd ap Cynwrig at 6s 8d because he was repairing it at his

110 Glyn Roberts, 'Wyrion Eden', pp.206-10; Gwilym's rise is discussed in Chapter 7.
111 *Calendar of Ancient Deeds* v, A13604; BUASC Penrhyn 10.
112 TNA SC6/1152/4.
113 TNA SC6/1152/1, m.2b.
114 TNA SC6/1152/2, m.3b.
115 TNA SC6/1152/2, mm.2b, 3b.
116 TNA SC6/1152/5, mm.3b, 4a. In 1393-4 the raglotry of Menai had been worth three pounds and in 1359-60 it had been worth fifteen (TNA SC6/1151/9, m.4b; 1149/9, m.6a).

own expense and Maredudd was also paying two pounds for Rhosyr mill on condition that he rebuilt it.[117] Beaumaris now had its new town wall, a clear case of shutting the stable door after the horse had bolted. Lands in Porthaethwy, Perthgyr and Bodynwy were without tenants and in Malltraeth land was let for grazing at £1 15s 5½d; in Menai Maredudd ap Cynwrig was farming Maeselidir in Ysgeifiog at fifteen shillings when it was worth £1 6s 8d and he was also paying an annual rent of £1 7s 4d for the bond township of Bodrida.[118]

In the next year's account two pounds of the rent of assise were respited in Dindryfwl and 11s 3d in Trefdraeth Ddisteiniaid because all the royal bondmen there had died in the revolt and their lands were unoccupied. There were similar cases in Menai and in 1418-9 the *rhingyll* of that commote was still referring to the destruction caused by the rebels, which suggests that this part of Anglesey had suffered particularly badly.[119] The small bond township of Bodfardden in Talybolion seems to have been completely depopulated, being recorded as waste and uncultivated; the *rhingyll* was pardoned the rent of assise and the grazing was let for 13s 4d.[120] The account for 1420-1 records that Cleifiog and Llanllibio had been leased by the community[121] There had been 30 named tenants there, all contributing to the rent, but there were not enough to do so now because of their poverty and because of the destruction caused by the rebels. In Menai Ysgeifiog was in decay; before the revolt it had been worth seven pounds but it was now without tenants. Once there had been eighteen bondmen, all contributing to the rent, but now there were only three old men who had been pardoned the rent because of their poverty.[122]

Rents were still being respited in 1421-2; the bondmen of Bodrida in Menai had all died in the revolt so the whole sum due had to be written off as there was nobody to pay it.[123] One would expect the situation to improve, especially since an agrarian society should be able to recover from the effects of war fairly quickly, but this was certainly not the case in many townships. In Menai in 1424-5 the hamlet of Bodlew was let for 15s 4d and more rents had been respited while in Talybolion the annual respite now stood at £12 16s 4d, ostensibly because of the damage caused by the revolt.[124] An increasing number of mills was reported as being derelict; in 1437-8 that of Dindryfwl had not been

---

117 Melin Newydd had been farmed at five pounds and Hirdre-faig at four in 1359-60 (TNA SC6/1149/9, m.6a).
118 TNA SC6/1152/5, mm.4a, 3a, 4b.
119 TNA SC6/1152/6, mm.4a, 7a; 1152/7, m.4a.
120 TNA SC6/1152/7, m.6b.
121 TNA SC6/1152/9, m.4a.
122 TNA SC6/1152/9, m.6b; it was said that the bondmen had left the township.
123 TNA SC6/1153/1, m.6b.
124 TNA SC6 /1153/2, mm.1b, 3b.

repaired, while that of Hirdre-faig was completely destroyed.[125] Subsequent accounts show no improvement; in 1441-2 all the bond tenants of Bodfardden had gone and part of one rent at Trefadog in Talybolion was written off because the tenants were too poor to pay.[126] At Ysgeifiog a whole free *gwely* was let and 90 acres in Tre Feibion Pill and Tregarwed in Menai yielded only 1s 8d for grazing.[127]

Decayed rents in Talybolion in 1449-50 came to £18 16s; in Carneddor and Llanfigel some bond tenants had died in the revolt and some had left.[128] In Menai some amercements could not be collected because of the disappearance of some tenants and the poverty of others.[129] In Llifon in 1451-2 the respites were twelve pounds and at Bodynolwyn the three remaining bond tenants could not pay the rent.[130] By 1464-5 yet more land was in decay and more customary lands written off and the following year's account painted an even blacker picture. In Talybolion lands in Botan and Bodfardden and the entire townships of Carneddor, Llanol and Aberalaw were now leased out, while in Twrcelyn the same was true of the *tir cyfrif* townships of Bodhunod, Rhosmynach, Deri and Bodednyfed.[131] In 1466-7 Tre Feibion Meurig and Bodynolwyn in Llifon and Bodronyn in Talybolion were also farmed out; Carneddor was let to two bond tenants and Llanol to three.[132] All these townships continued to be leased; there was to be no return to the old system.

All the foregoing evidence points very clearly to a decline in the unfree population and the depopulation of bond townships in Anglesey in the fifteenth century. It was easy for contemporary officials to lay the blame for this on the effects of the Glyn Dŵr revolt and in the early years of the century the revolt must, indeed, have left its mark. But the roots of the crisis lay in the years before 1400. Under normal circumstances an economy based on agriculture should have been well on the way to recovery soon after the revolt. But circumstances were not normal; the fact that they were not probably contributed to the revolt of Owain Glyn Dŵr in the first place. The fiscal burden carried by bond tenants had been a heavy one before the end of the fourteenth century; now, in the fifteenth, they voted with their feet and left depopulated townships in the hands of the crown and yielding no revenue.[133] Some certainly died in rebellion but

---

125  TNA SC6/1153/4, mm.3b, 7a.
126  TNA SC6/1153/5, m.5a.
127  TNA SC6/1153/5, mm.6a, 9b.
128  TNA SC6/1153/6, m.6b.
129  TNA SC6/1153/6, m.11a.
130  TNA SC6/1153/8, m.5a.
131  TNA SC6/1154/6, mm.4b, 6b
132  TNA SC6/1155/1, mm.3b, 6b; E163/8128, m.3b.
133  J. Beverley Smith, 'Crown and community in north Wales in the reign of Henry Tudor', 152-7.

many more departed during the century. The heaviest burden had been born by the *tir cyfrif* tenants and their townships all seem to have been abandoned. Excavation might well reveal deserted settlements in places like Llanol and Deri and many isolated churches and vanished chapel-of-ease bear witness to the disappearance and contraction of communities between 1350 and 1450.[134] Some bond tenants must have become landless labourers but others prospered, as the escheators' accounts of the late fifteenth century show. Thus the causes of the problems of the fifteenth century are not to be laid at the door of Owain Glyn Dŵr; the process had begun a long time earlier and its consequences were to trouble royal and seigneurial administrators in Wales for many years to come. And it was not only a Welsh problem; in fifteenth-century England more and more holdings became vacant and the demand for land diminished. There, too, an agricultural depression which had begun in the mid-fourteenth century or earlier continued.[135] The effects of the revolt were on individuals rather than on communities; the real loser in Anglesey was the Penmynydd family while the gainer was Gwilym ap Gruffudd, whose descendants were to dominate Gwynedd for a century. Other new families also emerged, above all the great house of Bulkeley whose history was to be bound up with that of the county for so long. Plague, slump and rebellion all left their mark and in many ways the world could never be the same again; '... a new society was emerging from the cracking shell of the old'.[136]

134  This is discussed in Chapter 1.
135  M.M. Postan, 'The fifteenth century', in *Essays in Medieval Agriculture and General Problems of the Medieval Economy*. pp.42-4.
136  Gwyn A. Williams, op.cit., p.177.

# Appendices

## *Appendix A : **Genealogical Tables***

1  Wyrion Eden lineage  . . . . . . . . . . . . . . . . . . . . . . . . . . . . . . . . . 262

2  Lineage of Llywarch ap Bran . . . . . . . . . . . . . . . . . . . . . . . . . . 264

3  Lineage of Hwfa ap Cynddelw . . . . . . . . . . . . . . . . . . . . . . . . 266

4  Lineage of Iarddur  . . . . . . . . . . . . . . . . . . . . . . . . . . . . . . . . . . 268

5  Lineage of Carwed  . . . . . . . . . . . . . . . . . . . . . . . . . . . . . . . . . . 269

These tables list the most prominent members of the lineages whose names appear in the text. Each table is followed by a list of the most important marriages of their members.

For more detailed tables see:
   P.C.Bartrum, *Welsh Genealogies AD 300-1400* (8 vols., Cardiff, 1974)
   and idem, *Welsh Genealogies AD 1400-1500* (18 vols., Aberystwyth, 1983).

# 1 : The Wyrion Eden lineage

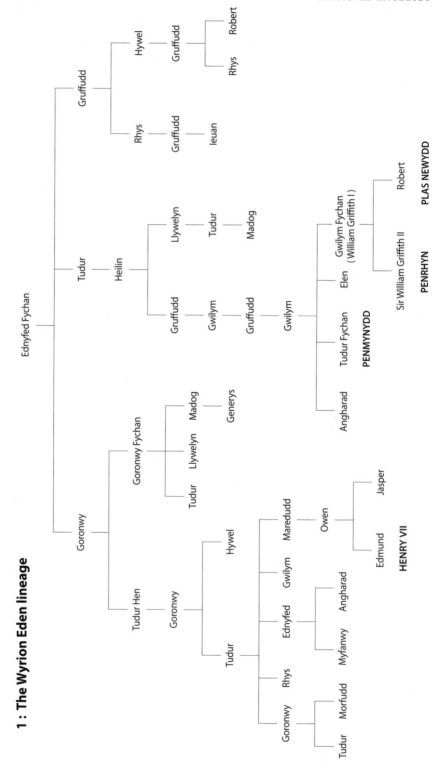

*Notes*

## DEATHS

| | | | | |
|---|---|---|---|---|
| Ednyfed Fychan | 1246 | | Owen Tudor | 1461 |
| Goronwy ab Ednyfed | 1268 | | Edmund Tudor | 1456 |
| Tudur ab Ednyfed | 1278 | | Jasper Tudor | 1495 |
| Tudur Hen | 1311 | | Gruffudd ap Gwilym ap Gruffudd | 1405 |
| Goronwy ap Tudur Hen | 1331 | | Gwilym ap Gruffudd ap Gwilym | 1431 |
| Madog ap Goronwy Fychan | 1348 | | Gwilym Fychan | 1483 |
| Tudur ap Goronwy ap Tudur | 1367 | | Sir Gruffudd ap Rhys | 1335 |
| Hywel ap Goronwy ap Tudur | 1366 | | Hywel ap Gruffudd ab Ednyfed | 1282 |
| Goronwy ap Tudur ap Goronwy | 1382 | | Sir Rhys ap Gruffudd | 1356 |
| Ednyfed ap Tudur ap Goronwy | 1382 | | Rhys ap Tudur ap Goronwy | 1411 |

## MARRIAGES

**Goronwy ap Tudur:** Myfanwy ferch Iorwerth Ddu ab Ednyfed Gam (Pengwern)

**Ednyfed ap Tudur:** Gwenllian ferch Dafydd ap Bleddyn Fychan (Flintshire)

**Maredudd ap Tudur:** Margaret ferch Dafydd Fychan ap Dafydd Llwyd (Trefeilir)

**Morfudd ferch Goronwy ap Tudur:** Gwilym ap Gruffudd ap Gwilym (Penhwnllys, later Penrhyn) *

**Myfanwy ferch Ednyfed ap Tudur:** Rhys ap Cynwrig ap Roppert (Coedymynydd)

**Angharad ferch Ednyfed ap Tudur:** Ieuan ab Adda ab Iorwerth Ddu (Pengwern)

**Generys ferch Madog ap Goronwy Fychan:** Gruffudd ap Gwilym ap Gruffudd (Nant, Flintshire) *

**Gwilym ap Gruffudd ap Heilin:** Efa ferch Gruffudd ap Tudur (Penhwnllys)

**Gruffudd ap Gwilym ap Gruffudd:** Generys ferch Madog *

**Gwilym ap Gruffudd ap Gwilym:** (1) Morfudd ferch Goronwy ap Tudur* (2) Joan Stanley

**Angharad ferch Gwilym ap Gruffudd:** Dafydd ab Ieuan ap Hywel (Llwydiarth Esgob)

**Elen ferch Gwilym ap Gruffudd:** William Bulkeley the elder (Beaumaris)

**Gwilym Fychan (William Griffith I):** Alice Dalton (Gwenllian ferch Iorwerth was the mother of Robert and two other sons)

*\* Marriages within the lineage*

# 2 : The lineage of Llywarch ap Bran

## (a) Iorwerth ap Llywarch

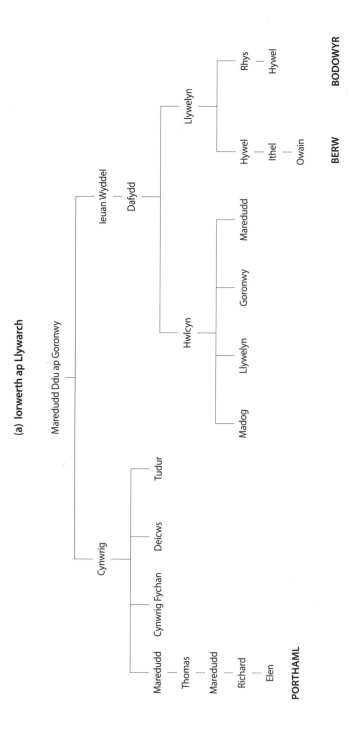

## (b) Cadwgan ap Llywarch

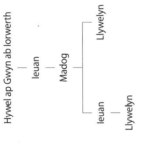

Hywel ap Gwyn ab Iorwerth

Ieuan

Madog

Ieuan      Llywelyn

Llywelyn

**PLAS COCH**

*Notes*

**MARRIAGES**

**Maredudd Ddu:** (1) Nest ferch Ithel Fychan (Englefield)

**Cynwrig ap Maredudd Ddu:** Angharad ferch Madog ap Gruffudd Fychan (Hwfa ap Cynddelw)

**Arddun ferch Maredudd Ddu:** Hywel ap Gwyn ab Iorwerth (Plas Coch) *

**Maredudd ap Cynwrig:** Annes ferch Robert Puleston (Maelor Saesneg)

**Nest ferch Maredudd ap Cynwrig:** Hwlcyn Llwyd (Glynllifon)

**Thomas ap Maredudd ap Cynwrig:** Angharad ferch Hywel y Farf (Treiorwerth)

**Elen ferch Richard ap Maredudd:** William, son of Rowland Bulkeley

**Ieuan ap Hywel ap Gwyn:** Annes ferch Hywel ap Cynwrig (Llwydiarth Esgob)

**Ieuan ap Madog ab Ieuan:** Mallt ferch Madog ap Hwlcyn ap Dafydd ab Ieuan Wyddel *

*  *Marriages within the lineage*

## 3 : The lineage of Hwfa ap Cynddelw

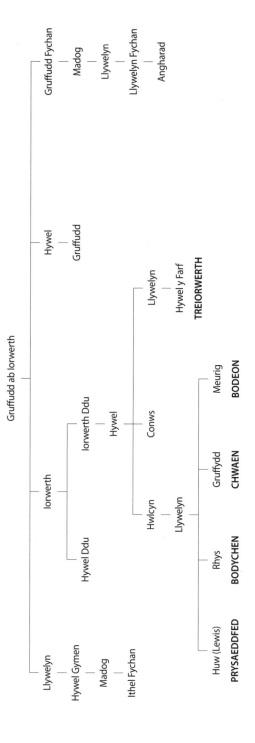

**(a) Matusalem ap Hwfa**

**(b) Iorwerth ap Hwfa**

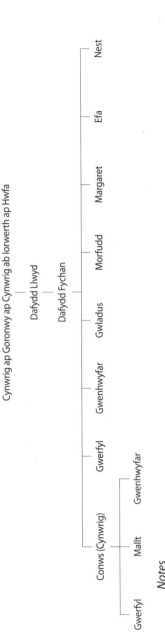

Cynwrig ap Goronwy ap Cynwrig ab Iorwerth ap Hwfa

Dafydd Llwyd

Dafydd Fychan

| Conws (Cynwrig) | Gwerfyl | Gwenhwyfar | Gwladus | Morfudd | Margaret | Efa | Nest |

Mallt     Gwenhwyfar

Gwerfyl

## Notes

### MARRIAGES

**Iorwerth Ddu ab Iorwerth ap Gruffudd:** Gwenllian ferch Maredudd Benhir

**Hywel ab Iorwerth Ddu:** Angharad ferch Hywel ap Cynwrig Fychan (Is Aled)

**Hwlcyn ap Hywel ab Iorwerth Ddu:** Erddylad ferch Dafydd ab Iorwerth (Llywarch ap Bran, Twrcelyn)

**Llywelyn ap Hwlcyn:** (1) Mali ferch Ieuan Llwyd ap Gruffudd (Gorddinog). (2) Angharad ferch Dafydd ap Cynwrig ap Goronwy*

**Meurig ap Llywelyn ap Hwlcyn:** Margaret ferch Ieuan Fychan ab Ieuan ab Adda (Pengwern)

**Rhys ap Llywelyn ap Hwlcyn:** Margaret ferch Rhys ap Cynwrig ap Roppert (Coedymynydd)

**Huw Lewis:** Sioned (Joan) Bulkeley (Beaumaris)

**Angharad ferch Llywelyn Fychan ap Llywelyn:** Llywelyn ab Ieuan ap Tudur Llwyd (Iarddur)

*Trefeilir*

**Dafydd Fychan ap Dafydd Llwyd:** (1) Angharad ferch Gruffudd ap Dafydd ap Tudur (Iarddur). (2) Nest ferch Ieuan ap Gruffudd (Bron-y-foel)

**Conws ap Dafydd Fychan:** Mallt ferch Gruffudd ap Madog Gloddaith (Gloddaith)

**Gwerfyl ferch Dafydd Fychan:** Rhys ap Gruffudd ap Madog Gloddaith

**Gwenhwyfar ferch Dafydd Fychan:** (1) Madog ap Hywel Gymen*. (2) Gruffudd ab Ieuan ap Gruffudd (Bron-y-foel)

**Gwladus ferch Dafydd Fychan:** Llywelyn Fychan ap Llywelyn*

**Morfudd ferch Dafydd Fychan:** Ieuan ap Hywel ap Cynwrig (Llysdulas and Llwydiarth Esgob)

**Margaret ferch Dafydd Fychan:** Maredudd ap Tudur ap Goronwy (Wyrion Eden)

*\* Marriages within the lineage*

# 4 : The lineage of Iarddur

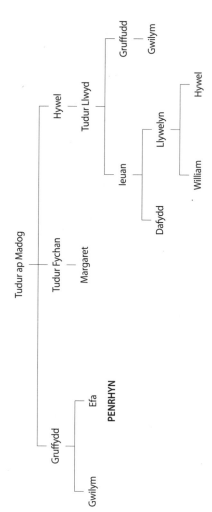

*Notes*

**MARRIAGES**

**Gruffudd ap Tudur Llwyd:** Angharad ferch Hywel ap Gruffudd (Llywarch ap Bran)

**Margaret ferch Tudur Fychan:** Dafydd Llwyd ap Cynwrig (Trefeilir)

**Gwilym ap Gruffudd ap Tudur ap Madog:** Gwenllian ferch Madog

**Efa ferch Gruffudd ap Tudur ap Madog:** Gwilym ap Gruffudd ap Heilin (Wyrion Eden)

**Llywelyn ab Ieuan ap Tudur Llwyd:** Angharad ferch Llywelyn Fychan (Hwfa ap Cynddelw)

**Gwilym ap Gruffudd ap Tudur Llwyd:** Nest ferch Ieuan ap Gruffudd (Bron-y-foel)

# 5 : The lineage of Carwed

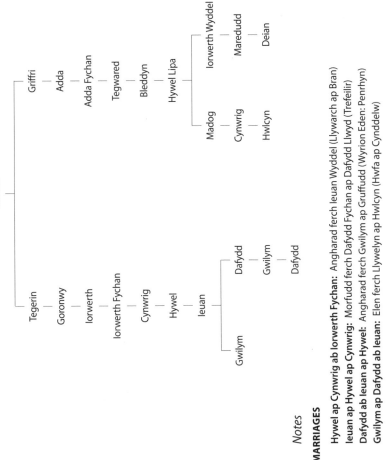

*Notes*

**MARRIAGES**

**Hywel ap Cynwrig ab Iorwerth Fychan:**  Angharad ferch Ieuan Wyddel (Llywarch ap Bran)

**Ieuan ap Hywel ap Cynwrig:**  Morfudd ferch Dafydd Fychan ap Dafydd Llwyd (Trefeilir)

**Dafydd ab Ieuan ap Hywel:**  Angharad ferch Gwilym ap Gruffudd (Wyrion Eden: Penrhyn)

**Gwilym ap Dafydd ab Ieuan:**  Elen ferch Llywelyn ap Hwlcyn (Hwfa ap Cynddelw)

# Appendix B : **Maps**

1  Anglesey : cantrefs and commotes . . . . . . . . . . . . . . . . . . . . . . 272

2  Dindaethwy . . . . . . . . . . . . . . . . . . . . . . . . . . . . . . . . . . . . 273

3  Menai . . . . . . . . . . . . . . . . . . . . . . . . . . . . . . . . . . . . . . . . 274

4  Malltraeth . . . . . . . . . . . . . . . . . . . . . . . . . . . . . . . . . . . . . 275

5  Llifon . . . . . . . . . . . . . . . . . . . . . . . . . . . . . . . . . . . . . . . . . 276

6  Talybolion . . . . . . . . . . . . . . . . . . . . . . . . . . . . . . . . . . . . . 277

7  Twrcelyn . . . . . . . . . . . . . . . . . . . . . . . . . . . . . . . . . . . . . . 278

8  Ecclesiastical lands . . . . . . . . . . . . . . . . . . . . . . . . . . . . . . 279

9  Townships affected by the Black Death . . . . . . . . . . . . . . . . 280

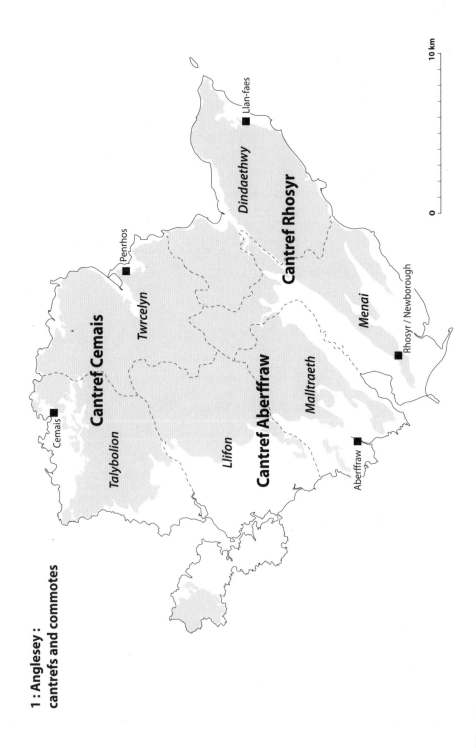

**1 : Anglesey :
cantrefs and commotes**

Cantref Cemais

Cantref Aberffraw

Cantref Rhosyr

Talybolion

Twrcelyn

Llifon

Malltraeth

Menai

Dindaethwy

Cemais

Penrhos

Llan-faes

Rhosyr / Newborough

Aberffraw

0                10 km

# 2 : Dindaethwy

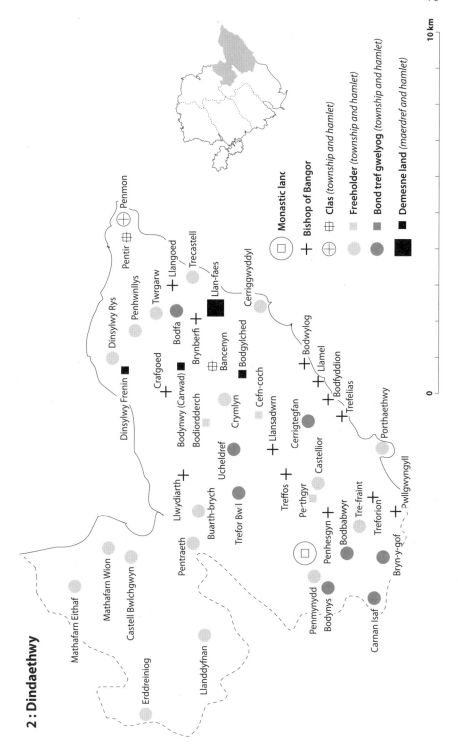

Mathafarn Eithaf

Mathafarn Wion

Castell Bwlchgwyn

Erddreiniog

Llanddyfnan

Pentraeth

Buarth-brych

Llwydiarth

Ucheldref

Trefor Bwl

Penmynydd

Bodynys

Carnan Isaf

Treffos

Perthgyr

Castellior

Cerrigtegfan

Penhesgyn

Bodbabwyr

Tre-fraint

Treforion

Bryn-y-gof

Pwllgwyngyll

Porthaethwy

Trefelias

Bodfyddion

Llamel

Bodwylog

Cerrigtegfan

Dinsylwy Frenin

Crafgoed

Bodynwy (Carwad)

Bodiordderch

Crymlyn

Cefn-coch

Llansadwrn

Bancenyn

Brynberfi

Bodgylched

Dinsylwy Rys

Penhwnllys

Twrgarw

Bodfa

Llangoed

Trecastell

Llan-faes

Cerriggwyddyl

Dinsylwy Rys

Pentir

Penmon

Monastic lanc

Bishop of Bangor

Clas *(township and hamlet)*

Freeholder *(township and hamlet)*

Bond tref gwelyog *(township and hamlet)*

Demesne land *(maerdref and hamlet)*

0       10 km

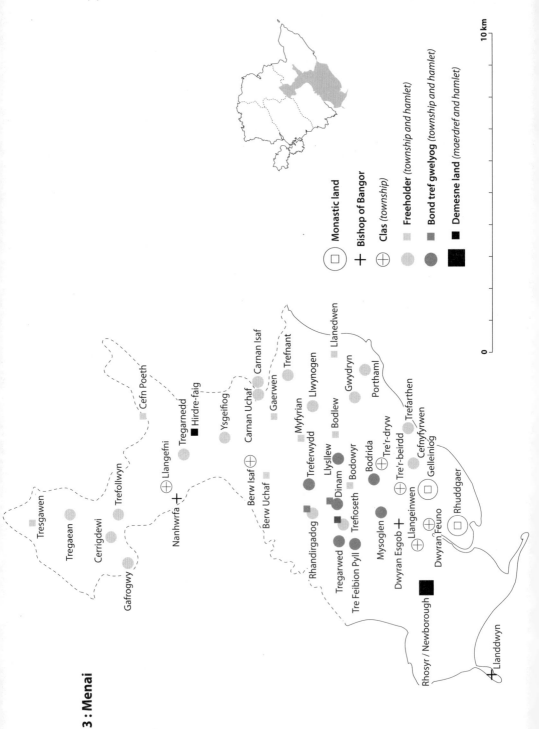

**3 : Menai**

Monastic land

Bishop of Bangor

Clas (township)

Freeholder (township and hamlet)

Bond tref gwelyog (township and hamlet)

Demesne land (maerdref and hamlet)

10 km

Tresgawen
Cefn Poeth
Trefollwyn
Tregarnedd
Hirdre-faig
Ysgeifiog
Carnan Uchaf
Carnan Isaf
Gaerwen
Trefnant
Llanedwen
Myfyrian
Llwynogen
Gwydryn
Berw Isaf
Bodlew
Porthaml
Treferwydd
Berw Uchaf
Llysllew
Bodowyr
Tre'r-dryw
Trefarthen
Tregaean
Cerrigdewi
Nanhwrfa
Llangefni
Dinam
Bodrida
Tre'r-beirdd
Cefnyfyrwen
Gafrogwy
Rhandirgadog
Trefloseth
Gelleiniog
Rhuddgaer
Tregarwed
Mysoglen
Dwyran Esgob
Llangeinwen
Tre Feibion Pyll
Dwyran Feuno
Llanddwyn
Rhosyr / Newborough

# 4 : Malltraeth

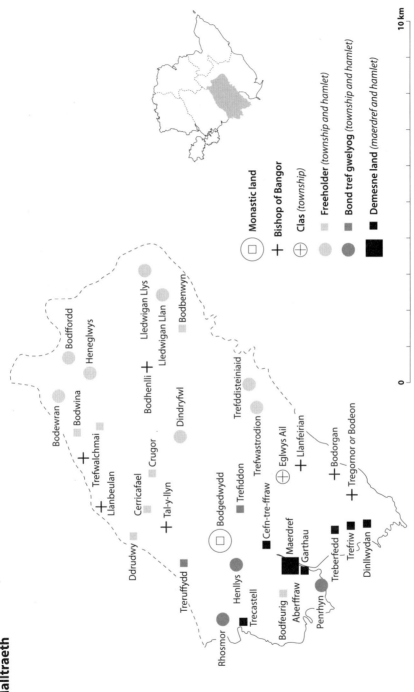

Monastic land

Bishop of Bangor

Clas (township)

Freeholder (township and hamlet)

Bond tref gwelyog (township and hamlet)

Demesne land (maerdref and hamlet)

Bodffordd
Heneglwys
Lledwigan Llys
Lledwigan Llan
Bodbenwyn
Bodewran
Bodwina
Bodhenlli
Dindryfwl
Trefwalchmai
Crugor
Trefddisteiniaid
Cerricafael
Trefwastrodion
Llanbeulan
Tal-y-llyn
Eglwys Ail
Ddrudwy
Trefiddon
Llanfeirian
Bodgedwydd
Bodorgan
Cefn-tre-ffraw
Tregornor or Bodeon
Treruffydd
Maerdref
Garthau
Henllys
Treberfedd
Trecastell
Trefriw
Rhosmor
Bodfeurig
Aberffraw
Dinllwydan
Penrhyn

0                                10 km

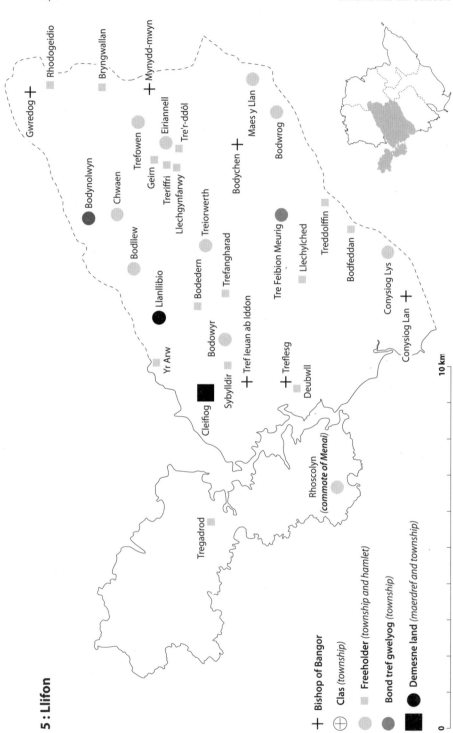

**5 : Llifon**

Rhodogeidio

Bryngwallan

Mynydd-mwyn

Gwredog

Eiriannell

Trefowen

Tre'r-ddôl

Maes y Llan

Geirn

Bodwrog

Bodynolwyn

Treriffri

Chwaen

Llechgynfarwy

Bodychen

Treiorwerth

Bodllew

Bodedern

Trefangharad

Tre Feibion Meurig

Llechylched

Treddolffin

Llanllibio

Bodfeddan

Yr Arw

Conysiog Lys

Bodowyr

Tref Ieuan ab Iddon

Conysiog Lan

Sybylldir

Treflesg

Cleifiog

Deubwll

Rhoscolyn
*(commote of Menai)*

Tregadrod

10 km

0

**Bishop of Bangor**

**Clas** *(township)*

**Freeholder** *(township and hamlet)*

**Bond tref gwelyog** *(township)*

**Demesne land** *(maerdref and township)*

**6 : Talybolion**

Monastic land

Bishop of Bangor

Clas *(township and hamlet)*

Freeholder *(township and hamlet)*

Bond tref gwelyog *(township and hamlet)*

Demesne land *(maerdref and hamlet)*

Maerdref Cemais

Tre'r Gof

Llanfechell

Rhosbeirio

Clegyrog

Cafnan

Caerdegog

Llanddygfael

Coeden

Llanol

Llanfflewyn

Bodronyn

Gwaunydog

Bod-Ddeiniol

Cemlyn

Cornwy Lys
*(Aberconwy abbey)*

Cornwylan

Bodegri

Ucheldref

Cnwchdyrnog

Meiriogen

Tre Feibion
Maelog
*(Aberconwy abbey)*

Alaw'r Beirdd

Tremoelgoch

Carneddor

Trefednyfed

Bodwigan

Botan

Llanfigel

Trefadog

Bodfarthen

Trelywarch

Dronwy

Aberalaw

Caergybi

**Commote of Llïfon**

10 km

0

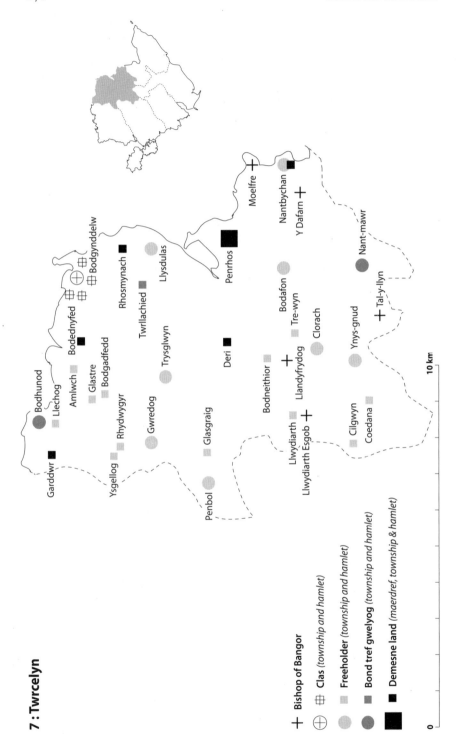

7 : Twrcelyn

Moelfre
Nantbychan
Y Dafarn
Nant-mawr
Tal-y-llyn
Penrhos
Bodgynddelw
Rhosmynach
Llysdulas
Bodafon
Tre-wyn
Bodednyfed
Twrllachied
Clorach
Bodhunod
Amlwch
Glastre
Bodgadfedd
Trysglwyn
Deri
Bodneithior
Ynys-gnud
Llechog
Rhydwygyr
Gwredog
Llandyfrydog
Ysgellog
Glasgraig
Llwydiarth
Cilgwyn
Garddwr
Penbol
Llwydiarth Esgob
Coedana

Bishop of Bangor
Clas (township and hamlet)
Freeholder (township and hamlet)
Bond tref gwelyog (township and hamlet)
Demesne land (maerdref, township & hamlet)

10 km

0

## 8 : Ecclesiastical lands

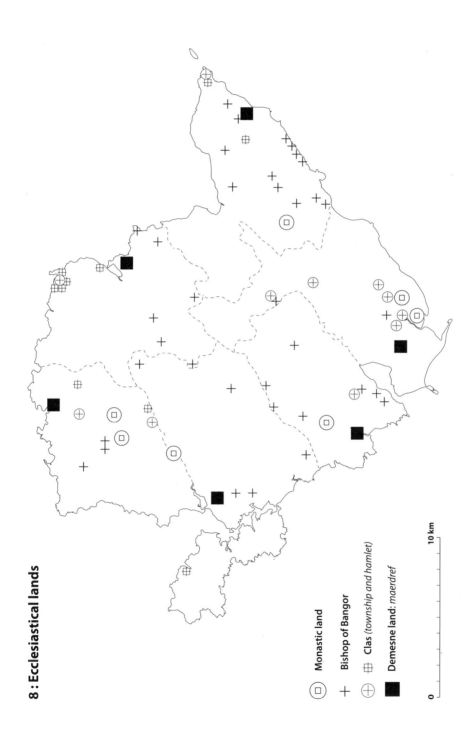

Monastic land

Bishop of Bangor

Clas (township and hamlet)

Demesne land: maerdref

0                                                                    10 km

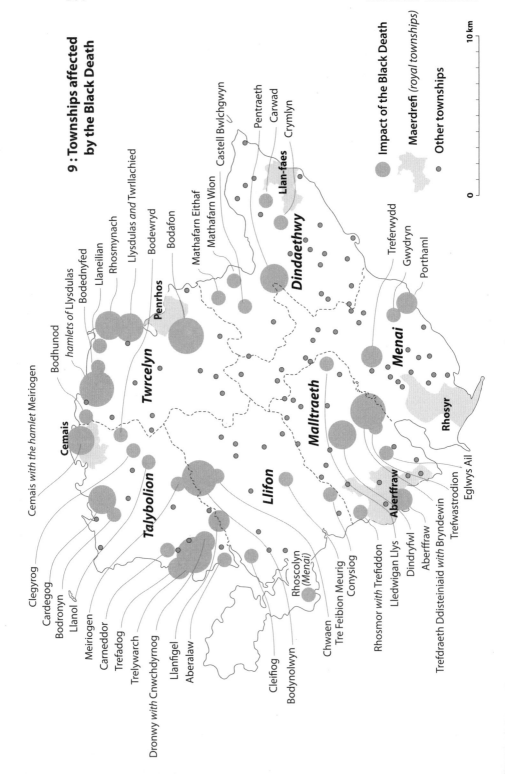

9 : Townships affected
by the Black Death

**Impact of the Black Death**

Maerdrefi *(royal townships)*

Other townships

10 km

0

Dindaethwy

Castell Bwlchgwyn

Pentraeth

Carwad

Crymlyn

Llan-faes

Treferwydd

Gwydryn

Porthaml

Menai

Rhosyr

Eglwys Ail

Trefwastrodion

Trefdraeth Ddisteiniaid *with* Bryndewin

Aberffraw

Dindryfwl

Lledwigan Llys

Rhosmor *with* Trefiddon

Aberffraw

Malltraeth

Conysiog

Tre Feibion Meurig

Chwaen

Mathafarn Eithaf

Mathafarn Wion

Bodewryd

Bodafon

Llysdulas *and* Twrllachied

Rhosmynach

Llaneilian

Bodednyfed

*hamlets of* Llysdulas

Penrhos

Twrcelyn

Bodhunod

Bodynolwyn

Cleifiog

Llifon

Rhoscolyn
*(Menai)*

Cemais *with the hamlet* Meiriogen

Cemais

Talybolion

Clegyrog

Cardegog

Bodronyn

Llanol

Meiriogen

Carneddor

Trefadog

Trelywarch

Dronwy *with* Cnwchdyrnog

Llanfigel

Aberalaw

# Bibliography

## A  Original sources : unpublished

1  *The National Archives, Kew*

EXCHEQUER
E101: Accounts (Various) 119/33; 120/1
E163: Miscellanea 6/38; 8/28; 24/1
E179: Subsidy Rolls 3/2,5; 242/49
E315: Augmentations: Miscellaneous Books 21; 122; 166
E326: Ancient Deeds 7201

SPECIAL COLLECTIONS
S.C.2: Court Rolls 215/1-11
S.C.6: Ministers' Accounts 1143/25; 1149-1155; 1170/1-19; 1172/5-11; 1173/1-9; 1174/1-4;
    1211-1217; 1227-1229; 1233/1; 1287/1-3; 1306/16; Hen. VIII 4705, 4972

KING'S BENCH
K.B.9: Ancient Indictments 204/K18-21

COURT OF REQUESTS
Req 2/6/214

PALATINATE OF CHESTER
Chester 25: Indictment Rolls 24

LAND REVENUE
L.R. 2/205


2  *National Library of Wales, Aberystwyth*

Bodewryd Correspondence 1034
Bodewryd MSS.
Carreglwyd MSS.
Church in Wales Records: B/MISC. VOLS./27
Llanfair and Brynodol MSS.
Lleweni MSS.
Peniarth MSS. 177; 405
Pitchford Hall MSS.

Sotheby MSS.
Thorne MSS.

### 3 *Bangor University Archives and Special Collections*

Bangor MSS. 1790; 1920(i); 26331
Baron Hill MSS.
Mostyn MSS.
Penrhos vii MSS.
Penrhyn MSS.
Penrhyn Further Additional MSS.
Plas Coch MSS.
Plas Newydd v MSS. 1434
Porth-yr-Aur Additional MSS. 178

### 4 *Flintshire Record Office, Hawarden*

D/MT: Mostyn of Talacre papers:1
D/NH: Nercwys Hall papers

### 5. *British Library, London*

Additional Charters 8642
Additional MSS. 33372

# B  Original sources : published

*Archaeologia Cambrensis, Original Documents* (1877)

Bartrum, P.C.: *Welsh Genealogies, A.D. 300-1400* (Cardiff, 1974)

Bede: *A History of the English Church and People*, trans. Leo Sherley-Price (Harmondsworth, 1955)

Board of Celtic Studies. *Mynegai i Farddoniaeth Gaeth y Llawysgrifau* (Cardiff, 1978)

Bowen, Ivor: *The Statutes of Wales* (London, 1908)

*Brut y Tywysogyon (Peniarth MS. 20 version)*, ed. Thomas Jones (Cardiff, 1952)

*Brut y Tywysogyon (Red Book of Hergest version)*, ed. Thomas Jones (Cardiff, 1955)

*Calendar of Ancient Correspondence concerning Wales*, ed. J.G. Edwards (Cardiff, 1935)

*Calendar of Ancient Deeds*

*Calendar of Ancient Petitions relating to Wales*, ed. William Rees (Cardiff, 1975)

*Calendar of the Caernarvonshire Quarter Sessions Rolls, 1541-1558*, ed. W. Ogwen Williams (Caernarfon, 1956)

*Calendar of Chancery Rolls Various*

*Calendar of Chancery Warrants*

*Calendar of the Charter Rolls*

*Calendar of the Close Rolls*

*Calendar of the Fine Rolls*

*Calendar of Inquisitions Miscellaneous*

*Calendar of Inquisitions Post Mortem*

*Calendar of Papal Letters*

*Calendar of the Patent Rolls*

*Cambrian Journal* (1863)

Carr, A.D.: 'The extent of Anglesey, 1352', *TAAS* 1971-2

*Cerddi Dafydd ap Gwilym* ed. D.Johnston et al. (Cardiff, 2010)

*Chartulary of Chester Abbey*, ed. J.Tait (Chetham Society, 1920)

*Chester Chamberlains' Accounts 1301-1360*, ed. R. Stewart-Brown (Lancashire and Cheshire Record Society, 1910)

*Close Rolls, 1227-1231*

*Close Rolls, 1247-1251*

*Close Rolls, 1256-1259*

*Councils and Ecclesiastical Documents relating to Great Britain and Ireland*, ed. R.W. Haddan and W. Stubbs, i (Oxford, 1869)

*Cywyddau Iolo Goch* ac *Eraill*, ed. Henry Lewis, Thomas Roberts and Ifor Williams (2nd edn., Cardiff, 1937)

*Episcopal Acts relating to the Welsh Dioceses, 1066-1272*, ed. J. Conway Davies (Cardiff, 1946-8)

*Eulogium Historiarum* iii, ed. F.S. Haydon (Rolls Series, 1863)

*Exchequer Proceedings concerning Wales in tempore James I*, ed. T.I. Jeffreys-Jones (Cardiff, 1955)

*Flintshire Ministers' Accounts, 1301-1328*, ed. Arthur Jones (Flints. Hist. Soc., 1913)

*Flintshire Ministers' Accounts, 1328-1353*, ed. D.L. Evans (Flints. Hist. Soc., 1929)

Florence of Worcester: *Chronicon ex Chronicis*, ed. B. Thorpe (English Historical Society, 1848-9)

Fryde, E.B., ed.: *A Book of Prests of the King's Wardrobe, 1294-5* (Oxford, 1962)

Fryde, Natalie, ed.: *List of Welsh Entries in the Memoranda Rolls, 1282-1343* (Cardiff, 1974)

Gerald of Wales: *The Journey through Wales* and *The Description of Wales*, trans. and ed. Lewis Thorpe (Harmondsworth, 1978)

Gresham, Colin A.: 'The Bolde rental' (Bangor MS. 1939), *TCHS* 26 (1965)

Griffiths, John: 'Two early ministers' accounts for north Wales', *BBCS* 9 (1937)

Griffiths, John: 'Early accounts relating to north Wales, *temp*. Edward I', *BBCS* 15 (1953), 16 (1954-6)

*Gwaith Bleddyn Fardd a Beirdd Eraill ail hanner y drydedd ganrif ar ddeg*, ed. Rhian M. Andrews et al. (Cardiff, 1996)

*Gwaith Dafydd ab Edmund*, ed. Thomas Roberts (Bangor, 1914)

*Gwaith Dafydd ap Gwilym*, ed. Thomas Parry (Cardiff, 1952)

*Gwaith Syr Dafydd Trefor*, ed. Rhiannon Ifans (Aberystwyth, 2005)

*Gwaith Gruffudd ap Maredudd* (i): *canu i deulu Penmynydd*, ed. Barry J. Lewis (Aberystwyth, 2003)

*Gwaith Gruffudd ap Maredudd* (ii); *cerddi crefyddol*, ed. Barry J. Lewis (Aberystwyth, 2005)

*Gwaith Gruffudd Gryg*, ed. Barry J. Lewis and Eurig Salisbury (Aberystwyth, 2010)

*Gwaith Guto'r Glyn*, ed. Ifor Williams and J. Llywelyn Williams (2nd edn., Cardiff, 1961)

*Gwaith Hywel Cilan*, ed. Islwyn Jones (Cardiff, 1963)

*Gwaith Iolo Goch*, ed. D.R. Johnston, (Cardiff, 1988)

*Gwaith Lewys Glyn Cothi*, ed. Dafydd Johnston (Cardiff, 1995)

*Gwaith Lewys Môn*, ed. Eurys I. Rowlands (Cardiff, 1975)

*Gwaith Llywarch ap Llywelyn 'Prydydd y Moch'*, ed. Elin M. Jones (Cardiff, 1991)

*Gwaith Llywelyn Goch ap Meurig Hen*, ed. Dafydd Johnston (Aberystwyth, 1998)

*Gwaith Rhys Goch Eryri*, ed. Dylan Foster Evans (Aberystwyth, 2007)

*Gwaith Sefnyn, Rhisierdyn, Gruffudd Fychan ap Gruffudd ab Ednyfed a Llywarch Bentwrch*, ed. Nerys Ann Jones and Erwain Haf Rheinallt (Aberystwyth, 1995)

*Gwaith Tudur Aled*, ed. T. Gwynn Jones (Cardiff, 1926)

*Gwaith Tudur Penllyn ac Ieuan ap Tudur Penllyn*, ed. Thomas Roberts (Cardiff, 1958)

Hall, Edmund Hyde: *A Description of Caernarvonshire (1809-11)*, ed. E. Gwynne Jones (Caernarfon, 1952)

*Historia Gruffud vab Kenan*, ed. D. Simon Evans (Cardiff, 1977)

*The History of Gruffudd ap Cynan*, ed. Arthur Jones (Manchester, 1910)

Jones, G.P.: 'Anglesey court rolls, 1346', *TAAS* 1930, 1932, 1933

Jones, G.P.: *The Extent of Chirkland (1391-3)* (Liverpool, 1933)

Jones, G.P. and Hugh Owen: *Caernarvon Court Rolls, 1361-1402* (Caernarfon, 1951)

Leland, John: *The Itinerary in Wales in or about the years 1536-1539*, ed. L. Toulmin Smith (London, 1906)

*Letters and Papers, Foreign and Domestic, of the Reign of Henry VIII*, Vols. I, IX, XII (i), XIII (i, ii)

Lewis, E.A.: 'The account roll of the chamberlain of the principality of north Wales from Michaelmas 1304 to Michaelmas 1305', *BBCS*, 1 (1923)

Lewis, E.A.: 'The proceedings of the small hundred court of Ardudwy in the county of Merioneth from 8 October 1325 to 18 September 1326', *BBCS* 4 (1928)

*Littere Wallie*, ed. J. G. Edwards (Cardiff, 1940)

*Llawysgrif Hendregadredd*, ed. J. Morris-Jones and T.H. Parry-Williams (Cardiff, 1933)

*Llyfr Colan*, ed. Dafydd Jenkins (Cardiff, 1963)

*Llyfr Iorwerth*, ed. Aled Rhys Wiliam (Cardiff, 1960)

*Monasticon Anglicanum*, ed. J. Cayley, H. Ellis and B. Bandinel (London, 1817-30)

*The Plea Rolls of Anglesey*, ed. Hugh Owen (Supplement to *TAAS*, Llangefni, 1927)

*The Poetry in the Red Book of Hergest*, ed. J. Gwenogyryn Evans (Llanbedrog, 1911)

Pryce, A. Ivor: 'The register of Benedict, bishop of Bangor, 1408-1417', *Arch. Camb.*, 1922

Pryce, A. Ivor: *The Diocese of Bangor in the Sixteenth Century* (Bangor, 1924)

Pryce, Huw, ed.: *The Acts of Welsh Rulers 1120-1283* (Cardiff, 2005)

Public Record Office (The National Archives): *List of Sheriffs for England and Wales from the earliest times to A.D. 1831* (TNA Lists and Indexes, IX, 1898)

Pugh, T.B.: *The Marcher Lordships of South Wales, 1415-1536* (Cardiff, 1963)

*Records of the Court of Augmentations relating to Wales and Monmouthshire*, ed. E.A. Lewis and J. Conway Davies (Cardiff, 1954)

*Register of the Black Prince* (1930-8)

*Registrum vulgariter nuncupatum The Record of Caernarvon*, ed. H. Ellis (London, 1838)

*The Register of Henry Chichele, Archbishop of Canterbury, 1414-1443*, i, ed. E.F. Jacob (Canterbury and York Society, 1943)

*Registrum Caroli Bothe, episcopi Herefordensis, A.D. MDXVI-MDXXXV*, ed. A.T. Bannister (Canterbury and York Society, 1921)

*Registrum Richard Mayew, episcopi Herefordensis, A.D. MDIV-MDXVI*, ed. A.T. Bannister (Canterbury and York Society, 1919)

*Registrum Thome Millyng, episcopi Herefordensis, A.D. MCCCCLXXIV-MCCCCXCII*, ed. A.T. Bannister (Canterbury and York Society, 1920)

*Registrum Thome Spofford, episcopi Herefordensis, A.D. MCCCCXXII-MCCCCXLVIII*, ed. A.T. Bannister (Canterbury and York Society, 1919)

*Registrum Roberti Winchelsey Cantuarensis Archiepiscopi*, i, ed. R. Graham (Canterbury and York Society, 1952)

Roberts, Glyn: 'The Anglesey submissions of 1406', *BBCS*, 15 (1952)

Roberts, Tomos 'Englynion Gwynedd gan Gruffudd ap Maredudd ap Dafydd', *TAAS* 1982

Robinson, W.R.B.: 'Dr. Thomas Phaer's report on the harbours and customs administration of Wales under Edward VI', *BBCS*, 24 (1972)

*Rotuli Parliamentorum* (London, 1783)

*Rotuli Scotiae*, i (London, 1814)

Rowlands, Henry: 'Antiquitates parochiales', *Arch. Camb.*, 1846-9

Rowlands, Henry: *Ideae Agriculturae* (1704) (reprinted in *TAAS* 1934, 1935, 1936)

*Royal and Historical Letters during the Reign of Henry IV*, ii (*1405-1413*), ed. F. C. Hingeston (Rolls Series, 1965)

Rymer, T.: *Foedera, 1066-1383*, ed. A. Clarke, J. Caley, J. Bayley, F. Holbrooke and J.W. Clarke (London, 1816-69)

Smith, G. Rex: 'The extent of Anglesey, 1284', *TAAS* 2009

Smith, G. Rex: 'The manor of Aberffraw, 1284-1339', *Cambrian Medieval Celtic Studies* 60 (2010)

Sturluson, Snorri: *Heimskringla: the Norse King Sagas*, trans. S. Laing, ed. P. Foote (London, 1961)

*Survey of the Honour of Denbigh, 1334*, ed. P. Vinogradoff and F. Morgan (London, 1914)

*Taxatio Ecclesiastica Angliae et Walliae, auctoritate Papae Nicholai IV, circa 1291*, ed. S. Ayscough and J. Caley (London, 1802)

*Treaty Rolls, 1337-1339*

*Valor Ecclesiasticus, temp. Henrici VIII, auctoritate regia institutus*, ed. J. Caley and J. Hunter (London, 1810-34)

*The Valuation of Norwich*, ed. W.E. Lunt (Oxford, 1926)

Wade-Evans, A.W.: 'Parochiale Wallicanum', *Y Cymmrodor*, 22 (1910)

*The Welsh Assize Roll, 1277-1284*, ed. J. Conway Davies (Cardiff, 1940)

William Williams: 'Historia Bellomarisci' (*Arch.Camb. Supplement*, 1917)

Williams-Jones, Keith: *The Merioneth Lay Subsidy Roll, 1292-3* (Cardiff, 1976)

William Worcester: *Itineraries*, ed. J.H. Harvey (Oxford, 1969)

Wynn, Sir John: *History of the Gwydir Family and Memoirs*, ed. J. Gwynfor Jones (Llandysul, 1990)

# C Secondary sources

Allmand, C.T.: 'Wales and the Hundred Years War: a French provost of Holyhead', *TAAS* 1964

Bassett, T.M. and James, Geraint: 'Coalmining in Anglesey', *TAAS* 1969-70

Barnes, F.A., 'Land tenure and landscape in Llanynghenedl, Anglesey, *TAAS* 1988

Bartlett, Robert: *The Making of Europe: conquest, colonization and cultural change, 950-1350* (London, 1993)

Baynes, E. Neil: 'The old monasteries, abbeys and chapels of Anglesey', *TAAS* 1920

Bebb, W. Ambrose: *Machlud yr Oesoedd Canol* (Swansea, 1951)

Bell, Colin and Rose: *City Fathers: the Early History of Town Planning in Britain* (Harmondsworth, 1972)

Benedictow, Ole: *The Black Death 1346-1353: a general history* (Woodbridge, 2004)

Beresford, M.W.: *The Lost Villages of England* (London, 1954)

Beresford, M.W.: *New Towns of the Middle Ages* (London, 1967)

Bloch, Marc: *Feudal Society*, trans. L.A. Manyon (London, 1965)

Bloch, Marc: 'From the royal court to the court of Rome: the suit of the serfs of Rosny-sous-Bois', in S.M. Thrupp, ed., *Change in Medieval Society: Europe North of the Alps, 1050- 1500* (London, 1965)

Bolton, Jim: 'The world turned upside down' in W.M. Ormrod and P. Lindley, eds., *The Black Death in England* (Stamford, 1996)

Bowen, E.G., ed.: *Wales, a Physical, Historical and Regional Geography* (London, 1965)

*Y Bywgraffiadur Cymreig hyd 1940* (London, 1953)

*Y Bywgraffiadur Cymreig, 1940-1950* (London, 1970)

Cam, Helen M.: *The Hundred and the Hundred Rolls* (London, 1930)

Carr, A.D: 'An aristocracy in decline: the native Welsh lords after the Edwardian conquest', *WHR*, 5 (1970)

Carr, A.D.: 'Rhys ap Roppert', *TDHS* 25 (1976)

Carr, A.D.: 'Medieval Gloddaith', *TCHS* 38 (1977)

Carr, A.D.: 'Medieval fisheries in Anglesey', *Maritime Wales* 3 (1978)

Carr, A.D.: 'The making of the Mostyns: the genesis of a landed family', *THSC* 1979

Carr, A.D.: 'Rhai beirdd ym Mon', *BBCS* 28 (1980)

Carr, A.D.: 'Anglesey and war in the later middle ages', *TAAS* 1984

Carr, A.D.: 'The priory of Penmon', *Jnl. of Welsh Eccl. Hist.* 3 (1986)

Carr, A.D.: 'The bondmen of Penrhosllugwy: a community's complaint', *TAAS* 1988

Carr, A.D.; 'Gwilym ap Gruffudd and the rise of the Penrhyn estate', *WHR* 15 (1990)

Carr, A.D.: *Owen of Wales: the end of the house of Gwynedd* (Cardiff, 1991)

Carr, A.D.: 'Tregarnedd', *TAAS* 1992

Carr, A.D.: 'The coroner in fourteenth-century Merioneth', *JMHRS* 11 (1992)

Carr, A.D.: 'Maredudd ap Cynwrig: a medieval public person', *TAAS* 1998

Carr, A.D.: 'The Black Death in Caernarfonshire', *TCHS* 61 (2000)

Carr, A.D.: 'The Penmon Valor, 1374', *TAAS* 2005

Carr, A.D.: 'The wealth of the medieval Welsh gentry: the case of Gwilym ap Gruffudd of Penrhyn' in *Proceedings of the Harvard Celtic Colloquium* 20-21, 2000, 2001 (Cambridge, Mass., 2007)

Carr, A.D.: 'The Black Death in Anglesey', *TAAS* 2010

Clarke, M.L.: *Bangor Cathedral* (Cardiff, 1969)

Creighton, C.: *A History of Epidemics in Britain from A.D. 664 to the Extinction of Plague* (Cambridge, 1891)

Davies, H.R.: *A Review of the Records of the Conway and the Menai Ferries* (Cardiff, 1942)

Davies, J. Conway: 'Felony in Edwardian Wales', *THSC* 1916-7

Davies, R.R.: 'Owain Glyn Dŵr and the Welsh squirearchy', *Trans. Cymm.* 1968

Davies, R.R.: 'Colonial Wales', *Past and Present*, 65 (1974)

Davies, R.R.: *Lordship and Society in the March of Wales, 1282-1400* (Oxford, 1978)

Davies, R.R.: 'The status of women and the practice of marriage in late medieval Wales', in Dafydd Jenkins and Morfydd E. Owen, eds.: *The Welsh Law of Women* (Cardiff, 1980)

Davies, R.R.: *Conquest, Coexistence, and Change: Wales 1063-1415* (Oxford, 1987)

Davies, R.R.: *The Revolt of Owain Glyn Dŵr* (Oxford, 1995)

Davies, Wendy: *Patterns of Power in Early Wales* (Oxford, 1990)

Delaney, C.J. and Soulsby, I.N.: 'The archaeological implications of redevelopment in the historic towns of Anglesey: Ynys Môn' (Cardiff, 1975)

Dickinson, J.C.: *The Origins of the Austin Canons and their Introduction into England* (London, 1950)

Dixon, Philip: 'Hafoty, Llansadwrn, Anglesey: excavations and survey of a medieval house', *Studia Celtica* 29 (1995)

Dolley, M.: *Anglo-Norman Ireland* (Dublin, 1972)

Duby, Georges: *Rural Economy* and *Country Life in the Medieval West*, trans. Cynthia Postan (London, 1968)

Edwards, J.G.: 'Sir Gruffudd Llwyd', *EHR* 30 (1915)

Emden, A.B.: *Biographical Register of the University of Cambridge to 1500* (Cambridge, 1961)

Emden, A.B.: *A Biographical Register of the University of Oxford to A.D 1500* (Oxford, 1957-9)

Emery, F.V.: *Wales* (London, 1969)

Evans, D.L.: 'Some notes on the history of the principality of Wales in the time of the Black Prince', *THSC* 1925-6

Evans, D.L.: 'Walter de Mauny, sheriff of Merioneth, 1332-72', *JMHRS* 4 (1963)

Evans, H.T.: *Wales and the Wars of the Roses* (Cambridge, 1915)

Fryde, Natalie: 'Welsh troops in the Scottish campaign of 1322', *BBCS* 26 (1974)

Genicot, Leopold: 'Crisis: from the middle ages to modern times', *Camb. Econ. Hist.*, i (2nd edn., Cambridge, 1966)

Godfrey, John: *The English Parish, 600-1300* (London, 1969)

Green, E. Tyrrell: 'The ecclesiology of Anglesey', *Y Cymmrodor* 40 (1929)

Greenly, E.: *The Geology of Anglesey* (Geological Survey, 1919)

Gresham, Colin A.: 'The Aberconway charter', *Arch. Camb.* 94 (1939)

Gresham, Colin A.: 'A further episode in the history of Clynnog Fawr', *THSC* 1966

Gresham, Colin A.: *Medieval Stone Carving in North Wales* (Cardiff, 1968)

Gresham, Colin A.: 'The parish of Beddgelert', *TCHS* (1969)

Griffith, J.E.: *Pedigrees of Anglesey and Caernarvonshire Families* (Horncastle, Lincs., 1914)

Griffiths, John: 'The revolt of Madog ap Llywelyn', *TCHS* 16 (1955)

Griffiths, Ralph A.: 'Some partisans of Owain Glyndŵr at Oxford', *BBCS* 20 (1963)

Griffiths, Ralph A.: 'The Glyndŵr rebellion in north Wales through the eyes of an Englishman', *BBCS* 22 (1967)

Griffiths, Ralph A.: *The Principality of Wales in the Later Middle Ages: the structure and personnel of government, I: South Wales, 1277-1536* (Cardiff, 1972)

Griffiths, Ralph A.: 'Wales and the marches', in S.B. Chrimes, C.D. Ross and Ralph A. Griffiths, eds., *Fifteenth Century England, 1399-1509* (Manchester, 1972)

Griffiths, Ralph A.: 'Patronage, politics and the principality of Wales, 1413-1461', in H. Hearder and H.R. Loyn, eds., *British Government and Administration: studies presented to S.B. Chrimes* (Cardiff, 1974)

Griffiths, Ralph A.: 'Richard, duke of York and the royal household in Wales, 1449-1450', *WHR* 8 (1976)

Griffiths, Ralph A.: 'An immigrant elite in the later middle ages: locating the De Parys family in north Wales and Chester', *WHR*, 25 (2010)

Gummer, Benedict: *The Scourging Angel: the Black Death in the British Isles* (London, 2009)

Hallam, H.E.: *Rural England, 1066-1348* (London, 1981)

Harding, Alan: *The Law Courts of Medieval England* (London, 1973)

Haslam, R., Orbach J. and Voelcker, A.: *The Buildings of Wales: Gwynedd* (London and New Haven, 2009)

Hatcher, John: *Plague, Population and the English Economy, 1348-1530* (London, 1977)

Hayman, Richard: 'Architecture and the development of Beaumaris in the nineteenth century', *Arch. Camb.* 153 (2004)

Hays, R.W.: *The History of the Abbey of Aberconway, 1184-1536* (Cardiff, 1963)

Heald, G.O.: 'Pentrefoelas mill, 1900-49', *TDHS*, 25 (1976)

Heer, Friedrich: *The Medieval World*, trans. Janet Sondheimer (New York, 1963)

Hewitt, H.J.: *Medieval Cheshire: an economic and social history of Cheshire in the reigns of the three Edwards* (Manchester, 1929)

Hilton, R.H.: *The Decline of Serfdom in Medieval England* (London, 1969)

Hilton, R.H.: *Bond Men Made Free* (London, 1973)

Hilton, R.H.: *The English Peasantry* in *the Later Middle Ages* (Oxford, 1979)

Hindle, Paul: *Medieval Roads and Tracks* (3rd edn., Princes Risborough, 1998)

Hoskins, W.G.: *The Making of the English Landscape* (Harmondsworth, 1970)

Hoskins, W.G.: *Fieldwork in Local History* (London, 1967)

Hoskins, W.G. and Stamp, L. Dudley: *The Common Lands of England and Wales* (London, 1963)

Hunnisett, R.F.: *The Medieval Coroner* (London, 1961)

Hyams, Paul R.: *Kings, Lords and Peasants in Medieval England: the common law of villeinage in the twelfth and thirteenth centuries* (Cambridge, 1980)

Insley, C.: 'Fact and fiction in fourteenth-century Gwynedd: the Aberconwy charters', *Studia Celtica* 33 (1999)

Jack, R. Ian: *Medieval Wales* (London, 1972)

Jack, R. Ian: 'The cloth industry in medieval Wales', *WHR* 10 (1981)

Jenkins, Dafydd: 'A lawyer looks at Welsh land law', *THSC* 1967

Jenkins, Dafydd: 'The significance of the law of Hywel', ibid., 1977

Jenkins, Dafydd: *Cyfraith Hywel* (Llandysul, 1970)

Johns, C.N.: 'The Celtic monasteries of north Wales', *TCHS* 21(1960)

Johnstone, Neil: 'An investigation into the royal courts of thirteenth-century Gwynedd' in Nancy Edwards, ed., *Landscape and Settlement in Medieval Wales* (Oxford, 1997)

Johnstone, Neil: 'Cae Llys, Rhosyr: a court of the princes of Gwynedd', *Studia Celtica* 33 (1999)

Johnstone, Neil: '*Llys* and *maerdref;* the royal courts of the princes of Gwynedd', *Studia Celtica* 34 (2000)

Jones, Arthur: 'The property of the Welsh friaries at the dissolution', *Arch.Camb.*, 1936

Jones, D. Cyril: 'The Bulkeleys of Beaumaris, 1440-1547', *TAAS* 1961

Jones, Evan J.: 'The enclosure movement in Anglesey 1788-1866', *TAAS* 2002, 2003

Jones, Francis: *The Holy Wells of Wales* (Cardiff, 1954)

Jones, Francis: 'The heraldry of Gwynedd', *TCHS* 24 (1963)

Jones, Glyn Penrhyn: *Newyn a Haint yng Nghymru* (Caernarfon, 1963)

Jones, Glyn Penrhyn: 'Some aspects of the medical history of Caernarfonshire', *TCHS* 23 (1962)

Jones, G.R.J: 'The distribution of medieval settlement in Anglesey', *TAAS* 1955

Jones, G.R.J: 'Anglesey portrayed', ibid., 1974

Jones, G.R.J: 'The tribal system in Wales: a re-assessment in the light of settlement studies', *WHR* 1 (1961)

Jones, G.R.J: 'The distribution of bond settlement in north-west Wales', ibid., 2 (1964)

Jones, G.R.J: 'Rural settlement in Anglesey', in G.R.J. Jones and S.J. Eyre, eds., *Geography as Human Ecology* (London, 1966)

Jones, G.R.J: 'The defences of Gwynedd in the thirteenth century', *TCHS* 30 (1969)

Jones, G.R.J: 'Post-Roman Wales', in H.P.R. Finberg, ed., *The Agrarian History of England and Wales, I-ii;A.D. 43-1042* (Cambridge, 1972)

Jones, G.R.J.: 'Multiple estates and early settlement', in P.H. Sawyer, ed., *English Medieval Settlement* (London, 1979)

Jones, G.R.J.: 'Early customary tenures in Wales and open-field agriculture', in Trevor Rowley, ed., *The Origin of Open Field Agriculture* (London, 1980)

Jones, G.R.J.: 'The multiple estate: a model for tracing the inter-relationships of society, economy and habitat' in Kathleen Biddiss, ed., *Archaeological Approaches to Medieval Europe* (Kalamazoo, 1984)

Jones, Gwilym T.: *The Fords of Anglesey / Rhydau Môn* (Bangor, 1992)

Jones, Gwilym T. and Roberts, Tomos: *Enwau Lleoedd Môn / The Place-Names of Anglesey* (Bangor and Llangefni, 1996)

Jones, H. Longueville: 'Mona Medieva XVI', *Arch. Camb.* 1855

Jones, Rhys: "The formation of the *cantref* and the commote in medieval Gwynedd', *Studia Celtica* 32 (1998)

Jordan, William Chester: *The Great Famine: northern Europe in the early fourteenth century* (Princeton, 1996)

Kershaw, Ian: 'The Great Famine and agrarian crisis in England, 1315-1322', in R.H. Hilton, ed., *Peasants, Knights and Heretics* (Cambridge, 1976)

Koebner, R.: 'The settlement and colonisation of Europe', *Camb. Econ Hist.* i

Laughton, Jane: *Life in a Late Medieval City: Chester 1275-1520* (Oxford, 2008)

Le Neve, J.: *Fasti Ecclesiae Anglicanae 1300-1541: XI: the Welsh Dioceses*, ed. B. Jones (London, 1965)

Lewis, Ceri W.: 'The treaty of Woodstock, 1247: its background and significance', *WHR* 2 (1964)

Lewis, E.A.: 'The decay of tribalism in north Wales', *THSC* 1902-3

Lewis, E.A.: 'The development of industry and commerce in Wales during the middle ages', *TRHS* (N.S.), 17 (1903)

Lewis, E.A.: 'A contribution to the commercial history of medieval Wales', *Y Cymmrodor*, 24 (1913)

Lewis, E.A.: *The Mediaeval Boroughs of Snowdonia* (London, 1912)

Lewis, Saunders: 'Dafydd ab Edmwnd', in J.E. Caerwyn Williams, ed., *Ysgrifau Beirniadol*, 10 (Denbigh, 1977)

Lloyd, D. Myrddin: 'The later Gogynfeirdd', in A.O.H. Jarman and Gwilym Rees Hughes, eds., *A Guide to Welsh literature*, ii (Swansea, 1979)

Lloyd, J.E.: *A History of Wales from the Earliest Times to the Edwardian Conquest* (3rd edn., London, 1939)

Lloyd, J.E.: *Owen Glendower* (Oxford, 1931)

Longley, David: *Medieval Settlement on Anglesey: an assessment of the potential for fieldwork* (GAT, n.d.)

Longley, David: 'Medieval settlement and landscape change on Anglesey', *Landscape History* 23 (2001)

Longley, David: 'The royal courts of the Welsh princes in Gwynedd' in Nancy Edwards, ed.,

*Landscape and Settlement in Medieval Wales* (Oxford, 1997)

Longley, David: *St Eilian's Church, Llaneilian* (GAT Report 559, Bangor, 2004, revised 2005)

Longley, David: *St Seiriol's Church and Priory House, Penmon* (GAT Report 648, Bangor, 2006)

Lynch, Frances: 'Report on the re-excavation of two Bronze Age cairns in Anglesey: Bedd Branwen and Treiorwerth', *Arch. Camb.* 120 (1971)

Macfarlane, Alan: *The Origins of English Individualism* (Oxford, 1978)

McKisack, May: *The Fourteenth Century 1307-99* (Oxford, 1959)

Messham, J.E.: 'The county of Flint and the rebellion of Owen Glyndwr in the records of the earldom of Chester', *JFHS* 23 (1967-8)

Miller, E. and Hatcher, J: *Medieval England: Rural Society and Economic Change, 1086-1348* (London, 1978)

Milward, Roy and Robinson, Adrian: *Landscapes of North Wales* (Newton Abbot, 1978)

Moore, David: 'Gruffudd ap Cynan and the medieval Welsh polity' in K.L. Maund, ed., *Gruffudd ap Cynan: a collaborative biography* (Woodbridge, 1996)

Morrall, John B.: *The Medieval Imprint: the founding of the western European tradition* (Harmondsworth, 1967)

Morris, Christopher: 'Plague in Britain', in Local Population Studies: *The Plague Reconsidered: a new look at its origins and effects in sixteenth and seventeenth century England* (Matlock, 1977)

Morris, J.E.: *The Welsh Wars of King Edward the First* (Oxford, 1901)

Morris, T.J.: 'The Liber Pontificalis Aniani of Bangor', *TAAS* 1962

Newton, K.C.: *Thaxted in the Fourteenth Century* (Chelmsford, 1960)

Newton, K.C.: *The Manor of Writtle* (Chichester, 1970)

Owen, Dorothy: 'Chapelries and rural settlement: an examination of some of the Kesteven evidence', in P.H. Sawyer, ed., *English Medieval Settlement*

Owen, Edward: 'Owain Lawgoch: Yeuain de Galles', *THSC* 1899-1900

Owen, Edward: 'The fate of the structures of Conway abbey and Bangor and Beaumaris friaries', *Y Cymmrodor*, 27 (1917)

Owen, Geraint Dyfnallt: *Elizabethan Wales* (Cardiff, 1966)

Owen, Hugh: 'Llanddwyn Island', *TAAS* 1920

Owen, Hugh: *Hanes Plwyf Niwbwrch ym Môn* (Caernarfon, 1952)

Owen, Morfydd E.: 'Functional prose: religion, science, grammar, law', in Jarman, A.O.H. and Hughes, Gwilym Rees, eds., *A Guide to Welsh Literature*, I (Swansea, 1976)

Owen, William: *Hanes Owain Glandwr, Blaenor y Cymry mewn Rhyfel* (Caernarfon, 1833)

Palmer, A.N.: 'The portionary churches of medieval north Wales', *Arch. Camb.*, 1886

Parain, C.: 'The evolution of agricultural technique', *Camb. Econ. Hist.* i

Peate, Iorwerth: *The Welsh House* (Liverpool, 1944)

Peate, Iorwerth: 'The antiquity of leprosy in Wales', *BBCS* 26 (1975)

Pierce, T. Jones: 'Some tendencies in the agrarian history of Caernarvonshire during the later middle ages', idem, *Medieval Welsh Society* (Cardiff, 1972)

Pierce, T. Jones: 'An Anglesey crown rental of the sixteenth century', ibid.

Pierce, T. Jones: 'The growth of commutation in Gwynedd in the thirteenth century', ibid.

Pierce, T. Jones: 'The *gafael* in Bangor MS. 1939', ibid.

Pierce, T. Jones: 'Medieval settlement in Anglesey', ibid.

Pierce, T. Jones: 'Medieval Cardiganshire: a study in social origins', ibid.

Pierce, T. Jones: 'The old borough of Nefyn, 1355-1882', *TCHS* 18 (1957)

Pierce, T. Jones: 'Landlords in Wales: the nobility and gentry', in Joan Thirsk, ed., *The Agrarian History of England and Wales, iv, 1500-1640* (Cambridge, 1967)

Platt, Colin: *The English Medieval Town* (London, 1979)

Platt, Colin: *Medieval England:* a *social history and archaeology from the conquest to A.D. 1600* (London, 1978)

Postan, M.M.: 'The fifteenth century', idem., *Essays on Medieval Agriculture and General Problems of the Medieval Economy* (Cambridge, 1973)

Postan, M.M.: 'Economic foundations of medieval society', ibid.

Postan, M.M.: 'Some agrarian evidence of declining population in the later middle ages', ibid.

Postan, M.M.: 'Medieval agrarian society in its prime; England', *Camb. Econ. Hist.* i

Postan, M.M.: *The Medieval Economy and Society* (Harmondsworth, 1975)

Powicke, F.M.: *The Thirteenth Century, 1216-1307* (Oxford, 1953)

Pratt, Derrick: 'Medieval people: the advowry tenents of Bromfield and Yale', *TDHS* 36 (1987)

Redknap, Mark: 'Llanbedrgoch: an early medieval settlement and its significance', *TAAS* 2007

Rees, William: *South Wales and the March, 1284-1415:* a *social and agrarian study* (Oxford, 1924)

Rees, William: 'The Black Death in Wales', in R.W. Southern, ed., *Essays in Medieval History* (London, 1968)

Rhys, John and Jones, D. Brynmor, *The Welsh People* (4th edn., London, 1906)

Richards, Melville: 'Gwŷr, gwragedd a gwehelyth', *THSC* 1965

Richards, Melville ed.: *An Atlas of Anglesey* (Llangefni, 1972)

Richards, Peter: *The Medieval Leper and his Northern Heirs* (Cambridge, 1977)

Robinson, A.H.W.: 'The sandy coast of south-west Anglesey', *TAAS* 1980

Roberts, E.: *The County of Anglesey* (Memoirs of the Soil Survey of Great Britain, 1958)

Roberts, Glyn: 'The Glynnes and the Wynns of Glynllifon', idem, *Aspects of Welsh History* (Cardiff, 1969)

Roberts, Glyn: 'Wyrion Eden', ibid.

Roberts, Glyn: 'The Dominican friary of Bangor', ibid.

Roberts, Glyn: 'Teulu Penmynydd', ibid.

Roberts, Glyn: 'Wales and England: antipathy and sympathy, 1282-1485', ibid.

Roberts, R.O.: 'The mills of Anglesey', *TAAS* 1958

Roberts, Tomos: 'Safle Capel Mair o Ddindryfwl', *TAAS* 1976-7

Rörig, Fritz: *The Medieval Town* (London, 1967)

Rowlands, E.I.: 'Nodiadau ar y traddodiad moliant a'r cywydd', *Llên Cymru*, 7 (1963)

Rowley, Trevor: *Villages in the landscape* (London, 1978)

Royal Commission on Ancient and Historical Monuments for Wales and Monmouthshire: *An Inventory of the Ancient Monuments in Anglesey* (London, 1937)

Russell, J.C.: *British Medieval Population* (Albuquerque, 1948)

Seebohm, F.: *The Tribal System in Wales* (London, 1895)

Sherborne, James: 'Richard II's return to Wales, July 1399', *WHR* 7 (1975)

Shrewsbury, J.F.D.: *A History of Bubonic Plague in the British Isles* (Cambridge, 1970)

Sims-Williams, Patrick: 'Edward IV's confirmation charter to Clynnog Fawr' in Colin Richmond and Isobel Harvey, eds., *Recognitions: essays presented to Edmund Fryde* (Aberystwyth, 1996)

Smith, J. Beverley: 'Crown and community in the principality of north Wales in the reign of Henry Tudor', *WHR* 3 (1966)

Smith, J. Beverley: 'Owain Gwynedd', *TCHS* 32 (1971)

Smith, J. Beverley: 'Gruffudd Llwyd and the Celtic alliance, 1315-6', *BBCS*, 26 (1976)

Smith, J. Beverley: 'Edward II and the allegiance of Wales', *WHR* 8 (1976)

Smith, J. Beverley: *Llywelyn ap Gruffudd, Prince of Wales* (Cardiff, 1998)

Smith, Llinos Beverley: 'The gage and the land market in late medieval Wales', *Econ. H.R.* 29 N.S. (1976)

Smith, Llinos Beverley: '*Tir Prid:* gages of land in late medieval Wales', *BBCS* 27 (1977)

Smith, Llinos Beverley: 'The *gravamina* of the community of Gwynedd against Llywelyn ap Gruffudd', *BBCS* 31 (1984)

Smith, Llinos Beverley: 'Towards a history of women in late medieval Wales' in Michael Roberts and Simone Clarke, eds., *Women and Gender in Early Modern Wales* (Cardiff, 2000)

Stephenson, David: *The Governance of Gwynedd* (Cardiff, 1984)

Stratton, J.M. and Brown, J. Houghton: *Agricultural Records, A.D. 220-1977* (2nd edn., London, 1978)

Taylor, A.J.: *The King's Works in Wales, 1277-1330* (London, 1974)

Thierry, Augustin: *La Conquête d'Angleterre par les Normands* (4th edn., Paris, 1859)

Thomas, Colin: 'Thirteenth-century farm economies in north Wales', *AHR* 16 (1968)

Thomas, Colin: 'Livestock numbers in medieval Gwynedd: some additional evidence', *JMHRS* 7 (1974)

Thomas, Colin: 'Peasant agriculture in medieval Gwynedd: an interpretation of the documentary evidence', *Folk Life* 1975

Titow, J.Z.: *English Rural Society, 1200-1350* (London, 1969)

Tout, T.F.: 'Wales and the march in the Barons' Wars', idem, *Collected Papers*, ii (Manchester, 1934)

Tout, T.F.: The captivity and death of Edward of Caernarvon', idem, *Collected Papers*, iii (Manchester, 1934)

Tout, T.F.: 'Medieval town planning', ibid.

Tout, T.F.: *Chapters in the Administrative History of Medieval England*, v (Manchester, 1933)

Trueman, A.E.: *Geology and Scenery in England and Wales* (Harmondsworth, 1949)

Usher, Gwilym: 'Holyhead as a fourteenth-century port', *BBCS* 15 (1954)

Usher, Gwilym: 'The foundation of an Edwardian borough: the Beaumaris charter, 1296', *TAAS* 1967

Usher, Gwilym: 'The Black Prince's Quo Warranto', *WHR* 7 (1974)

Waters, W.H.: *The Edwardian Settlement of North Wales in its Administrative and Legal Aspects, 1284-1343* (Cardiff, 1935)

White, Richard B.: 'The Llangadwaladr east window: an examination of the inscription and its personae', *TAAS* 1969-70

White, Richard B.: 'Excavations at Arfryn, Bodedern, long-cist cemeteries and the origins of Christianity in Britain', *TAAS* 1971-2

White, Richard B.: 'Rhosgoch to Stanlow Shell Oil pipeline', *BBCS* 27 (1977)

Wiliam, Dafydd Wyn: 'Llys Bodychen', *TAAS* 1966

Wiliam, Dafydd Wyn: 'Y traddodiad barddol ym mhlwyf Bodedern, Môn', *TAAS* 1969-70, 1971-2, 1973, 1974, 1975

Wiliam, Dafydd Wyn: 'Dafydd Benfras a'i ddisgynyddion', *TAAS* 1980

Williams, C.R.: *The History of Flintshire* (Denbigh, 1960)

Williams, Glanmor: *The Welsh Church from Conquest to Reformation* (Cardiff, 1962)

Williams, Glanmor: *Owen Glendower* (Oxford, 1966)

Williams, Glanmor: 'The Reformation in sixteenth-century Caernarfonshire', *TCHS* 27 (1966)

Williams, Gwyn A.: 'Owain Glyn Dŵr', in A.J. Roderick, ed., *Wales through the Ages*, i (Llandybïe, 1959)

Williams, John: *The History of Berw* (supplement to *TAAS* Llangefni, 1915)

Williams, W. Ogwen: *Tudor Gwynedd* (Caernarfon, 1958)

Williams, W. Ogwen: 'The social order in Tudor Wales', *THSC* 1967

Williams-Jones, Keith: 'Caernarvon', in Ralph A. Griffiths, ed., *Boroughs of Medieval Wales* (Cardiff, 1978)

Williams-Jones, Keith: 'The taking of Conwy castle, 1401', *TCHS* 39 (1978)

Willis, Browne: *A Survey of the Cathedral Church of Bangor* (London, 1721)

Wylie, J.H.: *History of England under Henry IV* (London, 1884-98)

# D Theses

Carr, A.D.: 'The Mostyn family and estate, 1200-1642', (Ph.D. Wales, 1975)

Evans, Colin M.: 'The medieval borough of Beaumaris and the commote of Dindaethwy, 1200-1600' (M.A. Wales, 1949)

Jones, D. Cyril: 'The Bulkeleys of Baron Hill, 1440-1621' (M.A. Wales, 1958)

Jones, J. Rowland: 'The development of the Penrhyn estate up to 1431' (M.A. Wales, 1955)

# INDEX

*abadaeth* 215, 217, 226

Aberalaw 68, 73, 178, 240, 258

Aber Braint 217

Aberconwy abbey (Caerns.) 26&n., 84, 85, 213

  abbot of 42, 46, 59, 214

  lands of 46, 214-5

  treaty of (1277) 30-31

Aberffraw 8, 10, 14, 17, 27, 33&n., 49, 57-8, 64, 65&n., 66, 67, 72, 80, 83, 87, 88, 93, 94, 95, 97n., 99n., 103, 110, 138, 140, 205n., 212, 213, 222, 224, 241

  cantref of 67, 85, 95, 97n., 107, 109-10, 239n.

  court buildings 86&n., 101, 108

  farmer of 57, 245. *See also* Bulkeley, William, sen.; Bulkeley, William jun.; Dafydd Goch ap Gruffudd; St. Peter, Sir John de

  renders and services of bondmen 94-5

  *rhaglaw* of *See* Goronwy ap Tudur (d.1331); Hywel ap Gruffudd

  *rhingyll* of. *See* Chebsey, Thomas de; Heyton, Roger de; Iorwerth Foel

Abergele (Denbs.) 29n.

Aber Lleiniog 22

Abermalltraeth 49, 81

Abermenai (Southcrook) 5, 8, 9, 21, 23, 24n., 80, 85

  ferry 9, 207, 245, 256

Abingdon, Richard de 97

accounts 41-2, 58-60, 79, 86-9, 115-6, 256-8

  bailiffs' 193-5, 207

  chamberlains' 59-60, 73, 80, 86-8, 251, 254-5

  coroners' 70, 135

  escheators' 40, 70-71, 89, 104, 121, 123-6, 135-7, 207, 253-4

  *rhingylls'* 41-2, 59-60, 72-3, 80, 239-41

  sheriffs' 37-9, 42-3, 58-60, 83, 120, 129-30, 185-6, 246

Adda ab Adda Fawr 137

  ab Einion 65

  ab Ieuan ap Madog 126

Goch 49

Grwn 223-4

Was 240

*affers* 64&n., 65, 69, 70, 136

Agnes, widow of Nicholas le Barber 204

Alaw, river 11, 77

Alaw'r-beirdd 217

Alcock, Hugh, dean of Bangor 217n.

Alice, wife of John Lagan 201

Amlwch 12, 14n., 50, 71, 73, 92, 174, 211, 213, 218, 219, 224, 241

*amobr* 83, 94, 95, 96n., 99, 100, 101, 107n., 112, 121

Angharad ferch Cuhelyn 135

  ferch Dafydd ap Cynwrig 182

  ferch Ednyfed ap Tudur 165

  ferch Gruffudd 93

  ferch Gruffudd ap Dafydd ap Tudur 183

  ferch Gwilym ap Gruffudd 179, 231

  ferch Hywel ap Cynwrig Fychan 182

  ferch Hywel y Farf 182

  ferch Ithel Fychan ab Ithel Gam 181

  ferch Madog ap Gruffudd Fychan 181

  ferch Madog *Talior* 70

  ferch Tudur ap Goronwy 181

  wife of Gruffudd ap Cynan 23

  wife of Henry de Trim 197

  wife of Madog Sionc 135

  wife of Rhys ap Tudur ap Syr Dafydd 132

Anglesey, archdeacon of 51, 102, 205, 212, 218, 225, 253. *See also* Einion

  coroner of 39&n. *See also* Gwilym ap Gruffudd ap Hywel; Hywel Lipa; Madog ab Einion

  escheator of 40, 48, 52. *See also* Clerk, Henry; Dafydd Fychan ap Dafydd Llwyd; Gwilym ap Gruffudd ap Hywel; Huntingdon, William de; Ieuan ap Tudur Llwyd; Maredudd ap Cynwrig; Maredudd ap Tudur; Pykemere, Richard de; Rhys ap Tudur ap Goronwy

  extent of, 1284 30, 59, 66-8, 80, 89, 94-5, 96-101, 138-9, 185-7 extent of, 1352  28, 42, 43, 52, 59, 84, 95-101, 101n., 107-9, 112, 121-2, 133, 208, 209, 241-2

sheriff of  34, 37-9, 42, 50-52, 59-60, 75, 129, 188, 238. *See also* Barton, Ralph de; Clerk, Adam; Cynwrig ap Gruffudd; Danvers, Thomas; Einion ab Ieuan; Ellerton, William de; Golding, Richard; Gruffudd ap Madog Gloddaith; Gruffudd ab Owain; Gruffudd ap Rhys; Gwilym ap Gruffudd ap Gwilym; Harborough, Thomas; Ieuan Chwerw; Madog Llwyd; Pykemere, Richard de; Pulesdon, Roger de; Rhys ap Llywelyn ap Hwlcyn; Rhys ap Tudur ap Goronwy; Stanley, John; Strangeways. Roger; Walsh, John; Winchester, Walter de; Wode, John del

Archwedlog (Denbs.)  107

Arddun ferch Gruffudd  113, 232

   ferch Maredudd Ddu  181-2

Ardern, Thomas  221

Ardescote, William, prior of Penmon  228, 229

Ardudwy (Mer.)  138

Arfon (Caerns.)  21, 28

Arw, Yr  110

assise, rents of (quit-rents)  38, 41, 94-5, 96-7, 98-9, 101, 107-8, 215-6, 257

Audlem, John  205

Augmentations, Court of  234

Augustinian Canons  215-6, 227&n.

avowry  13, 102, 115-6, 130, 136, 240, 241, 242

Babham, Thomas  56

Bagnall, Sir Henry  170

Bala (Mer.)  190, 197

Baldwin, archbishop of Canterbury  3, 25

Bancenyn  215, 233

Bangor (Caerns.)  9, 22, 25, 202, 213, 238, 246, 250

  bishop of  33n., 38, 42, 46, 59, 84, 93, 97n., 107, 122, 164, 192, 213-4, 229, 238 *See also* Cliderow, John; Bulkeley, Arthur; Dean, Henry; Pigot, de; Salcot, John; Swaffham, John

  bishop of, lands of  123, 213n., 213-4

  bishop of, lands of, extent of, 1306  8, 13, 68, 77, 84-5, 94, 120-1, 123, 124, 139, 213-4

  cathedral  218, 225

  dean of  189, 218, 225. *See also* Alcock, Hugh; Bondeby, Nigel; Kyffin, Richard; Martyn, John; Morgan, Hugh

  diocese of  219, 222-3, 224-5

  Dominican friary  69, 229, 231

prior of. *See* Llywelyn, Brother

Barker, David le  208

barley  63, 65, 66, 67&n., 68, 70, 71, 84, 89, 94, 139

Barmouth (Mer.)  75

Barneby, Thomas  250-1, 251n., 253, 255

Barton, Ralph de  51

Bate, John  176, 203, 228

battles

  Aberconwy  26

  Bosworth  173

  Bron-yr-erw  21

  'Coedaneu'  26

  Largs  30

  Mynydd Carn  21

  Pentraeth  25

  Poitiers  57

  Porthaethwy  26

  Shrewsbury  250

  Tal Moelfre  24-5

Beaumaris  5&n., 8, 9, 14, 34, 38, 43, 46, 51, 55, 59, 63, 76, 79, 86, 114, 116, 125, 128, 135, 137, 138, 174, 175-7, 179, 185, 187, 189-205, 206, 208, 210, 228-9, 231, 238, 240-1, 245, 249n., 250, 251, 252, 253, 256

  alderman of  196. *See also* Bulkeley, Richard; Bulkeley, William, sen.; Bulkeley, William, jun.; Golding, Richard; Ingram, William; Norreys, Thomas; Russell, Peter

  bailiffs of  60, 177, 190, 191n., 193-4, 193n., 195-6, 199-201, 202, 209

  borough, lands of  9, 125, 190-1, 202

  burgesses of  5, 51, 52, 55, 76, 78, 80, 116, 137, 175, 190-5, 196-201, 204-5, 208, 210, 230, 245, 250

  castle  34, 60, 79, 86, 120, 189, 190, 191-2, 193, 195, 200, 203-4, 216, 250, 251, 252, 255

  castle, prisoners in  88, 203-4, 250

  castle, repairs to  86, 87-8, 204

  charter of  175, 190, 196

  church  176&n., 192&n., 202, 204-5, 232, 233

  constable of  48, 190, 196, 204, 206, 250 *See also* Bold, Thomas; Goronwy ap Tudur (d.1382); St. Peter, John de; Sapy, John de; Vielville, Sir Rowland

  deputy-constable of  175 *See also* Bulkeley, Rowland; Bulkeley, William, sen.; Moyle, John

  ferry  9, 188, 193, 194

  markets and fairs  72, 187-8, 188n., 192, 193

port of 8, 73, 78-80, 192-3
town walls 86, 192, 195, 234, 257
trade 192-3
Welshmen in 196-9, 223-4
Bedd Branwen 4n.
Beddgelert, prior of 216n
    See also Deicws ap Cuhelyn
    priory 216, 219n., 224, 227
Bede 3, 63
bequests 69-70, 113, 167-8, 176-7, 230-1, 232
Berw 129, 171-2, 182, 209
Berw Isaf 17, 129, 216
Berw Uchaf 110, 129
Beuno, tenants of 46-7, 73, 106, 217
Bickerstaff, Thomas 201n.
billetting 95n., 96, 100-1, 122
Bispham (Lancs.) 202
Black Death 15, 40, 41, 71, 78, 116, 121, 124,
    125, 129, 226, 239-43, 244, 246
Black Prince. See Edward, prince of Wales
Bleddyn ap Cynfyn 21
    ap Llywelyn Croen, sons of 92
    Fardd 178
Bodafon 48, 48, 51, 77, 108, 120, 122, 174,
    254
Bod-Ddeiniol 11n.
Bodedern 9, 14, 19, 44, 93, 110, 113, 117, 122,
    224n., 232
Bodednyfed 49, 100, 240, 258
Bodegri 120
Bodeon 104, 123, 173, 182-3
Bodewran 108
Bodewryd 34, 179, 215
Bodfa 50
Bodfardden 124, 257, 258
Bodfeddan 110
Bodffordd 9, 14, 29n., 45, 124, 133, 179, 253
Bodffyddion 107n.
Bodgedwydd 215
Bodgylched 191
Bodhunod 100, 240, 258
Bodlew 100, 129, 257
Bodorgan 120-1
Bodowyr 110, 171
Bodrida 257
Bodronyn 125, 240, 254, 258
Boduan (Caerns.) 50
Bodwigan 121
Bodwrdin 27n., 93

Bodwrog 17, 18, 47, 138, 173
Bodwylog 120
Bodychen 138, 172, 173, 183, 213
Bodynolwyn 5, 67, 101, 159, 240, 241, 258
Bodynwy (Carwad) 7, 191n., 194, 257
Bold, Thomas 251, 255
Bolde, Alice 175n., 177
    Bartholomew de 175n., 177
Bondeby, Nigel, dean of Bangor 221
bondmen, bond tenants 12-13, 43, 66-8, 75,
    83, 85, 87, 91-107, 110, 114, 123, 133, 136-
    7, 186-7, 206, 220, 226, 238, 239, 240, 257-
    9, 257n.
    sale of 92-3, 167
borough courts 46, 190, 193, 195-6, 206
Borth Wen, Y 16
Botan 122, 258
Boteler, Sir Ralph 58
Botell, Robert 210
Bourgneuf 247n.
Brecon, lordship of 106
brewing 44, 63-4&n., 66, 74, 138, 139, 186,
    188
Bristol 78
Brittany 79
Bromfield, Richard 224,
    and Yale, lordship of (Denbs.) 115n., 242
Bron-y-foel 165
Brut y Tywysogyon 30
Bryan, David 136
Brynberfi 77
Bryngwallan 129
Bryn-y-chwil 132
Bryn yr Hen Bobl 4n.
Buarth-brych 77
Buckingham duke of 106
Bulkeley (Ches.) 190
    family 137, 168, 174-7, 202-3, 233-4, 259
    of Porthaml, family 171
    Arthur, bishop of Bangor 225.
    Bartholomew 177n.
    David 249n.
    Edmund 132, 176-7
    Elen 7, 131-2, 175-6, 224
    Hugh 176-7
    Hugh (Llanfechell) 225
    Richard 176-7, 203
    Sir Richard 214, 229, 233, 234
    Rowland 92, 132, 133, 170n., 170-1, 176-7

Sioned 179, 183

Thomas 234&n.

Thomas (Llangefni) 225

William, sen. 80, 131-2, 174-7, 175n., 179, 183, 202-3, 204-5, 224, 232

William, jun. 57&n., 177&n., 203

William, son of Rowland 170-1, 214

Bunbury (Ches.) 190

burgages 125, 176, 186-7, 188&n., 191, 193-5, 198-9, 198n., 201-3, 204, 207-10, 228, 245

Burgh, Hubert de 27

Burnedish, Benedict de 222

Burnell, Robert 32

William 63

Burton (Ches.) 75

Roger de 196-7

Bwrdd Arthur 8


Cadnant 9

Cadrod Hardd, lineage of 108, 160, 198n.

Cadwaladr, St. 85, 219

ap Gruffudd ap Cynan 24&n.

Cadwgan ap Bleddyn 22-3

ap Llywarch 171

Boatman 79

Cae Glas, Y (Llanbedr-goch) 16

Maes Yrron (Penhwnllys) 16

Mawr (Llanfechell) 16

Caerdegog 72, 108, 125, 240, 241, 254

Caergybi. See Holyhead

Caernarfon 5n., 9, 22, 32, 34, 39, 42, 49, 51, 52, 55, 79, 81, 85, 86n., 109, 116, 140n, 161, 175n., 182, 185, 186, 191, 192, 193, 195&n., 196-7, 198, 201&n., 206, 208, 237-8, 245, 250, 251n.

Exchequer of 37-8, 54, 106

Caernarfonshire 5, 28, 42, 50, 51, 60-1, 75n., 105, 128, 166-7, 176, 189, 197, 238, 244-5, 249, 255, 256

Caerwys (Flints.) 205, 209

Cafflogion (Caerns.) 64, 65, 66, 239

Cafnan 240

Canterbury, archbishop of. See Baldwin; Warham, William; Winchelsey, Robert

Cantref, deanery of 211, 213

Capel Halen 19

Caradog, river 10

Cardiganshire 101, 180-1

Cari ferch Iorwerth Tew Tastour 104

Carmarthenshire 180, 190n.

Carnan 109n., 116n.

Uchaf 131

Carneddor 103, 178, 240, 258

carpenters 5, 82, 86-8

Carwad. See Bodynwy

Carwed, lineage of 12, 53, 108, 160, 161, 162, 173-4, 183

Castell, John, prior of Penmon 228

Castell Bwlchgwyn 75, 109, 131-3, 176

Castellior 29n., 130, 191

cattle 65, 68, 69-71, 73, 89, 112, 114, 136-7

Cecilia Anglica 116

Cefn-coch 33

Cefn Cwmwd 9

Cefni, river 6

Cefn-poeth 110

Cemais 14, 15, 63, 57, 80, 93, 97n., 110, 140, 205n., 215, 241

bond tenants and services 95-6, 98-9

court buildings 86, 105

farmer of. See Bulkeley, William, sen.; Llywelyn ap Hwlcyn ap Hywel; Ieuan ap Tudur Llwyd; Maredudd ap Cynwrig; Missenden, Thomas de

Cemlyn 8, 80, 81, 107, 108, 125, 134, 176, 254

Ceri (Mont.) 181

Cerrigcafael 110, 241

Cerrigceinwen 71, 218

Cerrigdewi 47

Cerrig-gwyddyl 190-1, 191n.

Cerrigtegfan 109

Chamberlain Robert de 125

chantries 199, 202, 204, 218, 222

chapels-of-ease 18-9, 224, 232n., 259

Cheadle (Ches.) 174, 202

Chebsay, Thomas de 55

Cheshire 5, 51-2, 174, 176, 190, 201, 202, 248

Chester 22, 24, 25, 26, 32, 75, 78-9, 80-1, 165, 193n. 249-50, 255, 261

earldom of 41

Chirkland (Denbs.) 62

churches 5, 13-14, 17-19, 18n., 23, 34, 48, 71, 113, 168, 172, 173, 204-5, 208, 210, 211-3, 213n., 215-9, 222, 224, 227&n., 230-3

Cinque Ports 30, 32&n.

Cistercians 214-5

Clafdy 140

Clark, Margaret 203n.

clasau 14, 18-9, 212, 215, 216-8, 218n., 226

Clegyrog 27n., 108

Cleifiog  11, 35, 57, 104n., 108, 116, 173, 175, 241, 245, 254, 257
Clement, Hugh  223
clergy  204-5, 218-26, 253
Clerk family  137, 199-200
  Adam  51, 200, 203n
  Henry (1301)  199, 208
  Henry (escheator)  52, 114, 199-200
  Hugh  200, 203n.
  John  200
  Nicholas  200
  Richard  200
  Robert 200
  Thomas  194, 200
  William  200
Cliderow, John, bishop of Bangor  231
Clorach  12n., 70-1, 73, 124-5, 136, 164, 253, 254
cloth  70, 72-3, 79, 82, 136, 186, 193
Clun (Salop)  242n.
Clynnog Fawr  46-7, 216-7, 225, 226, 233
  Fechan  217
Cnwc y Tair Lôn  132
Cnwchdyrnog  77, 240
coal-mining  74
Cobham, Eleanor, duchess of Gloucester  203-4
Cochwillan family  166
Coedana  122
Coedcadw  5-6
Colle, Thomas de  55
Coluddyn Ci  48&n.
commortha  133
commote  24, 37, 40-1, 50, 60
  court (hundred court)  38, 41, 42, 4, 45-6, 60, 74, 103-4, 105, 107, 121, 122, 138
commutation  95-6, 107-8, 108n., 119, 121-2, 215-6
Conquet  79
Conws ap Hywel ab Iorwerth Ddu  183
Conwy  51, 79, 80, 175n., 177, 186, 191&n., 192, 193, 195, 196, 197, 198, 199, 202, 203, 214, 237-8, 245
  castle  165, 177, 249, 254
  river  25, 26, 31
  William  230n.
Conysiog  67, 108, 110, 122, 181, 212
  Lan  13, 110, 123
  Lys  11-12, 13, 110
Cookes, Robert  56
Cornwall  45n., 227n

Cornwy  77, 102, 178
  Lan  77, 120
  Lys  39, 215
coroner  39-40, 39n., 40n., 70
Cororion (Caerns.)  166, 168
Cors y Bol  3, 6
  Ddyga. See Malltraeth Marsh
  Erddreiniog  7
  Llanddyfnan  7
county court  23, 37-9, 43-4, 107, 111, 112, 121, 122, 210
  gaol  39&n.
court, suit of  107, 112, 121, 122, 214
Crafgoed  18n.
Cranwell, William de  84, 125, 201-2
Creuddyn (Caerns.)  64, 68
Cricieth (Caerns.)  79, 193, 198n.
crime  48-50
Cristin, wife of Owain Gwynedd  25
Cromwell, Thomas  233-4
Crosby (Lancs.)  190
Crymlyn  114, 133n., 215, 234, 254
Crymlyn y Mynydd  117
customs  76, 78, 186
Cwm-hir abbey (Rad.)  216n.
Cybi, St.  218, 252
cyfran  12
cylchoedd (circuits)  95&n., 96, 98, 100, 101, 121-2
Cynan ab Iago  21
  ab Owain Gwynedd  28, 33
  ab Owain Gwynedd, sons of  26
Cynddelw ap Conws  21
  ap Thomas  115
Cynlas  226
Cynllaith Owain (Denbs.)  181
cynnwys  130, 169
Cynwrig ap Dafydd ab Ithel Fychan  180
  ap Dafydd Fychan  183
  ap Gruffudd  51
  ap Hywel ap Cynwrig  174
  ab Ieuan ap Llywelyn  69, 231, 232
  ap Madog, carpenter  87
  ap Madog ap Cynwrig  124
  ap Maredudd Ddu ap Goronwy  170, 182
  ap Meurig  69
  ap Thomas  115
Cynwrig Fychan  254
  Teg  33, 124

Dafarn, Y 18n.
Dafydd ab Adda 115
    ab Angharad ferch Gaynor. *See* Dafydd ap
        Hywel ap Gruffudd
    ap Bleddyn, Brother 285n
    ap Cynwrig 70
    ap Dafydd ap Gwilym 174
    ap Dafydd ap Symon (Dafydd ap Dew Moel)
        104-5, 226
    ap Deicws ap y Gof 136
    ab Edmwnd 179
    ab Einion 61, 191&n., 196
    ab Einion ab Iorwerth 135
    ab Einion Ddu 136
    ab Elis 49
    ap Gruffudd 31, 33
    ap Gruffudd ap Dafydd ap Hywel 7
    ap Gwilym 111, 209
    ap Gwilym ap Dafydd 174, 179
    ap Hwlcyn ap Goronwy 132
    ap Hywel (1328) 238
    ap Hywel ap Griffydd (Ddydd ab Angharad
        ferch Gaynor) 113, 133
    ap Hywel ap Gruffudd (Dafydd ab Angharad
        ferch Iolyn) 16
    ap Hywel Ddu 135
    ab Ieuan ap Hywel 56n., 122, 174, 179, 199,
        231
    ab Ieuan ab Iorwerth ap Hwfa 132
    ab Ieuan ap Tudur Llwyd 221, 254
    ab Ieuan Moel 71, 104, 137
    ab Ieuan Wyddel 53
    ab Iocyn 70
    ab Ithel 135
    ab Ithel (Dinsylwy) 140
    ab Ithel ap Gwyddel 50
    ab Ithel ab Ieuan 99n.
    ap Jack ap Diarmed 117
    ap Llywelyn 27&n., 215
    ap Llywelyn ap Hywel 132
    ap Llywelyn ap Maredudd 34-5
    ab Owain Gwynedd 23-5
    ap Rhys ap Dafydd 174
    ap Rhys ap Llywelyn ap Gruffudd 17
    ap Tangwystl ferch Gwenhwyfar ferch Madog
        131
    ap Tegwared ap Madog 102
    ap Tegwared Ddu 106
    ap Tudur ap Dafydd ap Gwyn 131

    Benfras 178
    Chwith 30n.
    Chwith Bach 93
    Ddu 69
    Ddu ap Tegwared 74
    Don 77
    Ffon 105
    Fychan (Eiriannell) 68
    Fychan ap Dafydd Llwyd 40, 93, 129, 183
    Goch ap Gruffudd 252
    Hakeney 133&n.
    Hir ap Madog ab Ieuan ab Einion 70
    Llwyd (Tre Fraint) 121
    Llwyd ap Dafydd ap Tegwared 99
    Rwth ap Dafydd ap Goronwy 80
    Rwth ap Llywelyn Foel 120
    Trefor 225, 232n.
Dalton, Alice 169
    Sir Richard 169
Danvers, Thomas 86, 191, 201
David, ditcher 87
Daykyn Kat 79
Ddrudwy 110
Dean, Henry, bishop of Bangor 77
Degannwy (Caerns.) 27, 30, 239
Deheubarth 21, 24n., 180
Deicws ap Cuhelyn, prior of Beddgelert 136
    ap Cynwrig ap Maredudd 170&n.
    ap Hywel ap Dafydd ap Cadwgan 136
    ab Ieuan ap Tegwared 207
Deio ap Tudur 198
Delves, John de 28, 42, 52
Denbigh 185n., 195, 248
    lordship of 29n., 107, 222, 239, 249
Derby, earls of 202
Deri 14, 100, 105, 106, 135, 258, 259
Deubwll 110
diet 138-9
Dindaethwy, commote of 5, 6, 27, 29n., 33, 39,
    54, 68, 75-6, 77, 80, 83, 84, 92, 93, 107n.,
    109, 112, 115, 116&n., 117, 119, 120, 121,
    122, 123, 124, 126, 130-1, 163n, 166, 167,
    185, 192, 202, 213&n., 215, 240, 241, 244,
    246, 254
    commote court 44, 73, 116n.
    *rhaglaw* and raglotry of 54
        *See also* Cookes, Robert; Goronwy ap Tudur
        (d.1331); Goronwy ap Tudur (d.1382);
        Gwilym ap Gruffudd ap Gwilym; Hywel ap
        Tudur; Middlemore, Nicholas; Rossington,

Henry; Rhys ap Tudur ap Goronwy; Tudur ap Goronwy (Tudur Hen); Tudur ap Goronwy ap Tudur

*rhingyll* and ringildry of 54, 60, 80, 83, 244. *See also* Gwilym ap Gruffudd ap Gwilym; Gruffudd ab Einion Tew; Ieuan ap Dafydd ap Goronwy.

tourn 7, 50, 134, 140

Dindaethwy and Twrcelyn, deanery of 204, 211

Dindryfwl 7, 9, 19, 85, 104, 110&n., 133, 241, 257

Din Llugwy 19

Dinsylwy 126, 135, 140, 162n., 191n.

Rys 92, 126

Dolbadarn (Caerns.) 5n., 86, 88

Dolgynwal (Caerns.) 212

Doncaster, William de 79

Drogheda 79, 81

Dronwy 34, 77, 125, 178, 241, 247

Dryll y Pandy 72

Dublin 21, 22-3, 26, 27, 75, 81, 252

Dulas, port of 8, 80

Dun, Thomas 80-1

Dwygyfylchi (Caerns.) 50

Dwynwen 4, 231-2, 231n., 232n.

Dwyran 12n., 92n.

Beuno 217

Esgob 17n.

Dyddgu ferch Iorwerth ab Adda Ddu 243

Dyffryn Clwyd (Denbs.) 166&n., 242

Dynieton, Edmund 238

Edeirnion (Mer.) 180

Edmund ap Geoffrey 229n.

Ednyfed ap Tudur 164-5, 178, 181, 253

Fychan 29, 47, 48, 53, 109, 114, 124, 160-5, 162n., 175, 180-1, 246, 248, 255

Edward I 27, 30-4, 37, 43, 47, 55, 59, 61, 63, 94, 99n., 105, 125, 163, 166, 185, 187, 188, 189-90, 191, 196, 199, 208, 213, 215, 216n., 229

Edward II 30, 35, 45, 54, 61, 62, 88, 119, 134, 160, 161, 162, 192, 197, 200, 207, 212

Edward III 46, 55, 61, 162

Edward IV 217

Edward of Caernarfon. *See* Edward II

Edward, prince of Wales (the Black Prince) 41, 55, 57, 194, 196, 199, 222, 230

Edward ap Dafydd Was 134

Efa, ferch Dafydd Wyddel 117

ferch Gruffudd ap Tudur 164

ferch Gruffudd Goch

ferch Hywel ap Gruffudd ap Dafydd 141

ferch Hywel ab Ieuan ab Adda 106

ferch Madog ap Wyn 70, 136

Ddu 133

*Tope* 49

Eglwys Ail. *See* Llangadwaladr

Eifionydd (Caerns.) 182, 183

Eilian, St. 107, 218, 232

Einion, archdeacon of Anglesey 222n.

Brother, canon of Beddgelert 219n.

locksmith 88

Master 141, 188&n., 189n., 208

ap Deicws 65

ap Goronwy, prior of Penmon 228

ap Gruffudd 34n.

ap Gruffudd (1322-3) 115n.

ap Gwalchmai 177-8

ab Ieuan 51, 84, 161, 193, 197&n., 198

ab Ieuan ab Einion 105

ab Iocyn 64, 65, 66

ap Rhodri 108, 110

Bach 87-8

Ddu 188n.

Felyn 75

Goch 75

Goch Ffisigwr 208

Grach 70

Eiriannell 68, 69, 125, 141, 183, 191n., 221, 224, 254

Eleanor of Castile 45

daughter of Edward II 45n.

de Montfort, princess of Wales 229

ferch Gwilym ap Gruffudd 168

Elen ferch Gruffudd ap Hywel Escut 69, 113

ferch Gwilym ap Madog 209

ferch Llywelyn ap Hwlcyn 179-80

ferch Owain ap Thomas ap Llywelyn 181

ferch Richard ap Maredudd ap Thomas 170-1

wife of Cynwrig Fychan 254

Elidir Sais 178

Elis, Hugh 225

Elizabeth, daughter of Watcyn Fychan 183

ferch Gwilym ap Gruffudd 168

Ellerton, William de 38

Enlli (Caerns.) 227

Erddreiniog 29n., 47, 50, 109, 124, 163n., 164, 179

Erddylad ferch Dafydd ab Iorwerth 182

Ereswell, John de  161

escheator  39n., 40&n., 59, 70-1, 73, 89, 103,
    104, 119, 125, 136-7, 140, 195, 208, 253-4

escheats, escheat lands  38, 41, 48, 116, 119-20,
    121, 122, 124, 130, 170, 174, 240, 241, 242,
    244

fairs  72-3, 192, 205, 230
famine  237-8
Faversham, Simon de  81
Felton, William de  191
ferries  9, 230
Ffrwd-y-cleifion  140
Ffynnon y Badell  9
fish, fisheries  22, 76-8, 139
Flint  198n., 247, 248
Flintshire  41n., 58, 61, 128, 165, 166
food-renders  66-8, 91, 94, 98-9, 107n., 119,
    138-9, 214, 215-6
Forde, William  205
Forrest, John  196
Four Mile Bridge (Pont Rhyd-bont)  9-10
France  139, 186, 247
Franciscans  229-30
freemen, free tenants  14, 83, 85, 91, 107-8,
    115, 119, 122
Friend, Edward  79, 193&n.
Fryser, Robert  137

gafael, gafaelion  95-6, 97-9, 99n., 126, 241
Gafael Dafydd ap Tegwared  99
    Goronwy ab Edayfed  168
    Gwenllian  29n.
    Madog ab Adda  99
    Madog ap Cynwrig  99
    Madog ap Wyn  99
    Philip Môn  99n.
    y Porthorion  99n.
Gafrogwy  47&n., 57, 168, 175n.
Gallows Point  76
Garddau  95, 241
Garddwr  12
Gascony  190, 208
Geffrey, Rowland  229
Gelliniog  26n., 46, 214-5
Generys ferch Madog ap Goronwy Fychan
    114, 164, 166
Genilles ferch Philip ab Ithel  119
Geraint, lineage of  109, 160
Gerald of Wales  3, 4, 23, 25, 63, 138, 220n.,
    226-7

Gesail Gyfarch (Caerns.)  182
Glasgrug  20n.
Gloddaith (Caerns.)  183
Glyn, Dr. William  233
Glyndyfrdwy (Mer.)  181, 248
Glynllifon (Caerns.)  182, 233
gobrestyn  38, 44, 93, 101, 121, 224
Godfrey family  201, 228
    John, prior of Penmon  201, 228, 233-4, 234n.
    Thomas  201, 233n.
    Thomas, prior of Penmon  201, 228
    William  201
Godred Crovan, king of Man  22
Gogarth (Caerns.)  68
Golding, Richard  51, 125, 126, 201-2
Goodhew, John  195
Gorddinog (Caerns.)  182
Goronwy, rhingyll of Twrcelyn  34
    ap Dafydd ab Ithel  230n.
    ap Dafydd Fychan  132-3
    ab Ednyfed Fychan  48
    ab Einion ab Ieuan ap Madog  136
    ap Hwlcyn ap Dafydd  169
    ap Hywel Foel  198n.
    ab Ieuan  133n.
    ap Maredudd  103
    ap Rhirid Crydd  103
    ap Rhys ap Goronwy Pill  136
    ap Tudur (d.1331)  161, 162, 163, 180
    ap Tudur (d.1382)  137, 163, 164&n., 165,
        178, 181, 214n., 230-1, 233, 256
    ap Tudur ap Hywel  125
    Crach  54-5, 105
    Fychan  166
    Llwyd  169
    Teiliwr  136
Grace-Dieu abbey (Mon.)  216n.
grazing  11, 64, 65, 71, 121, 124, 186, 239, 240,
    241, 257, 258
Griffith family of Penrhyn (Caerns.)  77-8, 114,
    166n., 168, 202, 253
    Edmund  169, 222n.
    Margery  113-114
    Maurice  170
    Piers  168
    Reynold  234
    Robert  169-70, 169n.
    Rowland  113-114

William (Gwilym Fychan) 76, 77-8, 93, 168-9, 176
William (illegitimate son of Gwilym Fychan) 169
Sir William 168, 202
Griffri, sons of 108
Gruffudd ab Aron 128
ap Cynan 8, 21-3, 35, 117, 159&n., 162, 182, 212, 227
ap Cynan ab Owain Gwynedd 26&n., 85, 214
ap Dafydd ap Tudur 166
ap Dafydd Goch 122
ab Einion ap Hywel 207
ab Einion Tew 252-3
ap Goronwy 119
ap Gwenwynwyn 229
ap Gwilym ap Gruffudd 114
ap Hywel 33n.
ap Hywel ap Gruffudd 162
ap Hywel ap Gwerfyl 105
ap Hywel ab Iorwerth ab Ieuan Goch 102-3
ap Hywel ap Tudur ap Dafydd 16
ap Hywel Ddu 140
ab Ieuan ap Gruffudd 183
ab Iorwerth, sons of 97n.
ab Iorwerth ap Gwyddel 117
ab Iorwerth ap Maredudd 178
ab Iorwerth Foel 33, 99n., 208
ab Iorwerth Wyddel 117
ap Llywelyn 21, 217
ap Llywelyn ap Hwlcyn 173
ap Llywelyn ab Ieuan 93
ap Llywelyn ab Iorwerth 27
ap Llywelyn ab Iorwerth ap Rhys 141
ap Madog ap Goronwy 253
ap Madog Gloddaith 51, 130
ap Maredudd 27
ap Maredudd, heirs of 107
ap Maredudd, ap Dafydd 53&n., 164, 178, 240n., 246n., 247
ap Meurig 226
ab Owain 51
ap Rhys, Sir (Gruffudd Llwyd) 47, 51, 128, 160, 161, 162, 166, 180-1
ap Tudur 164
ap Tudur Llwyd 124, 253
Adarwr 6n.
Crythwr 135
Fychan, lord of Glyndvfrdwy 18

Fychan ap Gruffudd ab Ednyfed 178
Gethin 7
Gryg 53&n., 178
Sais (Gruffudd ap Dafydd ap Hywel) 247
Sais, lineage of 110
Nannau, Friar 230n.
Trefgoed 225
Grugor 29n., 110
Guto'r Glyn 6n., 179
Gwalchmai ap Meilir 24, 28-9, 29n., 108, 160, 177-8
Gwas Sanffraid ap Twrllach 117
Gwaunydog 215
Gweirydd ap Rhys Goch, lineage of 160
gwelyau 11-12, 11n., 13, 77, 83, 100-1, 101n., 107, 108, 119-24, 217, 220, 241, 258
Gwely Bleddyn ap Llywarch 121
Cadwgan ap Llywarch 120, 172
Conws 120
Cuhelyn ap Cadrod 84
Cynwrig ap Tegwared 122, 159n.
Goridyr 119
Goronwy ab Ednyfed 133
Goronwy Foel 120
Gwythur ap Cadrod 84
Hwfa ap Gwion 107
Hywel ap Llywelyn 84
Hywel ap Tudur 3n.
Iorwerth ap Hwfa 122
Iorwerth ab Ieuan 125
Iorwerth ap Llywarch 109n., 119, 120, 162n.
Madog ap Meilir 121
Maredudd ab Einion 122
Matusalem ap Hwfa 181
Philip ab Owain 162n.
Porthorion 83
Tegerin ap Carwed 173
Tudur ab Itgwon and Gothlon ab Itgwon 121
Wyrion ap Cynddelw 121
Wyrion Iarddur 121
Wyrion Sandde 120, 122
Gwenhwyfar ferch Conws ap Dafydd Fychan 183
ferch Dafydd Fychan 183
ferch Iorwerth ap Tegwared 112
ferch Llywelyn ap Hwlcyn 169
Gwenllian ferch Bleddyn ap Cyfnerth 103-4
ferch Cynan ap Maredudd 180
ferch Dafydd 92

ferch Dafydd ap Bleddyn Fychan 181
ferch Deicws 104
ferch Ieuan 235n.
ferch Ieuan Crythwr 135-6
ferch Iorwerth ap Dafydd 169
ferch Madog 232
ferch Maredudd Benhir 182
de Llŷn 198
widow of Dafydd ap Llywelyn ap Maredudd 35
wife of Heilin ab Ieuan ab Iorwerth 136
Wen 250
Gwerfyl ferch Adda 137
ferch Conws ap Dafydd Fychan 183
ferch Dafydd Fychan 183
ferch Gwenllian ferch Deicws 104
ferch Lleucu ferch Dafydd Brytaen 132
ferch Mab *Dummagh* 104
ferch Madog ap Gruffudd of Hendwr 180
ferch Rhys ap Tudur 165
daughter of Roger de Burton 196-7
Goch 49
Gwilym ap Dafydd ab Ieuan 174
ab Einion 207
ap Gruffudd ap Gwilym 51, 92, 102n., 112n., 114, 126-7, 164, 165-8, 167n., 175&n., 230, 253, 256, 259
ap Gruffudd ap Heilin 166
ap Gruffudd ap Hywel 40, 75
ap Gruffudd ap Tudur 69, 92, 128, 161, 162, 166&n., 168, 230, 232
ap Gruffudd ap Tudur Llwyd 125, 128, 253-4, 254n.
ap Gruffudd Trefgoed 225
ap Madog Crythwr 208
ap Philip 161&n.
ap Sefnyn 178
ap Tudur ap Goronwy 92, 163-5, 167, 209, 248-9, 249n., 253, 254, 255-6
Fychan. *See* Griffith, William
Rhyfel 25
Gwladus ferch Dafydd Fychan 183
*gŵr y farchnad* 186
Gwredog (Llifon) 11n., 17, 68
Gwredog (Twrcelyn) 29n., 47&n., 48, 109, 114, 124, 163n., 164, 166
Gwrgeneu ap Tegwared 65
Gwtyn ap Tegwared 102
Gwydryn 33, 109, 124, 129, 131, 242
Gwyn ab Iorwerth ap Cadwgan 172n.

Gwynedd 2, 10, 21-9, 30, 31, 37, 39n., 41, 43, 63, 64, 68, 73, 78, 79, 81, 88, 95, 101, 110, 117, 123, 139, 159, 160, 162, 163n., 164, 165, 168, 175, 181, 186, 187, 188, 189, 203, 208, 216, 217, 227, 233, 237, 246, 249, 259
kings and princes of 94. *See also* Gruffudd ap Llywelyn, Gruffudd ap Cynan, Owain Gwynedd, Dafydd ab Owain Gwynedd, Llywelyn ab Iorwerth, Dafydd ap Llywelyn, Llywelyn ap Gruffudd
seneschal of. *See* Goronwy ab Ednyfed
Gwynedd, John 217
*gwŷr gwaith* 95, 96, 98, 99
*gwŷr mâl* 95, 96&n., 98, 99&n.
*gwŷr tir bwrdd* 95, 96&n., 98

'Haf y Gwyddyl' 26
Hafod Grythwr 132
Hafoty 137, 138n.
Hale, Richard 235
Hambury, Robert de 47n., 162n.
Hampton, William de 55
Hanmer, Gruffudd 181
Jenkin 181
Harborough, Thomas 51
harbours 8, 78-81
Harlech 192, 197
castle 191n.
Harold Godwinson 26-7
Harrington, Sir William 38
Haryot, Edward 50, 136
Haunton, Walter 116
Haverfordwest (Pembs.) 78
Hawarden (Flints.) 62, 140n.
health 139-41
Hebrides 30
Heilin *Tuth* 121
Helpston, John de 201
Robert de 201
Thomas de 201
Henblas, Beaumaris 137&n., 176, 203&n.
Hendre Rhosyr 104, 106, 226
Hendwr (Mer.) 180-1
Heneglwys 45, 107, 133, 179n., 253
Hen Gapel Llugwy 19, 232n.
Henry I 25
Henry II 24, 27
Henry III 26, 27, 190
Henry IV 165, 195, 230, 249, 255
Henry V 50, 52, 58, 255

Henry VI 56, 203
Henry VII 52
  carpenter 86
  miller, of Newborough 83
  rector of Llaneilian 217
  Crach 188n.
  Fitz Henry 25
Hereford 34, 190
  bishops of 229
Hergest (Herefs.) 183
Heyrish, Patrick 117
Heyton Roger de 55
Hirdre-faig 18n., 102, 104, 226
Hodsock (Notts.) 83
Hoen ferch Tudur Ddu 106
holdings, size of 120-2, 123-6
Holland, Owen 171
  Sir Thomas 171
Holyhead (Caergybi) 2, 8, 9, 14, 33, 81, 103,
  125, 126, 196, 202, 252
  church of 18-19, 23, 26, 103, 109, 172, 177,
    211, 212, 213, 216, 218, 219-22, 224&n.,
    226, 232, 233
  provost of 212-3, 219, 224
  See also Bromfield, Richard; Clifford, Richard;
    Instructus, Master; Kettelbergh, Stephen
    de; Medford, Richard; Medford, Walter;
    Tiphaine, Jean; Wettenhall, Adam de;
    Windsor, Ralph of
  canons and prebendaries of 103, 109, 171,
    177, 219-22, 220n., 224, 225, 253, 254
Holy Island (Ynys Cybi) 1, 3, 8, 9-10
Honfleur 79
Hospitallers 212&n.
Hotspur. See Percy, Henry
houses 137-8
Housom, John de 230
Hugh, earl of Chester 22
  earl of Shrewsbury 22-3, 212
  ap Llywelyn ab Ieuan 172
  ap Robert ap Rhys 113-4
Hughes, Hugh 171
Humphrey, duke of Gloucester 203-4
hundred court. See commote court
Huntingdon, William de 40, 52
Huw ap Dafydd ap Gwilym 174
Hwfa ap Cynddelw 21n.
  ap Cynddelw, lineage of 12, 53, 67, 103, 107-
    10, 122, 159, 160, 161, 162, 172, 173, 178,
    181, 182, 183, 219, 220

  ab Iorwerth ap Hwfa 183
  ap Madog ap Dafydd 217
Hwlcyn ap Dafydd ap Goronwy ap Dafydd 140
  ap Dafydd ab Ieuan 7, 169, 171
  ap Hywel ab Iorwerth Ddu 172&n., 178-9,
    182, 183
  Llwyd 182
Hywel ab Adda Grwn 223-4&n.
  ap Conws ap Hywel 129
  ap Cynwrig 162&n., 173
  ap Dafydd 226
  ap Dafydd ab Ednyfed 70
  ap Dafydd ap Hywel 247
  ap Dafydd ap Hywel ap Tudur 132
  ap Dafydd ap Tudur 7, 131-2
  ap Dafydd Hir 70, 73, 106, 136
  ap Dafydd Llorpe 50
  ap Dafydd, wife of 112
  ap Deicws ap Llywelyn ap Llywarch 93
  ap Goronwy (1320) 33n.
  ap Goronwy ap Tudur 47, 114, 124, 130, 164,
    178
  ap Gruffudd ap Dafydd 141
  ap Gruffudd ab Ednyfed Fychan 32
  ap Gruffudd ap Hywel 125
  ap Gruffudd ab Iorwerth 161, 162, 197&n.
  ap Gwerfyl ferch Lleucu 132
  ap Gwyn ab Iorwerth 171-2, 182
  ab Ieuan ab Adda 106
  ab Ieuan ap Cynwrig 125, 182
  ab Ieuan ab Ednyfed 254
  ab Ieuan ap Gruffudd Ddu 70, 73, 136
  ab Iorwerth (1313) 128
  ab Iorwerth Ddu 172, 182
  ap Llywelyn ap Dafydd ab Ieuan 53, 74, 129,
    171, 182, 209
  ap Llywelyn ap Gwyn 247
  ap Llywelyn ap Hywel (Hywel y Farf) 173
  ap Llywelyn ab Ieuan ap Tudur Llwyd 224
  ap Madog ap Llywelyn 35&n., 124, 162&n.
  ab Owain Gwynedd 25, 159n.
  ap Rhys ap Llywelyn 53
  ap Rhys ap Tudur 250
  ap Robin ap Gruffudd 169
  ap Tegwared 77
  ap Tudur 166
  ap Tudur ap Goronwy 163
  Cilan 179
  Ddu ap Goronwy 33

Ddu ab Iorwerth ap Gruffudd 162
Fychan ab Ieuan 162
Lipa 39, 161&n., 162
Rheinallt 179
y Farf. *See* Hywel ap Llywelyn ap Hywel
y Fwyall, Sir 183

Iarddur, lineage of 109, 160, 162, 166, 183
Idwal, king 217
Ieuan, carpenter 87
  ab Adda of Pengwern 165
  ab Adda Grwn 223
  ap Dafydd 75
  ap Dafydd (Beaumaris) 191n.
  ap Dafydd (Trefdraeth Wastrodion) 49
  ap Dafydd ab Einion (1377-8) 135
  ap Dafydd ab Einion (1457) 76
  ap Dafydd ap Goronwy 252
  ap Dafydd ab Ieuan 49
  ap Deicws ab Ieuan *Toger* 136
  ab Ednyfed 207
  ab Ednyfed (Tre Fraint) 121
  ab Einion Bodfeurig 252
  ab Elidir 103
  ap Gruffudd ap Rhys 47
  ap Hywel ap Cynwrig 174, 183, 254
  ap Hywel ap Dafydd 132
  ap Hywel ab Ieuan ap Madog 104&n.
  ap Hywel ab Iorwerth 126
  ab Ieuan (Tre Fraint) 121
  ab Ieuan ap Gwyddel 117
  ab Ieuan Goch 102
  ab Iorwerth ab Einion 136
  ab Iorwerth ap Heilin 71
  ab Iorwerth Llwyd 208
  ap Madog ap Hwlcyn 169&n.
  ap Madog ab Ieuan 69-70, 172, 182, 232
  ap Mato ab Ieuan ab Einion 104
  ap Philip 69
  ap Rhys ab Ieuan Llwyd 132
  ap Rhys ap Roppert 247&n.
  ap Tegwared ap Dafydd 84
  ap Thomas ap Llywelyn 132
  ap Tudur Llwyd 40, 93, 124, 253-4
  Chwerw 51, 77
  Cwta 39n., 48
  Ddu (1321) 49
  Ddu ap Hwfa 246
  Deulwyn 179

Goch ap Rhirid 102
Llwyd Crydd 50
Teiliwr 117
Wyddel 117, 119, 162, 170
Ingram family 137, 200, 228
  John, sen 200
  John, jnr. 200
  John, prior of Penmon 179, 200
  Peter 200
  William 200&n.
Instructus, Master 212
Iocyn Fach 49
Iolo Goch 164, 165, 178
Iorwerth, carpenter 86
  prior of Penmon 227
  ap Brawdfaeth 116
  ap Dafydd (Trefadog) 48
  ap Dafydd (1312-3) 70
  ap Gruffudd ab Iorwerth 161, 162, 178
  ap Hwfa ap Cynddelw 247
  ab Ieuan ap Cyfnerth 135
  ab Ieuan ap Gwyddel 117
  ab Iorwerth Wyddel 117
  ap Llywarch 109, 119, 170, 171
  ap Madog (1391-2) 135
  ap Madog Offeiriad 225
  ap Philip Goch 30&n., 240
  Ddu ab Iorwerth ap Gruffudd 172, 182
  Foel 31, 33&n., 64, 65, 66
  Fychan 173
  Gam 70
  Tew *Tastour* 104
Ipswich (Suff.) 196n.
Ireland 21, 23, 24n., 25, 27, 81, 102, 117, 175,
  203, 204, 237, 238, 252
Irishmen 27n., 117, 252
Irish Sea 23, 26, 30&n., 76, 81
Irlam, John 216
Isabella, wife of Edward II 35, 38, 42, 45&n.,
  207
Is Aled (Denbs.) 182
Is Coed (Cards.) 181
Ithel ap Hywel ap Llywelyn 53, 171&n.
  ap Roppert 114
  Fychan ab Ithel Gam 181
  Fychan ap Madog ap Hywel 182

James of St. George 191
Jankyn ap Deicws ap Rhirid 117

ab Einion ap Tudur 136
Janyn Franc 116&n.
Joan, wife of Llywelyn ab Iorwerth 111, 229
John, king of England 190
　miller, of Newborough 83-4
　prior of Penmon 228
　son of Edward II 45n.
　ap Deicws Goch 137
Juliana, widow of Simon de Faversham 81
justice's sessions 38, 42-3, 46, 50, 85, 102, 104, 108, 109, 129, 130, 197, 198, 243

Katherine, wife of Henry V 58, 62, 75, 220
　daughter of William de Cranwell 125, 201-2
Kempe, Thomas le 194
Kennington (Surrey), petitions submitted at (1305) 97n., 101, 105, 127, 192, 205, 206
Kent, Thomas 209
Kernyther, Henry 196
Kettelbergh, Stephen de 221
Kyffin, Richard, dean of Bangor 218, 231
Kyghley, Sir John 202

labour services 15, 68, 85, 91, 94-5, 96-9, 100, 101, 105, 108, 121
Labourers, Statute of 1351 243
Lagan, John 201, 204
Lancashire 52, 202
Lancaster 190
land market 113, 127-33, 201-3, 210
Laurence ab Ithon 213n.
Laurenz, Adam 79
laws, Welsh 18, 72, 82, 113, 115, 119, 127-8, 130, 139
Le Croisic 79
Leicester 196n.
Leland, John 4, 74n.
Leominster, Hugh de 58
lepers 139-40, 140n.
Lewis Daron 232
　Glyn Cothi 179
　John 183
　Owen, bishop of Cassano 234
Lewys, Huw 6n., 173, 179, 183
Lewys Môn 178, 179, 223
Limoges 247n.
Lisbon 79
Liverpool 79, 87, 193
livestock epidemics 237-9

Llamel 120
Llanallgo 18n., 48, 224, 225
Llanbabo 14, 222, 225, 232
Llanbadarn Fawr (Cards.) 220n.
Llanbadrig 10, 110, 205n., 212, 215
Llanbedr-goch 16, 21
Llanbeulan 9, 211, 213, 226, 232
Llanddaniel 9, 216
Llanddeiniolen (Caerns.) 216
Llanddeusant 211-2, 222, 225
Llanddona 18n., 71, 215
Llanddwyn 4, 8, 71, 211, 219&n., 223, 224&n., 231-2, 231n., 251&n.
Llanddyfnan 7, 109, 119, 131-2, 176, 212, 213, 219&n., 223, 224, 247, 254
Llanddygfael 254
Llandegfan 192, 204
Llandrygarn 10, 18, 224n.
Llandyfrydog 12, 17, 23, 46, 82, 84, 123, 212
Llandygái (Caerns.) 168, 230
Llandysilio 224
Llanedwen 69, 110, 172, 216, 232
Llaneilian 14, 39, 49, 107, 179, 217-8, 223, 225, 228n., 232
　church 23, 213, 217-8, 223, 232-3
Llaneugrad 18n., 222n., 224, 225, 232
Llaneurgain (Flints.) 165
Llanfaelog 13, 140, 212, 226
Llan-faes 5-6, 6n., 9, 14, 28, 32n., 33, 34, 59, 63, 88-9, 93, 97n., 99, 140-1, 185-9, 190, 191, 192, 197, 198, 205&n., 208, 238
　agricultural activity at 63-4
　burgesses of 186-7, 188, 191n., 196, 205, 208
　church 9, 185, 187, 189&n., 201, 212, 216, 222&n., 228, 233, 234
　ferry 86, 186, 188
　friary 76, 168, 179, 185, 189, 195, 212, 224n., 226, 229-31, 231n., 233, 234, 249, 253
　herring fishery 76, 185, 186
　port of 78, 185-6, 187, 189
　services 66, 186
　trade 186, 193
　wood 6&n.
Llanfaethlu 225, 234
Llanfair Dyffryn Clwyd (Denbs.) 231
Llanfairfechan (Caerns.) 182
Llanfair-is-gaer (Caerns.) 169n., 216
Llanfair Mathafarn Eithaf 3
Llanfair Pwllgwyngyll 224

Llanfairynghornwy 213, 225, 232

Llanfair-yn-y-cwmwd 13, 212, 216

Llanfechell 11n., 14, 16, 213, 218, 221, 223, 232

Llanfeirian 33n.

Llanffinan 18n., 218

Llanfflewin 13, 18n.

Llanfigel 159n, 212, 240, 241, 258

Llanfihangel Dinsylwy 218

Llanfihangel Tre'r Beirdd 122

Llanfihangel Ysgeifiog 10, 218

Llangadwaladr (Eglwys Ail) 10, 14, 49, 85, 173&n., 218, 219, 224&n., 226, 234

Llangaffo 217

Llangefni 2, 9, 14, 128, 218n., 223, 224, 225, 234-5

Llangeinwen 25, 217, 226, 232

Llangoed 5, 11n., 68, 123, 218

Llangollen (Denbs.) 181

Llangristiolus 71, 218

Llangwyfan 18n.

Llangwyllog 215, 229, 234

Llangynhafal (Denbs.) 166n.

Llanidan 34n., 138, 216-7
 ferry 109, 170, 256

Llaniestyn 69, 92, 128, 161, 166, 218, 230, 232

Llanllibio 14, 15, 18n., 28, 35, 57, 102, 106, 172-3, 175, 245, 254, 257

Llannerch-y-medd 5, 10, 15, 28, 72-3, 127, 211, 213
 fairs 53, 72&n., 162n. 170, 174, 175, 256

Llanol 14, 15, 240, 258, 259

Llanrhuddlad 225

Llanrhwydrys 17, 232

Llanrwst (Denbs.) 5

Llansadwrn 137

Llantrisant 213&n., 219

Llanwenllwyfo 12, 218

Llanynghenedl 226

Llanynys (Denbs.) 14

Llanysgallog 218

Llechgynfarwy 69, 73, 110, 113, 116, 226

Llechog 30&n.

Llechylched 10, 103, 110

Lledwigan Llan 28, 35&n., 47-8, 124, 162

Lledwigan Llys 29n., 49, 70, 93, 107n., 109, 191n.

Lleucu ferch Dafydd Brytaen 131
 ferch Dafydd Foel 103
 ferch Iolyn 231

Llifon, commote of 5, 7n., 10-11, 12, 13, 14, 15, 27, 28, 39, 47n., 53, 54, 68-9, 72, 93, 95, 101, 104n., 108, 110, 112, 116&n., 117, 122, 123, 125, 128, 129, 160, 172-3, 178, 182, 183, 202, 211, 213&n., 240, 241, 242, 245, 253-4, 258

 commote court 44, 74, 104

 *rhaglaw* and raglotry of 44

 *See also* Cookes, Robert; Hywel ab Iorwerth Ddu; Lewis, Huw; Llywelyn ap Hwlcyn ap Hywel; Ieuan ap Tudur Llwyd; Llywelyn ab Ieuan ap Tudur Llwyd; Middlemore, Nicholas; Rossington, Henry

 *rhingyll* and ringildry of 44, 60, 24
  *See also* Cynwrig ap Dafydd Fychan; Dafydd Fychan ap Dafydd Llwyd; Hywel ap Llywelyn ap Hywel; Llywelyn ab Ieuan ap Tudur Llwyd

 tourn 69, 73, 115, 134

Lloyd, Thomas 174

Llwyd, Richard 25n.

Llwydiarth (Dindaethwy) 11n.

Llwydiarth Esgob (Twrcelyn) 12, 56n., 173-4, 179, 183, 199, 231

Llyn Alaw 3

Llyn Cefni 3

Llŷn (Caerns.) 5, 8, 21, 28, 31, 50, 65, 66, 68, 209, 238, 239

Llysdulas 1, 12, 105, 108, 122, 161, 162, 173-4, 183, 240

Llyslew 27n., 125

Llywarch ap Bran, lineage of 52-3, 57, 103, 108-10, 129, 159, 160, 162, 169, 170, 171-2, 181-2, 219, 220
 ap Maredudd 34n.

Llywelyn, Brother, Prior of Bangor 97
 ap Cynwrig ap Maredudd 170n.
 ap Cynwrig Ddu o Fôn 247-8
 ap Dafydd ab Ieuan Wyddel 53, 171
 ap Dafydd Fychan 124, 129
 ap Dafydd Goch 183
 ab Ednyfed, heirs of 107n.
 ap Goronwy Fychan 47
 ap Gruffudd 27, 28, 30-33, 55, 63, 105, 160, 163, 191n., 211n. 212, 215, 219
 ap Gruffudd ab Iorwerth 109
 ap Gutyn 6n.
 ap Hwlcyn ap Dafydd ab Ieuan 53, 169
 ap Hwlcyn ap Hywel 172-3, 179, 181-3
 ap Hwlcyn ap Llywelyn Moel 182&n.
 ap Hywel ap Cynwrig 216-7
 ap Hywel ap Dafydd 132

ap Hywel ab Iorwerth Ddu 173
ab Ieuan ap Dafydd 102, 104
ab Ieuan ab Iorwerth 253
ab Ieuan ap Madog 172&n.
ab Ieuan ap Tudur Llwyd 254
ab Iorwerth 25-6, 26n., 27, 28n., 29, 46, 47, 109, 111, 163, 185, 212, 214, 215, 216n., 227, 229, 248
ab Iorwerth ap Tegwared 112
ap Madog ab Ieuan 172
ap Maredudd, sons of 28
ap Maredudd Llwyd 103
ap Rhys ap Gruffudd ab Einion 17
ap Tudur ap Cynwrig 129
y Gwyddel 117
Foelrhon 101
Fychan ap Llywelyn 183
Goch ap Meurig Hen 178
Moel 122
Pengraith 136
Lollards 203
London 140
  Tower of 34
Ludlow (Salop) 190
Lygadbrith, Master David 223

Mab Brawdfaeth 115
Mabon Glochydd 109&n.
Macclesfield (Ches.) 190
  Alan de 208
Mac Cuter, Patrick 203
Mac Orlot, Andrew 203
Mac Steffan, Stephen 203
Madog, carpenter's mate 86
  ab Adda (Malltraeth) 115
  ab Adda (Penrhosllugwy) 99
  ab Adda Grwn 224
  ap Cynwrig 99
  ap Dafydd (1331) 197n.
  ap Dafydd ap Hywel 254
  ap Dafydd ab Iorwerth 104, 226
  ap Dafydd ap Tudur 166
  ap Dafydd Offeiriad 225
  ab Einion (coroner) 39
  ab Einion (Bodedern) 93
  ap Goronwy Fychan 114, 164, 166
  ap Gruffudd 121
  ap Gruffudd of Hendwr 180-1
  ap Hwlcyn ap Dafydd ab Ieuan 53, 169&n.,

171n., 182
  ap Hywel Gymen 183
  ab Idwal 121
  ab Ieuan (Bron-y-foel) 165
  ab Ieuan (Llaneillan) 49
  ab Ieuan ap Hywel 69, 121, 172
  ab Iorwerth ap Hywel ap Gruffudd 122
  ab Ithel 87
  ap Llywelyn 33-5, 47-8, 160
  ap Llywelyn, revolt of 33-5, 47, 61, 98, 124, 160, 187, 189
  ap Madog ab Einion Amlwch 243
  ap Tudur 162
  Ddu ap Meurig 130
  Dewi 230n.
  Gloddaith 130
  Llwyd 47, 51, 161
  Saer 87
Madyn Dysw 12
Maelgwn ab Owain Gwynedd 25
Maelor Saesneg (Flints.) 182
Maenaddwyn 122
maenol 110, 213
Maenol Badrig 110, 117, 125, 254
  Bangor 169
maerdrefi 10, 14, 16, 29-30, 57, 68, 93-100, 105, 121, 140, 186-7, 188, 189, 205, 212, 215, 222, 238, 239
Maeselidir 257
Magnus III (Bareleg), king of Norway 23&n.
Magnus VI (Haakonson), king of Norway 30
Mainwaring, John 255, 256
Mali ferch Ieuan Llwyd ap Gruffudd 182
Mallt ferch Conws ap Dafydd Fychan 183
  ferch Cynwrig Fychan 182
  ferch Gruffudd ap Madog Gloddaith 183
  ferch Madog ap Hwlcyn 182
  wife of Ieuan ap Rhys ab Ieuan Llwyd 132
Malltraeth, commote of 5, 6, 9, 27&n., 28, 29n., 39, 41, 54, 61, 70, 82, 93, 102, 104, 107, 108-9, 110, 115&n., 120, 123, 124, 125, 137, 160, 162n., 170, 173, 181, 182, 202, 211, 213&n., 225, 239, 241, 242, 244, 246, 257
  commote court 104
  rhaglaw and raglotry of 56, 57
    See also Cookes, Robert; Dafydd Fychan ap Dafydd Llwyd; Lewis, Huw; Llywelyn ap Hwlcyn ap Llywelyn Moel; Middlemore, Nicholas; Rossington, Henry
  rhingyll and ringildry of 60, 239 See also

Gruffudd Gryg, Dafydd Goch ap
    Gruffudd, Ieuan ab Einion Bodfeurig
subsidy assessment, 1292-3  61, 64-6, 135
tourn  7, 45, 49, 50, 69, 74, 81, 111-12, 115,
    133, 134, 140
    Marsh (Cors Ddyga)  2, 3, 6&n., 8, 17, 74, 82
malt  63-4, 67&n., 83, 84, 89, 139
Man, Isle of  3, 23, 30, 88, 204
    king of  227
    See also Godred Crovan; Rögnvaldr
Marchudd ap Cynan, lineage of  160
Maredudd ap Cynwrig  52, 53, 139, 170&n.,
    171&n., 179, 182, 209, 251-2, 251n., 254,
    256-7
    ap Dafydd ap Hywel  247
    ap Hwlcyn ap Dafydd  169
    ab Iorwerth  28n.
    ap Madog ap Llywelyn  35&n.
    ap Thomas ap Maredudd  170
    ap Tudur ap Goronwy  52, 164, 165, 181, 183,
        209, 224, 253, 255
    Benhir  159n.
    Ddu ap Goronwy  52-3, 160&n., 170, 172n.,
        181-2
    Ddu ap Gruffudd  181
Margam abbey (Glam.)  214
Margaret ferch Dafydd Fychan ap Dafydd
    Llwyd  181, 183
    ferch Gaynor  113
    ferch Ieuan Fychan ab Ieuan  182-3
    ferch Owain ap Thomas ap Llywelyn  181
    ferch Rhys ap Cynwrig ap Roppert  183
markets  72-3, 192-3, 205, 230
marriage  103-4, 106, 113-4, 180-4
Martyn, John, dean of Bangor  214n., 221
maslin  63, 83, 89
masons  86, 87, 88, 102, 233
Mathafarn, port of  8, 75, 80, 85, 87
    Eithaf  9, 16, 50, 72, 113, 122, 124, 132-3,
        254
    Wion  74, 109, 122, 132-3, 252, 254
Mato ab Ieuan Llwyd  50, 136
    ap Tudur Hen  50
    Wyddel  117
Matusalem ap Hwfa ap Cynddelw  172
Mauny, Walter de  55
Mawddwy (Mer.)  181, 183
Mawnog Ieuan Goch ap Madog ap Cynwrig  7
Mawnog Madog ap Gruffudd ab Einion  7
Maykyn, Thomas  79

Medford, Richard  221
    Walter  221
Meilir  177
    ap Goronwy  102
Meiriogen  96, 110, 240
Meirionnydd  22, 28, 34
Menai, commote of  5, 13, 15, 26n., 27&n.,
    28n., 32, 33, 39, 42, 45-7, 45n., 52-3, 54&n.,
    57, 58, 64, 67&n., 71, 73, 74, 83, 84, 85, 93,
    98, 101, 102, 104, 105, 108, 109, 110, 115,
    116n., 117, 119, 120, 125, 129, 137, 160,
    162n., 167, 168, 170, 188, 202, 205, 206,
    207, 209, 210, 211, 213n., 214, 216, 217,
    225, 226, 239, 240, 242, 244, 245, 247, 254,
    256, 257-8
    approvers of. See Madog ap Hwlcyn ap
        Dafydd ab Ieuan; Ithel ap Hywel ap
        Llywelyn; Llywelyn ap Hywel ap Madog;
        Owain ab Ithel ap Hywel
    commote court  45-6
    escheator of  46
    farmers and keepers of  See Leominster, Hugh
        de; Shalford, William de
    rhaglaw and raglotry of  54n., 160, 244, 256.
        See also Cookes, Robert; Hampton, William
        de; Llywelyn ap Dafydd ab Ieuan Wyddel;
        Maredudd Ddu ap Goronwy; Middlemore,
        Nicholas; Rossington, Henry; Dafydd ab
        Ieuan Wyddel
    rhingyll and ringildry of  46, 54, 85, 209, 244,
        257  See also Dafydd ab Ieuan Wyddel;
        Goronwy Crach; Hywel ap Llywelyn ap
        Dafydd ab Ieuan Wyddel; Hywel ap Rhys ap
        Llywelyn; Ithel ap Hywel ap Llywelyn;
        Llywelyn ap Dafydd ab Ieuan Wyddel;
        Llywelyn ap Hwlcyn ap Dafydd ab Ieuan;
        Madog ap Hwlcyn ap Dafydd ab Ieuan;
        Maredudd ap Cynwrig; Rhys ap Llywelyn
        ap Dafydd ab Ieuan Wyddel; Hywel ap
        Dafydd ap Hywel; Gruffudd ap Madog ap
        Goronwy; Llywelyn ab Ieuan ab Iorwerth
    stewardship of  46, 54, 170, 206, 210, 244
        See also Gwilym ap Gruffudd ap Gwilym;
        Maredudd ap Cynwrig
    tourn  46
Menai Bridge  2
Menai Straits  2, 5, 9, 22, 25, 30, 32&n., 168,
    186, 213, 214, 230, 255
Mercer, Richard le  188n.
Merioneth  5, 24, 52, 55, 60, 61, 75, 82n., 128,
    138, 141n., 197, 238n., 249
Meurig ap Bleddyn  124
    ap Llywelyn ap Hwlcyn  104, 173, 182-3
Middlemore, Nicholas  56

Milford (Pembs.) 78
military service 29&n., 162, 163&n., 214
mill, suit of 3n., 82-3, 84-5, 95-6, 98-9, 100, 101, 107, 109-10, 121
mills 3, 5, 38, 44, 53, 58, 59, 66, 67, 71, 80, 82-5, 105, 109-10, 121, 130, 138, 170, 213, 216, 238, 244, 257
  Aberalaw 15, 75, 84, 87, 138, 256
  Aberffraw 83, 84, 87, 95
  Bancenyn 85
  Beaumaris 84, 201
  Bodiordderch 85
  Bodronyn 75, 138, 241, 254
  Botan 241
  Bryn Gwydded 75, 84, 86, 98, 100
  Cefn-coch 6n., 75, 83, 86, 87, 201
  Cemais 75, 84, 86, 87, 98, 254, 256
  Chester 75
  Cleifiog 120
  Cornwy 85
  Cymynod 120
  Dindryfwl 5, 75, 85, 87, 101, 107, 257
  Dulas 75, 98, 100
  Hirdre-faig 245, 256&n., 258
  Holyhead 84n.
  Llanegryn (Mer.) 75
  Llaneilian 84
  Llan-faes 6n., 75, 83, 86, 87, 189, 201
  Llanfigel 241
  Melin Adda 5n., 86
    y Bont 5, 75, 87
    Braint 84, 121
    Esgob 84
    Gwna 126
    Hywel ap Rhys 84
    Newydd 83, 245, 256&n.
    Pwllfanog 84
  Moelfre 24, 97n., 123
  Newborough 75, 83-4, 85, 87, 105, 206, 207
  Penmynydd 85
  Rhosyr 208, 256-7
  Rhuddgaer 84
  Tal-y-bont 26n., 85
  Tre Feibion Meurig 101&n.
  Treffos 84
mills, fulling 72
  hand 85
  water 3&n., 83, 254
  wind 2, 83-4, 197, 206

millstones 74-6, 74n., 80, 85, 87, 100, 105, 216
millstone quarries 40, 74-6, 87, 216
Missenden, Thomas de 57
Moelfre 24, 97n., 123
Moel-y-don 9
Moldsdale (Flints.) 62
Montgomery, Treaty of 27, 29
Morfudd ferch Dafydd Fychan 183
  ferch Goronwy ab Ieuan ap Dafydd 114
  ferch Goronwy ap Tudur 114, 164, 167
  wife of Hywel ap Dafydd ap Tudur 132
Morgan ap Maredudd ap Dafydd 182
  Hugh, dean of Bangor 182
Mortimer, Hugh 167
  Roger 101n., 161, 198
Mostyn family 128, 165, 181
Moyle, John 178-9, 198n.
multure 66, 83, 84
Munster, king of 23
Myddfai (Carms.) 141
Myfanwy ferch Ednyfed ap Tudur 165
  ferch Hywel ap Dafydd ap Tudur 132
  ferch Iorwerth Ddu ab Ednyfed Gam 181, 230-1, 233
Myfyrian 110
Mynydd Bodafon 3, 122
Mynydd Llwydiarth 3
Mynydd Mechell 3
Mynydd-mwyn 11n., 68
Mynydd Parys (Trysglwyn) 1, 2, 74
Mynydd Trysglwyn. See Mynydd Parys

Nanhwrfa 120
Nant (Flints.) 166
Nantbychan 14
Nantconwy (Caerns.) 243
Nantmawr 18n., 19n., 33, 47, 57&n., 83, 122, 160, 163, 166, 174, 245
Nefyn (Caerns.) 22, 64, 185, 189, 209
Nesse, Thomas de 201
Nest ferch Cynwrig ap Maredudd Ddu 182
  ferch Ieuan Ddu 70
  ferch Ithel Fychan ap Madog ap Hywel 182
  ferch Maredudd ap Dafydd ap Hywel 103, 125-6
  wife of Dafydd Fychan ap Dafydd Llwyd and Gwilym ap Gruffudd ap Tudur Llwyd 183, 254
Newborough 3, 4, 7&n., 9, 14, 46, 53, 59, 72, 73, 83-4, 99, 111, 112, 114, 137, 140, 141,

161&n., 163, 183, 188, 192&n., 196, 198, 205-10, 224&n., 232, 239, 242, 256
alderman of. *See* Maredudd ap Cynwrig
bailiffs of 50, 207, 224&n.
borough lands of 206, 207-8
burgesses of 5, 33, 136, 161, 187, 198, 206, 207, 208-9, 209&n., 224
charter 205-6, 205n.
farmers of 207&n., 208, 245 *See also* Deicws ab Ieuan ap Tegwared, Hywel ab Adda Grwn; Ieuan ab Ednyfed; Ieuan Llwyd; Maredudd ap Cynwrig; Maredudd ap Tudur ap Goronwy; William ap Madog
markets and fairs 192&n., 206
mayor of 206, 210
town cross of 87, 206, 209
Newborough, Morgan 225
Nicholas ap Dafydd ap Gwilym 92, 174
ab Elis 179, 223, 233
Feddyg 50
Normans 22, 26, 212, 227
Norreys, Sir Thomas 76, 202, 204
Northampton, Treaty of 203n.
Norway, king of *See* Magnus III (Bareleg); Magnus VI (Haakonson)
*Norwich, Valuation of* 17, 211, 233

oats 63-72, 64n., 67n., 83, 84, 89&n., 94, 101, 136, 138-9
Ogilby, John 9
open fields 16-17&nn., 69, 72
Overton, Peter de 60
Owain ap Gruffudd 27&n., 211n., 215, 216
ab Ithel ap Hywel 53, 171
ap Meurig ap Llywelyn 173
ap Thomas ap Rhodri (Owain Lawgoch) 246-8, 246n.
Glyn Dŵr, revolt of 15, 51, 56, 62, 80, 116, 125, 165, 166-7, 167n., 168, 169, 170, 171, 172, 175, 179, 182, 192, 195, 202, 203, 207, 208, 209, 219, 223, 228, 230&n., 244, 248-56, 258, 259
Gwynedd 23, 24&n., 25, 35, 248
Owen, John 171
William 249&n., 252
oxen 64-6, 69, 70-1, 127, 238
Oxford 203, 223

Paimpol 79
parliament 96, 97n., 161, 175, 199, 200, 210
Parys, Robert de, sen. 48, 208

Robert de 167, 251
patronage, bardic 177-80
ecclesiastical 218-23
royal 55-8
earl of 51
Penbol 12
*pencenhedlaeth* 109
Pengwern (Denbs.) 165, 181, 183
Penhesgyn 136
Penhwnllys 16, 109, 166
Peniarth (Mer.) 128
Penllyn (Mer.) 31
Penmarc 79
Penmon 50, 71, 74, 88, 212
church of 23, 215, 232
prior of 46, 76, 92, 212, 216, 218, 219, 224, 225, 227, 228
*See also* Ardescote, William; Castell, John; Einion ap Goronwy; Godfrey, John; Godfrey, Thomas; Ingram, John; Iorwerth; John
priory 68&n., 85, 189, 212, 215-6, 216n., 222, 226-9, 233-4
priory, lands of 215-6, 233-4
Penmynydd 17, 29n., 47, 109, 114, 124, 126, 161, 162&n., 163&n., 164&n., 168, 171, 179, 181, 209, 212, 215, 218, 222n., 224, 225, 226, 230, 233, 233, 256
Penrhosllugwy 14, 16, 19, 33, 41, 47n., 53, 57&n., 65, 71, 72, 73, 93, 98&n., 99&n., 105, 106, 108, 112, 122, 136, 138, 140, 189, 205n., 212, 216, 217, 222, 228, 232n.
bondmen of, dispute 29-30, 30n., 96-8, 105, 238
bond renders and services 67, 72, 96-8
court buildings 86, 100, 105
farmer and farm of 245. *See* Bulkeley, William, jun.; Clerk, Adam; Dafydd ap Gwilym ap Dafydd; Dafydd ab Ieuan ap Hywel; Gwilym ap Dafydd ab Ieuan; Ieuan ap Tudur Llwyd; Maredudd ap Cynwrig; Ravensholme, John de
*rhaglaw* of 97n.
Penrhyn (Caerns.) 93, 164, 168, 169, 176
Isaf, Y 7
Mawr 3
Pentraeth 109, 121, 122, 125, 126, 132, 133, 134, 243, 253, 254
Percy, Henry (Hotspur) 56, 249, 250, 251
Perthgyr 130, 191n., 257
Phaer, Dr. Thomas 6, 8
Philip, carpenter 87

miller, of Newborough 83
ab Ieuan Dommok 135
ap Robyn 197
Ffwlbart 49
physicians 140-1, 188
Pigot, Thomas, bishop of Bangor 224
pigs 5, 65, 67, 69-71, 89, 91, 101, 136, 186
pilgrimages 231-2
Plas Berw 138, 171
Plas Bodewryd 138&n.
Plas Coch 131, 131, 182
Plas Hywel ap Dafydd ap Tudur 131
Plas Newydd 1, 4, 168-9, 170, 171
Plymouth 78
poetry 111, 139, 164, 177-80, 179n., 209, 223
Pole, William de la 181
Pont Rhyd-y-defaid 10
Pont Rhyd-y-sbardun 9
population 19, 23-4, 141
Porthaethwy 14, 73, 109, 130, 257
  ferry 9, 86, 136, 240, 256
Porthaml 52, 108, 109&n., 110, 113, 117, 119,
  120, 131, 139, 160n., 162&n., 168-9, 171-2,
  172n., 179, 181, 209, 217, 247, 254
Porth Eilian 81
Porthesgob ferry 9, 214
Porth Swtan 8n.
Porth Trefadog 8n.
Porth Wygyr 8n.
Porthyllongdy 132
Powys 22, 180
Praty, Richard 223
prices 86, 88-9
Priestholm, Ynys Seiriol, (Ynys Lannog) 8, 79,
  215, 226-7, 226n.
private jurisdictions 46-8
Prydydd y Moch 26n.
Prysaeddfed 6n., 172, 173, 179, 183
Pulesdon, Roger de 34, 98&n.
Puleston, Annes 182
Pwllgwyngyll 130-1
Pwllheli (Caerns.) 140n., 185, 189, 209
Pykemere, John 74
  John (1437) 175n.
  Leticia 175n.
  Richard de 51, 52

quit-rents. See assise, rents of
Quo Warranto, 1348 164, 206, 214

Ravensholme, Sir John de 57
Record of Caernarvon 71, 221
Red Wharf Bay. See Traeth Coch
Reformation 233, 234
relief 38, 41, 44, 93, 95, 96n., 99, 100, 101,
  107n., 115, 121, 224
Requests, Court of 76, 216
revenue 38-9, 58-61
rhaglaw 40-1, 101, 105, 108
Rhandirgadog 83
rhingyll 41, 53-4, 57, 59-60, 108, 239
Rhirid ab Iorwerth 33
Rhisierdyn 178
Rhodogeidio 129
Rhodri ap Gruffudd 31-2
  ab Owain Gwynedd 25-6, 28, 108, 120, 247
  Mawr 217
Rhoscolyn 16n., 129, 213, 224n., 225
Rhos Fawr 249
Rhosgoch 47n.
Rhosmeirch 252
Rhosmor 7, 18n., 102, 104, 239
Rhosmynach 85, 100, 105, 137, 258
Rhosneigr 3
Rhosyr 5, 7-8, 14, 16n., 24, 28, 33&n., 45n.,
  53, 57, 69, 93, 97n., 99n., 140, 170, 188,
  205, 206, 207-8, 212, 222, 231, 239, 256-7
  bond tenants and services 67, 72, 97n., 98-9,
    99n.
  farmer of See Hwlcyn ap Dafydd ab Ieuan;
    Maredudd ap Cynwrig
  Roger of 205
Rhuddgaer 84, 214
Rhuddlan 32, 33, 37, 165n., 198&n., 202, 205-
  6, 229, 248
Rhyd-yr-arian 10
  -y-clafdy 10, 140
  -y-clafdy (Caerns.) 140n.
  -y-delyn Fach 10
  -y-delyn Fawr 10
  -y-fotyn 9
  -y-groes 10
Rhys, foster brother of Rhys ap Tudur 250
  ap Cynwrig ap Roppert 165, 183
  ap Dafydd ap Gwilym 174
  ap Dafydd ap Rhys 113, 232
  ap Gruffudd (Lord Rhys) 180
  ap Gruffudd, Sir 162&n.
  ap Gruffudd ap Madog Gloddaith 130, 183
  ab Ieuan ab Einion 207

ap Llywelyn ap Dafydd 53, 171
ap Llywelyn ap Hwlcyn 84&n., 173, 183
ap Llywelyn ap Hywel 132
ap Madyn Espyn 49
ap Tewdwr 21
ap Tudur ap Sir Dafydd 132
ap Tudur ap Goronwy 51, 163-4, 165, 181,
    209, 248, 249, 250, 253, 255
Goch, lineage of 108, 109
Goch Eryri 139, 179
Goch Glyndyfrdwy 179
Sion Dafydd 234
Wyn ap Llywelyn ap Tudur 179&n.
Richard II 42, 55, 165, 194, 203, 248, 255
bishop of Bangor 212
duke of York 175, 204
Ringstead, Thomas de, bishop of Bangor 214
Robert ap Gruffudd 166
ab Ithel 189
ap Rhys ap Llywelyn ap Hwlcyn 113
of Rhuddlan 21-2
Robin ap Gruffudd ap Gwilym 166
Rögnvaldr, king of Man 26
Rossington, Henry 56n.
Rowlands, Henry 25n., 72, 110
Russell, Peter 196, 199, 200, 204
Ruthin (Denbs.) 201, 239, 248
rye 67, 70, 138-9

St. Albans (Herts.) 190
St. Asaph, bishop of 222
St. Briavels (Gloucs.) 34
St. Bride's (Trearddur Bay) 8
St. Ives (Cornwall) 78
St. Malo 79
St. Patrick's (Cemais) 8&n.
St. Peter, Sir John de 6, 245
St. Pol-de-Leon 79
Salcot, John, bishop of Bangor 214
Salghall, John 255
Salmon family 200
Henry 200, 203n.
Nicholas 200
Rees 203n.
Robert 198, 200
Roger 200
William 200
William Roberson 198
Sandbach (Ches.) 190
Adam 78, 193

Sapy, John de 39n.
Sardon, John de 87
Scalby, John 250
Scales, Roger de 222
Scarisbrick family 201
Thomas 201n.
Scotland 21, 237, 238, 249
Scots 81, 162, 194, 195, 203&n., 216, 251,
    256
Scrope, Stephen 252
Sir William le 55&n.
Seiriol, St. 218, 226.
Shalford, Henry de 198, 246
William de 58, 161, 197
Shedle, Richard 79
sheep and lambs 65&n., 66-9, 68n., 70, 71, 72,
    89, 94, 96, 100, 112, 136, 138, 215, 234
sheriff, office of 33, 37-9, 40, 42, 44, 46, 59-60
sheriff's tourn 37, 38, 44-5, 49, 59, 62, 96, 112
Sherwin, Thomas 76
ships 78-81, 185-6, 187, 188, 192, 251
George of Plymouth 78
James of Caernarfon 81
Le Mariot of Conwy 237
Mary of St. Ives 78
Michael of Dulas 80
Saint Mary cog of Bristol 78
Shrewsbury 26, 34
Silcock, John 223
Skerries (Ynysoedd y Moelrhoniaid) 4, 21, 22,
    77-8
slates 75n., 86
Snowdon 31
Snowdonia 2, 5, 27, 32
Southcrook. See Abermenai
Spain 139
Sparkford, Thomas 221
Spencer, Thomas 115
Stanley family 167
Lady Eleanor 202
John 52
Jonet 164, 167, 175&n.
Sir Thomas of Alderley 175
Sir William of Hooton 167, 175
staurum principis 41, 95, 99, 244
Stephen, smith 87
Strangeways, Roger 52
Stretton family 201
Hugh 201, 231

Roger 201

William 201

subsidies, lay 61-2, 61n., 64-6, 81, 89, 238&n.

subsidies, clerical 189, 211, 219, 223-4, 224n., 228

Suetonius Paulinus 4

Suffolk, duke of 56, 176

Swaffham, John, bishop of Bangor 214

Sylkeston, Matthew de 87

Sym ap Dafydd Goch 129

Tacitus 4

Talbot, Gilbert, Lord 256

Talybolion, commote of 12, 13, 34, 39, 48, 54, 67, 68, 72, 75, 84, 87, 93, 102, 105, 107, 108, 112, 116, 117, 120, 121, 122, 123, 124, 125, 128, 133&n., 140, 160, 167, 170, 172-3, 182, 192, 198n., 211, 213&n., 215, 217, 225, 240&n., 241, 242, 247, 254&n., 257, 258

    *rhaglaw* and raglotry of 160
        *See also* Gruffudd ap Maredudd ap Dafydd; Lewis, Huw; Tudur ap Gruffudd; Gruffudd ap Tudur Llwyd; Gwilym ap Gruffudd ap Tudur Llwyd

    *rhingyll* and ringildry of 76, 240, 241, 256, 257 *See also* Chebsay, Thomas de; Dafydd ap Cynwrig ap Goronwy; Gruffudd ap Tudur Llwyd; Hwlcyn ap Hywel ab Iorwerth Ddu; Hywel ab Ieuan ab Ednyfed; Ieuan ap Tudur Llwyd; Llywelyn ap Hwlcyn ap Hywel; Overton, Peter de

tourn 49, 69, 73, 77, 133, 134

Tal-y-bont (Mer.) 45n.

Tal-y-foel 25

Tal-y-llyn 13

Tangwystl ferch Dafydd ap Madog 131

    ferch Ieuan ap Gwerfyl 105

    ferch Maredudd Llwyd 103

Tano ferch Ieuan ab Adda 136

Tany, Luke de 32

Taunton (Som.) 88

Tegeingl (Flints.) 181, 183

Tegwared, King 217

    ap Bleddyn 230n.

    ap Dafydd Gest 49

    ap Goronwy ap *Sildrig* 247&n.

    ab Owain 73

    ap Rhys ap Hwfa 70

    le Swan 243

    Porthmon 73

thatchers 82, 88, 138

Thaxted (Essex) 88

Thomas ap Dafydd ap Gwilym 174

    ap Dafydd ap Tudur 131-2, 224

    ab Ieuan ap Rhys 133

    ap Llywelyn ap Hywel 132

    ap Maredudd ap Cynwrig 170, 171n., 182, 209

    ap Rhys Wyn 222

Thomelyn ap Dafydd Was 134

Tintern abbey (Mon.) 214

Tiphaine, Jean 220-1

*tir bwrdd* 96, 98

    *corddlan* 14, 95n.

    *cyfrif* 12, 14, 15-16, 18n., 99-100, 240, 258

    *gwelyog* 12-13, 18n., 83, 85, 100-1, 123

    *prid* 127-32, 162n., 166, 169, 198, 202, 253

tithes 71, 212, 213, 215, 218, 220, 231

tolls 72-3, 78, 186, 192, 193, 194, 205, 207, 208, 256

trade 112, 135, 185-6, 187, 192-3

Traeth Coch, port of 8, 80

Trahaearn ap Bleddyn 34

Treban 10

Treberfedd 66, 95

Trecastell 17, 29n., 47, 109, 124, 163n., 164

Treddolffin 116, 241

Trefadog 48, 84, 108, 220n., 240, 241, 258

Trefangharad 110

Trefarthen 108, 129

Trefdraeth Ddisteiniaid (Trefddisteiniaid) 29n., 33n., 49, 50, 81, 107n., 109, 119, 121, 126, 129, 133, 239, 241, 257

Trefdraeth Wastrodion (Trefwastrodion) 29n., 49, 50, 81, 83n., 107n., 109, 112, 159n., 182, 241, 253

Trefeddygon 240

Trefednyfed 6&n., 69, 108, 133

Tre Feibion Maelog 212, 215

Tre Feibion Meurig 5, 67, 68, 70, 71, 101&n., 258

Tre Feibion Pyll 8, 67, 105, 258

Trefeilir 129, 179, 181, 183

Trefelias 77

Treferwydd 105, 242

Treffos 68, 93-4, 213, 214

Trefiddon 239

Trefieuan 125

Tref Ieuan ab Iddon 213

Trefnant, Geoffrey, Provost of Clynnog 217

Trefollwyn 120, 125, 202
Treforion 254
Trefowain 108, 125, 129, 213n.
Tre Fraint 109, 120
Tref Was Padrig 94
Tregadrod 93, 110
Tregaian 165
Tregarnedd 29n., 47, 109, 160, 163n., 180-1, 183
Tregarwed 8, 67-8, 105, 258
Tregornor 83n., 120
Tregwehelyth 162n., 178
Tregwŷr-rhyddion (Caerns.) 131
Trehwfa 113
Treiorwerth 172, 173, 182
Trelywarch 103, 108, 109n., 241, 247
Tre'r-beirdd 172n., 216&n.
  -ddôl 72, 116, 240, 241
  -dryw 47, 217&n.
Treriffri 110
Trescawen 110
Trewalchmai 29n., 33, 39, 109, 110, 191n., 241
Trim, Henry de 197
Trussell, William 25
Trysglwyn 12, 109, 162, 163n., 244, 254, 164
Trysglwyn Ednyfed 130, 161&n.
Tudor of Penmynydd family 164, 165, 246&n., 255-6, 259
Tudor, Owen 165, 255
Tudur ap Cynwrig ap Maredudd 170&n.
  ab Ednyfed Fychan 114, 166
  ab Einion Goch ap Llywelyn 130
  ap Goronwy (d.c.1400) 164
  ap Goronwy ab Ednyfed Fychan (Tudur Hen) 160, 163
  ap Goronwy ap Hywel ap Gruffudd Trefgoed 132
  ap Goronwy ap Tudur 124, 162, 163, 164, 165, 178, 181, 209, 248
  ap Goronwy Fychan 48&n.
  ap Gruffudd (1301) 160
  ap Gruffudd ap Meurig 49
  ab Ieuan ab Ieuan ap Madog 126
  ab Ithel Fychan 128
  ap Llywelyn 161&n., 162
  ap Madog 48
  ap Madog (lineage of Iarddur) 166
  ap Madog Offeiriad 225
  Aled 179, 223, 228, 233n.
  Cayr 230n.

Ddu 106
Fychan 33, 47, 105, 160-1, 166
Fychan ap Gwilym ap Gruffudd 164, 168
Penllyn 179
turbaries 7, 67, 105, 119, 125
Twrcelyn, commote of 12, 14, 15, 27, 29n., 30, 33, 39, 47&n., 48-9, 51, 53, 54, 58, 67, 68, 70-1, 75, 77, 80, 83, 84, 86, 87, 93, 100, 105, 107, 108, 112, 114, 115, 116n., 117, 120, 122, 123, 124, 130, 133n., 160, 161, 163n., 164, 167, 173-4, 182, 192, 199, 213&n., 217, 240, 241, 242, 244, 245, 247, 253, 254, 258
  commote court 44, 69, 105, 112
  rhaglaw and raglotry of 41, 47n., 56, 97n., 160-1, 254
    See also Babham, Thomas; Colle, Thomas de; Dafydd ab Ieuan ap Hywel; Griffith, Sir William; Hywel ap Cynwrig; Ieuan ap Hywel; Ieuan Chwerw; Iorwerth Fychan; Tudur Fychan
  rhingyll and ringildry of 41, 47n., 48, 56&n., 72, 80, 98n., 161, 254, 256. See also Colle, Thomas de; Dafydd ab Ieuan ap Hywel; Goronwy; Ieuan Chwerw; Tudur ap Llywelyn; Ereswell, John de; Ieuan ap Hywel; Dafydd ap Gwilym ap Dafydd
  tourn 49, 85
Twrgarw 102n., 109, 126
Twrllachied 12n., 117, 240
Twyn-y-Parc 10
Tyddyn Ieuan ap Cadwgan 131
  Gobaith Bran 132
  Llwyn Goronwy 132
Tyddynod Mab Cynwrig Goch 131
Tywyn (Mer.) 185, 189
  Aberffraw 3
  Trewan 3

Ucheldref (Dindaethwy) 7
  (Talybolion) 215
uchelwyr 180, 183, 209, 223
usury 134-5
Uwch Aled (Denbs.) 107

Valle Crucis abbey (Denbs.) 215
Valley 3
Valor Ecclesiasticus 71, 211, 214, 216
Vaughan, Richard 225
  Robert, of Hengwrt 42, 243, 253n.
Venables, William, of Kinderton 251
Ventadour 247
Vielville, Sir Rowland 202, 231n.

wages 83-4, 86-8

Wales, north, chamberlain of 38, 59, 73, 80, 86, 168, 201, 206. *See also* Barneby, Thomas; Griffith, Sir William; Parys, Robert de; Stanley, Sir Thomas; Wettenhall, Adam de

north, deputy-justice of. *See* Delves, John de

north, justice of 42, 59, 61, 80, 187, 202, 214, 228, 237. *See also* Mortimer, Roger; Percy, Henry; Stanley, Sir Thomas

Wales, Statute of 33, 37, 39, 50, 127, 130

Walker, William 79

Walsh, John 52

Warham, William, archbishop of Canterbury 224, 228

Waterford, John 222

Wauncey, Sir Edmund de 57

weavers 72, 73, 82

weirs 76-7, 107n., 130

Werdale, William de 222&n.

Wettenhall, Adam de 220

Whalley (Lancs.) 18

wheat 65-8, 67n., 70, 71, 79, 83, 89&n., 94, 101, 115, 138-9

Whitford (Flints.) 128, 225

Wilcock ap Wathampton 116&n.

William I 22

William II 22

ap Dafydd ap Gwilym 174

ap Llywelyn ab Ieuan ap Tudur Llwyd 224

ap Madog 207

Anglicus 116

Friar, guardian of Llan-faes 229

Fychan 251

wills 69-70, 104, 167-8, 172, 176-7, 204-5, 230-1, 231n., 232

Winchelsey, Robert, archbishop of Canterbury 227

Winchester, bishop of 88

Walter de 38, 191

Windsor, Ralph of 220

wine 78-9, 81, 139, 185-6, 189, 193

Wode, John del 51

Richard del 209

women 73-4, 111-14, 134-5

Woodhouse, John 92

Woodstock, Treaty of 27

wool 69, 71-3, 79, 112, 193

Worcester, Richard of 222

William 4

works and services

building 85, 95, 98, 100, 101, 107-8

carrying 15, 66-8, 85, 95, 96, 97, 98, 100, 101, 105

day- 66, 94, 97

harrowing 66-8, 94, 97, 98

manuring 67, 72&n., 97

ploughing 64, 65, 67, 69, 215-6

reaping 65-8, 97, 98, 100, 215-6

Wrexham (Denbs.) 140n.

Wygyr, river 10

Wyn ap Madog 99

Wyrion Eden 1090, 163

Ynys Gadarn (Ynys Dulas) 76

Lannog. *See* Priestholm

Seiriol. *See* Priestholm

Young, Gruffudd 251

Ysgeifiog 28n., 74, 163n., 257

## Astudiaethau Hanes Môn / Studies in Anglesey History

1  *Copper Mountain*, John Rowlands 1966, reprinted 1981

2  *Natural History of Anglesey*, edited by W Efion Jones 1966

3  *Prehistoric Anglesey* The archaeology of the island to the Roman conquest
Frances Lynch 1970

4  *Ships & Seamen of Anglesey 1558-1918*, Aled Eames 1973

5  *Two Centuries of Anglesey Schools: 1700-1902*, David A Pretty 1977

6  *Medieval Anglesey*, A D Carr 1982

7  *Portraits of an Island* Eighteenth century Anglesey, Helen Ramage 1987
ISBN 0 9500199-5-X

8  *A New Natural History of Anglesey*, edited by W Efion Jones 1990
ISBN 0 9500199-6-8

9  *Prehistoric Anglesey* The archaeology of the island to the Roman conquest
Frances Lynch. Second edition 1991, ISBN 0 9500199-7-6

10  *Portraits of an Island* Eighteenth century Anglesey, Helen Ramage
Second edition 2001, ISBN 0 9500199-8-4

11  *Power, Politics & County Government in Wales* Anglesey 1780-1914
W P Griffith 2006, ISBN 0 9500199-9-2

12  *Medieval Anglesey*, A D Carr
Second edition 2011, ISBN 978-0-9568769-0-4